THE CAVALRY OF CLASSICAL GREECE

THE CAVALRY OF CLASSICAL GREECE

*A Social and Military History with
Particular Reference to Athens*

I. G. SPENCE

CLARENDON PRESS · OXFORD

Oxford University Press, Walton Street, Oxford OX2 6DP
Oxford   New York
Athens   Auckland   Bangkok   Bombay
Calcutta   Cape Town   Dar es Salaam   Delhi
Florence   Hong Kong   Istanbul   Karachi
Kuala Lumpur   Madras   Madrid   Melbourne
Mexico City   Nairobi   Paris   Singapore
Taipei   Tokyo   Toronto
and associated companies in
Berlin   Ibadan

Oxford is a trade mark of Oxford University Press

Published in the United States
by Oxford University Press Inc., New York

British Library Cataloguing in Publication Data
Data available

Library of Congress Cataloging in Publication Data
The cavalry of classical Greece : a social and military history
with particular reference to Athens / I.G. Spence.
Includes bibliographical references and index.
1. Greece—Army—Cavalry—History.   I. Title.
UA724.S64   1993   357'.1'0938—dc20   93-442
ISBN 0-19-815028-8

1 3 5 7 9 10 8 6 4 2

Printed in Great Britain
on acid-free paper by
Biddles Ltd.,
Guildford and King's Lynn

To my wife Christine

ACKNOWLEDGEMENTS

I WOULD like to express my thanks to the many people who contributed to the completion of this book and the Ph.D. research on which it is based. I could not have undertaken my original research in London and Athens without the financial assistance of the Keith and Dorothy McKay Travelling Scholarship (awarded by the University of New England, Australia) and the Australian Archaeological Institute at Athens Fellowship for 1987. Both these sources of income were regularly and generously supplemented by my mother and stepfather, Valerie and Geoff Frazer. The final transformation of Ph.D. thesis into book was made possible by a grant from the Australian Research Council, administered by the University of Queensland and the University of New England.

Dr Sally Humphreys made the original suggestion to look at the Athenian cavalry and was my supervisor in the important first year of my Ph.D. studies at University College, London. While studying there my task was made much easier by the help of Dr John Wood, the assistance of the staff at the Institute for Classical Studies, the Senate House Library, and the British Museum, and by the supervision of Dr John North. Dr Tim Cornell and Mr John Lazenby played no small part in getting my thesis accepted for publication and provided useful advice on several points. Dr Neil Adams and his wife Julie and Ken and Lynda Ward contributed invaluable support with accommodation and transport— particularly on subsequent visits to the UK. My research in Athens was assisted by conversation with Dr Hector Catling, Mrs Sheilagh Crowther, and Ms Karen Stears, and by the help of the staff of the National, Epigraphical, and Eleusis Museums. Without the help and friendship of Dr Jill Carington Smith, then Deputy Director of the Australian Archaeological Institute at Athens, I would have been able to achieve little of what I had planned to do in Greece.

I would also like to thank my colleagues in the Department of Classics and Ancient History at the University of New England, with many of whom I have discussed aspects of my work: in particular Associate Professors Greg Stanton and Peter Toohey, Dr Minor Markle, and Colonel Alan Treloar; Mr Roger Pitcher very kindly gave up some of his precious study leave to check references for me in London in early 1992. Ms Patricia Kokori and Mr Nick Machalias, of the Division of Modern Greek, provided timely assistance when my modern Greek proved lacking and Mr Wayne Higgins of the Zoology department provided information on the modern dietary requirements of horses. Mr Ray Nyland, with help from Garth Barker, checked most of the references in the body of the book and, in the final weeks, Drs Tom Hillard and Lea Beness of Macquarie University raced around Sydney checking references and material which were unavailable to me in the rural confines of New England. Dr N. V. Sekunda, late of ANU, also gave generously of his time. My Commanding Officer, Lieutenant Colonel Chris Donovan, helped considerably with his understanding attitude towards the need for leave from my regimental duties in the final stages of the project. Lucy Gasson steered the whole book through the publication process with unfailing patience and calmness – for which I am very grateful.

Finally, and most importantly, I would like to thank my wife Christine and my children James, Christopher, and Mary. The reader should be grateful to Christine for the many suggestions she made for improving the phrasing and the flow of the argument, and the whole family patiently endured my studies with a devotion above and beyond the call of duty.

I.G.S.

Armidale, NSW
1992

CONTENTS

LIST OF PLATES

between pages 154 and 155

LIST OF TABLES

ABBREVIATIONS

APART from its first appearance (when it is given in full) an item in a footnote normally occurs in a shortened, but readily identifiable, form of its entry in the select bibliography. This list therefore contains only particularly shortened forms, those few journal titles which are not abbreviated in accordance with the scheme in *l'Année Philologique*, and other abbreviations used. To aid the non-specialist reader, where a variant title of an ancient work exists in either the Penguin or Loeb edition, this is given in brackets at the end of the entry. In the case of ancient works, the abbreviated titles are listed alphabetically under the author's name.

AAG	A. M. Snodgrass, *Arms and Armour of the Greeks* (London, 1967)
ABV	J. D. Beazley, *Attic Black-Figure Vase-Painters* (Oxford, 1956)
ACGC	C. M. Kraay, *Archaic and Classical Greek Coins* (Berkeley, Calif., 1976)
Add.	L. Burn and R. Glynn, *Beazley Addenda* (Oxford, 1982)
*Add.*²	T. H. Carpenter, *Beazley Addenda*, 2nd edn. (Oxford, 1989)
AGH	J. K. Anderson, *Ancient Greek Horsemanship* (Berkeley, Calif., 1961)
Agora xv	B. D. Meritt and J. S. Traill, *The Athenian Agora*, xv (Princeton, NJ, 1974)
AIF	Australian Imperial Force
Ain. Takt.	Aineias Taktikos
Aisch.	Aischylos
Pers.	*Persai* (*The Persians*)
Prom.	*Prometheus Bound*
ALH	Australian Light Horse
Andok.	Andokides
AO	R. Develin, *Athenian Officials 684–321 BC* (Cambridge, 1989)
APF	J. K. Davies, *Athenian Propertied Families 600–300 BC* (Oxford, 1971)
Ar.	Aristophanes
Acharn.	*Acharnians*

Ekkl.	*Ekklesiazousai (The Assemblywomen* or *The Parliament of Women)*
Kn.	*Knights*
Lysis.	*Lysistrata*
Thes.	*Thesmophoriazousai (The Poet and the Women)*
Arist. *Pol.*	Aristotle, *Politics*
Arr.	Arrian (Flavius Arrianus)
Anab.	*Anabasis*
Takt.	*Taktika*
*ARV*²	J. D. Beazley, *Attic Red-Figure Vase-Painters*, 2nd edn., 3 vols. (Oxford, 1963)
Ath. Pol.	*Athenaion Politeia (Constitution of Athens*, often ascribed to Aristotle)
ATL	B. D. Meritt, H. T. Wade-Gery, and M. F. McGregor, *The Athenian Tribute Lists*, 4 vols. (Cambridge, Mass., and Princeton, NJ, 1939–53)
BM	British Museum (London)
BSA	British School at Athens
Chenevix-Trench	C. Chenevix-Trench, *A History of Horsemanship* (London, 1970)
CAH	J. B. Bury, S. A. Cook, and M. A. Adcock (eds.), *The Cambridge Ancient History*, vol. 6 (Cambridge, 1953)
CIL	*Corpus Inscriptionum Latinarum*
Conze	A. C. L. Conze, *Die attischen Grabreliefs*, 6 vols. (Berlin, 1893–1922)
CVA	*Corpus Vasorum Antiquorum*
DAI	Deutsches Archäologisches Institut
Dein.	Deinarchos
Dem.	Demosthenes
Diod. Sic.	Diodorus Siculus (Diodorus of Sicily)
Diog. Laert.	Diogenes Laertius
Dion. Hal.	Dionysios of Halikarnassos
EJEA	*Empire Journal of Experimental Agriculture*
EM	Epigraphical Museum (Athens)
Eur.	Euripides
El.	*Elektra*
Hek.	*Hekabe (Hecuba)*

Her.	*Herakles (Hercules, The Madness of Hercules)*
Hipp.	*Hippolytos*
IA	*Iphigeneia in Aulis*
IT	*Iphigeneia in Tauris*
Or.	*Orestes*
Phoin.	*Phoinissai (The Phoenician Women)*
Rh.	*Rhesos*
Fairbanks, *AWL*	A. Fairbanks, *Athenian White Lekythoi*, vol. 2 (University of Michigan Studies in Humanities, vol. 7; New York, 1914)
FGH	F. Jacoby (ed.), *Die Fragmente der griechischen Historiker*, parts 1–3 (Leiden, 1954–64)
GC	C. M. Kraay, *Greek Coins* (London, 1966)
GCV	D. R. Sear, *Greek Coins and their Values*, 2nd edn., 2 vols. (London, 1978–9)
GMAW	F. E. Adcock, *The Greek and Macedonian Art of War* (Berkeley, Calif., 1967)
GSAW	W. K. Pritchett, *The Greek State at War*, 4 vols. (Berkeley, Calif., 1971–85)
Hammond and Griffith	N. G. L. Hammond and G. T. Griffith, *A History of Macedonia*, vol. 2 (Oxford, 1979)
HCT	A. W. Gomme *et al.*, *A Historical Commentary on Thucydides*, 5 vols. (Oxford, 1970–81)
Hdtos	Herodotos
Helbig	W. Helbig, 'Les ἱππεῖς athéniens', *Mémoires de l'Institut National de France*, 37/1 (1904), 157–264
Hell. Oxy.	*Hellenika Oxyrhynchia*
HMND	W. W. Tarn, *Hellenistic Military and Naval Developments* (Cambridge, 1930)
Hom.	Homer
Il.	*Iliad*
Od.	*Odyssey*
Hyper.	Hypereides

IG	*Inscriptiones Graecae*
Isok.	Isokrates
Kroll	J. H. Kroll, 'An Archive of the Athenian Cavalry', *Hesperia*, 46 (1977), 83–140
Kyle, *AAA*	D. G. Kyle, *Athletics in Ancient Athens* (Leiden, 1987)
LSJ	H. G. Liddell and R. Scott, *A Greek–English Lexicon*, 9th edn., rev. S. Jones and R. McKenzie (Oxford, 1978)
Lyk.	Lykourgos
Markle, 'Macedonian Arms'	M. M. Markle, 'Macedonian Arms and Tactics under Alexander the Great', *Studies in the History of Art*, 10 (1981), 87–111
Markle, 'Macedonian Sarissa'	M. M. Markle, 'The Macedonian Sarissa, Spear, and Related Armor', *AJA* 81 (1977), 323–39
Markle, 'Use of the Sarissa'	M. M. Markle, 'Use of the Sarissa by Philip and Alexander of Macedon', *AJA* 82 (1978), 483–97
Mat. SSSR	*Materialy i issledovanija po arkheologii SSSR*
MT	J. K. Anderson, *Military Theory and Practice in the Age of Xenophon* (Los Angeles, 1970)
NM	National Museum (Athens)
OCD²	N. G. L. Hammond and H. H. Scullard (eds.), *The Oxford Classical Dictionary*, 2nd edn. (Oxford, 1978)
OPW	G. E. M. de Ste. Croix, *The Origins of the Peloponnesian War* (London, 1972)
PA	J. Kirchner, *Prosopographia Attica*, 2 vols. (Berlin, 1966)
Para.	J. D. Beazley, *Paralipomena* (Oxford, 1971)
Pl.	Plato
Parmen.	*Parmenides*
Repub.	*Republic*
Symp.	*Symposion*
Plut.	Plutarch
Ages.	*Life of Agesilaos*

Alex.	*Life of Alexander*
Alk.	*Life of Alkibiades*
Arat.	*Life of Aratos*
Arist.	*Life of Aristeides*
Dem.	*Life of Demetrios*
Kim.	*Life of Kimon*
Mor.	*Moralia*
Nik.	*Life of Nikias*
Pelop.	*Life of Pelopidas*
Per.	*Life of Perikles*
Philop.	*Life of Philopoimen*
Phok.	*Life of Phokion*
Pyrr.	*Life of Pyrrhos*
Them.	*Life of Themistokles*
Timol.	*Life of Timoleon*
PP	T. B. L. Webster, *Potter and Patron in Classical Athens* (London, 1972)
RE	G. Wissowa *et al.*, *Paulys Real-Encyclopädie der classischen Altertumswissenschaft* (Stuttgart, 1894–1970)
SEG	*Supplementum Epigraphicum Graecum*
Sekunda, *AG*	N. V. Sekunda, *The Ancient Greeks* (London, 1986)
SIG³	W. Dittenberger (ed.), *Sylloge Inscriptionum Graecarum*, 3rd edn., 4 vols. (Leipzig, 1915–24)
Soph.	Sophokles
OC	*Oedipus at Colonus*
TAPA	Ταμείο Ἀρχαιολογικῶν Πόρων καὶ Ἀπαλλοτριώσεων
Thucy.	Thucydides
Xen.	Xenophon
Ages.	*Agesilaos*
Anab.	*Anabasis*
Hell.	*Hellenika* (*A History of My Times*)
Hipparch.	*Hipparchikos* (*On the Cavalry Commander*)
Lak. Pol.	*Lakedaimonion Politeia* (*Constitution of the Lacedaemonians*)
Mem.	*Memorabilia*
PH	*Peri Hippikes* (*On the Art of Horsemanship*)
Symp.	*Symposion*

INTRODUCTION

THIS book is a revision and expansion of my Ph.D. thesis on the Athenian cavalry which was presented at the University of London in October 1988. Although the emphasis on Athens remains, the book has been expanded to include a more comprehensive discussion of the cavalry of other Greek states. This was done to increase its usefulness to readers who are interested in Greek warfare and society in general. I hope it will also be of use to social historians and literary scholars, as one of the main focuses is on the place of the *hippeis*, (the cavalry or cavalry class) in Athenian society; this is identified through a detailed examination of the contemporary literature.

The Athenian *hippeis* is a field of study which has the potential to illuminate important areas of Athenian society and yet has been generally neglected in the past.[1] A recent work by Glenn Bugh does provide a chronologically based history of the Athenian cavalry, but, as it concentrated mainly on the cavalry's financial and administrative aspects, a clear need for a study focused on its military role remained.[2] My book is designed to fulfil that need; its particular emphasis on the factors affecting the military use of horsemen has been determined largely by intriguing contradictions in the way the *hippeis* are presented by both ancient and modern writers.

Ancient writers often neglect the cavalry, even to the extent of providing battle descriptions which detail the ebb and flow of the hoplite clash but omit any real information about the cavalry, other than its presence at the start of the engagement.[3] Modern

---

[1] Until recently the only two specialist works on the cavalry were A. Martin, *Les Cavaliers athéniens* (Bibliothèque des Écoles Françaises d'Athènes et de Rome, fasc. 47; Paris, 1886) and W. Helbig, 'Les ἱππεῖς athéniens', *Mémoires de l'Institut National de France*, 37/1 (1904), 157–264. On the importance of the subject see Martin, *Cavaliers*, pp. vii ff.

[2] G. R. Bugh, *The Horsemen of Athens* (Princeton, NJ, 1988), an extensive revision of his 1979 dissertation from the University of Maryland. See my review of this book in *Gnomon*, 62 (1990), 420–3 and J. K. Anderson's review, *JHS* 110 (1990), 251.

[3] For example: Delion (424 BC), Thucy. 4. 93–7; Amphipolis (422 BC), Thucy. 5. 2, 10; Mounychia (404 BC), Xen. *Hell.* 2. 4. 10–22; Nemea (394 BC), Xen. *Hell.* 4. 2. 16–23.

authors usually follow suit and tend to dismiss the mounted arm as ineffectual and therefore as peripheral to the study of ancient warfare. However, if this were truly the case, it seems remarkable that Athens, for example, spent nearly forty talents a year in order to ensure she had a cavalry force ready for almost immediate action.[4] The Boiotian League had a force of 1,100 men and even the hoplite-dominated Peloponnesian cities developed their mounted arms in the fourth century. In addition, states like Thessaly, Macedonia, and the Greek settlements in Italy and Sicily, relied very heavily upon their cavalry arm. These considerations cast doubt on the modern view that ancient Greek cavalry was essentially useless, and this doubt is confirmed by a close examination of the available evidence. This shows that cavalry could, and often did, play a far from negligible role in ancient Greek warfare.[5]

The general effectiveness of Greek cavalry in combat is discussed in Chapters 2 and 3 and it is clear that despite the prevailing view they did possess considerable potential against hoplites. This was particularly true when they were well-trained and aggressively led, as was the case with the Syracusan cavalry in 369 BC. Xenophon describes how a mere fifty of them herded a large force of Theban hoplites around the plain of Corinth with apparent impunity.[6] However, despite this, and other Greek cavalry successes, the general military standing of cavalry at Athens, the state for which we have the most evidence, seems to have followed a pattern of sporadic triumph and prominence separated by longer periods of obscurity, neglect, and even unpopularity. The aim of this book is to explain why cavalry remained a subordinate arm at Athens, and in Greek warfare in general, during the fifth and fourth centuries BC. The Athenian emphasis results not only from the importance of the city but also from the relative lack of evidence for the other Greek states, a factor which prevents an equally comprehensive coverage of all. However, while certain influences (notably social and political) are specific to Athens, many of the factors which determined

---

[4] Xen. *Hipparch.* 1. 19.
[5] Y. Garlan, *War in the Ancient World*, trans. J. Lloyd (London, 1975), 120, is one of the few modern authorities to acknowledge that, although secondary, the role of cavalry was not negligible.
[6] Xen. *Hell.* 7. 1. 20–1.

Athenian attitudes towards its cavalry also applied to other Greek states. Where this was the case, valid comparisons may be made between Athens and the rest of Greece.

The priorities, therefore, are to establish first, exactly what sort of combat potential the *hippeis* had; second, how they were used in combat; third, which factors influenced their employment; and fourth, which of these determined their subordination to the hoplite arm. The most usual explanation for the limited role of cavalry in classical Greece is that without stirrups it was simply ineffectual against formed bodies of heavy infantrymen. However, while deficiencies in equestrian equipment did play a part in hindering the use of the cavalry arm, its failure to reach its full potential was due primarily to social attitudes and conditions. The most important of these in much of Greece was the domination of military thinking by the hoplite ethos and traditions—although the high cost of owning a horse also contributed by restricting the number of cavalrymen available. At Athens, the unpopularity of the *hippeis* after the rule of the Thirty Tyrants (an extreme oligarchy in power from 404 to 403 BC) also played a major role, but this did not apply to other states.

Because this book is directed towards answering the specific question of why Athenian and other Greek cavalry remained subordinate to the hoplites, a chronological approach is not appropriate. Therefore, while the question of date and the temporal pattern of developments is kept firmly in focus, the discussion does not sequentially detail the history of Greek, or even Athenian, cavalry from *c*.500 to 300 BC—the general period covered by this book.

Although evidence is drawn from throughout the fifth and fourth centuries, I have concentrated on the years from *c*.450 to 320 BC. As far as the Athenian cavalry is concerned, this is not only the best-documented period but probably also the most important. Between *c*.450 and 320 Athens was a fully autonomous city, or *polis*, and her *hippeis* consisted of one thousand men. Prior to this, the cavalry was a much smaller body and consequently much less able to exercise any influence in battle. After 320 BC the domination of Greece by Alexander's successors (the *diadochoi*) meant that Athens could not always order her military affairs as she wished and her armed forces consequently had a

vastly reduced role.[7] The period between *c*.450 and 320 BC is
therefore a coherent and distinct one which properly forms the
basis of any analysis of the military role and social position of
the Athenian *hippeis*. To keep the book to a manageable length,
the discussion is largely restricted to this core period—with the
exception of occasional forays outside it for comparative purposes, and parts of the general survey of Greek cavalry history
in Chapter 1.

Unless otherwise specified, the following conventions apply to
the rest of this work: dates are BC, translations are my own, and
Greek quotations are from the relevant Oxford text. To aid the
reader without Greek, all quotations appear in translation (however, the original is also supplied wherever necessary). In translit-
erating Greek names, a continuing problem for more recent
scholars, I have generally avoided Latinized forms, preferring 'k'
to 'c', 'ai' to 'ae' and 'os' to 'us'. The more familiar 'Pericles'
therefore appears as 'Perikles', 'Plataea' as 'Plataia', and 'Lama-
chus' as 'Lamachos'. However, I have not been quite able to steel
myself to render χ as 'kh' (as in 'Akhilleus' instead of 'Achilles')
and have retained the more traditional 'ch'. Wherever major
confusion seemed likely to arise I have retained the traditional
Latinized spelling. It has also proved impossible to be completely
consistent with the titles of ancient works. I have adopted the
broad principle that titles should be given in the form best known
to the majority of readers. They are therefore generally given in
translation or as transliterations of the original Greek—the more
traditional Latin titles are increasingly less familiar to students
and to the general reader.

References to ancient authors are by the traditional method. In
the case of Aristotle's *Politics* and *Poetics*, the standard book and
chapter reference (used, for example, in the Penguin edition) is
supplied in brackets after the initial reference. In the case of
orators, speeches are not referred to by title, but by the traditional
number which appears in the Loeb editions[8] (probably the most

---

[7] Compulsory military service was abolished at the end of the 4th cent. and an
inscription (inv. no. 767, ll. 6–11) indicates that recruiting for the cavalry was
limited by the Macedonians. See J. Threpsiades and E. Vanderpool, "Πρὸς τοῖς
Ἑρμαῖς", *AD* 18 (1963), 104–5, 106.

[8] Note that although the Loeb edition of Isokrates' speeches lists those in vol. 2
according to a different system, the traditional numbers are given in brackets after
each title.

readily accessible edition to English-speaking readers) and in some or all of the Oxford, Teubner, or Budé texts. The speech numbers used also accord with the work number in the *Thesaurus Linguae Graecae Canon of Greek Authors and Works* (3rd edition), except for Deinarchos, Hypereides, and Demosthenes. However, in the case of Demosthenes, the editors have placed the traditional number in brackets after the title of each speech. Where the traditional authorship is incorrect, doubtful, or disputed, the author's name appears in square brackets.

To avoid duplicating information about the careers of cavalrymen or the museum details of vases and reliefs listed in the appendices, when these appear in the body of the text the appropriate appendix reference numbers are supplied (although in the case of the men this is usually done only when they are first mentioned).

THE EVIDENCE

The foundation of any piece of historical writing is its sources of information and, as this book is designed to cater for the more general reader as well as the specialist, it is appropriate to consider briefly both the extent and state of the available material and the principles I have adopted for its use. As noted, the evidence is largely (but not entirely) Athenian and includes literary, epigraphic, and artistic material. The most important of these is the literature, which supplies most of our information on the position of cavalry in Greek society and warfare. However, there are gaps, particularly for the smaller or less well-documented states.[9] Although this does not really affect our knowledge of cavalry equipment, tactics, and employment (these seem to have varied little from city to city during the classical period), the evidence is often insufficient to reconstruct the social history of cavalry in Greek states other than Athens.

There is quite a large body of information about cavalry matters distributed through the writings of a number of ancient authors, but Xenophon is by far our most important informant. His

---

[9] Cf. H. D. Westlake, *Thessaly in the Fourth Century BC* (London, 1935), p. v, maintaining that the ancient authors are insufficient to reconstruct a continuous account of 6th- and 5th-cent. Thessaly.

technical works, the *Hipparchikos* and the *Peri Hippikes*,[10] provide much of our information on cavalry organization, training, and equipment, and on equestrian techniques. His historical works on the other hand provide a significant proportion of the evidence for the use of cavalry in warfare from 411 to 362. Xenophon's importance also derives from his military and cavalry qualifications. His campaigns in Asia Minor and his close contacts with the Peloponnesians during his exile gave him a wide experience of practical soldiering and a knowledge of the military practices of other states. In addition, he was almost certainly a serving cavalryman at Athens in the last decade of the fifth century and his close links with the Athenian cavalry were renewed when his sons (Appendix 5.55, 72) enlisted after the family returned from exile, *c*.369.

But experience is by itself no guarantee of skill. As Frederick the Great remarked in his memoirs, 'a mule who has carried a pack for ten campaigns under Prince Eugene will be no better a tactician for it, and it must be confessed . . . that many men grow old in an otherwise respectable profession without making any greater progress than this mule.'[11] Xenophon's testimony is doubly valuable because he clearly thought deeply about military affairs and had the ability to apply his practical knowledge to other situations. As rearguard commander of the Ten Thousand (a predominantly infantry force) he initially used contingents of men, or *ekdromoi*, to charge out against Persian cavalry attacks. This was the standard Greek tactic, but as the *ekdromoi* were on foot and the Persians mounted it proved a failure. However, when criticized later Xenophon admitted his error and proposed a logical and ultimately successful solution to the threat.[12]

Other evidence too suggests he was not the sort of soldier who believes all the answers are in the tactics manuals and blindly follows stock solutions or set patterns. For example, after describing several useful stratagems in his cavalry commander's manual, he is careful to point out quite firmly that, 'to read these a few

---

[10] For Xenophon see App. 5.192; the *Hipparchikos* is a manual for the aspiring cavalry commander, the *Peri Hippikes* is an equestrian manual. They are often referred to as *Eq. Mag.* and *Eq.* respectively (abbreviations of their Latin titles).

[11] Quoted in Liddell Hart, A. and B. (eds.), *The Sword and the Pen: Selections from the World's Greatest Military Writings* (New York, 1976), 114.

[12] He raised a scratch force of cavalry and slingers and used them to keep the enemy cavalry at bay, Xen. *Anab.* 3. 3. 6–4. 6.

times will suffice, but it is always necessary for him (i.e. the hipparch) to keep whatever happens in mind and, on examining the present circumstances, to work out the best course. To write down everything it is necessary to do is no more possible than to know everything which will occur.'[13]

Given this level of both experience and ability, Xenophon's value as an informant about Greek cavalry in general and the Athenian cavalry in particular is considerable. The *Hipparchikos* and the *Peri Hippikes*, for example, are sound practical manuals for the cavalry officer and horse-owner alike[14] and allow a real insight into the military theory and practice of the fourth century. However, one ostensible difficulty is determining how far they are proposing innovation or talking theoretically rather than describing existing usage. Fortunately, this difficulty is more apparent than real because Xenophon often makes it perfectly clear when he is suggesting a departure from contemporary practice. This is certainly the case when he recommends using a straight-legged seat instead of a chair seat, two javelins instead of a spear, or suggests innovations in parade manœuvres.[15]

Further confirmation can be provided by using alternative sources of information to check whether his advice reflects contemporary usage. This often seems to be the case for the recommendations or practices in the *Peri Hippikes*, many of which are attested on vase-paintings. At 7. 1 he describes how to mount with the aid of a javelin and a cup, illustrated at Plate 1, shows a youth practising to do precisely this. Xenophon, too, cautiously approves a rider training his horse to crouch down to assist him to mount—as long he knows how to mount quickly by other methods in an emergency. This practice is apparently attested on a red-figure vase dated to after 430.[16] His advice at 5. 3 to muzzle horses for safety reasons is confirmed by vase-illustrations of muzzles in use.[17] Finally, the practicality of his advice to use

[13] Xen. *Hipparch.* 9. 1.
[14] Chenevix-Trench (an ex-cavalry officer) praised the *PH* (at 28, 30, 42, 35, 299, 314), claiming that, apart from a misconception about the function of the horse's frog, many of its recommendations could still be followed today. At 300 he notes that this same misconception was current among British grooms as late as this century.
[15] Xen. *PH* 7. 5; 12. 12; *Hipparch.* 3. 1–14, esp. 5.
[16] *PH* 6. 16; Vase 107.
[17] Vases 3, 4, 12, 13, 17, 103; all 6th cent. except 103 (*c*.450–420).

blunt javelins for realistic, but risk-free, training is supported by
the appearance of such weapons on vases dating from the second
quarter of the fifth century.[18]

The *Hipparchikos* seems equally reliable as many of the tactics
it suggests are recorded in contemporary Greek warfare.[19] In
fact, the only two areas of detail in the manuals which may
represent considerable departures from existing practice are those
concerning the cavalry command structure in *Hipparchikos*, 2. 1–
7, and some of the more exotic pieces of defensive armour in *Peri
Hippikes*, 12. Both these questions are discussed in more detail in
Chapter 2 but it is appropriate to note here that while the *phyle*,
or squadron, organization was most probably an innovation it was
based on a proven system already operating with the Spartan
infantry. Similarly, the items of armour were almost certainly
modelled on Persian equipment and perhaps even worn by a few
Athenian *hippeis*.[20]

However, although Xenophon's manuals are accurate in detail,
by themselves they cannot indicate the extent to which their
advice was followed. While the use of the chair seat and *kamax*
spear, which Xenophon rejects, and his recommended
alternatives—the straight leg seat and two javelins—are all attested
in vase-paintings, it is not possible to establish the proportion of
hippeis using them.[21] In addition, Xenophon himself concluded a
list of tactical practices with the remark: 'nearly everyone then
knows these things but not many regularly pay attention to
them.'[22]

I suspect too that it would have been an above average hipparch
who would have operated the cavalry exactly according to Xenophon's instructions. Xenophon's whole treatise on the cavalry
commander's duties assumes that the hipparchs' individual skills
and actions determine the cavalry's efficiency. Philopoimen's
transformation of the Achaian League's cavalry from a worthless

[18] *PH* 8. 10; cf. Pls. 1 and 15(?) which may portray these (the photographs
available suggest there were no points). The use of such a practice weapon on foot
is attested as early as *c*.480, cf. *ARV*² 203.95.
[19] See Ch. 3.
[20] The number who did so, though, was probably small. See 'protection',
Ch. 2.
[21] *PH* 7. 5–7; 12. 12. Chair seat: Pl. 7; straight leg seat: Pls. 2, 8, 13. Most
vases portray cavalrymen with two javelins but a few portray them with the
kamax. See 'mobility' and 'weaponry', Ch. 2.
[22] Xen. *Hipparch*. 4. 5; cf. *Oik*. 20. 6–9.

body into an impressive fighting arm confirms the assumption, and graphically illustrates the vast difference in standards which could apply in the same unit under different commanders.[23] Although we can from time to time read between the lines, no theoretical handbook can tell us exactly what real standards were like and the level of expertise certainly varied with commanders.

The equestrian and cavalry manuals probably represent a high state of the equestrian and cavalry commander's arts rather than the average level of achievement. However, they are accurate in detail, carefully constructed, and lucidly presented. As such, they are an invaluable aid to the reconstruction of Athenian cavalry training, organization, tactics, and equipment, and of equestrian practices in general. Xenophon's remaining works are also useful for supplementing these details, but are more important for what they show of the tactical and strategic employment of cavalry in real combat and of its role and position at Athens, especially under the Thirty Tyrants. In the field of tactics, the manuals tell us what it was possible to achieve; his histories tell us what actually was achieved.

The other literary evidence for the cavalry consists primarily of separate references in a variety of works of different genres: history, oratory, drama, and philosophy. The contemporary historians, naturally enough, provide the best information on the military use of cavalry. Thucydides is most important for the fifth century, although Herodotos also supplies some information for the start of that period, while Xenophon, as already stated, is our best source for the late fifth century and the first half of the fourth. Although only small portions survive, the *Hellenika Oxyrhynchia* is also occasionally useful for parts of the same period. I have supplemented these accounts with those of later writers such as Diodorus Siculus, Plutarch, and Arrian. Diodorus Siculus, despite his frequently catalogued faults and inaccuracies, has the cardinal virtue on occasion of providing an account of periods or events not covered by either Xenophon or Thucydides. The same is true of Plutarch. Arrian is particularly valuable as his military background would have assisted him in sifting the available evidence: he too was a cavalryman in the days before stirrups and his descriptions of military activities are likely to be basically sound.

[23] Plut. *Philop.* 7. 2–5; cf. Xen. *Mem.* 3. 3. 1–15.

However, the extent to which the work of these three later writers was derived from earlier authors, and the accuracy of their sources, are the subject of controversy. It is beyond the scope of this book to examine these 'lost sources' of Plutarch, Diodorus, or Arrian and to decide which parts of which authors are based on the 'best' authorities. To attempt to create a ranking of these authors' reliability according to their sources is in any case an oversimplification[24] and instead I have followed the general practice of preferring the accounts of the contemporary writers like Xenophon and Thucydides to those of the later authors—except when there were specific reasons for not doing so.

Although the historians do provide useful information on attitudes to the cavalry and its position within society, most of this evidence comes from playwrights, orators, and to a lesser extent, the philosophers. All of these authors were either Athenian or residents of Athens and their evidence almost exclusively refers to that city. Because of the pattern of survival, drama is most useful for the fifth century and oratory for the fourth. Or, and it is a better division for the history of attitudes to the Athenian cavalry, drama provides most of the information prior to the Thirty Tyrants while oratory provides most of the information after them.

While orators undoubtedly exaggerated whenever they felt they could get away with it, forensic speeches can be used to good effect in identifying the general climate of opinion towards the cavalry.[25] The orators' arguments must have been designed to appeal to the majority of the jury and this majority, as Markle has recently demonstrated, was composed of the 'poor' (i.e. those who 'had little or no leisure').[26] They also constituted the majority of the Athenian population. The same argument can be applied, although less securely, to the work of the Attic dramatists. One of their main aims was presumably to win first prize (despite Aris-

[24] Cf. N. G. L. Hammond, *Three Historians of Alexander the Great* (Cambridge, 1983), 167.
[25] On the general value of oratorical evidence, see K. J. Dover, *Greek Popular Morality in the Time of Plato and Aristotle* (Oxford, 1974), 8–14.
[26] M. M. Markle 'Jury Pay and Assembly Pay at Athens', in P. A. Cartledge and F. D. Harvey (eds.), *Crux: Essays Presented to G. E. M. de Ste. Croix on his 75th Birthday* (History of Political Thought, vol. 6, Issue 1/2; Exeter, 1985), 265–97, esp. 265–6, 285–9.

tophanes' remark that a poet's purpose should be to educate his fellow-citizens); Aristotle for one certainly believed that the competition affected both plot and form in tragedy.[27] Where a particular play or speech is known to have been victorious, this gives some slight additional grounds for believing that on a general level it was in tune with contemporary views.

However, this can only provide a very rough indication. In the case of plays our knowledge of how the prize was awarded is not sufficient to say whether theme, presentation, or treatment was the most important criterion for success.[28] Similarly, the outcome of legal cases must have been affected not only by the appeal of the arguments but also by other factors such as the popularity of the protagonists, the quality of the opposing speech (which in most cases is not extant), or even the facts of the case. Antiphon's defence oration of 410 could not overcome his unpopularity and save his life, even though that famous connoisseur of speeches, Thucydides, described it as 'the best up to my time'.[29]

There are in addition other influences on the dramatic and forensic material: actors' interpolations in the former and the revision of speeches for publication in the latter. Luckily several factors minimize the potential effect of these upon the evidence. The majority of passages I have cited from tragedy are, according to Page at least, probably unaffected by interpolations. In addition, and this applies to comedy as well, the main period for interpolations was in the fourth and third centuries. Given the very high standing of actors in the fourth century this would seem to be the most likely period for interpolations from this source.[30] If this is so, then many modifications to the original texts would continue to represent opinion from the period considered in this book. The main effect of an interpolation therefore would be to render the dating of a particular remark less precise. Actors' interpolations then are not really a problem and the editing of speeches prior to written dissemination is also unlikely to have markedly affected their value as evidence. This is because

[27] Ar. *Frogs*, 1008–10; Arist. *Poetics*, 1451^{b}33–9 (9); 1453^{a}30–5 (13).
[28] Although there are exceptions: Dikaiarchos fr. 84 in F. Wehrli, *Die Schule des Aristoteles*, i (Basle, 1967), 31 states that the unprecedented award of first prize and repeat performance of Aristophanes' *Frogs* was because of the plea it contained to restore the exiles (see also Wehrli, 67, 68–9).
[29] Thucy. 8. 68. 2.
[30] D. L. Page, *Actors' Interpolations in Greek Tragedy* (Oxford, 1934), 14–15.

it seems improbable that an orator would replace a popular argument with a less popular one, even though he might be more inclined towards manipulating the facts of the case than when subject to immediate contradiction by his adversary in open court.

In general then, while it is clearly impossible to use every dramatic or forensic line as if it were representative of Athenian opinion, the frequency with which a particular attitude or idea appears or is implicit (particularly if it occurs in several authors) can indicate whether it was widespread or of particular interest at the time. By adopting these guidelines, it is possible to use Attic drama and oratory in conjunction with other evidence to reconstruct the attitudes to the cavalry and its position within Athenian society. Occasionally the speeches may also be useful for more basic information on cavalry deployments or its organization at specific times.[31] This type of information tends to come from minor or background detail which would hardly have been worth inventing, particularly as the opposition would often have had the opportunity to correct any blatant lies or misrepresentations on the spot.

The main importance of the literary evidence lies in identifying cavalry theory and practice (which is generally applicable to all of Greece), the social position of the Athenian *hippeis*, and the attitudes of the remainder of Athenian society towards them. The artistic material (again largely Athenian) contributes a rather more narrow range of evidence which particularly concerns basic cavalry equipment and techniques. Despite some interpretational problems, it is a valuable source of information on the cavalry and the cavalry class. The artistic material can conveniently be divided into two types: painting and sculpture. The former consists almost exclusively of vase-paintings, although there are some extant descriptions of lost murals, while the latter, and smaller group, includes grave-reliefs and larger works such as the Parthenon frieze.

The vast bulk of the pictorial evidence for the period under consideration consists of Athenian red-figure vase-paintings.[32] The pottery from other states is limited (although in some cases it

[31] Cf. Aischines, 3. 140; [Lysias], 20. 23–5, 28.

[32] There are numerous 5th- and 4th-cent. Attic vases with equestrian scenes, most dating *c*.500–420; see App. 1.

can be partially replaced by coin art) and Athenian black-figure painting went into a fairly rapid decline in the early part of the fifth century. With the exception of Panathenaic prize amphoras (see Plate 8 for an example), it had died out by about 450[33]—a little before the Athenian cavalry was increased to a strength of 1,000 men. The ceramic evidence can help provide details of cavalry training and perhaps also an indication of the relative popularity of the *hippeis* at different times—if only as subjects for vase decoration. However, it is most useful for supplying particulars of dress, equipment, equestrian technique, and the use of weapons on horseback. Almost all the vases can be used in this way as there appears to be no difference in the riding habit and practices of the military and civilian rider, except for the use of armour.

This is clear from a comparison of military scenes, where the riders are obviously serving cavalrymen, with hunting or travelling scenes where the horsemen are probably civilians.[34] Confirmation of this is supplied by the sculpture which shows a variety of dress in the field and indicates that a *hippeus* on active service merely added armour to his normal riding costume, and sometimes did not even do this. For example, one stela base (relief 27) depicts a horseman in action on three of the four sides. One wears a petasos (a broad-brimmed hat), a chiton (tunic), muscle cuirass, and boots (Plate 2); the second a petasos, chiton, cloak, boots, and slung sword; the third a petasos, chiton, cloak, and boots.[35] The similar dress of horsemen on active service and non-military riders is not surprising; the cavalry was not a standing unit of professional soldiers but consisted of volunteers drawn from the upper echelons of Athenian civilian society and mobilized only when needed.

Therefore, unless the subject is a foreigner, it is possible to consider almost any Athenian painting of a rider as evidence for local equestrian or cavalry practices. Fortunately, it is usually possible to identify foreigners because Attic vase-painters were

[33] J. D. Beazley, *The Development of Attic Black-figure* (Sather Classical Lectures, 24; Berkeley, Calif., 1951), 87.

[34] For example, cf. vases 19 and 34. *PP* 181 comments on the difficulty of differentiating between cavalrymen, hunters, and even jockeys.

[35] Athens, NM 3708 (relief 27). Cf. the stela base 2744 in the same museum (= relief 25; Pl. 13) which portrays the cavalryman in a petasos-style helmet, chiton, and wearing a sword but with bare feet.

generally careful to distinguish different nationalities. In her useful study of Scythian archers on archaic Attic pots, Vos convincingly identifies clear differences in the way Greeks, Scythians, Persians, and Thracians were depicted.[36] The last group is particularly important as some fifth-century Athenian cavalrymen adopted items of Thracian dress, thereby raising the possibility of mistaken identification.

For example, several riders on the Parthenon frieze, and who are therefore undeniably Athenian, wear the Thracian alopekis (fox-skin) cap.[37] Vases too have examples of this, and also of a shorter version of the long Thracian cloak, the zeira. However some cavalrymen on vases are clearly Thracian: they wear both the alopekis and the long zeira (a distinguishing feature of the region) and in addition have the distinctive van Dyck beard used by vase-painters to distinguish northern foreigners.[38] This can be seen particularly well in a group of vases dating to *c*.450–420.[39] These confirm Vos's conclusion that Attic vase-painters 'tried to reproduce faithfully the more noticeable features of the different foreign costumes' and that they seem to have been quite skilled at doing so.[40] This cluster of vases depicting Thracians also suggests that vase-painters may be reasonably useful for identifying changing patterns in fashion.

While this apparent care in the portrayal of foreign dress gives grounds for confidence in the general accuracy of the pot-painters, it really only shows that they could be accurate when they

[36] M. F. Vos, *Scythian Archers in Archaic Attic Vase Painting* (Groningen, 1963), 43–7.

[37] There are twelve examples of the alopekis on the Parthenon (by frieze, slab, and number): South: I 2, 3, 4; xv 40, 41; West: iv 8; viii 15; x 19; North: xxxv 108; xxxvi 110; xxxviii 117; xxxix 120. South ii and xiv may have traces of the alopekis on figures 6 and 38 respectively but this is not certain given the state of the stone.

[38] An excellent example of an alopekis-style cap and a short zeira worn together is vase no. 20, but see also mixed dress (alopekis and chlamys or petasos and short zeira) on the same man: nos. 3, 5, 132, and the right-hand rider, Pl. 8. See too, groups of cavalry with differently dressed individuals (some with items of Thracian dress and some without): nos. 14, 20, 27. Van Dyck beard: Vos, *Scythian Archers*, 56–7; cf. the older groom on vase no. 103.

[39] Vases 81 and 94. As can be seen from the beardless youths on BM E 481 (*ARV*² 1090.33), the use of beards alone to identify Thracians is not helpful with younger men. However, the full length zeira seems to be particularly associated with Thracians and these youths should almost certainly be identified as such.

[40] Vos, *Scythian Archers*, 45–7. Cf. the sudden appearance of Scythians on vases *c*.530, suggesting the artists were depicting a novel subject, ibid. 43, 59–60.

wished. Whether they always chose to be so is a different matter, and the question of consistent accuracy in terms of Athenian cavalry dress and equipment remains open, particularly as there is some discrepancy between the literary accounts of cavalry dress and equipment and the pictorial representations of it. This will be discussed in more detail in Chapter 2.

Another minor uncertainty with some of the ceramic evidence is its date. To make the fullest use of vases as evidence it is desirable to date them as accurately as possible. Sadly this cannot always be done with a great degree of precision. I do not claim to be an expert in dating vases, a skill which takes many years of practice to acquire. In addition I have been further limited by an enforced reliance in most cases (except in the UK and Greece) upon photographs of vases rather than on an examination of the pots themselves. However, the general chronological scheme for the corpus of red-figure vases is now essentially agreed upon by scholars in the field,[41] and where experts do disagree the difference is seldom large. While it is still sometimes unwise to press the dating of a particular vase too far (despite T. B. L. Webster's claim that 'any painted pot can be dated within ten years'),[42] we can usually be pretty certain of its general date.

In order to provide a firm chronological framework for my discussion of the ceramic evidence I have adopted the following dates for Beazley's stylistic periods:

Early Red-Figure	*c.*530–500
Late Archaic	*c.*500–475
Early Classic	*c.*475–450
Classic	*c.*450–420
Late Fifth Century	*c.*420–390
Fourth Century	*c.*390–300[43]

These are, however, approximate periods only and there is probably considerable overlap between them. Although the periods are much more detailed for the fifth century than for the

---

[41] G. M. A. Richter, *Attic Red-figured Vases: A Survey*, rev. edn. (New Haven, Conn., 1958), 22.

[42] *PP* 296.

[43] I have basically applied the dates in *PP* 27–41 to Beazley's periods in *ARV*². However, I have accepted the dates in Richter, *Attic Red-figured Vases*, 115, 139 and extend the lower dates of the 'Classic' and 'Late Fifth Century' periods by 5 and 10 years respectively.

fourth, the most useful fourth-century vases tend to be the earlier ones. The later vases decline in quality and their subjects are often stereotyped scenes such as amazonomachies and grypomachies[44] which are not so useful for a study of the cavalry. Because of the exotic dress and subject of these scenes I have only used them to corroborate the literary or other artistic evidence for equestrian techniques and the use of weapons from horseback— the most likely aspects of such vases to correspond to reality. Vase-paintings are therefore useful but, when doubts exist about their accuracy and date, they are best used in conjunction with other evidence.

One question remains before leaving the artistic material, the accuracy of sculpture in general and in particular the identity of the riders on the Parthenon frieze. The first part of this can be dealt with fairly quickly as the fourth-century grave stelae seem to agree with the detail in Xenophon's testimony. Several riders are shown in exactly the type of cuirass and pteryges (strips of leather to protect the groin and thigh) recommended by Xenophon, and wearing the Boiotian helmet he prefers. A high proportion of them are booted, a measure he suggests for protecting the legs, and (unlike those depicted on the vase-paintings) many wear swords.[45] The sculpture therefore seems to be accurate in matters of detail, although even it portrays slightly fewer cavalrymen wearing basic items of armour than one would expect from the literary evidence.

The Parthenon frieze, however, is rather more controversial and, since Boardman's suggestion that the mounted figures are really the heroized dead from Marathon, it is no longer possible simply to assume without discussion that they are *hippeis*.[46] Despite this, and for the reasons given in Appendix 3, I find Boardman's argument unproven—although he does cast some doubts on the traditional interpretation. Nevertheless, the horse-

---

[44] On the story of the Arimasps and gryphons cf. Aisch. *Prom.* 803–6.

[45] For example, cuirass: 6, 7, 24, 27 (Pl. 2), 30 (Pl. 12); boots: 7, 27 (all 3 riders; see Pl. 2), 30 (Pl. 12, both riders), 31; helmet: 7, 13, 17, 25 (Pl. 13), 26, 29; sword: 8, 10–11, 12 (Pl. 11), 13, 20 (Pl. 9), 25 (Pl. 13), 27, 29, 33. Quite a few other reliefs, though, show cavalry in ordinary dress without protection—except for boots, (cf. two of the riders on relief 27).

[46] J. Boardman, 'The Parthenon Frieze—Another View' in U. Höckmann and A. Krug (eds.), *Festschrift für Frank Brommer* (Mainz am Rhein, 1977), 39–49.

men certainly represent the *hippeis* who participated in the procession and this is confirmed by their dress, which fits the pattern of cavalry costume in other sculptures and paintings.[47] The frieze can also be dated with more precision than much of the other pictorial or sculptural evidence, a valuable asset when dealing with changes of costume over time. Only the West frieze could be earlier than 442 and the East, South, and North friezes were probably completed by 438, although the finishing touches to the last two of these could slightly postdate this.[48] The sculptures, however, do suffer from one deficiency: the weapons carried by the carved *hippeis* were either bronze attachments or were painted on.[49] As these no longer survive they cannot contribute to our knowledge of cavalry weaponry.

The epigraphic material is the last and smallest body of evidence available for the cavalry but it is by no means negligible. It is particularly important for the light it sheds on details of cavalry numbers, organization, and administration. *IG* I³ 375 for example, which I have examined in detail elsewhere,[50] can be used to determine that the number of Athenian cavalry serving in 410/09 was closer to 600 than to 1,000. Two series of lead tablets from the fourth and third centuries discovered in the Kerameikos and the Agora at Athens[51] help to explain several details concerning the financial administration of the corps. They are particularly important in illustrating the *timesis* or valuation of the horses and the level of financial support given to the *hippeis* by the state; this in turn is invaluable for calculating the financial resources necessary to be a member of the hippic class. Inscriptions also provide much of the information for constructing a cavalry prosopography, a very valuable tool for examining the social composition of

[47] In a conversation with Professor Boardman in 1987, he suggested that, although unable to accept the traditional interpretation, he was happy to allow my argument that the horsemen were depicted as cavalrymen—which he considered did not affect his basic theory. He also states, 'The Parthenon Frieze', 40, that there are sufficient differences in the dress of the riders to 'help define the groups, all in terms of contemporary Athenian dress, military or otherwise.'

[48] B. Ashmole, *Architect and Sculptor in Classical Greece* (London, 1972), 126–7, 141–2.

[49] Ibid. 117. On the origins of carrying weapons in the Panathenaic procession see *Ath. Pol.* 18. 4.

[50] I. G. Spence, 'Athenian Cavalry Numbers in the Peloponnesian War: *IG* I³ 375 Revisited', *ZPE* 67 (1987), 167–75.

[51] See K. Braun, 'Der Dipylon-Brunnen B1, die Funde', *MDAI(A)* 85 (1970), 129–269; Kroll, 83–140.

the *hippeis*.[52] Finally, they can sometimes be useful in supplementing the literary record of cavalry deployments: without *IG* I[3] 365, for example, we would not know that Athenian cavalry served in Macedonia in 432/1.

The total body of evidence available for an examination of the Athenian *hippeis* from *c*.450 to 320 is therefore quite considerable. There are also numerous scattered references to the cavalry of other Greek states, including the depiction of non-Athenian cavalry in local sculpture and coinage. These show that south of Thessaly it was basically equipped and handled in the same way as the Athenian horse. In Thessaly and Macedonia cavalry forces were larger and handled more effectively, but essentially equipped in the same way—until the 330s when the Macedonian arm seems to have adopted the long Macedonian lance or *sarissa* as a cavalry weapon. Although the evidence is not uniformly good for all states or for all periods, if used carefully it is more than adequate to allow valid conclusions to be drawn concerning the wartime use of Greek cavalry. It is also good enough, for Athens at any rate, to reveal the cavalry's peacetime training and administration, and its place within society.

[52] See App. 5 for a list of cavalrymen and a more detailed discussion of the evidence available for its reconstruction.

Rome

CAMPANIA

Neapolis

Poseidonia

Taras

R. Siris

Siris

Thurii

Kroton

Tyrrhenian Sea

Messana

Rhegion

Himera

N

S I C I L Y

Katane

Selinous

Morgantine

Leontine

Akragas

Syracuse

Gela

Kamarina

Land over 1000 metres

0   50   100 miles

0   50   100   150 km

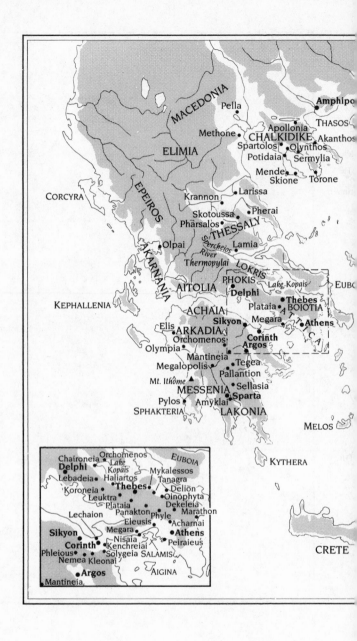

MACEDONIA
Pella
Methone
ELIMIA
Apollonia
THASOS
CHALKIDIKE Akanthos
Spartolos Olynthos
Potidaia Sermylia
Mende Skione Torone
Amphipo

CORCYRA
EPEIROS
AKARNANIA
Krannon
Larissa
Skotoussa Pherai
Pharsalos THESSALY
Olpai
Spercheios River
Lamia
Thermopylai
LOKRIS
PHOKIS Lake Kopais
AITOLIA Delphi
EUBO
ACHAIA
Thebes
Plataia BOIOTIA
Sikyon Megara ATTICA Athens
KEPHALLENIA
Elis
ARKADIA
Orchomenos
Corinth
Olympia
Argos
Mantineia
Megalopolis Tegea
Pallantion
Mt. Ithôme
Sellasia
MESSENIA Amyklai Sparta
Pylos LAKONIA
SPHAKTERIA
MELOS

KYTHERA

Chaironeia Orchomenos EUBOIA
Delphi Lake Kopais
Mykalessos
Lebadeia Haliartos Tanagra
Koroneia Thebes Deliōn
Leuktra Oinophyta
Plataia Dekeleia
Lechaion Panakton Phyle Marathon
Eleusis Acharnai
Sikyon Megara Athens
Nisaia Peiraieus
Corinth Kenchreiai
Phleious Solygeia SALAMIS
Nemea Kleonai
Argos AIGINA
Mantineia

CRETE

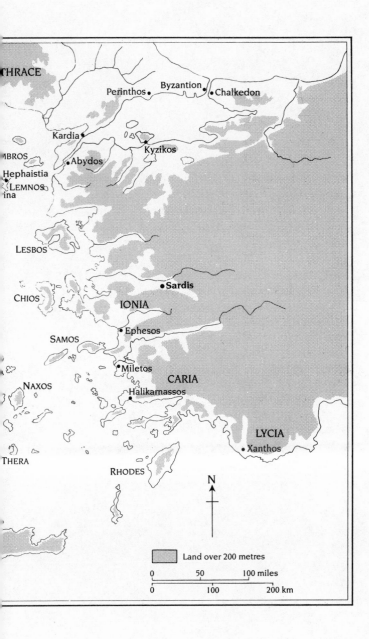

THRACE

Perinthos• Byzantion• •Chalkedon

Kardia•

IMBROS

Hephaistia
LEMNOS
ina

Abydos•

Kyzikos•

LESBOS

CHIOS

SAMOS

NAXOS

Sardis•

IONIA

•Ephesos

•Miletos

CARIA

Halikarnassos•

LYCIA

•Xanthos

THERA

RHODES

N

Land over 200 metres

| 0 | 50 | 100 miles |
| 0 | 100 | 200 km |

I

Greek Cavalry c.500–300

THIS chapter outlines the main features of Greek cavalry in the fifth and fourth centuries, placing the cavalry in its historical context, and providing the reader with a quick introductory survey of its history and organization in the different *poleis* (cities). The survey is organized geographically, covering four broad areas: the Peloponnese, Central Greece, Northern Greece, and Italy–Sicily. Each of these regions placed rather a different emphasis on its cavalry arm, with the role of cavalry in mainland Greece becoming increasingly important, and the cavalry tradition increasingly strong, the further north one looks.

THE PELOPONNESE

The Peloponnesians in general apparently had little in the way of a cavalry tradition and most states do not seem to have had any true cavalry to speak of until either the end of the fifth or the start of the fourth century. The Peloponnese is not for the most part particularly good cavalry country—Homer described one region, Arkadia, as the place where 'Mount Kyllene towers . . . (and) . . . men are hand-to-hand fighters'.[1] Peloponnesian states produced hoplites, and good ones at that, rather than cavalry. The Peloponnesian League, which included most Peloponnesian states under the leadership of Sparta, and which was the pre-eminent military alliance during the sixth and fifth centuries, could muster between thirty and sixty thousand hoplites in 431. However, all the cavalry was provided by three allies from outside the Peloponnese itself—Boiotia, Phokis, and Lokris.[2] Neverthe-

---

[1] *Il.* 2. 603–4.

[2] Plut. *Per.* 33. 4 gives the hoplite total as 60,000 but this seems very high and Gomme's estimate (*HCT* ii. 13) of approximately 30,000 is more likely. Whatever the size of the force, it represented two-thirds of the total League army, Thucy. 2. 10. 2, 47. 2; 3. 15. 1. Cavalry: Thucy. 2. 9. 3.

less, by about 370 most Peloponnesian states seem to have had cavalry forces which were often used in close conjunction with the picked troops, or *epilektoi*, which became increasingly fashionable in the fourth century. The evidence suggests that, as was the case at Athens and elsewhere, the cavalry of the Peloponnesian states was drawn from the wealthiest level of society, except for Sparta where the wealthy only paid for cavalry horses and did not serve in person.

Sparta

The Spartans had a much less well developed cavalry tradition than Athens—very early on they had wholeheartedly embraced the hoplite arm and put all their energy into creating good heavy infantrymen. However, they did retain a strong equestrian tradition amongst the wealthy and aristocratic which led to an impressive string of victories in the four-horse chariot race, the most expensive event at the Olympic games.[3] In the fourth century, riding and equestrian activities were part of the leisure pursuits of the royal families.[4] Their army also contained a unit (probably the Kings' bodyguard) called the *Hippeis*, which clearly fought on foot during the classical period,[5] but whose name suggests that in an earlier period it must have been either a cavalry or mounted hoplite corps. In fact, Thucydides states that the Spartans only established a force of 400 cavalry in 425/4 in order to cope with Athenian coastal raids, emphasizing that this was 'contrary to their usual practice'.[6]

We know nothing about this fifth-century body apart from its size, but there is rather more information available for the fourth-century corps. The Spartan army had the same number of cavalry and infantry *morai* (units)—six,[7] but the size of the cavalry *mora* is uncertain. However, there seem to have been five *morai* of hoplites at Nemea in 394 and 600 cavalrymen and, if all of these

[3] See S. Hodkinson, 'Inheritance, Marriage and Demography: Perspectives upon the Success and Decline of Classical Sparta' in A. Powell (ed.), *Classical Sparta: Techniques behind her Success* (London, 1989), 96–100.

[4] Kastor and Polydeukes, the two divine horsemen, were Spartan, Hom. *Il.* 3. 236–42. Royal families: Xen. *Hell.* 5. 3. 20; *Ages.* 9. 6.

[5] See J. F. Lazenby, *The Spartan Army* (Warminster, 1985), 10–12.

[6] Thucy. 4. 55. 2.

[7] Xen. *Lak. Pol.* 11. 4.

were Spartans and the same number of cavalry and infantry units were deployed, this would mean five cavalry *morai* of 120 men. This would give a total force of 720 horsemen.[8] Each *mora* was commanded by an officer called a *hipparmostes* and the whole cavalry force may have been commanded by at least one hipparch; Xenophon, for example, uses this term to describe Polycharmos, the Spartan cavalry commander killed at Olynthos in 382.[9] The cavalry included both Spartiates and Perioikoi in its ranks around 378[10] but its membership is otherwise unknown.

The quality of the Spartan arm does not seem to have been very high. Xenophon is particularly critical of its standard at the time of the Leuktra campaign (371), describing it as '*ponerotatos*' or 'very poor quality'. He blames this on the fact that the rich paid for the horses which were then ridden by other men who only collected together on mobilization, and who were drawn from those soldiers 'least physically fit and least keen to win honour (*philotimoi*)'. His remarks are confirmed by the defeat at Leuktra[11] and supported by other indications that the Spartan cavalry was not noted for its prowess. For example, it was also defeated and its commander killed outside Olynthos in 382, and ten years earlier a small group of Spartan cavalrymen under the *hipparmostes* Pasimachos actually chose to dismount and fight on foot against the Argives.[12] This last incident suggests that Spartans perhaps always felt more comfortable as hoplites than as cavalry.

One notable success was the vigorous pursuit in 368 following the 'Tearless Battle' (so called because not a single Spartiate was killed), but it is not entirely certain that the cavalry involved was Spartan. On this occasion, Xenophon fails to give the composition of their army so we do not know if the Spartan cavalry was present; his account of the pursuit mentions only 'the cavalry and the Celts'. It is therefore possible that the cavalry here was part of (or at least supplemented by) the allied force, which consisted of 'Celts, Iberians, and about fifty cavalry', sent over by Dionysios I of Sicily.[13]

[8] Xen. *Hell.* 4. 2. 16; Lazenby, *Spartan Army*, 12, 136.
[9] Xen. *Hell.* 4. 4. 10, 5. 12; 5. 2. 41.
[10] Ibid. 5. 4. 39.
[11] Ibid. 6. 4. 10–11, 13.
[12] Ibid. 4. 4. 10; 5. 2. 41.
[13] Ibid. 7. 1. 20, 28–32.

It is perhaps not surprising then, that, while campaigning in Asia Minor at the start of the fourth century, the Spartans asked for a force of 300 Athenian *hippeis* to assist them, or that Agesilaos later raised his own cavalry from the local Greek communities there.[14] The rigid Spartan *agoge*, or training system, was presumably not particularly effective in imparting flexibility—one of the key characteristics required of good cavalry. However, the Spartans cannot have been completely unskilled in the training and employment of cavalry as Agesilaos' force was able to defeat the renowned Thessalian arm on its own territory.[15] This was a feat of which he was particularly proud,[16] but he may have been working with better material than that normally available at Sparta. Teleutias, the general at Olynthos in 382, displayed a similarly good grasp of the principles involved—his foresight in keeping a mounted reserve, and his intelligence in committing it when he did, snatched victory from almost certain defeat.[17]

Argos

Like Sparta, its main Peloponnesian rival, Argos does not seem to have had much of a cavalry tradition (despite two references in Homer to 'horse-grazing' Argos),[18] and may not even have had any cavalry at all until the fourth century. It signed a mutual defence pact with Athens, Elis, and Mantineia in 420, which required the city which had requested help to pay the allied troops (including cavalry) ration money at set rates after thirty days' service.[19] Although this could imply that each state possessed cavalry, subsequent events suggest that one of the reasons for this treaty was to allow the Peloponnesian signatories access to the Athenian cavalry because they had none of their own. During his description of the campaign which followed the signing of the treaty, Thucydides records the Argives and their other Peloponnesian allies as surrounded and in some difficulty because

    [14] Ibid. 3. 1. 4, 4. 15.
    [15] Ibid. 4. 3. 3–8; for the training and recruitment methods used by Agesilaos see 3. 4. 15–16.
    [16] Ibid. 4. 3. 9; *Ages.* 2. 5; Plut. *Ages.* 16. 5.
    [17] Xen. *Hell.* 5. 2. 40–3.
    [18] Hom. *Il.* 2. 287; 15. 30.
    [19] Thucy. 5. 47. 6.

'they had no cavalry as the Athenians, alone of all their allies, had not yet arrived.'[20]

This deficiency had obviously been rectified sometime in the late fifth or early fourth century as Xenophon records the entire Argive cavalry in action *c.*370, posted with accompanying infantry as the rearguard. The contingent was routed by a spirited charge of sixty Phleiasian cavalrymen, although Xenophon does add that not many Argives were killed.[21] Unfortunately, this solitary reference is insufficient to tell us anything about the size of the force (although it cannot have been large if chased off by sixty men), its organization, equipment, or command structure. Its quality is also unknown but on this particular occasion it did not perform particularly well—perhaps because it seems to have been acting as a static blocking force instead of taking advantage of its mobility.

Corinth

The history of the Corinthian cavalry is similar to that of neighbouring Argos, as it too seems to have been created post-425. At any rate, Corinth's army was defeated while resisting an Athenian naval landing at Solygeia in that year, largely because of its lack of cavalry. The Corinthians had been forewarned of the Athenian attack and had mobilized their entire army to deal with it (although they left half of the force at Kenchreiai in case the Athenians diverted their fleet there).[22] If the Corinthians had possessed any cavalry they surely would have used it at Solygeia; the only plausible explanation for its absence is that they did not have any.

The likelihood is that the Corinthian cavalry came into being towards the end of the fifth or the start of the fourth century. Its first attested action was in 370/69 when it was mobilized, along with the Athenian *hippeis*, to locate the Theban army which was returning from an invasion of Lakonia.[23] It also took the field against the Thebans in the following campaign season, again deployed with the Athenian cavalry—although both contingents

[20] Ibid. 5. 59. 3.
[21] Xen. *Hell*. 7. 2. 4.
[22] Thucy. 4. 42–4.
[23] Xen. *Hell*. 6. 5. 52.

judged the Theban army too strong to attack.[24] Our only other
real source of information on the Corinthian arm is provided by
Plutarch. He tells us, for example, that Timophanes (brother of
the famous general Timoleon, and later assassinated when he
attempted to set up a tyranny) commanded the cavalry in action
against the Argives and Kleonaians c.368–366.[25]

Most of the remaining evidence concerns the cavalry under
Timoleon during his Sicilian campaigns, but it is often difficult
to tell whether the cavalry referred to is Corinthian, Sicilian, or a
mixture of the two. However, if the 200 cavalrymen sent to Sicily
in 345 with Timoleon[26] were citizens and not mercenaries, it is
likely that the total cavalry corps was considerably larger than
this—no state would have sent its entire corps on an overseas
expedition of this nature. In an interesting aside, Plutarch also
claims that the weather was so calm that the horses swam across
from Thurii to Sicily with their reins secured to the troop trans-
ports.[27] The last known activity of the Corinthian arm occurred
in the mid-third century, when, in a particularly poor display of
horse-management, it ruined most of its horses while hurrying to
rendezvous at Argos with King Kleomenes III of Sparta.[28]

Phleious

Phleious was a small state, rather unfortunately situated between
Sikyon and Argos in the north-east of the Peloponnese. Despite
its size, we do know something of Phleious' cavalry in the second
quarter of the fourth century—largely because Xenophon's
imagination was caught by its exploits as a faithful ally of Sparta.
In 370, during Agesilaos' invasion of Arkadia, the Phleiasian
horse saved some mercenary colleagues who were being roughly
handled by the Mantineians.[29] The next few years saw them
paying dearly for this support as they were subjected to constant
pressure from their powerful neighbours, Sikyon and Argos, and
also suffered the occasional Theban invasion. According to Xeno-

[24] Ibid. 7. 1. 22.
[25] Plut. *Timol.* 4. 1 (for the tyranny and assassination—in which Timoleon was
involved—see ibid. 4. 2–5; Diod. Sic. 16. 65. 4; Cornelius Nepos, *Timoleon*, 1. 3–4).
[26] Plut. *Timol.* 16. 1–2.
[27] Ibid. 19. 3.
[28] Plut. *Kleom.* 19. 2.
[29] Xen. *Hell.* 6. 5. 13–14.

phon, though, they acquitted themselves very well—largely because of the energy and aggression of their cavalry and *epilektoi*
who regularly took the field together. We know nothing of the
Phleiasian cavalry's organization and equipment, apart from the
fact that the men wore breastplates and there were at least sixty of
them, but the quality of its performance recorded by Xenophon
suggests they were well trained and well led.[30] Its activities
against the larger forces of the neighbouring states certainly seem
to have impressed him, and he was a good judge of cavalry.

Elis

Elis is situated in the south-west of the Peloponnese. It apparently
had a reputation for horse-breeding[31] but, like most of the other
poleis of the area, Elis too may have had no real cavalry in the
fifth century (see the discussion on Argos). Eleian cavalry first
appears in our sources in the fourth century, and seems to have
been drawn from the upper echelons of society—together with
'the Three Hundred' (presumably the Eleian *epilektoi*) it was
prominent in putting down a democratic revolution in the city
c.365.[32] Its size, organization, and command structure are unknown but it may have been commanded by a single hipparch.
One holder of this office, Andromachos, killed himself in 365
after an attack he had suggested against the Arkadians failed and
another, Damophantos, was killed in single combat with the
Achaian general Philopoimen at the River Larissos in 209/8.[33]

Despite the personal failures of its commanders on these occasions, the Eleian cavalry generally seems to have been quite
competent. At the start of the war against Arkadia in 365 it
played a major part in driving the enemy out of Elis itself—even
though they had apparently penetrated as far as the *agora*
(market-place).[34] During the same war it also proved very successful against the democratic exiles and neighbouring Pylians and in
362, at the battle of Mantineia, it saved the Athenian hoplites

[30] Ibid. 7. 2. 4, 10–23.
[31] Hom. *Od.* 21. 347 refers to 'horse-pasturing Elis'; cf. *Od.* 4. 634–7 and *Il.*
11. 671–81.
[32] Xen. *Hell.* 7. 4. 15–16.
[33] Ibid. 7. 4. 19; Plut. *Philop.* 7. 6–7—the word *hipparchos* is used on both occasions.
[34] Xen. *Hell.* 7. 4. 14.

from disaster by launching an attack on the Boiotians who were pressing them hard.[35] Eleian cavalry may also have served under Alexander if the 150 soldiers who arrived to join him after Granikos were, as Arrian implies, horsemen.[36]

Achaia

The last Peloponnesian area to be examined is Achaia, situated on the north coast of the peninsula, and organized as a confederacy from at least the fourth century onwards. No real comment can be made about the cavalry forces of the individual cities of the area but the Achaian Confederacy apparently sent a contingent of horse which served with Alexander at the battle of Gaugamela in 331. Its size is unknown, but it cannot have been large as it was brigaded with the cavalry of 'the Peloponnesians'.[37]

We know considerably more about its history in the third and second centuries as the Achaian Confederacy was reorganized in 280 and soon came to play a prominent part in Peloponnesian and Greek affairs. The force was clearly aristocratic and wealthy as Plutarch described its members as 'the most esteemed of the citizens'.[38] At the battle of Sellasia in 222 its members were equipped with heavy armour, numbered 1,000, and were accompanied by another thousand horsemen from the Arkadian city of Megalopolis (which had joined the Confederacy in 235).[39] The normal establishment of the Achaian cavalry corps (excluding Megalopolis) at this time seems to have been 1,000 and this was certainly the number deployed against the Spartans at Pallantion in 228,[40] but it is impossible to know how many cavalrymen they had in the fifth and fourth centuries. Their standard in the third and second centuries seems to have been quite high—although two of their commanders, including the famed Philopoimen, were killed or captured when they got into difficulties on rough terrain.[41] However, the quality of any arm fluctuates over time and,

---

[35] Ibid. 7. 4. 26 (Pylos); Diod. Sic. 15. 85. 6–8 (Mantineia).
[36] Arr. *Anab.* 1. 29. 4.   [37] Diod. Sic. 17. 57. 3–4.
[38] Plut. *Philop.* 18. 4; cf. 6. 3.
[39] Sellasia: ibid. 6. 1–4; Polybios 2. 66. 7. Megalopolis' admission to the Confederacy: Polybios, 2. 44. 5.
[40] Plut. *Kleom.* 4. 4.
[41] Plut. *Philop.* 18. 5–7; the other was Lydiadas the ex-tyrant of Megalopolis, Plut. *Kleom.* 6. 3; *Arat.* 37. 1–3. Both men may have been generals on these occasions.

although Philopoimen brought the Achaian cavalry to a high
standard during his command in 209/8, it was apparently in a
pretty poor state when he took it over, largely because it was
difficult to discipline a body of men drawn from the most prominent and influential group in the cities.[42]

CENTRAL GREECE

For the purposes of my discussion, Central Greece includes all
states north of Corinth and south of Thessaly. However, apart
from Athens, only three areas within the region, Lokris, Phokis,
and Boiotia, stand out as cavalry states. As noted, these supplied
the cavalry for the Peloponnesian League army in the second half
of the fifth century[43] and they also maintained their cavalry
forces into the fourth century. Central Greece is generally more
suited to cavalry actions than the Peloponnese because it contains
some quite large areas of flat ground—especially the large plains
of Boiotia. Another incentive for the states north of Athens to
develop cavalry expertise was the presence of Thessaly, a major
cavalry power, on their northern borders.[44]

Athens

The Athenian cavalry seems to have gone through four main
phases in its development between c.500 and 300. The first of
these was a force of 96 cavalrymen, levied on the basis of two
from each of 48 administrative units (*naukrariai*) which also
supplied ships and crews for the navy. Although this force may
have been abolished at the end of the sixth century, it more
probably continued until the second phase which began with the
establishment of a corps of 300 men c.477 (or possibly later). It is
not known on what basis this enlarged force was recruited but it
is possible that thirty men were drawn from each *phyle*, or tribe.
It was probably divided into three equal-sized squadrons, each
commanded by a hipparch. The third stage of development, and
the one which forms the basis of this book, was the expansion of

---

[42] Plut. *Philop*. 7. 2–5.
[43] Thucy. 2. 9. 3.
[44] Cf. N. H. Demand, *Thebes in the Fifth Century* (London, 1982), 9.

the cavalry to a corps of 1,000, some time between c.445 and 438. This corps was divided into ten tribal squadrons of 100 men with each squadron (also called a *phyle*) commanded by a phylarch elected from within that tribe. Overall command was vested in two elected hipparchs of equal status. Each cavalryman received a state establishment loan (*katastasis*) to help set himself up in the corps and in addition was given a daily allowance (*sitos*) to assist with feeding his horse. The cavalry basically retained this structure and organization until c.320 after which, and under the influence of Macedonian domination, it entered its fourth phase—a reduction in strength to a force of 200–300 men.

However, because of the lack of evidence, many of the details (particularly of the first two stages) are impossible to recover or are the subject of considerable debate. For example, whether sixth-century Athens even had a cavalry which normally fought while mounted has been questioned. Helbig, for one, maintained that until c.477 it possessed no proper cavalry and that prior to this all Athenian military horsemen were mounted hoplites who rode to the battlefield but dismounted there and fought on foot.[45] His argument was based largely on the fact that most of the riders depicted on sixth-century vases are equipped as hoplites. However, there is a small but significant number of scenes which show horsemen dressed and equipped in the same way as the true cavalry of the fifth and fourth centuries. Helbig argued that such riders are either Thessalian cavalrymen or the grooms of mounted hoplites who hovered on the edges of the mêlée rendering what assistance they could.[46]

This, however, is not wholly convincing and Alföldi in particular has disagreed with it. He argues that Athens did have a true cavalry force in the sixth century but that heroic survivals in the vase-painting tradition meant that the majority of horsemen were depicted as mounted hoplites.[47] Despite the fact that his thesis is flawed by faulty argument and at times an over-imaginative interpretation of the pictorial evidence, he does manage to cast serious doubts upon Helbig's assessment of the ceramic mater-

[45] Helbig, 170 ff.; cf. P. A. L. Greenhalgh, *Early Greek Warfare* (Cambridge, 1973), 75–7.

. [46] Helbig, 208–21.

[47] A. Alföldi, *Die Herrschaft der Reiterei in Griechenland und Rom nach dem Sturz der Könige*, (*Antike Kunst*, Beiheft 4; Bern, 1967), 13–47. See also Martin, *Cavaliers*, 79 ff.

ial.[48] Alföldi's view gains further support from a vase near the style of the Thalia Painter which depicts what is apparently a *dokimasia* or inspection of the cavalry. This vase (no. 14), dated to between *c.*510 and 500, shows youths dressed in chlamydes and petasoi or in chitones and alopekides, leading horses forward for some sort of examination.[49] These youths were certainly not mounted infantry and, although Bugh speculates they may be young men about to participate in a procession,[50] the most natural interpretation of this scene is that Athens possessed some sort of cavalry force shortly before the end of the sixth century. Therefore, although many of the 'cavalrymen' on sixth-century Attic pottery are portrayed as mounted hoplites, Helbig is incorrect to state categorically that there were no proper cavalrymen at Athens during this period.

It also seems sensible to identify the youths in the *dokimasia* scene with the 96 naukraric cavalry attested for this date.[51] These were possibly established during Solon's reforms (traditionally dated to his archonship of 594/3).[52] Given that Athenian cavalry is not attested during the Persian Wars (490 and 480/79), it is possible that this force had been disbanded, perhaps during Kleisthenes' reforms at the end of the sixth century (*c.*508/7).[53] However, this is not certain as the *naukrariai* themselves were probably not abolished at this time but continued until Themistok-

---

[48] For example, although he produces several illustrations to support the existence of *amphihippoi*, men who rode into battle with a spare horse, to leap on to if necessary, none of them actually depicts a man doing so. Most show a rider mounted on a single horse and dismounting at the run. In addition, he also misrepresents Helbig's arguments concerning the purpose of the naukraric cavalry and the possibility of riding with greaves: Alföldi, *Herrschaft der Reiterei*, 14, 20, (cf. Helbig, 169, 189). However, his section on heroic survivals in vase-paintings (16 ff.) does seriously weaken Helbig's interpretation of the painted material.

[49] For a detailed discussion of this piece of pottery and others like it, see H. A. Cahn, 'Dokimasia', *RA* (1973), 3–22.

[50] Bugh, *Horsemen*, 18, but at 19 he states his belief that they are in fact cavalrymen.

[51] Pollux, 8. 108.

[52] Martin, *Cavaliers*, 79 ff., following the *Ath. Pol.* and rejecting Hdtos. C. Hignett, *A History of the Athenian Constitution* (Oxford, 1958), 316 ff., dates Solon's reforms to a later period.

[53] Bugh, *Horsemen*, 5–6; cf. *AGH* 130. For the suggestion that Kleisthenes' reforms had a distinct military purpose see P. Siewert, *Die Trittyen Attikas und die Heeresreform des Kleisthenes* (Vestigia, Beiträge zur alten Geschichte, 33; Munich, 1982), *passim*.

les' naval reforms of c.483.[54] It is also quite possible that the 96
naukraric cavalrymen were not deployed as a unit during the two
Persian invasions simply because they would have been helpless
against the vast number of enemy horsemen.[55] Because of this,
the naukraric cavalry could have survived until the abolition of
the naukraries which supplied them. Whether they did or not, at
some time prior to c.450 they were replaced by an enlarged force
of 300 men.

Unfortunately, the lack of reliable evidence for this period
means that the exact date of this reform is impossible to reconstruct with any real certainty. Bugh, for example, believes that
the corps of 300 was created in 'the relatively brief period between
Tanagra (458/7) and Oinophyta (457)'.[56] His argument is that the
early years of the Delian League (c.477–460) show an emphasis
on the fleet and, to a lesser degree, the hoplites, with no cavalry
involvement attested for Eurymedon or the Mount Ithôme campaign. He claims this situation changed in 460/59 with 'Athens'
involvement in the affairs of mainland Greece' and that the
desertion of their Thessalian cavalry allies at Tanagra in 458/7
provided the impetus for Athens to expand her cavalry corps to
300 men. Bugh also suggests that this date is confirmed by
Andokides, 3. 4–5 and Aischines, 2. 172–3 which, he argues
elsewhere, refer to this expansion.[57]

Helbig on the other hand opted for a date of c.477, although
admittedly while trying to prove the erroneous view that the
Athenians possessed no true cavalry until after the Persian Wars.
Although his main thesis is incorrect, his arguments for dating
the creation of the 300-strong corps to c.477 have some merit. He
concludes that the reform must date between 479 and 458/7 as
there were no Athenian cavalrymen at Plataia but that they were
present at Tanagra. He suggests that this range can be narrowed
by considering the influence of Thracian costume on various

---

[54] Hignett, *Athenian Constitution*, 21–2, 69–70, *contra* the testimony of *Ath.
Pol.* 21. 5. Unless the Athenians had decided to do without cavalry entirely, the
naukrariai would presumably have continued to furnish horsemen as well as ships
until this date.

[55] See also Bugh, *Horsemen*, 11–13.

[56] Ibid. 47.

[57] Bugh, *Horsemen*, 40–2, 47, and 'Andocides, Aeschines, and the Three Hundred Athenian Cavalrymen', *Phoenix*, 36 (1982), 306–12, esp. 309 ff. However,
this support only arises if the redating of Kimon's return in W. E. Thompson,
'Andocides and the Peace of Cimon', *Phoenix*, 38 (1984), 216–20 is accepted.

vases, supporting a date between 479 and 455 (when Athens again had close links with the region), and a cavalry allusion in Aischylos' *Seven against Thebes*, line 393, which suggests the reform took place prior to 467.[58] He finds further support in the statement in Plato, *Meno*, 93d that Themistokles had his son Kleophantos trained to be an excellent *hippeus*. Taking *hippeus* here as 'cavalryman' and not 'rider', he argues that this must have occurred prior to Themistokles' exile which he dates between 474 and 472.[59] Finally, he argues that the change was likely to have occurred closer to 477, when the Athenians were still impressed by the need for cavalry shown by Plataia, and while they were instituting the military reforms associated with the foundation of the Delian League.[60]

Both theories are open to criticism, but this reflects the quality of the evidence rather than the quality of the arguments. For example, Bugh believes that the Athenian cavalrymen which were probably at Tanagra[61] were naukraric cavalry and not part of the corps of 300. If so, they must have continued in existence for at least twenty years after the abolition of the naukraries, the administrative unit from which they had been drawn. This seems highly unlikely and suggests that the cavalrymen at Tanagra were, as Helbig concludes, members of the new corps. In this case its institution must pre-date the battle and therefore also Bugh's preferred date. In addition, as Bugh accepts,[62] there are still chronological problems with Andokides, 3. 4–5; if the traditional dating of 451 for Kimon's return is retained, this passage cannot support a date as early as 457 for the cavalry reform. Finally, the argument that there was no cavalry activity prior to 460 is rather tenuous. Certainly they are not mentioned in our sources, but these are particularly slim for this period and Bugh himself admits that the logistics of transporting cavalry by sea to Eurymedon might have been the reason they were not used there.[63] Their omission from the Ithôme campaign could readily be explained by the fact that cavalry can play little if any part in a

[58] Helbig, 229–35.

[59] Ibid. 235–6. Bugh, *Horsemen*, 13–14 argues that this is probably what Plato intended; whether Plato was correct is another matter.

[60] Helbig, 236.

[61] Bugh, *Horsemen*, 43–5; but the evidence for their presence is not absolutely certain.

[62] Ibid. 47.   [63] Ibid. 41.

siege and the Athenians therefore may simply not have sent any.[64] Given our lack of evidence, the argument from silence is particularly dangerous here, especially as the Athenian cavalry are not even attested at the battles of Oinophyta (457) or Koroneia ten years later,[65] both of which took place after Bugh's date for the reform.

Similarly, Helbig's account is open to queries. The Aischylos reference is a cavalry simile which could be understood by anyone who had seen warhorses ready for action and therefore need not necessarily refer to the corps of 300. The dating of the Thracian influence on the vases to c.479 to 455 is also open to question as Athens had had a long history of involvement in that area, including the period prior to the Persian Wars.

The evidence is therefore ambiguous, but on balance perhaps favours the earlier date. This is further strengthened by a comparison of two *dokimasia* scenes. The scrutineer on the cup near the Thalia Painter already mentioned (vase 14, c.510–500) seems to be a member of the cavalry, while his equivalent on a later cup (vase 32, Plates 3–5, dated to c.480–470) seems to be a civilian official; this suggests that between the two paintings the state may have become more involved with the cavalry organization. This is most likely to be linked with the creation of the corps of 300. In addition, a reform of the cavalry at the same time (c.483?) as the abolition of the naukraries from which the original force was drawn seems logical. However, neat logic does not always apply in such situations and it remains possible that Bugh's date of 457 is correct.

The best we can probably say is that at some stage prior to c.450 the naukraric cavalry was restructured to become a larger force of 300 men and horses. This date is based on an inscription, *IG* I[2] 400, which mentions three hipparchs of apparently equal rank who served together in the same action or actions. This almost certainly refers to the 300-man cavalry organization and not to the naukraric cavalry or the 1,000-strong corps. The naukraric cavalry of 96 men was too small to have had three hipparchs and, although the 1,000-strong corps had two hipparchs in Athens with an additional hipparch of lower status on Lemnos

[64] Cf. the Syracusans who dismissed their cavalry during a siege in 404 because they thought it was useless in this phase of war, Diod. Sic. 14. 9. 1.

[65] See Bugh, *Horsemen*, 46–7 (Oinophyta) and Helbig, 242 (Koroneia).

(see Appendix 6), these were not of equal rank and presumably would not have campaigned together. The most probable explanation is that the hipparchs of this inscription were in fact equivalent to squadron commanders, with each leading a force of 100 men.[66] Unfortunately the date of the inscription is variously assessed as 'shortly after 457', '*c.*446', and, perhaps most safely, the 'mid-fifth century'.[67] In addition, there is nothing in the inscription to support Anderson's claim that it may have 'celebrated the foundation of the new corps as much as its first success'[68]—it could date from any point in the corps' existence. All it can tell us about the date of the reform is that the expanded corps of 300 most probably already existed *c.*450.

In general terms then, Athens probably possessed a force of naukraric cavalry, numbering only 96 men, from the time of Solon's reforms to about 483. At around this date, or sometime later, the force was replaced by a corps of 300. The next change was the reform which established the cavalry in its classic organization of 1,000 men, although the exact date for this is again subject to debate. Helbig, for example, suggests a little before 438/7, Martin argues for sometime between 445 and 438 (with 442 as his preferred choice), while Bugh opts for 'sometime between 445 and 431'.[69] The upper date is fairly secure, but Bugh is perhaps a little over cautious with the lower date. Given the identification of the riders on the Parthenon frieze as members of a cavalry corps apparently divided into ten sub-units (see Appendix 3), 439/8 would be the latest date for the reform.[70] The current state of the evidence does not allow any greater precision within the period *c.*445–438, but it is possible to say that the reform may well have been associated with Perikles (Appendix 5.142). He certainly had strong links with the cavalry class; he was of hippic status himself and his sons (nos. 140, 189) were trained as good

---

[66] *HCT* i. 328 n. 1; cf. Bugh, *Horsemen*, 49–50.

[67] A. E. Raubitschek, *Dedications from the Athenian Akropolis* (Cambridge, Mass., 1949), 151 (no. 135*b*); von Gaertringen (*IG* I² 400); Dittenberger, *SIG*³ 51.

[68] *AGH* 131.

[69] Helbig, 242; Martin, *Cavaliers*, 131–4; Bugh, *Horsemen*, 76 (Bugh's remarks, 49, 76, imply he favours a date shortly after Pleistoanax of Sparta successfully invaded Attica in 446).

[70] Ashmole, *Architect and Sculptor*, 126–7, 141–2 argues that the friezes were probably largely complete by 438.

riders.[71] In addition, his use of the cavalry in defence of Attica during the Peloponnesian War shows a sound knowledge of the characteristics of the mounted arm.[72]

This reform created a corps of 1,000 men, commanded by two hipparchs and subdivided into ten squadrons or *phylai*, each led by a phylarch. The individual *hippeis* were essentially volunteers, although possession of a certain level of wealth rendered citizens liable for compulsory cavalry service. To ease the financial burden the state paid an establishment grant or *katastasis* to assist with the initial purchase of horse and equipment. This was a loan which was repaid when a cavalryman retired from the service. It is possible that the institution of this grant coincided with the creation of the corps of 300,[73] but this would seem highly unlikely if this did take place in the 480s or 470s. It is preferable to associate the introduction of this payment with the expansion of the cavalry to 1,000 members as this increase is more likely to have required the service of men who were on the borderline of being able to keep horses than the earlier increase from 96 to 300. It would also fit better with a date after the middle of the fifth century, when the principle and practice of state pay and allowances was firmly established. At any rate, the earliest mention we have of *katastasis* is for the year 404/3.[74] The only evidence for the amount is for 1,200 drachmas, but this is a sizeable sum and the grant may well not have been as large as this from its inception.[75] In addition to this, a daily *sitos* payment was made to assist with feeding the horse.

Down to sometime between 395 and *c*.365 the corps was supplemented by 200 *hippotoxotai*, or mounted archers, and the existence of *hamippoi* (infantrymen attached to the cavalry) is attested from *c*.365 onwards. Although subject to minor organiza-

---

[71] Pl. *Meno*, 94b.

[72] See 'mobile defence', Ch. 3.

[73] Bugh, *Horsemen*, 52–3.

[74] Lysias, 16. 6–7. Bugh, *Phoenix*, 36 (1982), 309 ff. makes too much of καθ-ίστημι and κατάστασις as technical terms. As he himself points out, ibid. 311–12, the former could be used in a non-technical sense. As Andokides applied the term in the same sentence both to cavalry and to archers (who did not receive *katastasis*), it seems more likely that he was using it in this way. If Andokides' intention really was to correct his predecessors and to show that *katastasis* was first instituted at this time, he surely would have done so much more explicitly than Bugh's theory suggests.

[75] See also my review of Bugh, *Horsemen*, in *Gnomon*, 62 (1990), 423.

tional changes and occasionally fluctuating numbers, this was the essential form of the cavalry from the time of the major reform of c.445–438 up until the period of Macedonian interference after about 320.

The corps served with some distinction during the Peloponnesian War but adversely affected its popularity, and probably also its future employment, by its involvement in the oligarchic movements at the end of the fifth century. A period of neglect followed which included a reduction in the peace-time rate of *sitos* payment, the forced repayment of the *katastasis* by those *hippeis* involved in the oligarchy, and even one case where cavalrymen were sent overseas with the thought that their loss in action would be of no great concern to the democracy. This phase seems to have lasted until c.362, when the memory of the oligarchy had faded somewhat and the cavalry had provided a major boost to morale by its action against the Thebans at Mantineia—the only success of that campaign. The remainder of its fourth-century history was characterized by an increased emphasis on the value of cavalry in public thought and debate, culminating perhaps in its use, along with the cavalry of allied Greek states, as the main striking arm against the Macedonians at Krannon and Lamia. After about 320 the cavalry, like Athens itself, went into a decline and probably had its establishment reduced by various Macedonian rulers. The abolition of compulsory military service at the end of the fourth century, and an associated reluctance on the part of the wealthy to undertake civic service, also undoubtedly helped to reduce numbers at this time. The last recorded military action of the *hippeis* occurred against the Gauls at Delphi in 279, where, ironically, they were unable to contribute to the battle because of the rugged terrain.[76]

Lokris and Phokis

Although they are separate states, it is convenient to treat the neighbouring regions of Lokris and Phokis together. Like Athens, both seem to have raised a proper cavalry corps in the period between the end of the Persian War (479) and the start of the Peloponnesian War (431). With one possible exception, all known Phokian and Lokrian troops serving in the Persian War (whether

---

[76] Pausanias, 10. 20. 3 ff.

on the Greek or Persian side) were hoplites,[77] and the first mention of their cavalry is in Thucydides' description of the Peloponnesian League forces at the outbreak of the war against Athens in 431. Unfortunately he does not indicate the size or organization of the contingents and fails to provide any further details of their cavalry contribution to the war-effort. However, it is probable that the Lokrians who arrived just in time to join in the pursuit at Delion in 424 were cavalrymen;[78] it seems unlikely that hoplites would have been able to catch up with the Athenian infantry as it fled from the field.

The cavalry of both states played an important part in the Sacred War of 355–346, serving as usual on opposite sides. In 354/3 the Phokian cavalry defeated the Lokrian and Boiotian horse on Lokrian territory but the numbers on each side are unknown. A year later, at the battle of the Crocus Plain, the Phokian army was decisively beaten, apparently because the 500 Phokian horse were insufficient to overcome the 3,000 Thessalian cavalry who opposed them. Later in the war the Phokian cavalry lost a large number of men in a mounted engagement against the Boiotians near Chaironeia.[79] Unfortunately for modern scholars examining the Phokian cavalry arm, one of the reasons the fairly small state of Phokis could resist so many powerful enemies at once was because it used the sacred treasures at Delphi to pay for large numbers of mercenaries.[80] It is therefore difficult to know whether the Phokian cavalry recorded during this war was Phokian, mercenary, or (more likely) a mixture of the two. However, the number of cavalry available locally was probably not large as the Phokians could only deploy 500 troopers in the early stages of the war, at a time when they still had plenty of money. Later in the war they responded to a Spartan request for aid by sending 3,000 infantry and no cavalry to the Peloponnese.[81] The size of the Lokrian force is also unknown. Under the surrender terms at

[77] Both regions were forced to join the Persians after Thermopylai. For their troops see Hdtos 7. 203 (with 212, 217–18); 9. 17–18, 31. The possible exception is the Phokian group which refused to submit to the Persians, harrying their rear area instead (Hdtos 9. 31). These men may have included cavalry but their mountain base makes it more likely that they were infantrymen.

[78] Thucy. 2. 9. 3; 4. 96. 8.

[79] Diod. Sic. 16. 30. 3, 35. 4–6; cf. Hammond and Griffith, 273–8. Chaironeia: Diod. Sic. 16. 38. 7.

[80] See Diod. Sic. 16. 30. 1–3.

[81] Ibid. 16. 39. 3.

the end of the Sacred War the Phokians were deprived of their arms and horses and forbidden to purchase new ones until they had repaid the sacred monies they had used for the war and this must have destroyed their cavalry corps for some time afterwards. However, by 331 they had recovered sufficiently to join with the Lokrians in sending a cavalry contingent to fight on Alexander's side in the final battle against Darius at Gaugamela.[82]

Boiotia

Boiotia is basically a large plain surrounded by mountains and containing (in antiquity) several large lakes but little high ground.[83] It was good cavalry country and the Boiotians in general seem to have had a long equestrian tradition.[84] The Boiotian plain supported many settlements which together developed into a federal league of autonomous cities, known as the Boiotian League. Although Thebes was the largest city in the region and from time to time dominated the federal organization (especially in the fourth century), the Boiotian League was a true federation with its own political and military organization. The discussion which follows therefore largely deals with the League as a whole and not with the individual member states.

However, the first mention of Boiotian cavalry was in service with the Persians at the battle of Plataia in 479 and the force did not include contingents from all states. After Thermopylai, most of Boiotia joined the Persians but Plataia and Thespiai refused to Medize and continued to fight on the allied side.[85] The Boiotians contributed both hoplites and cavalry to the Persian cause and at Plataia their cavalry in particular seems to have distinguished itself against the allied Greek army. Herodotos records that at the end of the fight it placed itself between the fleeing Persians and their pursuers and assisted the invaders as much as possible. It was certainly effective in this role as Theban horsemen, under the hipparch Asopodoros, cut down 600 Megarian and Phleiasian

[82] Ibid. 16. 60. 1–4; 17. 57. 3–4. Q. Curtius Rufus, 4. 13. 29 only records the presence of the Lokrians.

[83] The most famous of these lakes, Kopais, is now drained.

[84] Cf. the Mycenaean bronze horse-bit on display in case 16 at the Archaeological Museum of Thebes. The Thebans are also called the 'horse-racing Kadmeians' in Hom. *Il*. 4. 391.

[85] Hdtos 8. 50; 9. 28, 30–1.

hoplites who had imprudently broken their phalanx to chase the Persians.[86] To inflict so many casualties this cavalry contingent must have been quite large, but it is impossible to tell its precise size or what proportion it formed of the Boiotian cavalry as a whole.

Although Thebes' enthusiastic support of the Persians lost her the dominant position in Boiotia for some time, she had largely regained it by 446—when the region broke free from a period of Athenian control. From this date down to its temporary dissolution by the Spartans in 386 the Boiotian League probably fielded a cavalry corps of 1,100 men—a large force by Greek standards. This figure is derived from a description of the Boiotian federal constitution written in the fourth century.[87] Although the relative positions of the cities within the League fluctuated between 446 and 386, and parts of the description clearly apply to post-427 (when Plataia fell to Thebes), the general military and political organization probably applied throughout the period.[88] Given the oligarchic nature of the League constitution, it is certain that the cavalry was recruited from those who could supply their own horse and equipment—in short, from the wealthiest class in each city. Contingents were supplied as follows: Thebes contributed 400; Orchomenos and Hyettos (called Hysiai in the text) together sent 200; 200 were jointly contributed by Thespiai, Eutresis, and Thisbai; 100 came from Tanagra; 100 from Haliartos, Lebadaia, and Koroneia combined; and Akraiphnion, Kopai, and Chaironeia jointly contributed a further 100.[89]

Other sources confirm that the Boiotian League could deploy around 1,000 cavalrymen in the fifth century. It had this number in defence of its own territory at Delion in 424 and is supposed to have sent 900 to raid Attica from Dekeleia in 408. However, as might be expected, fewer than this were usually employed in expeditions outside Boiotia and in such cases 500–600 men was the norm.[90] Despite the League's temporary disbandment from 386 to 378 and some fighting between member states in the

---

[86] Ibid. 9. 68–9.

[87] *Hell. Oxy*. 11. 2–4, dated to the period 386–356, J. M. Moore, *Aristotle and Xenophon on Democracy and Oligarchy* (London, 1975), 125.

[88] Cf. Moore, loc. cit.

[89] *Hell. Oxy*. 11. 3–4.

[90] Thucy. 4. 93. 3; Diod. Sic. 12. 69. 3–4; 13. 72. 4 (Delion and Dekeleia). Thucy. 4. 72. 1; 5. 57. 2 (500–600 men).

following years,[91] in the fourth century its cavalry remained basically the same size. During this period it was normally deployed as a body of 500–700 men, although 1,300 were mobilized to aid Ptolemy against Demetrios in 313.[92]

The corps' command structure is unknown but as each district of the League contributed a squadron of about 100 men[93] it seems logical that each of these was commanded by a local officer. In battle the cavalry seems to have been commanded directly by the Boiotarchs (generals) of the League and it is possible that there was no equivalent to the Athenian position of hipparch—although Thucydides does use this term to describe the leader of a Boiotian cavalry contingent in 424. However, as was the case at Athens, the Boiotian arm was strengthened by the attachment of *hamippoi*, infantrymen trained to operate with the cavalry. These are attested as early as 418 and were apparently deployed on the basis of one *hamippos* per cavalryman. Boiotian cavalry also operated closely with Thessalian light troops at Mantineia in 362.[94] Its members were apparently regularly equipped with armour in both the fifth and fourth centuries, and this practice may have dated as far back as 500.[95] Their armament included the sword and javelin, although the outflanking movement at Mantineia (362) suggests that they may have had a thrusting spear at that date.[96]

The quality of the Boiotian cavalry seems to have been fair. In 431 it defeated the Athenian horse in the initial action of the first annual invasion of Attica, and a flanking movement by two

[91] Xen. *Hell.* 5. 4. 10; 6. 3. 1, 5, 4. 10; Diod. Sic. 15. 46. 4–6.

[92] Plut. *Pelop.* 35. 1; Diod. Sic. 15. 68. 1, 71. 3; 16. 39. 2; but cf. 15. 94. 2 (300 men). For the aid to Ptolemy see Diod. Sic. 19. 77. 4.

[93] *Hell. Oxy.* 11. 3–4; some cities of course controlled more than one district.

[94] Boiotarchs: Thucy. 4. 96. 5 and (less certainly) 7. 30. 3. Hipparch: Thucy. 4. 72. 4. *Hamippoi*: Thucy. 5. 57. 2. Mantineia: Diod. Sic. 15. 85. 4–5.

[95] Thucy. 4. 72. 4; Xen. *Hell.* 7. 5. 20. A 4th-cent. relief in the courtyard of the Thebes Museum depicts a rider in a helmet and a cuirass with pteryges; a rider on a relief from Thespiai (Athens, NM 828) may be wearing a breastplate under his chlamys. A warrior on an equestrian grave-relief of *c.*500 in the Boston Museum of Fine Arts (= Demand, *Thebes*, pl. 3) wears a crested Corinthian helmet, breastplate, greaves, and slung sword. Enough of the monument survives to show he was not carrying a shield and therefore probably should not be identified as a mounted hoplite.

[96] Sword: see preceding note; javelins: Xen. *Hell.* 5. 4. 40 (although he uses the term '*dorata*', the weapons were thrown); Mantineia: Diod. Sic. 15. 85. 7.

squadrons resulted in an important victory at Delion in 424.⁹⁷ In
the fourth century it performed particularly well under Epameinondas, showing its full potential at the battle of Mantineia in
362. On this occasion, mixed with *hamippoi* and deployed in a
wedge, it cut right through the opposing cavalry (deployed in a
tetragonal formation) and played an important part in the resultant victory.⁹⁸ Some years earlier, again under Epameinondas'
command, it showed that on a good day, and when aggressively
handled, it could even match the renowned Thessalian arm.⁹⁹

However, its combat record is otherwise mixed. It was being
worsted in the second engagement in the 431 campaign by a joint
Athenian–Thessalian force until the Boiotian hoplites arrived to
help,¹⁰⁰ and in the fourth century showed itself capable of basic
errors. One group, for example, misjudged the speed of attacking
cavalry and hoplites under Agesilaos and, behaving 'as men who
had drunk at midday', discharged their javelins too early and left
their withdrawal too late; twelve died. On another occasion, while
fighting Alexander the Great, the cavalry fled in some disorder,
trampling its own infantry on the way and killing several of its
own number when it rode into a collection of narrow alleys and
trenches.¹⁰¹

NORTHERN GREECE

The main cavalry powers in Northern Greece were Thessaly,
Macedonia, and the cities of the Chalkidike. The Thessalians
were always regarded as having the best cavalry in Greece proper
but were later overtaken by the Macedonians under Philip and
Alexander. The Macedonians, however, were on the fringe of
Greek culture and society—some Greeks at any rate regarded
them as ill-bred, semi-barbarians, who drank their wine neat and

⁹⁷ Thucy. 2. 19. 2; 4. 96 (but see Diod. Sic. 12. 70. 2–3 for a contradictory—
and less plausible—account featuring a fairly standard reversal of fortunes).
⁹⁸ Xen. *Hell.* 7. 5. 23–4. Diod. Sic. 15. 85. 7 states that it then went on to
threaten the flank of the Athenian phalanx and this may well be true—despite
Xenophon's remark that the cavalry did not pursue far, he records that the
hamippoi did reach the Athenians.
⁹⁹ Diod. Sic. 15. 71. 6.
¹⁰⁰ Thucy. 2. 22. 2.
¹⁰¹ Xen. *Hell.* 5. 4. 40; Diod. Sic. 17. 12. 5.

engaged in unseemly and drunken parties. Because of this, and
the fact that a proper analysis of Macedonian cavalry tactics and
organization would require a volume of its own, this book contains
only a brief sketch of the Macedonian arm. This is included
largely because the Macedonian cavalry tradition and performance, and its attitude to mounted warfare, makes an interesting
contrast to the state of affairs in most of Greece. Although the
cavalry of the various Thracian tribes played an important part in
the military history of this region, it is omitted because of its
non-Hellenic nature and the very patchy state of the evidence
concerning it.

Thessaly

Thessaly is a basically flat and agriculturally rich region which
lent itself to the breeding and use of horses.[102] Its early society
was a feudal aristocracy which formed a loose confederation,
traditionally consisting of four administrative districts or tetrarchies.[103] However, by the mid-fifth century the cities of the
region had become powerful enough to challenge the feudal lords
and from this point on played an important part in the history of
Thessaly. The fourth century saw the rise of dynasts who con-
tended with each other for the control of the region, but by 320
Thessaly had lost its independence to Macedon and no longer
figured as an independent entity.[104]

Unlike many Greek states, Thessaly possessed a sizeable force
of true cavalry in the sixth century[105] and these must have been
provided under the system of tetrarchies. Each tetrarchy was
divided into blocks called *kleroi*, each of which supplied forty
cavalrymen and eighty peltasts.[106] The large feudal estates were
also able to provide horsemen—Menon of Pharsalos sent 200–300

[102] Several Thessalian cities regularly depicted horses or horsemen on their
coinage, see *GC* coins 466–8 (Larissa); *ACGC* pl. 21, coins 373, 385, 392, 395–6
(Larissa), 379 (Skotoussa), 381–2, 391 (Pharsalos), 387–8 (Pherai); T. R. Martin,
Sovereignty and Coinage in Classical Greece (Princeton, NJ, 1985), pl. 1, coins 1–4
(Larissa); see also n. 117 below.

[103] V. Rose, *Aristotelis Fragmenta*, 3rd edn. (Leipzig, 1886), F 497; Westlake,
Thessaly, 21–3.

[104] See Westlake, *Thessaly*, 29, 235.

[105] Cf. Hdtos 5. 63–4.

[106] Rose, *Aristotelis Fragmenta*, F 498 (accepting Cobet's emendation of
πελταστὰς for the MS ὁπλίτας).

for a campaign against the Persians in 476/5.[107] However, by 431 the Thessalian League's cavalry was organized on a city basis with each *polis* supplying one or more contingents commanded by a local officer. Larissa apparently supplied two squadrons at this time, one commanded by Polymedes, the other by Aristonous; a Menon commanded the Pharsalian contingent. This system continued throughout the fourth century and lasted until at least 331, when the Pharsalian force was described as the best of the Thessalian contingents in Alexander's army.[108]

As might be expected, considering Thessaly's fairly volatile history, the size of the individual contingents and of the total League force fluctuated—especially during the dynastic struggles of the fourth century. However, it was always larger than the cavalry arms of other contemporary Greek states. At the end of the sixth century, when Athens may have had a force of 96 cavalrymen, the Thessalians were able to send 1,000 troopers to assist them against Sparta.[109] As *Tagos* (head) of the Thessalian League in 375, Jason of Pherai could claim that he had 6,000 cavalry available to him and this was swollen to 8,000 when his allies were included.[110] This seems to have represented the height of the Thessalian League's military power, but later in the century it was still regularly capable of fielding around 2,000 horsemen[111]—a very large force by Greek standards.

Although not as heavily equipped as the Persian cavalry, the Thessalian cavalry did make use of armour. A coin of Alexander of Pherai (369–358) depicts a rider in a helmet, breastplate, and boots and another coin shows that the local cavalry used the combination side and thigh pieces to protect both horse and rider.[112] A fragmentary relief from Larissa confirms that heavy boots were worn and also depicts a spear with a butt-spike, which suggests that at least some Thessalian cavalrymen carried a thrusting spear. This could have been quite effective when used with

[107] Dem. 23. 199; [Dem.] 13. 23.
[108] City contingents: Thucy. 2. 22. 2–3; Xen. *Hell*. 4. 3. 3–5; 6. 4. 31. Pharsalians: Arr. *Anab*. 3. 11. 10.
[109] Hdtos 5. 63–4; *Ath. Pol*. 19. 5.
[110] Xen. *Hell*. 6. 1. 8, 19. These figures may have included his mercenary troops (which included cavalry, ibid. 6. 4. 28), Westlake, *Thessaly*, 106.
[111] Diod. Sic. 17. 17. 4 (1,800); 18. 15. 2 (2,000).
[112] Q. Curtius Rufus, 3. 11. 14–15; *GC* no. 471; J. K. Anderson, 'Notes on Some Points of Xenophon's Περὶ Ἱππικῆς' *JHS* 80 (1960), 7–8.

the diamond or rhomboid formation favoured by the Thessalians.[113]

Throughout its history, Thessaly was famous for its cavalry and its horsemanship.[114] Thessalian cavalry defeated the redoubtable Spartan hoplites near Athens in 510 and Alexander the Great certainly regarded the contingents which served with him in Asia Minor very highly.[115] Their performance at the battles of the Crocus Plain (353) under Philip II of Macedon and at Gaugamela (331) under Alexander seem to have been particularly notable.[116] This is perhaps not surprising given their numbers but their equestrian skills were also high—several Thessalian cities issued coins depicting young men chasing bulls on horseback and then dismounting to wrestle them to the ground.[117]

However, no force is invincible, and even the Thessalian cavalry had its share of reverses. It was defeated (with the loss of forty men) in its second engagement against the Spartans in 510 and some time prior to 480 was humiliated by the Phokians who created the ancient equivalent of a minefield by burying jars in a plain. When the Thessalians charged, their horses stepped in the jars and broke their legs; the Thessalians never forgave the Phokians and took their revenge during the Persian Wars.[118] This defeat was perhaps more a case of poor observation than poor combat skills but on occasion the Thessalians also failed against opposing cavalry. When Agesilaos of Sparta was crossing Thessaly in 394, he used his cavalry (recruited from the Ionian Greeks but trained under his supervision) aggressively and drove the Thessalians from the field—Polycharmos, the commander of the Pharsalian contingent was amongst the casualties. About thirty years later, Pelopidas again proved that when well and aggressively led the cavalry of other states could defeat the Thessalian arm.[119]

[113] Relief: L 393, Volos, Athanassakeion Archaeological Museum, in Sekunda, *AG* 17. Formation: Arr. *Takt.* 16. 1–5; Asklepiodotos, 7. 2.

[114] Cf. Pl. *Meno*, 70a–b.

[115] Hdtos 5. 63; Plut. *Alex.* 24. 1; 42. 3.

[116] Crocus Plain: Diod. Sic. 16. 35. 5 (but they did outnumber the enemy). Gaugamela: Arr. *Anab.* 3. 15. 3; Diod. Sic. 17. 60. 5–8; Q. Curtius Rufus, 3. 11. 13–15.

[117] The coins normally portray the man and the bull on one side and the recently abandoned steed on the other—see *GC* no. 466 and *ACGC* pl. 21, coins 375–8, 383, 386 (in the last the rider is still mounted).

[118] Hdtos 5. 64; 8. 27–32.

[119] Xen. *Hell.* 4. 3. 5–8; *Ages.* 2. 2–5; Plut. *Ages.* 16. 5 and *Pelop.* 32. 2.

Macedonia

Macedonia was a monarchy, but one in which the nobility played an important part—particularly in the period down to Philip II when the central authority was often weak. The area had reasonably large plains, particularly in the Bottiaian region and eastwards into the Chalkidike and, in common with other aristocratic societies, possessed a strong cavalry tradition. Horses and horsemen are frequently portrayed on Macedonian coinage in the classical and hellenistic periods, particularly on regal coins dating from Alexander I (*c*.495–452) onwards. This same Alexander is recorded riding to the Greek camp at Plataia in 479 to advise them of the Persian situation and intentions.[120] The tradition was maintained throughout the fifth century—Macedonia supplied sufficient cavalry to their Peloponnesian allies during the Olynthian campaign of 432 for Perdikkas to be appointed commander of the allied cavalry.[121] When the Thracian chief Sitalkes invaded with a large army three years later, the Macedonians adopted the strategy of mobile defence and relied on their cavalry to provide some protection to the countryside. Except when completely outnumbered, this proved quite effective because they were 'good horsemen and protected by armour'. Armour is certainly attested on early fifth-century coinage,[122] but the majority of horsemen depicted are lightly equipped and may represent hunters or light cavalrymen. However, there is no reason to doubt Thucydides' testimony here and the Macedonian cavalry under Philip and Alexander was apparently also equipped with armour.

Down to the reforms of Philip II,[123] the Macedonian cavalry seems to have been fairly typical of other cavalry forces and possessed a fairly good reputation—although it was defeated by the Chalkidians outside Olynthos in 382 and was outshone by Derdas' Elimian horsemen in the rest of the campaign.[124] It was Philip's reforms which created the Macedonian army as an unusually professional fighting force, and this included the mounted

---

[120] *GCV* coins 1317–18, 1321–2, 1477, 1482–3, 1490–2, 1494, 1509, 1514; *ACGC* pls. 26–8, esp. coins 484, 491–500, 502, 504–6, 513; C. T. Seltman, *Greek Coins*, 2nd edn. (London, 1960), pl. 46, coins 1, 10–14. Plataia: Hdtos 9. 44–5.

[121] Thucy. 1. 62. 2.

[122] Thucy. 2. 100. 5. Coinage: *GCV* 1317; *ACGC* 491.

[123] For a general discussion of this, see Hammond and Griffith, 405–49.

[124] Xen. *Hell.* 5. 2. 40; cf. 5. 2. 41–2, 3. 1–2.

arm. Under Philip and Alexander the cavalry was used as the battle-winning arm, reaching its perfection in the well-timed charges which Alexander employed to shatter the enemy's battle-lines in Asia.[125] However, this cavalry was rather different from the earlier Macedonian horse. It used a wedge-shaped formation, apparently introduced by Philip II (who may have borrowed the idea from the Thracians, who in turn had got it from the Scythians).[126] Their equipment was also different—Macedonian scouts or *prodromoi* were also known as *sarissophoroi* (*sarissa*-bearers) and Markle makes a plausible case for the use of the long Macedonian lance or *sarissa* by other Macedonian cavalrymen.[127] It seems likely then, that at least some of the native Macedonian cavalrymen were regularly equipped with this weapon, but it is difficult to assess what proportion was armed in this way.

The Macedonian army, particularly after the absorption of Thessaly, could field a flexible and very large cavalry force which included both light and heavy cavalrymen.[128] The size of the mounted arm, its new disciplined organization, new tactics and equipment, the considerable experience acquired in almost continual warfare from the time of Philip II, and good leadership under both Philip and Alexander, made the Macedonian cavalry arguably the best in the world in the second half of the fourth century. Its history is beyond the scope of this book, and after Philip's reorganization it is rather atypical of the Greek arm in general, but it nevertheless illustrates something of the potential which all Greek cavalry possessed.

The Chalkidike

The Chalkidike was colonized by several Greek states during the eighth and seventh centuries. Its non-Greek neighbours to the

[125] Cf. Arr. *Anab.* 1. 14. 6 ff.; Diod. Sic. 17. 19. 6 ff. (Granikos). Arr. *Anab.* 2. 9 ff.; Diod. Sic. 17. 33. 5 ff.; cf. Q. Curtius Rufus, 3. 11. 2 ff. (Issos). Arr. *Anab.* 3. 8 ff.; Diod. Sic. 17. 60. 1–4; Q. Curtius Rufus, 4. 15 (Gaugamela).

[126] Arr. *Takt.* 16. 6; Aelian, *Takt.* 18. 3. Asklepiodotos, 7. 3 states that the Macedonians used the wedge but does not mention Philip by name.

[127] Markle, 'Macedonian Sarissa', 333–9, 'Use of the Sarissa', 489–91 (for supporting archaeological evidence see 'Macedonian Arms', 87–111).

[128] Alexander had over 2,000 Macedonian cavalry (and 1,800 Thessalian horse) with him at the start of his Asian campaign in 334, while Antipater still had 1,500 in Greece, Diod. Sic. 17. 17. 4–5 with R. D. Milns, 'Alexander's Macedonian Cavalry and Diodorus xvii. 17. 4', *JHS* 86 (1966), 167–8.

north and east, the Thracians, had a tribal organization with a fairly strong cavalry tradition; the Macedonians to the west were also noted cavalrymen. The equestrian influence on the Greek settlers is evident in the late sixth/early fifth century when at least one city, Sermylia, was issuing coins depicting horsemen.[129] In 432/1 several of the cities joined together to form the Chalkidian Confederation; this had a federal government, with the administrative centre at Olynthos, issued its own coinage, and had common laws. In 382 a proposal was passed which involved the member states in common citizenship with equal rights of intermarriage and property ownership. However, not all states in the region were happy with this and Akanthos and Apollonia appealed to the Spartans who promptly dispatched an expeditionary force to the area.[130] The Confederacy lost the war in 379 and was dissolved, with its member states forced to make separate treaties with Sparta. Although it later underwent a period of resurgence, Olynthos was conquered by Philip II in 348 and the member states became Macedonian subjects.[131]

The military history of the region therefore revolves around federal activities and in particular the conflicts with the Athenians, Macedonians, and Spartans in the period 432–379. The size of the united Chalkidian cavalry corps was probably around 1,000 strong. Demosthenes claims that Olynthos possessed a force of only 400 men prior to federation but had 1,000 afterwards. This is supported by both Thucydides and Xenophon and seems to have applied throughout the period 432–379.[132] Unfortunately we know very little of its organization and equipment. Presumably the member cities supplied contingents under the command of local officers and we know that in 348 two of the commanders at

---

[129] *GC* no. 394 (dated to *c.*500–480); Potidaia issued coins with a mounted Poseidon at the same time or rather earlier (ibid. no. 395; *ACGC* pl. 26, coins 471, 474; Seltman, *Greek Coins*, pl. 7, coins 4–5). Olynthos minted a coin depicting a horse *c.*440, *ACGC* no. 476.

[130] Thucy. 1. 58. 2; Xen. *Hell.* 5. 2. 11–24.

[131] For a general discussion of the Confederacy see J. A. O. Larsen, *Greek Federal States* (Oxford, 1968), 58–78.

[132] Dem. 19. 263, 266–7. Thucy. 1. 62. 3 records Perdikkas' cavalry at 200 and 4. 124. 1 states that his cavalry and the Chalkidian arm together was nearly 1,000 strong. If Perdikkas' force was the same size on both occasions then the Olynthian contingent was 800. This fits very well with Xen. *Hell.* 5. 2. 14 where the dissident states of Akanthos and Apollonia claim that with their cavalry added the Confederacy would have a total of 1,000.

Olynthos (called hipparchs in our Athenian sources) were Lasthenes and Euthykrates.[133] These could have been the leaders of the Olynthian contingent but, as they betrayed 500 cavalry-men into the hands of Philip II, it seems more likely that they commanded the entire league force. If this is so, the Chalkidian corps was similar to the Athenian one—about 1,000 men, com-manded by two hipparchs, but had individual city contingents led by local officers in place of the Athenian *phylai* or tribal squadrons.

The cavalry's equipment and dress is uncertain—the coin from Sermylia mentioned earlier depicts a naked horsemen who is clearly a hunter and not a soldier. However, as the Chalkidian troopers used javelins against the Athenian hoplites at Amphipolis in 422 they may have been fairly lightly equipped. There is no specific mention of *hamippoi* attached to the corps but on several occasions it operated very closely with javelin-equipped light troops[134] and this no doubt contributed to its success. Whether *hamippoi* were a formal part of the cavalry's organization or not, the Chalkidians clearly understood the principles of using cavalry and light infantry together.

In general, the quality of the Chalkidian cavalry seems to have been quite good and it was largely responsible for the defeat of the Athenian expeditionary forces to the region in 429 and 422.[135] This success was repeated against the Lakonian and Boiotian cavalry serving with the Spartans in 382, although clever use of a cavalry reserve by Teleutias (the Spartan commander) meant that the Chalkidian corps' success could not be exploited and their army had to retire within the walls of Olynthos. The corps was also very cool in action later in the same campaign, causing Teleutias to lose his temper and launch a premature attack on them which resulted in his death and the defeat of his army. However, a botched raid against a dissident member state shows it could also be overconfident and careless. In this case, a force of 600, confident in its size, had ridden right up to the suburbs of Apollonia in no sort of order. This left them vulnerable to a sudden cavalry charge from inside the city and, when it eventu-

[133] Hyper. fr. 76 (OCT) *Against Demades*, 1; Dem. 8. 40; 9. 66.
[134] Amphipolis: Thucy. 5. 10. 9–10. Light troops: ibid. 2. 79. 3–7; 5. 10. 9–11; Xen. *Hell.* 5. 3. 5–6.
[135] Thucy. 2. 79. 3–7; 5. 10. 9–11.

ated, the shocked Chalkidians were routed with the loss of eighty men.[136]

ITALY AND SICILY

The Greek cities of Sicily and southern Italy (often called Magna Graecia because of the number of Greek colonies there) had a long-standing equestrian and cavalry tradition—which perhaps influenced the development of the native arm.[137] Many cities, including Taras (Tarentum), Gela, and Syracuse, minted coins with victorious jockeys or charioteers as early as the end of the sixth or the start of the fifth century and Dionysios I, tyrant of Syracuse, sent several four-horse chariot teams to the Olympic games.[138] Several coin issues also portray military riders.[139] However, the importance of their mounted forces was not restricted to appearances on coins—cavalry played a large part in inter-city wars and (on Sicily) in the perennial struggle against the Carthaginians.

As early as c.490 Gela had an organized cavalry force with its own commander (called a hipparch by Herodotos) and the number of cavalry available to many states was large. Gelon, tyrant of Syracuse, was supposed to have offered 2,000 horsemen and 2,000 *hamippoi* to assist the mainland Greeks during the second Persian War of 480–79 and the Sicilians are supposed to have deployed 5,000 against the Carthaginians in 480.[140] Although these numbers may be exaggerated, it is clear from the weight of the evidence that Magna Graecia was rich in cavalry. Thucydides records that in 415 the Syracusans fielded 1,200 against the Athenians (including 200 from Gela and twenty from Kamarina) and Diodorus Siculus (a local historian) regularly

[136] Xen. *Hell.* 5. 2. 40–3, 3. 3–6 (cf. their solid performance against peltasts, ibid. 5. 4. 54). Apollonia: ibid. 5. 3. 1–2.

[137] M. W. Frederiksen, 'Campanian Cavalry: a Question of Origins', *Dialoghi di Archeologia*, 2 (1968), 3–31; see also Alföldi, *Herrschaft der Reiterei*, 31–45.

[138] *GCV* 40–5 (Taras); and (by coin number) 785–6, 789–96, 806–7 (Gela); 734–8, 913–16, 920–1, 923–4, 926–7, 931–7 (Syracuse); 749–50 (Akragas); 767–72 (Katane); 812–14, 818 (Himera); 823–7 (Leontine); 906–7, 910 (Selinous). Dionysios I: Diod. Sic. 14. 109. 1.

[139] *GCV* nos. 342, 344–5, 376, 378–9 (Taras); 713–14, 797, 800, 802–3 (Gela); 860 (Morgantine); *GC* nos. 313, 316 (Taras); 154, 156 (Gela).

[140] Hdtos 7. 154, 158; Diod. Sic. 11. 21. 1.

records forces of 1,000–3,000 troopers deployed during the fifth and fourth centuries.[141]

Most of the riders portrayed on the coins of the area are naked and probably represent jockeys or men and youths engaged in equestrian pursuits,[142] but some depict mounted warriors. These are equipped in a variety of ways, ranging from a helmet and spear only to a full panoply of helmet and breastplate. In general, the ones with full armour seem to date from the mid-fourth century onwards while the unprotected riders are earlier. However, the cavalry of Syracuse was certainly equipped with breast-plates *c*.399 as the tyrant Dionysios had a large number made for his cavalrymen, infantry officers, and mercenary bodyguard.[143] An interesting local phenomenon is the use of a shield on horseback—something not attested for Greece proper. Examples of this occur on coins from 430 onwards and consist of two types. On the first (all from Taras) naked riders, often in the process of dismounting, carry very small shields on their right forearm/hand. These appear to be participating in some sort of equestrian sport or game. The second type, much more military in character, depicts riders with a large shield and one or more spears. These come largely, but not exclusively, from Taras and date from the second half of the fifth century onwards.[144]

The history of Greek cavalry in Sicily and south Italy is too long to detail here, but the defence of Syracuse against the Athenians from 415 to 413 provides a good example of its use and quality. In a classic display of mobile defence, the cavalry was used to restrict Athenian movement, especially foraging for supplies. It was also employed in two pitched battles, performing sterling service in the first by protecting its own hoplites from annihilation when they fled. In the second engagement its charge

---

[141] Thucy. 6. 67. 2; Syracuse: Diod. Sic. 14. 100. 2 (1,000); 20. 56. 2 (1,200); 14. 47. 7, 58. 2 (3,000); 16. 9. 2 (10,000—surely exaggerated); Campania: 14. 9. 2–3 (1,200); Akragas: 20. 56. 1 (nearly 1,000); Thurii: 14. 101. 2 (1,000).

[142] See *GCV* nos. 331, 334, 340–1, 343, 350, 372, 736, 738, 786, 814, 826–7; *GC* nos. 66, 73, 77, 319.

[143] Gela has a series of coins dating from *c*.480 with riders equipped only with a helmet and spear—*GC* nos. 154, 156; *GCV* nos. 713–14, 800, 802–3. For examples of fuller panoplies see *GC* nos. 312–13, 316; cf. *GCV* nos. 378–9 (3rd cent.). Dionysios: Diod. Sic. 14. 43. 2–3.

[144] Type 1: *GC* nos. 306, 308–9 (*c*.380–345); *GCV* nos. 335 (*c*.420–380), 364 (*c*.302–281). Type 2: *GC* nos. 311–12 (*c*.344–334), 314 (*c*.300); *GCV* nos. 344 (*c*.344–334), 375–6 (*c*.272–235), 797 (Gela, *c*.430–425).

32   *Greek Cavalry* c.*500–300*

against the left flank of the Athenian phalanx caused it to break. This was a vital contribution to the war effort as this victory allowed the Syracusans to complete their cross-wall and ended any Athenian hope of blockading the city.[145] Syracusan or allied Sicilian cavalry also had some good successes against the Carthaginians[146] and other examples of their cavalry usage appear in Chapters 2 and 3. On one of the few occasions when Greek cavalry from Sicily was employed in mainland Greece, a force of fifty from Syracuse proved very successful against a Theban army which the Athenian and Corinthian horse considered too large and dangerous to attack.[147] In general, the cavalry of Magna Graecia seems to have been of about the same standard as the Thessalian arm and rather better than the corps of lesser cavalry states.

CONCLUSIONS

The history of Greek cavalry during the fifth and fourth centuries is a varied one, but several general points can be made. Like all citizen soldiers in classical Greece, cavalry was enrolled at the start of the year and mobilized as necessary; it was not a standing force. Greek cavalry was largely recruited from the wealthy classes, although at Sparta these paid for the horses but did not serve and in Thessaly it is clear that the retainers of the landed aristocracy also served in the cavalry—as was probably also the case in Macedonia. In general terms, the cavalry tradition in mainland Greece became stronger the further north one travelled, partly because of the more open country but also because of the stronger aristocratic elements in society. The history of Greek cavalry in Italy also confirms that a combination of an aristocratic tradition and open plains often led to the development of a powerful and important mounted arm. The cavalry of most states was equipped and handled in much the same way; it was essentially light horse, although some cavalrymen were armed with a thrusting spear rather than javelins and armour seems to have

---

[145] Mobile defence: Thucy. 7. 4. 6, 13. 2, 44. 8. Battles: ibid. 6. 70. 2–3; 7. 6. 2–4, 11. 2.
[146] Cf. Diod. Sic. 11. 21. 5—22. 1; 16. 80. 2.
[147] Xen. *Hell.* 7. 1. 20–2.

been relatively common. Macedonia provides an exception to this as, after Philip II, some of its cavalry units (including the *prodromoi*, or scouts) were equipped with a longer lance (the *sarissa*). Although the evidence is not comprehensive, many forces seem to have been organized in sub-units of approximately 100 men. The Thessalian and Macedonian arms were also organized, and presumably recruited, territorially, as was certainly the case for the Boiotian and Chalkidian League forces.

The history of the cavalry outlined above exhibits, in the case of Athens at least, a close association with the fortunes of the state as a whole. It was very expensive to own a horse and the strength of the cavalry was consequently dependent on the financial well-being of the city. Numbers were therefore affected by the level of wealth within society, and were dependent too upon the attitudes of the rest of Athens to her cavalry class. The general use of the mounted arm was also influenced by the social position of the *hippeis*: as will be seen, their subordination to the hoplite in battle was primarily the result of social and economic factors. All of these things illustrate not only the importance of considering Athenian (and Greek) military history and events within the wider social context but also the importance of the *hippeis* to an understanding of Athenian society. The following chapter examines the combat potential of ancient Greek cavalry, concentrating on the Athenian arm in particular.

2

The Combat Potential of the *Hippeis*

THE supreme test of any military organization's effectiveness is its performance in combat. However, success or failure in action are insufficient as a complete measure of an organization's military value. This is because a variety of influences outside a unit or arm's control can cause it to perform poorly in an action or series of actions. These influences include terrain, the information available, the size of the enemy, the physical condition of the force, and, not least of all, luck. For example, it is quite possible for a unit with a good combat record (or a high combat potential) to perform badly on unsuitable terrain, when overwhelmingly outnumbered or already exhausted from previous engagements, or when misused by the high command.

The early use of tanks provides an excellent example of this—as Plate 6 graphically illustrates. Prior to November 1917—when they were finally used properly, en masse and on the firm ground of Cambrai—they had been frittered away in penny packets in the quagmires of Flanders. Operation Market Garden of September 1944 provides another modern instance of an arm employed in less than ideal circumstances. In this operation, paratroopers were to seize bridges vital for a rapid advance on Germany, but errors in planning led to the British 1st Airborne Division landing at Arnhem at a time when two panzer divisions were resting in the area and the defences had been greatly strengthened. The opposition encountered was beyond the means of the lightly-equipped paratroopers and, despite valiant efforts, three-quarters of the division were killed or captured before the remnants withdrew.[1] In both these cases, failure did not result so much from the quality of the troops or their training, or from inherent problems with their organization and equipment,[2] but from miscalculation or misuse on the part of the commanders involved.

[1] See K. Macksey, *Military Errors of World War Two* (Poole, 1987), 179–200.
[2] Although inadequate radio equipment did contribute to the defeat at Arnhem, ibid. 198–200.

Because of the external factors which can affect actual performance, it is important to consider potential performance when
determining the combat value of any arm—including classical
Greek cavalry. Combat potential, or hitting power, is today
usually considered to be the product of mobility, firepower, and
protection.[3] However, as it omits important human influences,
this definition provides an oversimplified picture of how a force
ought to perform in battle. The combat potential of a force or
unit is in fact the product of all of its qualities or characteristics,
not just the three mentioned above. The hitting power of classical Greek cavalry, including the Athenian arm, was determined largely by eight major influences. These were: mobility,
weaponry, protection, leadership, training, motivation, flexibility,
and size. Other minor factors also played a part and many of the
major ones listed are closely interlinked: for example, mobility,
leadership, training, and motivation all contributed to combat
potential in two ways—directly and through their effect on flexibility. To some extent these divisions are therefore artificial, but
they do provide the necessary framework for a discussion of how
Greek cavalry ought to have performed in battle.

This chapter primarily concerns itself with potential; although
examples of performance are included to illustrate what was
possible, a detailed examination of the wartime employment of
the cavalry is held over to Chapter 3. In identifying the characteristics of the arm and how these determined its hitting power, I
have also attempted to chart (wherever the evidence permitted)
how these qualities changed over time. This has proved easier, or
even unnecessary, in the case of those characteristics which depended upon the physical nature of horse and rider. These include
mobility and, to a lesser extent, weaponry and protection—all of
which remained basically constant in the fifth and fourth centuries. However, the other characteristics: leadership, training,
motivation, flexibility, and size, were much more subject to fluctu-
ation over time (and from state to state). While the likely impact

[3] There are variants of this, cf. E. Luttwak, *A Dictionary of Modern War*
(London, 1972), 94 s.v. Fire Power. 'Hitting power' has been used to denote one
of the characteristics affecting combat potential (cf. T. Wintringham and J. N.
Blashford-Snell, *Weapons and Tactics* (Harmondsworth, 1973), 22 ff.). As this
involves both firepower and the means by which it is delivered, the term is
essentially the same as 'combat potential' and I have used it in this way throughout
the following discussion.

of these on the overall combat potential of the Athenian *hippeis* can often be determined in general terms, we cannot always be certain of their specific influence at a particular date.

MOBILITY

Ancient Greek cavalry possessed a considerable degree of mobility—an important asset in an era dominated by the relatively slow-moving hoplite. This mobility was largely determined by four factors: endurance, speed, terrain, and equestrian equipment. Endurance primarily affected strategic, or long-distance, movement, while speed had rather more influence on a tactical level. Terrain and equipment factors were closely linked and affected equally both strategic and tactical mobility.

Properly looked after, horses have considerable endurance and are capable of being ridden long distances—even under adverse conditions. This is particularly well illustrated in the modern era by the 1915–17 campaign in Palestine. This was fought in physical conditions not unlike those in ancient Greece, albeit somewhat harsher climatically. Chenevix-Trench, for example, recorded that his regiment, Hodson's Horse, advanced 56 miles (90 km.) in 26 hours and fought 'several stiff actions' on the way. Trooper Idriess of the 5th ALH Regiment noted that, while involved in continuous fighting during one advance, his unit's horses went without water on several occasions for periods of between 36 and 40 hours. He adds that New Zealand horses and those from other Australian units were reportedly without water for 60–70 hours.[4] The official figures for water usage during the sustained pursuit of the Turks after the Third Battle of Gaza in AD 1917 confirm that this was not unusual (see Table 1). While the horses did suffer from the lack of water, they were still able to function without it for considerable periods under combat conditions and to do so without incurring permanent damage. Idriess records that far from suffering any lasting ill-effects his regiment's horses 'bucked up wonderfully' after watering and a couple of day's rest.[5]

---

[4] Chenevix-Trench, 179; I. L. Idriess, *Desert Column* (Sydney, 1985), 256, 258, 264, 277.
[5] Idriess, *Desert Column*, 281.

TABLE 1. Water and ration usage in the pursuit, Gaza, AD 1917[a]

Formation or unit	Max. hours without water	Work done	Average amount of grain and fodder daily
Australian & NZ Mounted Division	72	continuous	9 lb. grain; 4 lb. fodder; 4 lb. tibben
Australian Mounted Division	72	continuous	8 lb. grain; 2 lb. fodder
Bucks Yeomanry	72	continuous	10 lb. grain and fodder (to 26 Nov.); forage obtained locally once
Dorset Yeomanry	54	60 miles	9 lb. grain; 7 lb. tibben occasionally
Lincoln Yeomanry	84	continuous	5 lb. grain (max. 9 lb. grain and 3 lb. hay from 1–5 Nov.); small amt. tibben
XX Brigade, Royal Horse Artillery	56	50 miles	9 lb. grain
54th Division Train	63	50 miles	10 lb. grain; 7 lb. fodder; a little grazing

[a] From Falls, *Military Operations Egypt and Palestine*, ii. 641.

Under better conditions, horses are capable of travelling particularly long distances—and faster than a man on foot. Baden-Powell conducted a 600-mile (960 km.) reconnaissance of the Drakensberg region in South Africa in 1885 and averaged 33 miles (53 km.) a day while living off the land. At the end of the trip, though, his horses were still in 'tip-top condition'.[6] There are many other documented examples of long-distance rides[7] or of horses having to fight after a period of hard work, including an Athenian cavalry advance to Mantineia in 362. In this case, the horses completed an overnight move of about 60 miles (96 km.) with only one break. Despite the lack of opportunity on arrival

[6] Cited in M. Lawrence, *Flyers and Stayers: The Book of the World's Greatest Rides* (London, 1980), 143–4.

[7] Ibid. 100–59.

for rest or food, they were able to perform well enough to allow the *hippeis* to distinguish themselves in an engagement with the Boiotian horse.[8] This incident clearly illustrates the advantages of being able to move mounted troops fairly long distances relatively quickly. During the Peloponnesian War, the Athenians also exploited this high level of strategic mobility, annually ravaging the Megarid with a large-scale cavalry incursion. Because the inhabitants had less time to evacuate it, the swift descent of the cavalry probably caused more damage to property than would have been the case with invasion by a more cumbersome hoplite force.[9]

However, although a horseman can generally move further and faster than a man on foot, a horse will eventually break down if excessive effort and inadequate feeding or watering are maintained for an undue length of time. As Xenophon points out, a horse naturally enjoys running 'unless forced to run past what is appropriate. Nothing taken to excess is pleasing to either horse or man.'[10] However, if a horse finally does break down, unlike a man it is often difficult to restore to health by rest and restorative diet. This was recognized by the British Army Veterinary Department which remarked in one of its manuals that 'once the troop horse is sick, injured or exhausted, he is only an encumbrance to a fighting unit and has to be left behind.'[11]

That horses could be pushed beyond their limits on campaign is attested in many periods—as late as 1914, for instance, the German advance on the Aisne was almost stopped 'not by battle casualties but by horse-wastage'. Cardigan's 'sore back reconnaissance' during the Crimean War killed 80 of the 196 horses involved and left many of the survivors permanently disabled— without any contact with the Russians.[12] However, there are also several examples of horses being over-extended in antiquity, sometimes (as in Alexander's pursuit of Darius after Issos)[13] because the military situation required that speed should be put before horse-care. At other times it apparently stemmed from a

[8] Xen. *Hell.* 7. 5. 15–17.

[9] Thucy. 2. 31. 3; cf. Xen. *Anab.* 7. 6. 27–8.

[10] Xen. *PH* 10. 14.

[11] Quoted in D. W. Engels, *Alexander the Great and the Logistics of the Macedonian Army* (Berkeley, Calif., 1978), 129 n. 31.

[12] Chenevix-Trench, 179, 308.

[13] Arr. *Anab.* 3. 15. 3–6; Plut. *Alex.* 42. 3 ff. For his motives, see Tarn, *CAH* vi. 382.

lack of due regard for the possible consequences. In the third century, for example, the Corinthians were so eager to join King Kleomenes III of Sparta in Argos that all their horses were ruined. More ambiguous is an incident in 313 when Demetrios lost most of his horses during a forced march made to surprise Ptolemy's army while it ravaged Cilicia.[14] Although his aim may have been sound, the planning certainly was not—Demetrios arrived too late to catch the enemy, but even if he had got there in time it is hard to imagine what he could have achieved with most of his cavalry out of action.

However, most of the known cases of horses being rendered unfit for action occurred in Asia Minor, presumably because campaigning distances there were longer and conditions harsher than in Greece. In fact, I have been able to find only one reference to horses suffering from overwork in Greece proper and this reflects abnormal conditions. Most Greek campaigns were conducted over short periods (usually around harvest time), but Thucydides records that from 413 onwards the Athenian cavalry rode out daily in defence of Attica, which was being ravaged on a continual basis by Peloponnesian League forces based in Dekeleia.[15] This was an unusually heavy workload for Greek cavalry and the normal campaigning conditions (including the preference for deciding wars by pitched battles on relatively flat ground) probably meant that horses were unlikely to break down on campaign in Greece, unless seriously neglected.

It also seems unlikely that such neglect was at all frequent. First of all, horses were an expensive commodity[16] which most owners would presumably have been loath to lose and, second, many *hippeis* undoubtedly had strong personal feelings towards their horses. The whole tone of Xenophon's *Peri Hippikes* attests to this and the affection of owner for mount in antiquity is confirmed by several anecdotes in writers such as Aelian.[17] Finally, the *hippeis* provided their own horses and, as there was no organized remount system, they would risk having to walk home

---

[14] Plut. *Kleom.* 19. 2. Diod. Sic. 19. 80. 2.

[15] Thucy. 7. 27. 4–5.

[16] See App. 4.

[17] Xenophon's training methods are based on kindness: *PH* 9. 2–12; 10. 3–5, 12–13. Aelian, *On Animals*, 11. 31 records a cavalry officer devoted to his horse; cf. Idriess, *Desert Column*, 257, 263 for the affection of Australian Light Horsemen for their mounts.

if they lost their mounts through neglect. Cavalrymen do not like
to walk. All these factors presumably encouraged, but did not of
course guarantee, good horse care in the field.

On a tactical level, the speed of the horse normally allowed
cavalry to overtake men on foot,[18] whether these were hoplites
(who were particularly encumbered by their panoply) or the more
lightly equipped peltasts. It could also be moved quickly around
the battlefield to meet emerging needs or changing circumstances
and this gave considerable flexibility to those commanders who
were inclined to use it. The number who did so was not always
large, but the potential importance of high mobility is shown by
the successful flanking movement of a Theban cavalry squadron
at Delion in 424, and by Derdas' timely charge outside Olynthos
in 382. In both of these cases the rapid redeployment of cavalry
across the battlefield decided the result of the engagement, and
at Olynthos even turned imminent defeat into victory.[19] It
was the Theban cavalry which was first to reach the small city of
Mykalessos when it was attacked by Thracian mercenaries in 413
and even managed to overtake the main enemy party on its way
back to its ships. In 396 the Boiotians again dispatched cavalry to
their east coast, but this time to prevent King Agesilaos performing a sacrifice at Aulis prior to his departure for Asia.[20] On both
these occasions hoplites would apparently have been unable to
arrive in time. Even the Spartans recognized the superior mobility
of horsemen—during the Peloponnesian War they responded to
Athenian raids on their coastline by raising a cavalry unit to act as
a quick reaction force. The Athenians too utilised the mobility of
their *hippeis* to minimize the damage to Attica during the same
war.[21]

However, limitations were imposed on both tactical and strategic mobility by the closely linked factors of terrain and equestrian
equipment. Apart from swamps and rivers, which posed problems
for all types of troops (except, apparently, Roman emperors),[22]
hilly or rough ground had the potential either to damage the

[18] Cf. Xen. *Hell.* 5. 4. 54.

[19] Thucy. 4. 96. 5; Xen. *Hell.* 5. 2. 41–2.

[20] Mykalessos: Thucy. 7. 29–30; the hoplites eventually caught up during the
course of the action. Aulis: Xen. *Hell.* 3. 4. 3–4.

[21] Sparta: Thucy. 4. 55. 1–2. Athens: see 'mobile defence', Ch. 3.

[22] Constantine is recorded as riding through a swamp to attack Sarmatians;
Anonymus Valesianus, *Life of Constantine*, 2. 3.

horse or to reduce the security of the rider's seat—at least in part because of deficiencies in the available horse-tackle. However, the difficulties arising from these limitations were not as serious as is often suggested.

To take the possibility of damage first: this is probably attested in Xenophon's account of the withdrawal of Greek mercenaries (later known as the Ten Thousand) after the untimely demise of their Persian employer had left them stranded in the middle of enemy territory. Xenophon records that in one engagement he led his troops on horseback until the ground became too rough and he was forced to dismount.[23] The problem of laming one's steed by injuring a leg on rocky or uneven ground has always been a problem for cavalrymen, but it is often assumed that this was compounded in classical Greece because of the lack of horse-shoes. These first appeared in slip-on form in the first century BC and in nail-on form in the first century AD.[24] Although protective coverings of cloth or leather were known in the classical period, metal hipposandals (the Roman term in common use), whether slip-on or nail-on, were not.[25] This lack of protection for the hoof is often cited as a disadvantage for ancient cavalry but, while one of Xenophon's treatises does imply that damage could occur to a horse's hooves,[26] the evidence suggests that its effects were limited.

Diodorus Siculus claims in one case that 'the horses' hooves had been worn thin through constant marching', but this refers to Alexander's cavalry after nearly eight years' campaigning in Asia.[27] The only example I can find which might refer to similar problems in mainland Greece, is Thucydides' previously mentioned comment about the damage to Athenian horses deployed against the Peloponnesian garrison in Dekeleia. According to this passage, wounds accounted for some injuries but, 'others were lamed both by the hard ground and through continual hard work'.[28] However, the phrase used for the laming (ἀπεχωλοῦντο ἐν

---

[23] Xen. *Anab.* 3. 4. 49.
[24] *AGH* 91–2; Chenevix-Trench, 300.
[25] P. Vigneron, *Le Cheval dans l'antiquité gréco-romaine* (Annales de l'Est, l'Université de Nancy, Mém. 35; Nancy, 1968), 45–50; cf. the protective coverings used in the snow in Armenia, Xen. *Anab.* 4. 5. 36.
[26] Xen. *Hipparch.* 1. 4, 16.
[27] Diod. Sic. 17. 94. 2; cf. Q. Curtius Rufus, 9. 2. 8–11.
[28] Thucy. 7. 27. 5.

γῇ ἀποκρότῳ) does not indicate whether this was because of injury to the legs, or hooves, or to both, and it is quite possible that it refers mainly to leg damage, which was presumably a real danger in the rocky foothills of Attica. J. K. Anderson certainly believes that the danger to hooves has been exaggerated, arguing that the effect of broken ground on unshod hooves was minimized because Greece possessed 'a climate and soil that would help to make hard well-formed hooves'. This is supported by C. P. Chenevix-Trench, who served as a cavalry officer in the Indian army, and who maintained that it is perfectly possible to do without horseshoes in countries where the ground is dry and hard;[29] ground in fact like that of much of Greece. The find pattern of hipposandals also suggests that even after their use became widespread they may have been considered unnecessary in Greece: most are found not in the drier Mediterranean area but in Gaul, Germany, and Britain, all areas with damper climates.[30]

Finally, even though Xenophon identified hoof damage as a possible problem, he believed that with proper care it was relatively easy to prepare the hooves so that the horses could be ridden 'even in rough country'. This was presumably to be achieved by his advice to keep the stable (and therefore the hooves) dry and to toughen the tender part of the hoof by grooming the animal while it stood on rounded stones.[31] An animal was arguably better off under this regime and unshod than wearing the early types of nail-on shoe which probably caused damage through placing the horse's weight on the front of the hooves.[32]

Horses could be lamed on rough terrain through leg injury, but hoof damage was perhaps only a minor consideration. Hilly or steep country, though, could pose problems for riders, as the following description of a horse race on a mountainside illustrates: 'on the way down the majority rolled over, while on the way up the sharp slope the horses scarcely managed a walk; whereupon there was much shouting, laughter, and cheering.'[33] This weak-

---

[29] *AGH* 92; Chenevix-Trench, 299, cf. 231, 241.
[30] Vigneron, *Cheval*, 46.
[31] Xen. *Hipparch.* 1. 4. Advice: Xen. *PH* 4. 3; *Hipparch.* 1. 16.
[32] Cf. Chenevix-Trench, 304.
[33] Xen. *Anab.* 4. 8. 28.

ness basically stemmed from loss of balance caused by the high centre of gravity of a mounted man but was exacerbated by the lack of stirrups. These probably evolved around the fifth century AD and were certainly unknown in Greece in the classical period.[34] The use of stirrups renders mounting easier, increases control over the horse, and results in a steadier seat, particularly in hilly or broken terrain.[35] Ancient riders of the pre-stirrup era certainly were less secure than their more fortunate successors, but the difference has been over-emphasized.

For example, the unsteadiness of the classical rider's seat is often assumed on the evidence of Xenophon's address to the Ten Thousand after the battle of Kounaxa. He argued that 'we are on a much more secure footing than cavalrymen. For they are suspended in the air on their horses, fearing not only us but also falling, while we, planted on the ground, will strike much harder blows if anyone approaches and are much more likely to hit whatever we choose.'[36] However, it is usually forgotten that these remarks formed an important part of Xenophon's attempts to raise the morale of his fellow mercenaries and are undoubtedly exaggerated. Although victorious on their part of the field, the death of their employer, Cyrus, had left them in a very awkward position. They were a hoplite force stranded thousands of miles from home and surrounded by the Persian army whose best troops were cavalrymen. Given the views expressed about cavalry in the *Hipparchikos* and the *Peri Hippikes*, and the nature of the existing threat at Kounaxa, it seems very likely that Xenophon's statement represents what he thought would be best for the soldiers to hear rather than his true beliefs about the value of cavalry.

Nevertheless, the relative instability of the ancient Greek rider was a fact of life: Aristophanes for example makes a ribald joke about falling off while 'riding' and Andokides records that he fractured his skull and broke his collar-bone in an equestrian accident in the Lykeion. Xenophon also stresses the lack of confidence felt by a cavalryman mounted on anything other than

[34] A. D. H. Bivar, 'The Stirrup and its Origins', *Oriental Art*, NS 1 (1955), 61–2; *GMAW* 49–50. Stirrups were apparently known elsewhere at an earlier date (Bivar, loc. cit.; *HMND* 75 n. 1) but were not widely used.

[35] Chenevix-Trench, 65–6; *AGH* 76; Wintringham and Blashford-Snell, *Weapons and Tactics*, 41.

[36] Xen. *Anab.* 3. 2. 19.

a well-trained and obedient horse.[37] This is of course a perennial problem—riders still fall off today—but it is now reduced by improved riding tackle and by the use of mares and geldings as mounts. However, the number of riders portrayed on stallions in Greek art suggests that ancient riders preferred these to the more temperamentally stable alternatives; almost all horses depicted on vases or in sculpture are stallions—as the fairly representative sample included in my plates shows. On the other hand, this may result from an artistic convention designed to heighten the impression of power and majesty often intended in representations of horses.[38]

The literary evidence, for example, suggests that the use of stallions was not as widespread as the artistic evidence implies. Aelian certainly records that mares were preferred for chariot-teams and Miltiades' famous team was no exception to this.[39] Vigneron too believes that the practice of gelding was very common in antiquity and this view gains some support from the remark in Xenophon that 'when spirited horses are gelded, they stop biting and prancing around but are no less suited for war'.[40] However, this is recorded in his work on the education of Cyrus the Great and he does not suggest this practice in either of his equestrian treatises. The extent to which stallions were used, particularly as warhorses, is therefore uncertain but it seems likely that few cavalrymen of sense would have chosen to risk their lives on a stallion of unstable temperament when a more placid mare or gelding was available.

Whether mounted on stallions or not, control problems affected all riders, both military and civilian, but the lack of stirrups presumably caused additional concern for the cavalryman who had to use his weapons while mounted. Adcock points out that without stirrups it is not possible to exert sufficient leverage to use a long slashing sword effectively from horseback.[41] Similarly, throwing the javelin while mounted was obviously an acquired skill which

[37] Ar. *Lysis.* 676 ff.; Andok. 1. 61; Xen. *PH* 3. 12. Cf. the riding accident on an Italian vase, P. Mingazzini, *Catalogo dei vasi della collezione Augusto Castellani*, ii (Rome, 1930), no. 746, pl. cxcix. However, I have not come across this subject on a Greek vase.

[38] Cf. the use of the horse to convey this in Athenian tragedy, below 196–8.

[39] Aelian, *On Animals*, 11. 36; 12. 40; Hdtos 6. 103.

[40] Vigneron, *Cheval*, 43–4; Xen. *Kyrop.* 7. 5. 62.

[41] *GMAW* 50; cf. Chenevix-Trench, 37.

not all horsemen were able to master with the same degree of expertise.[42] Another factor (believed by many to be the most important when considering the use of cavalry in an era dominated by the hoplite phalanx) was that without stirrups, or a saddle-tree with a high cantle, the horseman of antiquity was almost certain to be unseated if he attempted to ride into a compact body of foot while using a rigidly held lance or thrusting sword.[43] Therefore, true shock action was denied to the Greek cavalryman. However, as this particular effect of the lack of stirrups did not reduce the cavalry's mobility, it is best left to the discussion of shock tactics at the end of this chapter.

The relative instability of seat identified above obviously rendered Greek cavalry less effective in battle than forces of later periods equipped with the stirrup. However, if the problems arising from the lack of stirrups had been insurmountable then the Greeks would presumably have abandoned the use of cavalry in warfare. They patently did not do so, and the numerous successes outlined in the next chapter testify to the general ability of the cavalryman to keep his seat and to fight on horseback. This is because the Greeks developed practices which, while perhaps not as effective as the invention of stirrups in solving the mobility and weapon-handling problems, still considerably alleviated them.

In his works on horsemanship and cavalry generalship, Xenophon outlines techniques which were employed to aid control of the horse, to improve the rider's seat, and to facilitate mounting. For the latter he prescribes several different methods to assist the young (and not so young) trooper to mount in both normal and emergency situations. These range from mounting with a jump, using either the mane or a spear as an aid, to getting a leg up, or even having the horse crouch to assist the rider.[44] Two of these methods are illustrated in Attic red-figure vase-painting: mounting with the aid of a spear is illustrated in Plate 1 and a crouching horse is probably depicted on vase 107. A variant of the leg up is depicted in the boy's riding lesson on vase 96.

---

[42] Xen. *Hipparch.* 1. 21, 25; for a later period see H. Dessau (ed.), *Inscriptiones Latinae Selectae*, 2nd edn., i (Berlin, 1954), 2487.

[43] *GMAW* 50; *HMND* 54; cf. *AGH* 129.

[44] Mounting from the spring: *Hipparch.* 1. 5, 17; *PH* 7. 1–2. Leg up: *Hipparch.* 1. 17; *PH* 6. 12. Crouching horse: *PH* 6. 16.

To improve control of the horse, Xenophon advocated constant training and practice and also suggested the use of severe bits. These, as Xenophon describes, certainly would have discouraged the horse from taking the bit between his teeth.[45] Although I have obviously never experimented with this, it seems possible that the employment of a rough bit such as the Greeks used would be almost as effective for pulling up a horse as the modern combination of smooth bit and stirrups. Xenophon also proposes several measures specifically intended to improve the rider's stability. One was to adapt one's riding technique to the ground, for example collecting the horse when turning on a rough or slippery surface.[46] Another was to choose a horse with high withers and the right temperament. Xenophon claimed that the former helped to keep the rider in position and pointed out that both excessively timid and spirited horses could be instrumental in causing a fall. Conversely, he argued that an obedient horse inspired confidence in the rider particularly in war or 'in dangerous situations'.[47]

To achieve this obedience, and to improve the rider's seat, was the main function of the training and practice Xenophon consistently recommended. Apart from the breaking-in of the young horse (a task he advised leaving to professional horse-breakers), and its training in the basic skills required of a warhorse, he advocated more advanced training for both mount and rider. This training was to take place regularly and over all types of terrain.[48] If these recommendations were followed, the skill of the Athenian *hippeus* and his horse would have been improved considerably. This in turn would have increased the rider's control over his mount, particularly in dangerous situations or in rough terrain.

The rider's posture too was of course very important in ensuring that he kept his seat and here again Xenophon had some sensible advice for riders without stirrups. He suggested that, whether riding bareback or not, the aspiring rider should sit 'not as if on the seat of a chair . . . but as if standing upright with legs

---

[45] Xen. *PH* 10. 6–12; for examples of these, see *AGH* 71, pls. 33–4, 36.

[46] Xen. *PH* 7. 15.

[47] Ibid. 1. 11; 3. 9, 12.

[48] Horsebreaking: *PH* 2. 1–2. Basic training: ibid. 3. 8. Advanced training and practice: ibid. 8. 1 ff.; *Hipparch.* 1. 5–6, 18–20.

astride'. He goes on to explain that in this method the horse is
gripped with the thighs while the lower leg, from the knee down,
is allowed to dangle loosely. By doing so the rider will be able to
grip the horse firmly, but avoid the damage which might result
from an impact on the lower leg if it too were held stiffly. As a
final point, he added that 'the rider should also train himself to
keep the part of his body above the hips as flexible as possible,
for in this way he will be able to endure more and be less likely to
fall if anyone pulls or pushes him.'[49]

The chair seat criticized by Xenophon, and illustrated in Plate
7, was less secure than the straight leg seat, illustrated in Plates 2,
8, and 13. The efficiency of Xenophon's preferred posture is
attested by the fact that it became, and for centuries remained,
the standard riding seat in the European world.[50] However, the
fact that Xenophon has to discuss the relative merits of the two
alternatives before recommending the straight leg seat suggests
that some Athenians at least continued to use the chair seat. It is
difficult to ascertain which was preferred by the majority of
hippeis, but if the artistic evidence reflects reality in this case (and
there is nothing to suggest otherwise) the chair seat seems to have
been popular in the sixth and the early fifth centuries but by the
end of the fifth appears to have been largely supplanted by seats
which were either fully straight leg or fairly close to it.[51]

The seat advocated by Xenophon would not only result in a
general increase in security in all riding contexts but also, he
claims, assist in the use of weapons while riding.[52] It is clear then
that Greek equestrian techniques were far from rudimentary and
that the practices recommended by Xenophon or attested elsewhere would have considerably alleviated the effects of riding
without stirrups. Therefore, while the mobility of Greek cavalry
was undoubtedly curtailed by the hilly or rough terrain discussed
above, it is highly likely that the classical rider's seat was rather
more secure than is usually assumed. In addition, as we are
examining combat potential, it is important to consider these
limitations on mobility in the context of Greek warfare.

[49] Xen. *PH* 7. 5–7.
[50] Chenevix-Trench, 28.
[51] See vases 1, 5, 8, 9 (chair seat); 55, 120, 136, 202 (straight leg seat). All
riders in the Group G series use the straight leg seat, as do most other 4th-cent.
riders.
[52] Xen. *PH* 7. 5.

Given that Greece is predominantly mountainous, the weakness
of cavalry in steep country, and the possibility of leg or, to a
lesser extent, hoof damage on rough ground, placed some limitations on its use. However, the influence of this on military
practices was probably marginal for the simple reason that the
majority of engagements in the fifth and fourth centuries were
hoplite actions on plains. This is exactly the type of terrain on
which cavalry was most effective—at any rate the phrase 'to
challenge cavalry on the plain' was apparently proverbial in
fourth-century Athens for a rash action.[53] As a result, the combination of steep or rough terrain and the lack of stirrups would
normally only affect the cavalry's mobility to the extent that
hard-pressed infantry would have the chance to retire to the
relative safety of any high or broken ground within reach. The
relief felt by the Ten Thousand on reaching the mountains after
incessant harassment by the Persian horse is eloquent testimony
to the effectiveness of cavalry on the lowlands.[54]

However, retiring to the high ground would not always have
been possible for the infantry and would anyway limit the use of
the cavalry only in the pursuit and the attack phase of war.
Furthermore, once hoplites sought the protection conferred by
steep or rugged terrain they would generally have to abandon
their own formation, if they had not already done so—the phalanx
was also unsuited to this type of country. In this case, their
immediate value as a fighting force was ended because, whether
or not their formation disintegrated as a result of the move, once
in the upland areas they were no longer able to fight a battle or to
threaten the crops. This is precisely what happened to an Argive
and Arkadian army which a largely mounted contingent of Phleia-
sians and Athenians had restricted to the hills. The Argive force
took such care to keep to the high ground and avoid the crops on
the plain that Xenophon likened it to an army traversing friendly
territory.[55]

[53] This seems to be the meaning of the remark that 'challenging Sokrates to
argument is like challenging cavalry on the plain' (" Ἱππέας εἰς πεδίον" προκαλῇ
Σωκράτη εἰς λόγους προκαλούμενος), Pl. *Theaitetos*, 183d.
[54] Xen. *Anab.* 3. 4. 24; cf. Thucy. 7. 5–6; Diod. Sic. 14. 80. 1; 18. 15. 6 and the
advice (in a 6th cent. Byzantine work) to attack Persian invaders of the Roman
East in Colchis, where the rugged terrain made it difficult for their cavalry, John
the Lydian, *On the Magistracies of the Roman Constitution*, trans. T. F. Carney
(Sydney, 1965), 3. 34. 4.   [55] Xen. *Hell.* 7. 2. 10.

The lack of stirrups and the associated problems of steep slopes and rough terrain probably had only a relatively minor influence on the military employment of the *hippeis*. What effects they did have, apart from making Greek cavalrymen more prone to falls than stirrup-equipped horsemen of later times, was mainly to render the cavalry less secure in scrimmages with infantry in close formation, and to reduce casualties amongst fleeing infantry who were able to reach high or broken ground. The other effect was to allow commanders to secure their flanks from mounted attack by deploying their forces with steep hills or other obstacles such as rivers, ditches, or walls, to protect them. This however was not a purely anti-cavalry tactic as these types of obstacle would also preclude attack by hoplite formations.

WEAPONRY

The offensive weapons carried by the cavalry allowed the corps to employ both missile-fire and close-quarter combat in succession and this was further enhanced by attaching either infantry (*hamippoi*) or mounted archers (*hippotoxotai*) to the cavalry. In itself this facility was a major component of hitting power, but it also had further influence through its impact on the cavalry corps' flexibility.

The best evidence for cavalry weapons is Athenian but it seems likely that the cavalry of most other Greek states was equipped in a similar way—although the Macedonian cavalry did use the *sarissa* from about 338 onwards.[56] Basically, there was no standard set of cavalry weapons: individual *hippeis* sported a variety of weaponry in different combinations, apparently according to personal preference. The main armament could consist of two javelins, a single thrusting spear, or two javelins and a spear, and some at least also carried a sword. Although the evidence does not permit us to determine what proportion of the Athenian cavalry was equipped with each of these possible combinations, we can say that individual cavalrymen, each *phyle* (or squadron), and the corps as a whole, were apparently able to engage in both close-quarter and longer-range combat.

[56] Markle, 'Use of the Sarissa', 483–93.

This would certainly have been the case if Xenophon's advice was followed and two cornel-wood *palta* or javelins were adopted as the main armament for the cavalry.[57] The ceramic evidence suggests that this might indeed have been the most popular configuration as almost all armed riders on vases carry two javelins. However, other evidence renders this far less certain and even the pot scenes themselves exhibit some variation. For example, one vase (no. 95) depicts a horseman with three javelins and several exist with riders carrying only one. However, this last type probably portrays the rider after he has thrown one of the two weapons he originally carried. The retention of one javelin in combat certainly accords with Xenophon's advice on the type of javelin to be chosen and how it should be employed in battle. He specifically advocates the use of cornel-wood weapons because their strength would allow a rider who had thrown one javelin at the enemy to retain the other for close-quarter contact. His advice here seems based upon an incident where Greek cavalrymen were worsted in a mêlée because their inferior weapons broke when thrust at their Persian opponents.[58]

The use of the correct sort of javelin therefore allowed the *hippeus* to fight his opponent at close-quarters but its primary purpose was to be thrown from a distance. Unfortunately, the range of the weapon when thrown from horseback is unknown—although Xenophon sensibly argued that the further away from the enemy the javelin could be discharged the better.[59] Harris estimates a man on foot could throw a javelin 300 feet (91 metres) with the aid of a throwing loop,[60] but a horseman was essentially throwing with the power of his arm alone and without a run up must have been unable to throw as far as this. On the other hand, horsemen also employed the throwing loop to enhance the distance which could otherwise be achieved. This loop, or *amentum* (the conventional term derived from Roman usage) is illustrated in Plate 15. It was a loop of cord attached to the javelin and into which the thrower inserted his finger or fingers to allow him to impart spin when the weapon was discharged—see Plate 8 for the

[57] Xen. *PH* 12. 12.
[58] Loc. cit.; *Hell.* 3. 4. 14.
[59] Xen. *PH* 12. 13.
[60] H. A. Harris, 'Greek Javelin Throwing', *G&R* 10 (1963), 35.

technique involved.[61] This permitted a greater velocity than would be the case without one, resulting in an extended range.[62] However, the extent to which Athenian cavalrymen took advantage of this addition to the javelin is unknown: Xenophon neglects to mention it at all, but this could be because its use was so common as to require no comment. Similarly, its infrequent representation on vase paintings could be because it was a very small detail of precisely the type many artists would be likely to omit. All we can say is that it did exist and was used by some Greek cavalrymen.

Although we cannot be certain of its potential range, the javelin could be an effective and flexible weapon, particularly when fitted with an *amentum* and constructed either from cornel-wood or from a similarly strong material. However, it is clear that not all *hippeis* were armed in this way and some at least carried a weapon which appears identical to the hoplite spear.[63] To distinguish this weapon from the javelin in the discussion which follows I have either adopted N. V. Sekunda's practice of calling it a *kamax* (although this could refer to a longer weapon) or have simply referred to it as a *doru* or spear. Sekunda's terminology, used in what to my knowledge is the only treatment of this weapon, is adapted from the phrase *doratou kamakinou* of Xenophon's *Peri Hippikes* 12. 12.[64] Although the word '*kamax*' was almost certainly not used by itself in such a specialized sense in antiquity (it meant any pole, including a spear-shaft), it is a convenient shorthand term for this cavalry spear.

The *kamax* is attested in both art and literature, occurring in vase-paintings, on grave-reliefs, and in Xenophon's technical treatises. As in the case of the javelin, these sources can only show that the spear existed and how it was used—they cannot

[61] The loop is portrayed on vases 42, 44, and 202. Its existence is also strongly indicated, either because of the finger position or the existence of a band around the weapon, on vases 19, 29, 159, 198.

[62] On the use of loops see Harris, *G&R* 10 (1963), 28 ff.; E. N. Gardiner, 'Throwing the Javelin', *JHS* 27 (1907), 249–66.

[63] See vase 132; cf. 192, where cavalrymen and hoplites have the same type of spear.

[64] Sekunda, *AG* 16. This work, part of a series designed for wargamers and military modellers, is necessarily very limited in the space available for a detailed treatment of the subject. However, Dr Sekunda is currently preparing a much larger work on Hellenistic armies and equipment and I look forward to this publication with keen interest.

show what proportion of the cavalry carried it instead of, or as well as, the two javelins. For example, although the literary evidence suggests that its use may have been more common, I have been able to identify the *kamax* in only nine Athenian pottery scenes; it is also attested on an Argive relief of the early fourth century.[65] In addition, Sekunda's attractive suggestion that the *kamax* appears fairly frequently on grave-reliefs is not absolutely certain; while some reliefs clearly depict the *kamax*, on many others the weapon which was once painted on or attached is no longer extant.[66] Although cavalrymen apparently using thrusting weapons could, as Sekunda assumes, be using a *kamax*, it is also possible that they were wielding the *palton* advocated by Xenophon. Because Xenophon recommends using a javelin as a close-quarter weapon, missing thrusting weapons on reliefs should not automatically be reconstructed as *kamakes*.

Although Xenophon's testimony confirms the pictorial evidence (see vase 132) that the *kamax* was a close-quarter and not a missile weapon, it too does not reveal how widely it was employed by the Athenian *hippeis*. He argued against its use, claiming that it was 'weak and cumbersome'.[67] This shows that it was carried by some cavalrymen and may perhaps have been a fairly common weapon—his other references to it do suggest that its use was more widespread than the artistic evidence indicates. For instance, he advises how the spear should be positioned to allow groups of cavalrymen either to show themselves off to advantage in public displays or to give a false impression of their numbers during operations. He also describes how to mount using it as an aid and discusses its use in practice combat exercises.[68] It is worthwhile quoting the latter passage (*PH* 8. 10) in full because of the information it provides:

it is good training for two riders to co-operate. While one flees on

---

[65] Vases 34, 37, 53, 132, 135, 136(?), 139, 174(?), 192; relief: Athens, NM 3153.

[66] Sekunda, *AG* 18. Athenian reliefs with *kamax*: 4, 20 (Pl. 9). Examples of reliefs which may originally have depicted a *kamax*, although the weapon is no longer extant, are: 12, 25, 26, 27, 29, 30 (Pls. 11, 13, 2, 12).

[67] Xen. *PH* 12. 12. For close-quarter use see Xen. *Hell.* 3. 4. 14; Arr. *Anab.* 1. 15. 3–16. 1.

[68] Xen. *Hipparch.* 3. 3; 5. 6–7; *PH* 7. 1, 3, 8, 9; 8. 10; 12. 12. However, he occasionally appears to use *doru* as a generic term to cover all kinds of spear—cf. the plural '*dorata*' for spears which were thrown (and possibly therefore javelins), *Hell.* 5. 4. 40.

horseback across all types of terrain and retreats with his spear (*doru*) pointing backwards, the other chases with buttons on his javelins (*akontia*) and his spear (*doru*) modified in the same way. Whenever he gets within javelin range he hurls the blunted weapons at the fleeing man and whenever close enough for a spear-thrust, strikes his captive.

Xenophon seems to assume here that the cavalryman engaging in practice sessions will be equipped both with a *kamax* and two javelins, the former for close-quarter combat and the latter for missile-fire. However, to my knowledge there is only one illustration of a *hippeus* equipped in this way (see Plate 9) and on all other occasions when discussing weapon-training skills Xenophon refers only to the javelin.[69] Similarly, when giving his views on cavalry equipment, Xenophon advocates replacing the *kamax* by two *palta* in terms which suggest that two javelins be carried instead of the *kamax*, not that the *kamax* be dropped from an existing complement of two javelins and a spear.[70]

One solution to the apparent conflict and uncertainty in the sources over cavalry weaponry is that the use of a combination of *kamax* and two javelins, or of two javelins alone, represent patterns of armament which prevailed at different times.[71] However, there are problems with this viewpoint as both weapon configurations occur in the same treatise, the *Peri Hippikes*. Although this could be explained by dating section 12 of this work substantially later than sections 1–11, this particular argument is not entirely convincing.[72] In addition, Xenophon's treatise on the cavalry commander shows that the two patterns of armament did coexist. He states here that 'in my opinion the majority would practice throwing the javelin from horseback if you (i.e. the hipparch) were in addition to give notice to the phylarchs that they would have to ride to javelin practice at the head of the javelin throwers of their squadron (*tois tes phyles akontistais*).'[73] The use of the phrase *tois tes phyles akontistais* implies that some, but not necessarily all, members of each *phyle* were equipped with the javelin. It

[69] Xen. *Hipparch.* 1. 6, 21, 25; 6. 5.
[70] Xen. *PH* 12. 12.   [71] This was suggested to me by Dr N. V. Sekunda.
[72] Cf. E. Delebecque, *Essai sur la vie de Xénophon* (Paris, 1957), 242–4, 431–2. His argument that the *PH* is otherwise entirely civilian in nature is not correct (cf. 3. 7; 7. 3–5, 15–17; 8. 10–12; 9. 1) and the reference to the 'Athenian Eleusinion' is not proof it was written outside Athens—the term 'Eleusinion' was also used for the temple at Eleusis (cf. Aelius Aristeides, *Panath.* 373; *IG* II² 204, l. 7; 1672, l. 129).   [73] Xen. *Hipparch.* 1. 21.

seems certain, given the references to *dorata* already identified elsewhere in the same work, that the others were equipped with the *kamax*.

The existing evidence is insufficient to allow anything more than that some Athenian *hippeis* were equipped with javelins, some with a *kamax*, and some with a combination of both. Whether any one configuration predominated at a particular time is in my opinion impossible to ascertain. This is reinforced by the freedom of choice implicit in Xenophon's advice to the individual *hippeus* on the best weapon to adopt.[74] It appears most likely then that the differences in arms carried resulted more from individual preference than from any organizational specification of the number of spear- or javelin-bearing cavalrymen in each *phyle*.

The final offensive weapon of the cavalry was the sword. This, like the *kamax*, was a close combat weapon and where carried it was in addition to, not instead of, the main armament. Because of this it was presumably most often employed when the spear or javelins were either expended or broken.[75] According to Xenophon, the best type to have was that called the *machaira* or *kopis*, which seems to have been a shorter version of the more modern cavalry sabre. That it too was primarily a slashing weapon is confirmed by Xenophon's explanation of why it was more efficacious than the *xiphos*, a straight sword. This use is also corroborated by the artistic evidence which reveals that the most popular blow was an overarm stroke delivered from above the head or shoulder.[76]

Wielded in this way by a rider, the *machaira* was very probably a thoroughly effective weapon. The Hippokratic treatise *On Head Wounds*, generally dated to *c.*400, provides important evidence for this. It records that wounds delivered from above, as would be the case of those inflicted from horseback upon an infantryman, are worse than ones inflicted from the same level.[77] However, even the humble horizontal blow delivered from horseback had

[74] Xen. *PH* 12. 12.
[75] Xen. *Hell*. 3. 4. 14 and *PH* 12. 12 attest to the weakness of the *kamax*; the breakage of spears was common enough to be depicted on the funeral monument of Suagenes, a Theban hoplite who died *c.*424, Thebes Museum no. 56.
[76] Xen. *PH* 12. 11. For swords in vase-paintings see vases 26, 39, 50, 136, 145, all of *xiphos* type. Amazons or Arimasps: 63, 85, 90, 124. Overarm blow: vases 167–8, 184–5, 196; cf. reliefs 10, 13.
[77] *On Head Wounds*, 11.

considerable potential, as recent work on Japanese skeletal remains of the fourteenth century AD illustrates. Dr M. Shackley considers that these blows were possibly fatal, 'immediately rendering the warrior unconscious from loss of blood.'[78] Although the riders involved had stirrups, and the Japanese *tachi* or *katana* of the fourteenth century was undoubtedly sharper than the *machaira*, similar wounds to those shown in Shackley's plates may have been inflicted by ancient Greek cavalry. Even with stirrups, the Japanese were apparently not noted riders[79] and a horizontal blow is not so dependent on the use of stirrups anyway. Finally, although not as sharp as the Japanese weapon, the classical *machaira* was probably heavier at the point of impact. The Greek treatise confirms the effectiveness of the latter characteristic, stating that the worst wounds are inflicted by heavy blunt instruments and while the *machaira*, being edged, does not quite conform to this description it was certainly closer to it than the illustrations of *tachi* or *katana* which I have seen.[80]

However, the *machaira* could also be used against parts of the body other than the head, and wielded by a mounted warrior would presumably often have been directed at the neck and throat, the area most vulnerable on a hoplite. As far back as Homer, the unprotected area between breastplate and helmet was recorded as a favourite target and the overarm thrust with the hoplite spear at the neck is often illustrated in vase-paintings.[81] The *machaira* was undoubtedly a useful weapon well suited to close-quarter fighting from horseback—despite its shortness in comparison with the sabre used by more modern cavalry. However, as pointed out, the lack of stirrups would have made a longer weapon unmanageable and a shorter weapon was not

[78] M. Shackley, 'Arms and the Men; 14th-Century Japanese Swordsmanship Illustrated by Skeletons from Zaimokuza, near Kamakura, Japan', *World Archaeology*, 18 (1986), 251; her pls. 1 and 2 graphically illustrate the effect.

[79] Chenevix-Trench, 147. However, as my son James pointed out to me, this is apparently contradicted by some of the Japanese art in S. R. Turnbull, *The Book of the Samurai* (London, 1982), 18, 19, 24.

[80] *On Head Wounds*, 11. 31 ff.; for the *tachi* or *katana* see Turnbull, *Samurai*, 66, 144–6.

[81] The most famous, and a very early example, is the 'Chigi Vase' which depicts two rows of hoplites with spears poised for this thrust, Rome, Villa Giulia 22679. For Homer, see *Il.* 13. 387–8; 16. 330 ff., 339 ff. (2 cases); 20. 455 ff. The best example, which actually refers to the vulnerable point, is of course the death of Hektor, *Il.* 22. 315 ff.

necessarily a major disadvantage—as the Australian charge at
Beersheba in 1917 shows. Although not equipped with swords,
the 4th ALH Brigade successfully charged Turkish trenches on
horseback, armed with bayonets of approximately the same length
as the *machaira*.[82]

Unfortunately, as with both the javelin and spear, it is impossible to determine how many Athenian cavalrymen actually carried
a sword. Xenophon recommends it as if it were a standard item of
equipment[83] but the vase-paintings and sculpture only occasionally portray riders wearing one. Interestingly, the sword starts to
become more common on Athenian pottery from the Classic
Period onwards (largely worn by Amazons, although the Late
Fifth Century examples show either Athenian cavalry or horsemen accoutred as such).[84] It may be then that the sword became
a more common item of equipment in the late fifth century, with
its popularity continuing well into the fourth. Pots of this later
period frequently portray Arimasps and Amazons wielding
swords and the contemporary grave-reliefs too seem to suggest
that they were a fairly familiar sight on cavalrymen of this period
(cf. Plates 11, 13).[85]

In conclusion, the precise pattern of weaponry carried by the
hippeis is uncertain. Two javelins, a *kamax*, and a *kamax* and two
javelins, are all attested as possible combinations, with or without
a sword. However, whatever the exact array of weapons carried
by individual members of the cavalry corps, it is clear that as a
body the Athenian *hippeis*, and probably Greek cavalry in general,
were able to employ both close-quarter and longer-range missile
combat. This facility was also assisted at Athens and elsewhere by
the attachment of horse archers and infantry to the cavalry.

The Athenian horse archers, or *hippotoxotai*, formed a contingent of 200 hundred mounted archers who operated in wartime

---

[82] See H. S. Gullett, *The AIF in Sinai and Palestine* (The Official History of
Australia in the War of 1914–1918, vol. 7; St Lucia, 1984), 394–404; cf. Idriess,
Desert Column, 261, 275–6

[83] Xen. *PH* 12. 11.

[84] Non-Amazons with sword: Classic Period (*c*.450–420), vase no. 50; Late
Fifth Century (*c*.420–390; a period of low output because of the Peloponnesian
War), 136 and 145.

[85] Swords wielded in combat: see 54 n. 76 above. Grave reliefs with swords
carried: Introd. n. 45. In some of these, as in the case of some vase-paintings, the
sword is indicated only by the existence of a baldric, the rest of the weapon being
obscured.

with the *hippeis*. Vos suggests that in the sixth century such mounted archers serving in Athens were Scythian mercenaries.[86] This may also have been so for the early fifth century as the archer on the *dokimasia* cup of *c*.480–70 certainly looks Scythian (Plate 5). However, others have argued that, although of Scythian origin, the fifth-century *hippotoxotai* were public slaves.[87] This last view seems to be an assumption based on Andokides' reference to 300 slave archers (*toxotai*) who served as police[88] but this is not decisive evidence for the servile status of the *hippotoxotai*. The weight of the total evidence available for land warfare strongly indicates that slaves were not normally used as fighting troops by the Athenians. In addition, the existence of citizen foot archers in the mid-fifth century is attested by a casualty list of the Erechtheid tribe and the total at the height of the Athenian empire may have been as high as 1600.[89] It is therefore unwise to assume that all military archers were Scythian slaves. This is also true of the *hippotoxotai* as a speech of Lysias records that Alkibiades the Younger (Appendix 5.9) served with them in the expedition of 395.[90] Although Alkibiades seems to have been reduced to this because his phylarch had expelled him from the cavalry squadron, and it was obviously held as a posting of low reputation, this incident does show that it was at least possible for citizens to serve with the *hippotoxotai*.

Because of this their precise status is uncertain, although they were perhaps primarily mercenaries with a stiffening of citizens— but in what proportion it is impossible to say. Unfortunately this doubt also extends to their use in battle. Their availability undoubtedly added considerably to the hitting power of the *hippeis*, but we have no specific evidence for their use, apart from Xenophon's statement that they led the charge of the cavalry.[91] This suggests that one of their functions was to advance ahead of the *hippeis* and use their arrows to soften up an enemy formation, but this cannot be confirmed. All we do know is that twenty were

[86] Vos, *Scythian Archers*, 68–9.
[87] Lammert, *RE* viii. 1926, s.v. ἱπποτοξόται.
[88] Andok. 3. 5.
[89] R. L. Sargent, 'The Use of Slaves by the Athenians in Warfare', *CPh* 22 (1927), part I, 201–12. Citizen archers: *IG* I² 929; *Ath. Pol.* 24. 3. See also *HCT* ii. 41–2.
[90] Lysias, 15. 6.
[91] Xen. *Mem.* 3. 3. 1.

sent to Melos in 416, thirty to Sicily in 414, and that an unknown
number served at Haliartos in 395,[92] but these occasions have
led to differing interpretations of their function. Gomme, for
example, suggests that in the case of Melos they may have been
utilized for 'raiding isolated farms and hamlets'. Lammert, on the
other hand (and in line with his view that they were slaves)
maintains that they were '*Feldgensdarmen*' or military police.[93]
Gomme's opinion is the more likely—their equipment would
have particularly suited them to raiding and their use in this type
of combat-role is further supported by Aristophanes' *Birds*. This
pictures 30,000 hawk '*hippotoxotai*' being dispatched to inter-
cept Iris who was attempting to break a blockade.[94] The *hippotoxotai* are attested down to *c*.395 but sometime prior to *c*.365
seem to have been replaced by *hamippoi*, footsoldiers who were
posted with, and fought alongside, the cavalry. The reason for
their replacement is not known, but if the force was largely
composed of mercenaries then it is possible that the source of
supply had dried up, or that the Athenians simply decided that
their function could be performed better and more cheaply by
citizen footsoldiers.

The earliest evidence for *hamippoi* at Athens occurs in Xenophon's treatise on the duties of the hipparch, *c*.365. He argues
here that it is necessary for 'the hipparch to show how weak
cavalry without infantry is—compared to cavalry with *hamippoi*
attached—and, once the hipparch has got his infantry, to use
them.'[95] His tone here suggests that their existence depended at
least in part upon the persuasiveness of the hipparchs and that
they were not necessarily a permanent part of the cavalry establishment. However, other evidence suggests the opposite, at least in
the mid- to late fourth century. For example, the *hamippoi* were
checked by the *Boule*, apparently at the annual review of the
cavalry horses and the *prodromoi*, and any who were deemed
unsuitable forfeited their pay.[96] They may therefore have existed
as a formal body within the armed forces (and probably attached
to the cavalry) in the latter part of the fourth century. However,

---

[92] Thucy. 5. 84. 1; 6. 94. 4; Lysias, 15. 6.
[93] *HCT* iv. 155; Lammert, *RE* viii. 1926.
[94] Ar. *Birds*, 1178 ff.
[95] Xen. *Hipparch.* 5. 13.
[96] *Ath. Pol.* 49. 1.

this force may have existed as early as 362 if, as Sekunda suggests, the *psiloi* (light infantry) fighting alongside the Athenian cavalry at Mantineia are the *hamippos* corps.[97] Even if not formally constituted at this date, these troops certainly represent de facto *hamippoi*.

A fourth-century grave-relief in the Louvre, (no. 32; illustrated at Plate 10) confirms that these *hamippoi* were light-armed soldiers and also illustrates one of their tactics: charging into battle holding on to the tail of the cavalry mounts. This particular relief is reminiscent of the Stanley Berkeley painting of the cavalry charge of the Scots Greys at Waterloo, when infantry of the 42nd and 92nd Highland Regiments (the Black Watch and the Gordons) charged with the Greys while holding onto their stirrups.[98] Xenophon describes *hamippoi* involved in a similar charge when Epameinondas mixed them in with his cavalry at Mantineia in 362 to assist the mounted thrust into the opposing cavalry; Agesilaos did the same against Persian cavalry on the plain of Sardis.[99] However, *hamippoi* could also be used in other ways: Xenophon suggests they be hidden behind the cavalry and used to ambush the enemy, and elsewhere mentions Argive cavalry and infantry posted together to act as a rearguard in a withdrawal.[100] *Hamippoi*, therefore, could be used to stiffen cavalry in defence, to add weight to their attacks, or to stage ambushes. Unfortunately, our evidence does not permit us to state how large the Athenian *hamippos* corps was—although it has been plausibly suggested, on the basis of Boiotian practice at Delion, that there might have been one *hamippos* to each *hippeus*.[101]

Therefore, although some of the details are uncertain, the Athenian *hippeis* would have had a corps of 200 *hippotoxotai* and/ or an unknown number of *hamippoi* attached to them. Other states also used *hamippoi*, especially in the fourth century, but they are attested in Sicily as early as 480 and were in use in the

[97] Diod. Sic. 15. 85. 4, cited in Sekunda, *AG* 54.

[98] The incident is also described by W. Siborne, *History of the War in 1815*, quoted in Glasgow Herald, *Scotland Forever: A Gift-book of the Scottish Regiments* (London, 1915), 110–11.

[99] Xen. *Hell.* 7. 5. 23–5; Plut. *Ages.* 10. 3—Epameinondas used a wedge formation, Agesilaos' formation is unspecified.

[100] Xen. *Hipparch.* 8. 19; *Hell.* 7. 2. 4.

[101] J. Kromayer and K. Veith, *Heerwesen und Kriegführung der Griechen und Römer* (Munich, 1928), 93.

Boiotian army by 419/18.[102] The mounted archers would have
added significantly to the missile power of the cavalry while the
hamippoi would have improved its close-quarter combat capabilities. These would have contributed to its hitting power both
directly and via their influence on the cavalry's flexibility—already fairly high because of the mix of individual weapons within
the corps.

PROTECTION

The protection available to rider and horse in classical Greece
had two major effects on the cavalry's combat potential. First,
armour was likely to make the rider feel safer and more confident
and render him more enthusiastic in combat than if he were
unprotected. Second, it would reduce casualties and therefore
keep more soldiers in action during an engagement. This second
effect also conferred a longer term benefit because it reduced the
chance of death at a later date from what nowadays would be
regarded as fairly minor wounds. The worst of these in terms of
possible complications and subsequent death were those to head
or torso (although wounds to a limb could also prove fatal).[103] In
the case of torso wounds, John Keegan points out that, before
antiseptics or antibiotics, 'those which had pierced the intestines,
emptying its contents into the abdomen, were fatal: peritonitis
was inevitable. Penetrations of the chest cavity, which had probably carried in fragments of dirty clothing, were almost as certain
to lead to sepsis.'[104] While referring to AD 1415, his remarks are
arguably still true of antiquity—although the standard of medicine
then was probably better than in the medieval period.

Although there is some uncertainty about the proportion of
Athenian cavalry who wore protective dress, it seems that breastplate, helmet, and heavy boots (embades), were commonly used,
particularly in the fourth century. The first two of these, shown
in Plates 2 and 13 respectively, would have provided considerable
protection from the head and torso wounds which were so dangerous. The boots are worn by the right-hand youth on Plate 3 and

[102] Hdtos 7. 158 (*hippodromoi psiloi*); Thucy. 5. 57. 2.
[103] Hdtos 6. 134–6.
[104] J. Keegan, *The Face of Battle* (Harmondsworth, 1978), 113.

the riders on Plates 2 and 12 (although here only traces of the soles remain), and would have provided protection for both feet and lower legs.[105]

Many cavalrymen may even have been better off in this respect than hoplites, whose panoply (with the exception of the shield) seems to have grown progressively lighter during the fifth and fourth centuries.[106] This trend probably arose primarily from a desire to increase mobility, but presumably was also affected by considerations of comfort and cost—it was apparently quite expensive to have armour made to fit the individual.[107] The cavalry-man, however, was not so subject to these influences: his mobility was provided by his mount and so not appreciably reduced by the weight and encumbrance of armour. Many *hippeis* too would have been able to afford the made to measure items which fitted much more comfortably than cheaper pieces of armour. While some cavalrymen undoubtedly chose not to avail themselves of this protection,[108] it is apparent from the literary and sculptural evidence that many others regularly wore protective items (see Plates 2 and 12–13).

Demosthenes, for example, treats the wearing of a breastplate as standard practice, summing up Meidias' avoidance of cavalry service in the Euboian campaign with the remark 'he never put on his breastplate'. Xenophon too treats the cuirass as a major item of equipment[109] and seems to have worn one as a matter of course during his service in Persia. He describes the difficulty he had operating on foot while wearing cavalry armour as follows:

Soteridas the Sikyonian said 'You and I are not equal, Xenophon, as you are riding a horse while I am exhausted from carrying my shield (*aspis*).' When Xenophon heard this he dismounted from his horse, pushed him out of the rank, and taking his shield pressed on as fast as he was able. But, as he had on his cavalry breastplate, he was weighed down and

---

[105] Xen. *PH* 12. 10.
[106] *AAG* 109–10; *MT* 13–42, esp. 40–2.
[107] Cf. Xen. *Mem.* 3. 10. 9–15.
[108] Although it seems strange that men would wear less protection in battle than was available, this is not only an ancient Greek phenomenon. Major Peter Murphy, late of the Royal Australian Armoured Corps, told me that all the wounds suffered by his men while he was an APC troop commander in Vietnam could have been avoided or reduced in severity if they had been wearing the flak jackets and helmets issued. However, these were uncomfortable to wear and many soldiers removed them once away from their superiors.
[109] Dem. 21. 133; Xen. *PH* 12. 1–10.

could scarcely keep up, so he urged those in front to go on and those
behind to overtake. The other soldiers, though, struck, stoned, and
abused Soteridas until they forced him to take his shield back and
continue the march.[110]

The Achaian general Philopoimen had similar problems some
200 years later,[111] indicating not only that cavalry armour had
remained basically the same but that, as in Xenophon's era, it was
heavier than that worn by the infantry. Other writers confirm
that, in addition to the Athenians and the Achaians, the cavalrymen of many Greek states went to war in protective clothing.
Boiotian cavalry certainly did: dead ones were stripped of their
armour by the Athenians at Nisaia in 424, while Xenophon
describes live ones 'enthusiastically polishing their helmets' before
Mantineia some sixty-two years later.[112] The Macedonian cavalry
too seems to have worn armour in battle, as did the Thracian and
Sicilian mounted arms.[113] Xenophon also records that the ad hoc
cavalry force raised by the Ten Thousand after Kounaxa was
equipped with 'jerkins and breastplates' (*spolades kai thorakes*), as
if these were an essential and normal part of cavalry equipment.[114]

In the case of Athens at least, the literary evidence is supported
by fifth- and fourth-century sculpture in general, and by grave-
reliefs in particular. Although these show that some cavalrymen
disdained protection, they also confirm that others did wear
armour. For example, on the Parthenon frieze (which portrays a
religious procession for which many cavalrymen might well have
left their armour at home) 16 of the 114 cavalry figures in a
reasonable state of preservation wear body armour (excluding the
high boots which are very common indeed).[115] The proportion
on grave-reliefs is considerably higher. Of the 20 reliefs in Appendix 2 which depict cavalrymen and where the rider is extant, 10

[110] Xen. *Anab.* 3. 4. 47–9.
[111] Plut. *Philop.* 6. 4.
[112] Thucy. 4. 72. 4; Xen. *Hell.* 7. 5. 20.
[113] Macedonians: Thucy. 2. 100. 5, (but not so heavily armoured as Scythians:
Arr. *Anab.* 3. 13. 4). Thracians: Xen. *Anab.* 7. 3. 40. Sicilians: see 'Italy', Ch. 1.
[114] Xen. *Anab.* 3. 3. 20.
[115] These are (by frieze, slab, and number): South: v 13; x 26, 28; xi 29–31;
xiii 35–7; North: xxviii 86; xxxviii 116; West: ii 3; iv 7; vi 11; x 18; xi 20. A more
doubtful figure (not included in my total) is West vi 12 (wearing a helmet and
very similar to the dismounted rider, West xv 29, but not depicted with a horse).
See App. 1 and 2 for numerous examples of embades in Athenian art.

men wear items of protective dress.[116] These items are predominantly breastplates and helmets (especially the petasos-helmet identified by Sekunda;[117] see Plate 13) and embades. However, these are only some of the pieces available—others included protectors for both right and left arms and for the thigh. A complete list, and a discussion of each item, is given in Xenophon's outline of the essential armour required by an aspiring cavalryman.[118] However, even though the panoply he recommends would have afforded considerable protection, it is doubtful whether this quantity of armour was ever worn by many *hippeis*.

Two of the items suggested by Xenophon, the shoulder-to-hand guard for the left arm and the forearm guard for the right are, for instance, apparently unattested in Greek art or archaeological finds. A third item, the thigh-protectors, is to my knowledge attested outside Xenophon only in a relief from Xanthos (which may depict a Lycian cavalryman) and on a Thessalian coin.[119] However, it seems intrinsically unlikely that a soldier of Xenophon's experience and obvious practical bent would recommend mythical pieces of equipment, and recent research confirms this. N. V. Sekunda has shown that the arm-guards were used by the Persian cavalry and presumably observed by Xenophon some time before he wrote the *Peri Hippikes*.[120] The arm-guards and thigh-protectors therefore did exist and the latter were worn in Thessaly at least. In addition, these thigh-protectors were made of padded cloth so the chance of archaeological finds is extremely remote. Despite these considerations, though, the general lack of Athenian supporting evidence for these, and for the arm-guards in particular, strongly suggests that they were never widely adopted in Athens.

At this point, it is appropriate briefly to review the problem of the ceramic evidence which seems to indicate that even the more traditional cuirass and helmet were not widely worn. For example,

---

[116] Reliefs 6, 7, 13, 17, 24–7, 29, 30. Fragmentary reliefs, those with farewell scenes which do not include weapons and/or armour (and may therefore symbolise the parting of death rather than a departure for war), and those with victors in equestrian games are excluded from the total.

[117] Sekunda, *AG* 19.

[118] Xen. *PH* 12. 1–7.

[119] Xen. *PH* 12. 8–9. Relief: the 'Sarcophagus of Payava' in the BM (J. K. Anderson, *Xenophon* (London, 1984), pl. 7); coin: Anderson, *JHS* 80 (1960), 7–8.

[120] N. V. Sekunda, 'Some Notes on the Life of Datames', *Iran*, 26 (1988), 42.

of those vases in Appendix 1 which portray Athenian or Greek horsemen, only twelve depict armour.[121] Only one of these armoured riders is shown engaged in combat and few, if any, are likely to post-date the Athenian cavalry reform of *c*.445–438.[122] However, the weight of the literary and sculptural evidence suggests that the vase-paintings give a misleading impression of the frequency with which cavalry armour was worn. The exact reason for this is uncertain, although it probably arose from one or more of the following possibilities. First, that artists omitted armour in order not to spoil the line of their subjects' bodies and interfere with the ideal of heroic nudity. This, however, was not always the case as some cavalry (particularly non-Athenians) are portrayed in armour. Second, that many of the scenes represent training, or are based upon the painter's observation of training or of non-military equestrian activity where armour would not be worn. Third, and this receives some support from the increase in horsemen wearing armour on fourth-century grave-reliefs, that protective dress was less common in the fifth than in the fourth century. However, whatever the reason for the phenomenon, it is fairly clear that while vases can accurately portray individual items of armour they cannot be used to gauge the frequency with which they were worn.

The conclusions based on the written and sculptural evidence, therefore stand: not all cavalrymen wore protective dress, but it is likely that many regularly rode to battle in breastplate, helmet, and high boots. It is extremely doubtful, though, that the more esoteric items of equipment recommended by Xenophon were ever widely accepted (or possibly even worn at all), and the same is perhaps true of the horse armour he discusses. This is slightly surprising as horses were valuable possessions and, as Xenophon pointed out, a rider was in serious danger if his mount was injured.[123] To obviate this risk Xenophon proposed the use of head, chest, side, and belly armour. Their use by Greeks is attested by finds of equine face-guards, or champfreins, from

[121] Vases 13, 16, 21–3, 26, 30, 33, 35, 39, 43, 46; 23 is uncertain and 30 is probably a hoplite's attendant.

[122] Two are Early Red-Figure, five Late Archaic, and five Early Classic. Only very late vases in the last category could conceivably be contemporary with a reform *c*.445.

[123] *PH* 12. 8. See too Xen. *Kyrop.* 7. 1. 37–8; [Longinus], *de Subl.* 25.

Sicily and at Olympia,[124] and by the combination side and thigh
piece on the Xanthos relief and Thessalian coin already mentioned. As noted, because most of the items of horse armour
described by Xenophon were made of padded cloth, it is not
really surprising that none have survived to be included amongst
archaeological finds. However, like the arm-guards, their lack of
representation in sculpture or on vases suggests that the use of
equine armour was not common in Athens during the classical
and early Hellenistic periods.

Therefore, both *hippeus* and horse had the potential for considerable personal protection, although it seems likely that individual
preference inclined towards restricting body armour to helmet,
breastplate, and boots. Equipped in this manner, even though
they did not carry shields, the Athenian cavalry would probably
have been as well protected as the more lightly equipped hoplites
of the late fifth and the fourth centuries. This in turn would have
increased confidence and reduced casualties, and therefore added
to the combat potential of the corps.

LEADERSHIP

An important human factor in determining the hitting power of
any military arm is the quality of its leadership. As Xenophon
points out 'a man can shape nothing according to his wishes
unless the material he moulds is ready to obey the craftsman's
will. Nor indeed can one make anything of men unless, with the
god's help, they are prepared to view their commander with
friendly feelings and to consider him wiser than they in the
conduct of operations against the enemy.'[125] Good leadership
was particularly important in antiquity because most cavalry
forces, including the Athenian corps, were composed of part-time
soldiers who were essentially volunteers. With such organizations,
persuasion and example are usually much more important motiva-
tors than force or sanctions, which probably explains why Xenophon was so interested in leaders and how they were able to get
soldiers to follow them. The passage just quoted stresses the need

[124] Xen. *PH* 12. 8–9; cf. Xen. *Anab.* 1. 8. 6 and Arr. *Anab.* 3. 13. 4 for Persian
and Scythian horse armour. Champfreins: *AAG* 87.
[125] Xen. *Hipparch.* 6. 1.

for the officers to have the goodwill of the men and this is confirmed by several incidents described in Xenophon's *Anabasis*. In one case Klearchos was obeyed by the other officers 'not because they had chosen him leader but because they saw that he alone had the sort of wisdom a leader should have while the others were inexperienced.'[126] However, the Ten Thousand was a mercenary force with officers which in many cases it had elected itself and the dependence upon the soldiers' wish to obey was perhaps less marked in a citizen army.

This would have been particularly so at Sparta where discipline and obedience were instilled in the citizen as a matter of state policy, and very successfully too if Xenophon is to be believed.[127] But even the Athenians, who were regarded as more unruly than most,[128] may have been more amenable to discipline than mercenaries as their generals and junior officers were elected, not by the soldiers on campaign, but by the citizen body and the tribes respectively. Because of this, the *strategoi* and *hipparchoi* had the authority of the whole state behind them and the taxiarchs and phylarchs probably also derived some moral authority from their election. In one of Aristophanes' comedies a general ('Lamachos') responded to another character's taunts by appealing to the fact that both he and his colleagues were elected.[129] However, this had little effect in the play, and the extent of the moral authority in the case of the subordinate officers is even more difficult to ascertain. The taxiarch Laches, at any rate, seems to have derived no protection from his position when assaulted by a hoplite named Simon.[130] Whatever the degree of moral authority imparted to officers by state election, discipline problems undoubtedly still existed as the Athenian military command structure had fewer mechanisms for ensuring obedience than a modern army possesses.

There is, for example, no real evidence for a code of military behaviour enforced by sanctions in the field like those in modern armies, although there are some isolated examples of *strategoi*

[126] Xen. *Anab.* 2. 2. 5–6; see also 2. 6. 26 ff.; 5. 7. 27–34.
[127] Xen. *Lak. Pol.* 2. 14; cf. Demaratos' remarks on the influence of the laws, Hdtos 7. 104.
[128] Nikias complained to his fellow countrymen that his job as *strategos* was made difficult because 'you are by nature difficult to control', Thucy. 7. 14. 2.
[129] Ar. *Acharn.* 593–607.
[130] Lysias, 3. 45; but cf. Thucy. 2. 37. 3.

disciplining soldiers on active service. According to Lysias, the generals had the Simon referred to above banned by herald for insubordination—although he adds that Simon was the only Athenian to be punished in this way.[131] Another example is the (real) general Lamachos who executed a soldier for making traitorous signals to the enemy during the Sicilian campaign.[132] However, I can only find one case of an officer below the rank of *strategos* taking action against a soldier in the field, and this was more of an administrative matter. In this case the squadron commander expelled Alkibiades the Younger (5.9) from the cavalry *phyle* to which he had illegally attached himself. This cannot really be regarded as field punishment and it was the hipparch and not the phylarch who apparently then confiscated Alkibiades' horse.[133] Disciplinary powers in democratic Athens seem then to have been basically restricted to the *strategoi* and hipparchs, and this is confirmed by the case already mentioned involving Simon. One of his acts of insubordination was to strike the taxiarch Laches, yet the punishment meted out to him was ordered by the generals and not the assaulted taxiarch. It seems likely therefore that, while the hipparchs may have had the same authority over their men as *strategoi*,[134] the phylarchs had no great powers of direct punishment over their soldiers in the field.

While the question of discipline no doubt afflicted the Athenian army as a whole, it is possible that it was worse in the cavalry corps than in the hoplite force. The social homogeneity of the cavalry no doubt helped develop an *esprit de corps* and a sense of corporate identity, but it also created the potential for disciplinary problems.[135] This is because the *hippeis* were recruited exclusively from the upper echelons of society, from those who in their civilian life were used to giving orders rather than taking them, and who may well have regarded themselves as at least the

[131] Lysias, 3. 45; presumably the only one so punished on this expedition, rather than in the entire history of Athens.

[132] Lysias, 13. 67.

[133] Lysias, 15. 5–7.

[134] *Ath. Pol.* 61. 4. Xenophon's *Hipparch.* does not mention such powers, but 1. 24 (quoted in the next paragraph) suggests the ability to reward obedience and punish insubordination.

[135] On the other hand, such a force has many potential leaders who can step forward in an emergency. For its usefulness in WW II see H. B. S. Gullett's comments on the 2nd AIF, *Not as a Duty Only: An Infantryman's War* (Melbourne, 1976), 125.

social equals of their officers. Although there is no evidence that indiscipline affected the tactical use of the Athenian cavalry to any real degree, there are hints in the literature that controlling a body of wealthy men, many of whom were young, was not always easy. While Xenophon for example does not treat discipline as a major problem he does express concern about it.[136] He also advises the aspiring hipparch that 'in order to instil obedience in one's subordinates it is important both to lecture them on the many benefits of obedience and by your actions to confer advantage upon the disciplined and disadvantage, in all respects, upon the ill-disciplined.'[137] The sort of problem which could occur amongst the *hippeis* is demonstrated by Demosthenes' speech against Meidias. From this, it seems that an arrogant aristocrat like Meidias was not above going on campaign laden with luxury items and generally proving a disruptive influence upon his fellow soldiers.[138]

However, while they had fewer direct mechanisms for ensuring obedience than officers in a modern army, hipparchs and phylarchs were no worse off in this respect than either the rest of the Athenian armed forces or most other contemporary armies. Simon was apparently serving with the hoplites when he struck the taxiarch Laches, and Xenophon linked hoplites and cavalry together as the least well-behaved Athenian servicemen.[139] The worst indiscipline I have been able to find for the cavalry is the relatively minor case involving Meidias referred to earlier. Despite the lack of a military legal code and system of field punishment, indiscipline does not seem to have been a major problem. This was because the cavalry officers had four methods of encouraging obedience.

The first of these was to use the civil courts on return from campaign. While summary punishment in the field may have been restricted to the *strategoi*, anyone was presumably free to bring a court case against a soldier who had misbehaved. Most of the extant cases of this nature were, as far as we know, brought by men acting in a private capacity rather than by officers, but Xenophon certainly envisages cases preferred by the hipparchs to

[136] Xen. *Mem.* 3. 3.
[137] Xen. *Hipparch.* 1. 24.
[138] Dem. 21. 133–4.
[139] Xen. *Mem.* 3. 5. 19.

ensure that those who were eligible for service actually enrolled in the cavalry.[140] Similarly, prosecutions occasionally seem to have been made by a prominent figure in order to set an example—Lykourgos' action against Leokrates being a case in point. The accused here had fled from Athens after the battle of Chaironeia and on his return was charged with treason by Lykourgos, who at the time had a prominent role in governing the city.[141] The hipparchs and phylarchs therefore had recourse to the possibility of punishment after the event and this would certainly have helped to enforce discipline in the field. This is particularly so as penalties could be severe. Lykourgos for example demanded (and very nearly got) the death penalty in his speech against Leokrates, and Aischines lists several military offences for which disenfranchisement was the normal punishment.[142]

The second aid to maintaining discipline was the possibility of peer pressure to conform to accepted norms of behaviour. Xenophon relied on this to solve his problems with the disgruntled Soteridas (described above in the section on protection), although this is probably an extreme example as the pressure here involved physical as well as verbal abuse.[143] The former was probably less likely (although not impossible) in a citizen army, but the latter is attested in the case of Meidias who, according to Demosthenes, was subjected to ridicule by his fellow troopers because of his behaviour on campaign.[144] Although peer pressure appears to have failed with Meidias, it worked with Soteridas, and it does seem likely that in most normal cases the loss of reputation associated with acting outside the bounds of acceptable behaviour would have been an active inducement to obedience.

The third option for encouraging discipline was the now time-honoured one of making life unpleasant for the offender. This could involve minor actions in the field such as assigning the individual concerned to the less pleasant, or perhaps even the more dangerous, duties. This is what Xenophon presumably meant by the remark quoted earlier that the hipparch should 'confer . . .

[140] Xen. *Hipparch.* 1. 9–10.
[141] Lyk. *Against Leokrates*, 16–19.
[142] Ibid. 8; Aischines, 1. 28–9.
[143] Xen. *Anab.* 3. 4. 47–9.
[144] Dem. 21. 133–4.

disadvantage in all respects upon the ill-disciplined.'[145]

The fourth method of motivating the *hippeis* to obedience was by exercising good leadership, and in particular by leading through example and persuasion. This is stressed several times in the *Hipparchikos*, and by example as well as by the written word. Xenophon reinforced his recommendation that reason, not force, is the best motivator by taking care to persuade his reader of the need to adopt particular courses.[146] In fact the *Hipparchikos* displays a very sound grasp of the practicalities of good leadership. Xenophon's advice to look after the soldiers and to be competent in all the skills required of the trooper, as well as those required of a commander,[147] are classic aspects of leadership which are still stressed today. The cavalry commander or phylarch who followed these recommendations would probably have suffered minimal disciplinary problems among his troops.

However, getting the soldiers to follow is only half of the skill involved in good leadership and competence too is critical—a concept perhaps most economically illustrated by Siegfried Sassoon's poem 'The General':

> 'Good morning, good morning' the General said
> When we met him last week on our way to the line
> Now the soldiers he smiled at are most of them dead,
> And we're cursing his staff for incompetent swine.
> 'He's a cheery old card' grunted Harry to Jack
> As they slogged up to Arras with rifle and pack.
> But he did for them both by his plan of attack.[148]

The quality of the military decision-making clearly had a major impact on the combat potential of the cavalry, but neither tactical nor strategic decisions were exclusively the preserve of the cavalry officers. While they made the tactical decisions in independent operations and conducted the basic handling of the horse in supporting operations, it was presumably the *strategoi* who made

---

[145] Xen. *Hipparch.* 1. 24.

[146] Leading by example: 1. 21, 25; 6. 4–5. On reasons for learning see 2. 1, 6; 3. 5; 4. 2–6, 8, 13, 18–20; 5. 3–4; 6. 1; 7. 1, 5–8; 9. 1–2. Xen. also stresses the use of kindness not force for training both animals and humans: *PH* 10. 12–13; 11. 5–6; *Mem.* 2. 3.

[147] Xen. *Hipparch.* 6. 2–6; he emphasizes the latter point in *Mem.* 3. 3. 8–10.

[148] From B. Gardner (ed.), *Up the Line to Death: The War Poets 1914–18* (London, 1964), 97.

the major tactical decisions in joint operations and who also decided the strategic employment of the mounted arm. Although the lack of evidence makes it impossible accurately to ascertain the level of command expertise for any given date (particularly at the lower tactical level), there are some indications of the general trend. It is also quite possible to identify some of the factors which might have affected the basic quality of cavalry leadership in Athens. Because of this, it is worthwhile discussing the major issues even though the conclusions are necessarily tentative.

On balance, the evidence suggests that the Athenian *hippeis* were probably fairly well handled in most combat situations. This certainly seems to have been the case for independent or low-level operations where *strategoi* were unlikely to have been involved. The basic handling of the cavalry in the mobile defence role during the Peloponnesian War, the employment of the cavalry of the Ten Thousand under Athenian leadership, and the forced march and ensuing cavalry engagement at Mantineia in 362, all point to a reasonably good standard of leadership and decision-making by the officers involved.[149] On a higher level, the deployment of the *hippeis* at Solygeia, the decision to use them in defence of Attica in 431, and the intelligent positioning of the horse at Krannon and Lamia to take into account the composition of the opposing forces,[150] point to the fact that at least some *strategoi* had grasped the principles of cavalry usage. However, there are also some indications of problems, particularly at the higher level. The deployment of the cavalry at Delion in 424, for example, left something to be desired—as did the conduct of the large-scale reconnaissance towards Corinth in 370/69.[151] At a lower level, the premature charge of the cavalry at Tamynai in 348[152] at the very least points to a lack of control by the cavalry officer in charge.

The indications then are that the tactical handling of the

---

[149] See 'mobile defence', Ch. 3. For the Ten Thousand, see below, 143, 145 and Xen. *Anab.* 3. 3. 20 ff. Mantineia: Xen. *Hell.* 7. 5. 15–17.

[150] Thucy. 4. 42–4; Diod. Sic. 18. 15. 2–4, 17. 3.

[151] Delion: Thucy. 4. 93–4. The cavalry seems to have been split into three parts (the temple and both wings) thereby reducing its effectiveness—at any rate it was unable to prevent the flanking movement of the Theban squadron which caused the Athenian collapse (Thucy. 4. 96. 5). For the reconnaissance, see Xen. *Hell.* 6. 5. 52.

[152] See Plut. *Phok.* 13. 1–3.

cavalry was perhaps better in smaller-scale operations than in larger-scale ones; the advice provided by Xenophon's *Hipparchikos* on this lower level was certainly very sound. However, despite the quality of Xenophon's advice and the general trend apparent in the evidence, it is certain that the standard of cavalry leadership was not always consistently high. The battle of Tamynai provides us with one example of either poor decision-making or poor control and, as noted in Chapter 1, Xenophon's advice very probably represents an above average level of military skill. Finally, our evidence for minor cavalry actions is not extensive and, given the general limitations of Greek military expertise, there were undoubtedly many blunders of which we know nothing.

The performance of individual officers was obviously affected by normal variations in their levels of skill. This was particularly so as the general lack of a received body of military theory, or of anything remotely approaching a modern staff college, meant that there was little standardization in training, or even knowledge.[153] There seems to have been a proliferation of military manuals in later periods,[154] and some good works on military affairs did exist in the fourth century, but these were presumably not disseminated in any sort of organized fashion. Although Xenophon's manuals may have had a comparatively wide circulation in Athens, Alexander the Great is supposed to have kept beside him as 'a guide to the art of war', not contemporary handbooks, but the *Iliad*.[155] The lack of formal training may in part have resulted from Greek attitudes to warfare and the warrior mentality. While men like Xenophon could show an intense interest in the details of military practice, other Greeks undoubtedly viewed this as either unnecessary or excessive. The Athenian orator Isokrates was one who believed that, because everyone was equally qualified in this area, any man could pontificate about military matters.[156] The Achaian general Philopoimen's desire to perfect his military skills was viewed by some as immoderate and distasteful, and Plutarch implies that there was something rather unnatural about

---

[153] Lazenby, *Spartan Army*, 24 makes a similar point about Spartan military leadership.

[154] Cf. Plut. *Philop*. 4. 4–6.

[155] Plut. *Alex*. 8. 2.

[156] Isok. 6. 3.

the qualities and art of the soldier.[157] It is in just this sort of atmosphere, as Tarn points out, that new ideas often die with their creator or, if they do survive, are rigidly followed even when the circumstances are not quite the same.[158] Finally, the annual tenure of the hipparchy and phylarchy at Athens (and probably elsewhere) also had the potential to disrupt continuity of leadership, or to prevent the development of real expertise on the part of the command structure.

However, these were general problems which to some degree afflicted all classical Greek armies, not just the Athenian cavalry, and in some respects the *hippeis* were not as badly off as they might at first seem. For example, there was no limit to the successive number of hipparchies or phylarchies an individual could hold. So, although the system of annual command could theoretically result in new officers each year, it is likely that good or popular officers would regularly be re-elected to the same post. This certainly occurred with the *strategeia*, the military office for which we have the most evidence,[159] but even in the case of the hipparchy we know of two men who held the office more than once.

The first of these was Philokles, who was hipparch three or four times and *strategos* ten times before 323, the second was Theophrastos (of Lamptrai?) who served as hipparch in both 222/1 and 220/19.[160] In addition, someone like Meidias (Appendix 5.112), who was still a cavalryman at 50, was likely to have been hipparch on more than the one occasion for which we have evidence. Long service in the *hippeis* was by no means exceptional[161] and if men did hold the office of hipparch or phylarch over several years then they had the potential to build up consider-

---

[157] Plut. *Philop.* 3. 1–4; 4. 5–6. The same view is attested in Arist. *Pol.* 1253ᵃ 4–7 (1. 2) which talks of 'desire for war' (πολέμου ἐπιθυμητής) as one of the main characteristics of the citiless man who operated outside society's parameters.

[158] *HMND* 89–92 (Surenas) and 22–3, 42, 69 (Alexander). Epameinondas is another obvious case.

[159] Of the known *strategoi* between 481/80 and 405/4, forty-six held office more than once, see the list in C. W. Fornara, 'The Athenian Board of Generals from 501 to 404', *Historia Einzelschriften*, 16 (Wiesbaden, 1971), 41–71. In the period 338/7– 319/8 Phokion was *strategos* at least five times, Diotimos four times, Chares three times, and at least six others held the office twice, see T. Sarikakis, *The Hoplite General in Ancient Athens/The Generals of the Hellenistic Age* (Chicago, 1976), 125–32.

[160] Philokles (App. 5.153); Theophrastos: App. 5, part 2, no. 41.

[161] Dem. 21. 162–6; Lysias, 14. 10.

able expertise in commanding cavalrymen. In addition, it was apparently normal for cavalrymen to gain experience by serving in the ranks, and as phylarchs, before becoming hipparchs. Despite the relative patchiness of the prosopographic record, we know of at least four phylarchs who went on to become hipparchs and, although there could be exceptions, officers were generally expected to progress through the rank structure before achieving higher command.[162]

Cavalry officers were therefore likely to have been men of some experience and the electoral process would undoubtedly have ensured that most obvious incompetents would not have been re-elected—after all at least some of the voters had a personal interest in the appointment of cavalry officers who would not get them killed. This level of cavalry expertise may also have held true for the *strategeia*, Athens' high command. Although the election of *strategoi* often involved political considerations, at least eighteen (listed in Table 2) are known to have had previous service in the cavalry, and this undoubtedly explains why some generals were fairly adept at deploying or tasking the mounted arm. In fact, a remark in one of Xenophon's Socratic dialogues suggests that a man could be elected *strategos* without any military service except in the cavalry. Here, one character complains that another, Antisthenes, 'was elected (as general) although he has never served as a hoplite, nor achieved anything of note in the cavalry, and understands nothing but money.'[163]

Therefore, while it is impossible to assess the exact level of leadership or decision-making skills in the Athenian cavalry, there is nothing to suggest that the overall standard was lower than that in most other Greek citizen forces. What little specific information we possess indicates that the cavalry was generally fairly well led and that its commanders at least had the potential to gain experience before becoming hipparchs or phylarchs. In addition, after about 365, the Athenian cavalry officer may well have had access to Xenophon's *Hipparchikos*. This would have helped to improve, or possibly even partially standardize, com-

[162] App. 5: Dieitrephes (52), Kallisthenes (part 2, no. 12), Lykophron (103), and Pheidon (145)—the last less certainly. For the general expectation, see Xen. *Mem.* 3. 4. 1–2.

[163] Xen. *Mem.* 3. 4. 1; Sokrates' response was that Antisthenes' success in business (combined with his ambition to do well) admirably qualified him for the job.

mand skills and knowledge. Finally, as will be discussed in the
next section, the *hippeis* were involved in fairly regular training
sessions which would have assisted in raising the standard of the
officers as well as of the men. This would apply to both leadership
and tactical decision-making.

TABLE 2. Cavalrymen who became *Strategoi c.*450–200[a]

Name	App. 5 no.	Date in cavalry	Date *strategos*
Hipparchs	(*Part 1*)		
Lakedaimonios	99	*c.*450	433/2
Xenophon	191	*c.*450	441/40, 440/39(?), 439/8, 430/29
Pythodoros	168	*c.*420–10	414/3
Dieitrephes[b]	52	pre-414(?)	414/3 & 411[c]
Pamphilos	136	395/4	389/8
Euetion	67	*c.*350–325	323/2(?)
Kineas	87	*c.*350–275	*c.*350–275
Demetrios	46	pre-(?) 325/4	325/4, 324/3, 323/2(?)
Philokles	153	pre-324/3[d]	pre-324/3
APF lost name 8	196	pre-318	pre-318
	(*Part 2*)		
Demetrios	3	mid-3rd cent.	mid-3rd cent.
Kallisthenes	12	mid-3rd cent.	mid-3rd cent.
Theophrastos	41	222/1(?), 220/19	post 220(?)
Phylarchs	(*Part 3*)		
Glaukon	23	pre-*c.*280/79	pre-*c.*280/79
Aristophanes	7	pre-237(?)	237/6, 236/5
Cavalrymen	(*Part 1*)		
Alkibiades	10	424	at least 10 times from 420/19
Antisthenes	25	*c.*370(?)	*c.*370(?)
Asklepiades[e]	*PA* 2618	*c.*260–240	225/4

[a] The history of the period 320–200 shows that the chain of promotion was
sufficiently well established to continue after 320. Entries are listed (within
category) in chronological order. [b] Also a phylarch, Ar. *Birds*, 798–800.
[c] Under the oligarchy. [d] According to Dein. 3. 12 he had been hipparch three or
four times and *strategos* on ten occasions by this date. [e] Omitted from App. 5 as he
is outside the period covered by part 1 and is unattested as either a phylarch or
hipparch; his cavalry service is recorded on Braun, *MDAI(A)* 85 (1970), 208, no.
71.

TRAINING

As was the case with leadership, a high standard of skill was
necessary to allow the cavalry to function as a military arm. The
basic wartime function of cavalry, as it was for every component
of Greek city-state militias, was to kill the enemy, and if neither
individuals nor *phylai* were proficient in such skills as weapon-
handling or riding they would be unable to achieve this. Skill
basically derives from two things: natural ability and training. As
the first of these is impossible to examine at such a remove, this
section concentrates on the latter, which includes training or
practice conducted on both the individual and collective level.
The higher the standard of training, the better the hitting power
of the cavalry, not only because training had a beneficial impact
on such basic skills as riding (especially in formation) and
weapon-handling, but also because of its contribution to enhanced
flexibility.

Xenophon was quite correct in his belief that training for both
horse and rider was an essential step in building an effective
cavalry force. At Athens, the state certainly agreed as the Council,
or *Boule*, was apparently empowered to prescribe the amount of
collective training. However, despite the powers of the *Boule* in
this regard, the quantity as well as the quality of the training
probably varied according to the cavalry officers involved. At any
rate, when writing his cavalry commander's manual, Xenophon
considered the existing programme to be insufficient and advocated doubling it.[164] On the other hand, the cavalry was better
off in respect to training than some other cavalry forces and the
rest of the Athenian army (and indeed most other Greek armies).
Athenian hoplites, for instance, were apparently reviewed prior to
campaigns, but there is no evidence that they engaged in peacetime training; in fourth-century Sparta the cavalry seems to have
collected together only on mobilization.[165]

The Athenian *hippeis*, though, engaged in both individual and
collective training. Xenophon mentions individual rider education
and suggested that aspiring cavalry commanders could encourage
fathers to let their sons join up by the argument that 'if they
enlist under you, you will turn their sons away from expensive

[164] Xen. *Hipparch.* 1. 3–7, 13.
[165] Xen. *Hell.* 6. 4. 10–11.

things and mad horse-buying, and will take care to turn them quickly into horsemen.' Later on in the same work he suggested that 'we would persuade the young men to learn for themselves to mount their horses from the spring, but you would be justly praised if you provided an instructor.'[166] This type of practice, and the use of an instructor, occurs in Plate 1, which shows an older man teaching a youth how to mount with the aid of a javelin. Other vase-paintings show that cavalry training was a familiar and perhaps even frequent sight in classical Athens.[167] Although some scenes clearly show young men or even children of the horse-owning class being taught to ride (see vase 96), the inclusion of real or practice weapons in many others suggests that they depict cavalry training. This is confirmed by the presence of older, bearded, men (sometimes dressed and equipped as cavalry-men), who presumably represent the cavalry officers supervising training.[168]

Individual training relevant to active service would also accrue from participation in, and practice for, the equestrian events in festivals like the Panathenaia. Probably the most useful of these was 'throwing the javelin from horseback' (*aph' hippou akontizon*) which was not only a Panathenaic event but was almost certainly used as a cavalry training exercise as well.[169] The vase-paintings show that this was a realistic exercise involving riders throwing javelins at a target—usually a shield (see Plate 8; the range is shortened to fit both rider and target in the same scene). This would have improved weapon-handling skills, and other events (including the various horse races) would also have helped to improve general standards of equitation.[170]

Collective training for all the cavalry also seems to have been a fairly regular event. This included practice for, and participation in, the various sacred processions and the public displays in the Academy, the Lykeion, at Phaleron, and in the Hippodrome. The

[166] Xen. *Hipparch.* 1. 12, 17; cf. *PH* 7. 1.

[167] e.g. vases 24, 28, 42.

[168] See Pls. 14–15 and the discussion below 200; see also vase 28 (Pl. 1).

[169] Xen. *Hipparch.* 1. 21 emphasizes the need for developing javelin-throwing skills; for the Panathenaic event see also H. Metzger, *Les Représentations dans la céramique attique du IVe siècle*, i (Paris, 1951), 358–9. I have been able to find seven vases with mounted javelin-throwing at a target: App. 1, nos. 159, 161, 198, 202–3, and two black-figure vases: *ABV* 411.1 (Pl. 8) and Berlin 3980.

[170] For the equestrian events see Martin, *Cavaliers*, 226–58.

reviews at the Lykeion and the Hippodrome respectively involved displays of javelin-throwing and mock combat which would have been useful in war. This is because the men would have received valuable practice in weapon-handling and riding together in their *phyle* formations, while the officers would have benefited from the practice involved in controlling their men as a group. Xenophon attests to the realism provided by these displays, describing one manœuvre as being executed 'just as for battle'.[171] Their value as training was further enhanced by the fact that the *hippeis* apparently spent some time practising for them.[172]

Apart from these reviews and displays, however, Xenophon also envisaged the conduct of collective training at various times throughout the year. Even he, though, recognized that in peacetime it would be difficult to insist on a great deal of training. He therefore placed considerable emphasis upon individual cavalrymen practising in their own time.[173] The standard would have been high indeed if all *hippeis* behaved like the exemplary Ischomachos in Xenophon's *Oikonomikos*. In the spirit of the suggestion made in *Hipparchikos* 1. 18, this gentleman prepared for war by practising his horse over all kinds of terrain when riding on his country estate.[174]

With the various types of institutional training and the use of individual practice, a keen cavalryman would have been able to engage in quite a considerable amount of training in any one year. This was possible because the level of wealth required to be a *hippeus* allowed plenty of leisure time. However, less enthusiastic *hippeis* might well have limited their training to attending only the more prominent activities such as the public displays or processions. Even so, the cavalry certainly had the potential to develop a high level of skill, and this was no doubt facilitated by the fact that some cavalrymen and cavalry officers served year after year, providing a core of experienced soldiers and commanders.[175]

---

[171] Xen. *Hipparch.* 3. 6. Cf. 3. 5, 13 which suggest further improvement was possible and that there were annual variations not only in the standard achieved but also in the exact form of the display. This display is probably depicted in relief 36, illustrated in T. L. Shear, 'The Athenian Agora: Excavations 1970', *Hesperia*, 40 (1971), pl. 57*c* (= Bugh, *Horsemen*, fig. 7).

[172] See Xen. *Hipparch.* 1. 20.

[173] Ibid. 1. 17 ff; *PH* 2. 1.

[174] Xen. *Oik.* 11. 15–18.

[175] Lysias, 14. 10; see too the recurring service recorded on the lead cavalry tablets (esp. the Erechtheid *hippeis* in table 1 of Kroll, 90).

Although obviously subject to fluctuations, the net result of this was that the cavalry probably attained a relatively high standard of training which undoubtedly contributed to its combat potential, both directly, and by increasing its flexibility. This conclusion is supported by indications that the Athenian *hippeis* were fairly well regarded in the rest of Greece. While undoubtedly less renowned than the famous Thessalian horse, from time to time their services were in demand by other states. In 400, for example, Thibron requested that 300 Athenian *hippeis* be sent to him in Asia and in 338 the provision of cavalry and ships formed part of the peace settlement with Philip II.[176] Therefore, while the level of enthusiasm of the hipparchs, phylarchs, and soldiers would affect the frequency and quality of practice sessions, it seems safe to say that in general the Athenian cavalry probably enjoyed a reasonably high standard of training and skill.

MOTIVATION

Motivation is not only important in persuading soldiers to train but is also vital in getting them to fight, and to keep fighting. It therefore plays an extremely important part in determining a unit's combat potential. A force can be mobile, well trained, well led, and well armed, but if its soldiers are reluctant to fight, its hitting power will be very limited. Motivation is a product of several factors which operate on both the collective and the individual level. The collective influences are those of *esprit de corps* and leadership, the individual influences are the soldier's desire to win glory or avoid shame, and his commitment to the war or the engagement in hand. Leadership, and how officers could encourage troopers to fight, have already been covered and part of that discussion touched upon the general desire to be seen to be acting within the customary limits of behaviour. However, as it is also an important influence on motivation, it is necessary to examine the role of *doxa*, or reputation, in more detail.

The desire for a good reputation seems to have been regarded as an important factor in classical Athenian society—a speech

---

[176] Xen. *Hell.* 3. 1. 4; Plut. *Phok.* 16. 5.

ascribed to the Corinthians, for example, implies that this formed part of the Athenian character.[177] It was also thought that this desire for honour, *philotimia*, exercised considerable influence on men's actions. Xenophon states that 'the Athenians differ from others not so much in quality of voice or in physical stature and strength, as in their love of honour (*philotimia*), which is a particularly strong spur towards noble acts and deeds of honour.' Such a desire, if harnessed, could obviously be used to create a more effective army and (directly after the words just quoted) Xenophon has Sokrates ask the following question: 'Don't you think therefore . . . that if one also took the same care with the cavalry they would far surpass others in their weapons, horses, good order, and in their eagerness to face the enemy—if they considered that by doing these things they would acquire glory and honour?'[178] This is not an isolated instance of this idea in Xenophon's writings; earlier in the same work, he suggests that a love of fame was a motive of at least some who aspired to be cavalry commanders.[179] In his treatise on the cavalry commander's duties he advocates appointing file-leaders or dekadarchs 'from those at their physical peak and most keen for honour (*philotimotaton*) in doing some noble deed and hearing themselves called noble.' In the same work he also claimed that eagerness to win honour could be used to improve performance in javelin practice.[180]

Despite the literary emphasis on their own *philotimia*, the Athenians did not have a monopoly on this trait. Isokrates suggested in appeals to Philip of Macedon, Archidamos of Sparta, and Evagoras of Cyprus, that it was a universal motivator for military excellence, and the Spartan king Agesilaos capitalized on it to create an efficient army for his Asian campaigns of the early fourth century. On this occasion he used contests and prizes to create a healthy spirit of competition which led to a high standard of performance in all arms, including the cavalry.[181]

---

[177] Thucy. 1. 70. 6; cf. 2. 37. 3 for unwritten 'laws' which it was considered shameful to break.

[178] Xen. *Mem.* 3. 3. 13–14. Compare this with *Hipparch.* 1. 11, where he suggests capitalizing on 'the glamour of horsemanship' (τὰ ἐν ἱππικῇ λαμπρά) to aid recruiting.

[179] Xen. *Mem.* 3. 3. 1–2.   [180] Xen. *Hipparch.* 1. 21; 2. 2.

[181] Isok. 5. 134–5; 6. 107–9; 9. 3. Agesilaos: Xen. *Ages.* 1. 25; cf. *Hipparch.* 1. 26, which recommends this practice for Athens.

However, while this attitude could, and apparently did, moti-
vate Greek cavalry in both training and combat, it is very difficult
to assess how far it affected performance on particular occasions,
or how it held up under the stresses of active service. In most
cases, the lack of evidence means we cannot assess the commitment of the cavalry to individual campaigns or even to entire
conflicts—although there is some evidence of a collective reluctance on the part of the Athenian *hippeis* to fight in the closing
stages of the Peloponnesian War. This, however, was closely
linked with the cavalry's *esprit de corps*, or sense of corporate
spirit and identity.

Esprit de corps affects combat potential through its influence
upon collective performance and cohesion. A high level of corporate spirit and identity assists the standard of achievement
possible, and is also very important in ensuring a group does not
disintegrate under the stress of combat.[182] Conversely, a low
level of *esprit de corps* decreases performance and affects the
ability of a group, not only to function under pressure, but also to
survive. This clearly influences operational performance—the
higher the morale and team-spirit the more the soldiers can be
persuaded to do, or to attempt, and therefore the greater the
flexibility and hitting power available to their commander. While
it is obviously difficult from this distance to reconstruct the exact
level of cavalry *esprit de corps*, it is possible to state that, if Athens
was at all typical, most Greek cavalry corps probably had a strong
sense of identity.

In most states this would have been engendered primarily by
the social homogeneity of the cavalrymen, all of whom came from
the upper levels of society. At Athens, this was further enhanced
by their regular training, and the apparent tradition of family
service within the corps.[183] Presumably this was periodically
reinforced by the shared experiences and dangers of active service,
particularly marked during extended periods of hostility such as
the Athenians and others experienced during the Peloponnesian

[182] R. A. Gabriel, *The Antagonists: A Comparative Combat Assessment of the
Soviet and American Soldier* (Contributions in Military History, 34; Westport,
Conn., 1984), 140–2. See also Sobel's study of combat stress in J. C. Coleman,
Abnormal Psychology and Modern Life, 5th edn. (Glenview, Ill., 1976), 188.

[183] For discussions of cavalry homogeneity and tradition of service see below
180–90 and App. 5. The tradition of family service almost certainly applied in
other *poleis* too.

War. The relatively small number of cavalrymen would also accentuate the sense of group identity, particularly at *phyle* level, as the smaller the unit the closer its internal ties tend to be.

Although a strong sense of corps spirit and identity normally enhances combat performance, the opposite may occasionally be true.[184] In late fifth-century Athens, for example, this phenomenon resulted in cavalry participation in oligarchic movements and probably also in a reluctance to fight. This subject is dealt with in more detail in Chapter 4, but is worth briefly mentioning here. While some *hippeis* were undoubtedly oligarchically inclined anyway, the involvement of most in the coups at the end of the fifth century probably occurred more because they became frustrated with the conduct of the Peloponnesian War and their role in it. The horse-owning class certainly shouldered a large part of the financial burdens of war, a fact echoed in Sokrates' remarks to Kritoboulos in one of Xenophon's dialogues:

Moreover, I see that the city already requires a heavy contribution from you—keeping horses, paying for dramatic choruses, acting as gymnasiarch and *prostates*, and, if war occurs, I know that they will require you to maintain and captain a ship so often and pay so much *eisphora* (war tax) that you will not easily bear it. But, whenever you appear to be lacking in your performance of any of these, the Athenians will punish you no less than if they had caught you robbing them.[185]

However, in addition to this the cavalry was not only deployed daily in the defence of Attica from 413 to 404, but also took part in foreign expeditions (see Table 3). As the rest of the army played no part in the defence of Athens' agricultural hinterland, it would therefore be fairly easy for a member of the *hippeis* to feel that he and his companions were bearing an unfair burden of the war effort.[186] This no doubt would add to their sense of corporate identity, as collective grievances often do, and would have contributed strongly to their involvement in the oligarchic revolution of 404 as a group rather than as isolated individuals.

For some time after this, of course, the cavalry became an

[184] Australian and British troops have occasionally refused reallocation to other units because of their attachment to their Battalion or even Division—see R. Holmes, *Firing Line* (Harmondsworth, 1987), 327–8.

[185] Xen. *Oik*. 2. 6.

[186] Soldiers involved in continuous combat often feel that they have done their bit and that it is someone else's turn, see Holmes, *Firing Line*, 320–1.

TABLE 3. Athenian cavalry movements and activities 432–279

Year	Place	Number	References/Remarks
432/1	Macedonia		*IG* I³ 365; Thucy. 1. 61 ff. has no mention
431	Attica		Thucy. 2. 19. 2; lost minor action at Rheitoi
	Attica	1 *phyle*	Thucy. 2. 22. 2; supported by Thessalian horse against Boiotian cavalry at Phrygia
	Megarid		Thucy. 2. 31. 3; no specific mention of cavalry but reference to future annual operations.
430	Peloponnese	300	Thucy. 2. 56 ff.; seaborne raids with 4,000 hoplites. Horse transports used for first time; cf. Plut. *Per.* 35. 1
	Potidaia/ Chalkidike	300	Thucy. 2. 58. 1; 6. 31. 2; used with 4,000 hoplites to assist in the siege
	Megarid		? See 431
429	Chalkidike	200	Battle of Spartolos; see Table 5
	Megarid		? See 431
428	Attica		Thucy. 3. 1. 2; harassing invasion force
	Megarid		? See 431
427	Megarid		? See 431
426	Megarid		? See 431
425	Corinth/ Solygeia	200	See Table 5
	Megarid		? See 431
424	Kythera	'a small number'	Thucy. 4. 53. 1; minor action and coastal raids
	Megara	600	Thucy. 4. 68 ff.; with 4,000 hoplites. Night march, cavalry action against Boiotians, 4. 72. 3
424	Delion	all?	See Table 5
422	Amphipolis	300	See Table 5
420	Elis	'some'	Thucy. 5. 50; no action (waiting for Olympics)
418	Mantineia	300	Allied command; see Table 5
416	Melos	20	*Hippotoxotai*, Thucy. 5. 84, with 2,700 hoplites and 300 archers; cf. *HCT* iv. 155
416/5	Methone		Thucy. 6. 7; used with Macedonian cavalry; raids
415	Sicily	30	Thucy. 6. 43; one horse transport
414	Sicily/ Syracuse	250	Thucy. 6. 94. 4; they and 30 *hippotoxotai* sent without horses. With local cavalry and own infantry attack enemy horse, Thucy. 6. 98. 3–4 and Lysias, 20. 23–5; cf. Diod. Sic. 13. 7. 3 ff. See Table 5
413	Dekeleia	'the cavalry'	Thucy. 7. 27. 5; they rode out daily until 404

TABLE 3. (*contd*)

Year	Place	Number	References/Remarks
413	Syracuse	'a small force'	Thucy. 7. 51. 2; sallied out with some hoplites and lost 70 horses. Thucy. 7. 83. 1–2 and Plut. *Nik.* 27. 2 mention dispatch riders
412	Dekeleia		See 413
411	Attica	'the cavalry'	Thucy. 8. 71. 2; marched out with foot against Agis
	Dekeleia		See 413 and Lysias, 20. 28 (could also refer to 410)
410	Dekeleia		See 413 and 411; Lysias, 20. 28 (could also refer to 411)
	Athens/Ionia	100	Diod. Sic. 13. 52. 1; Xen. *Hell.* 1. 1. 33–4; after Kyzikos 100 cavalry and 1,000 hoplites voted to help Thrasyllos
409	Nisaia/Kerata	400	With 1,000 foot; Diod. Sic. 13. 65. 1–2
409	Ephesos/ Abydos	100	Xen. *Hell.* 1. 2. 1–17 (the force voted in 410); deployed with marines, separate from hoplites; see Table 5
	Dekeleia		See 413
408	Dekeleia		See 413
	Chalkedonia/ Bithynia	100?	Xen. *Hell.* 1. 3. 3–7; raids and a minor engagement
	Selymbria	300 +	Xen. *Hell.* 1. 3. 10; ravaging country (some cavalry possibly non-Athenian)
407	Attica	1,000?	Diod. Sic. 13. 72. 7 (for the date see Bugh, *Horsemen*, 84); beat enemy horse (very similar to Thucy. 8. 71 of 411)
	Dekeleia		See 413
	Ionia	150	Xen. *Hell.* 1. 4. 21
406	Dekeleia		See 413
405	Dekeleia		See 413
404	Phyle	'the cavalry'	Xen. *Hell.* 2. 4. 2–3; under the Thirty, retired because of snow
	Phyle	*c.*200	Xen. *Hell.* 2. 4. 4–7; left to protect against raids from Phyle, but surprised and routed in camp
	Eleusis	'the cavalry'	Xen. *Hell.* 2. 4. 8; occupy Eleusis
	Mounychia	'the cavalry'	See Table 5; after the battle they patrolled the city walls as hoplites, Xen. *Hell.* 2. 4. 24
400	Asia	300?	Xen. *Hell.* 3. 1. 4; under Spartan command
395	Haliartos?		Lysias, 16. 13; cf. Xen. *Hell.* 3. 5. 17 ff.; allied command, battle over before the Athenians arrived

TABLE 3. (*contd*)

Year	Place	Number	References/Remarks
394	Corinth/ Nemea	600	Allied Command; see Table 5
	Koroneia		See Table 5
394	Attica	'the cavalry'	Xen. *Hell.* 5. 1. 21–2; mobilized with foot against Teleutias; no action
379/8	Thebes/Boiotia	500	Diod. Sic. 15. 26; allied command? Used with 5,000 hoplites to aid Thebes; siege, but no recorded cavalry action
378	Attica	500	Xen. *Hell.* 5. 4. 20–1 (no nos. given); mobilized with foot against Sphodrias; cf. Diod. Sic. 15. 29. 5–7
	Thebes/Boiotia	200	Diod. Sic. 15. 32. 2–6; no battle; cf. Xen. *Hell.* 5. 4. 49 ff.
370/69	Arkadia/ Corinth		Xen. *Hell.* 6. 5. 49
	Oneion		Xen. *Hell.* 6. 5. 52; reconnaissance
369	Corinth		Xen. *Hell.* 6. 5. 49; allied command?
368	Phleious	'some'	Xen. *Hell.* 7. 2. 10; Phleiasian command?
364	Olympia	*c*.400	Allied command? See Table 5
363/2	Corinth		Xen. *Hell.* 7. 5. 16
362	Mantineia		Allied command? See Table 5
352	Phokis	400	Athenian command? Diod. Sic. 16. 37. 3 ff.
351?	Chalkidike		Dem. 4. 27; possibly non-Athenian
349/8	Olynthos	150	Philochoros, *FGH* 328 F50; possibly mercenaries
	Olynthos	300	Dem. 21. 197; Philochorus, *FGH* 328 F51
348	Euboia/ Tamynai		See Table 5
339	Thebes		Aischines 3. 140; no action?
338	Chaironeia	1,000?	Allied command? See Table 5
323	Plataia	500	See Table 5
	Lamia	500	See Table 5
322	Lamia	500?	See Table 5
	Krannon	500?	See Table 5
303/2?	?		*IG* II² 558; ransoming *hippeis*
279	Delphi	500	See Table 5

unpopular organization at Athens but in spite of this, or perhaps partly because of it, retained a sense of corps identity if not solidarity. The wording of the Dexileos monument (Plate 11) has been seen as a defensive reaction to this hostility and the collective cavalry monument from the same campaign may be a somewhat defiant reminder from the *hippeis* that they too served Athens.[187] In addition, what little evidence we have of cavalry membership at this time suggests that sons continued to follow fathers into the corps despite its apparent unpopularity with the rest of the population.[188]

The Athenian example illustrates the possible negative effects if a powerful sense of corporate identity is focused upon grievances rather than on the enemy. Apart from the political problems to which this contributed in 404, it is also likely that the degree of disaffection would make many *hippeis* unwilling to risk danger in what they saw as an unnecessary war to which they had already contributed more than their fair share. However, this is the only negative example I have come across, and it occurred during a period of hostilities unusually sustained and intensive for ancient Greece. The negative effect is in fact atypical and it seems quite clear that the usual effect of a high level of *esprit de corps* would be to act as a source of inspiration and cohesion in battle. Thus, motivation played an important role in determining the cavalry's hitting power—both directly and through its effect on the next characteristic, flexibility.

FLEXIBILITY

Flexibility is a major influence on combat potential,[189] but its close links with the other factors affecting battlefield performance also make it one of the most complex. It is affected by weaponry, organization, the quality of leadership and training, the degree of mobility, and the troops' level of motivation. With the exception of organization, these characteristics have already been discussed as separate factors in the combat potential of the cavalry, but it is now appropriate to examine how they contributed to the flexibility of the mounted arm.

---

[187] Monument = *IG* II² 5222; on this, see below 219–22.

[188] See App. 5, esp. Table 10.

[189] An excellent example of this is the 1940 campaign, where the French High Command and army organization proved too inflexible to cope with the pace of the German advance. As General Beaufre put it, the campaign was a 'nightmare . . . which . . . was from first to last an endless surprise exposing our inability to cope with the enemy's torrential advance', A. Beaufre, *1940: The Fall of France*, trans. D. Flower (New York, 1968), 179.

As used here, the general term 'flexibility' really covers two different, but interrelated, levels of this quality: operational and combat. 'Operational flexibility' is the ability to modify plans or activities rapidly and efficiently in response to changing circumstances during armed operations. This type of flexibility is primarily a function of organization, leadership, command structure, training, degree of mobility, and, to some extent, *esprit de corps*. At this level, for example, the hoplite can be seen as a relatively inflexible arm: once positioned there was little room for manœuvre or change in plan—although the Spartan army was an exception to this and could apparently execute comparatively complicated manœuvres on the battlefield.[190] 'Combat flexibility', is the ability to employ different modes of fighting and formation. An arm which possessed combat flexibility might, for example, be able either to utilize missile-fire or to engage in close-quarter combat, as well as to fight either in formation or as individuals. Here again the hoplite was fairly inflexible: his weapons really only allowed hand-to-hand fighting and he was essentially restricted to operating within the phalanx; outside it he could be very vulnerable indeed. Combat flexibility primarily derives from the equipment used by an arm, although it is also in part influenced by training.

Unlike hoplites, Greek cavalry had considerable flexibility. Operational flexibility existed because of the mobility of the mounted arm, the availability of couriers to disseminate orders quickly and, at Athens at any rate, its command structure. Combat flexibility existed because the offensive weapons carried by the cavalry allowed the corps to employ both missile-fire and close-quarter combat, and this was further enhanced by the attachment of *hippotoxotai* or *hamippoi*. Combat flexibility, though, has already been mentioned in the sections on weaponry and training and needs no further comment here. This section therefore deals with operational flexibility and, as the degree of mobility has already been discussed in detail, will particularly concentrate on the influences of command structure and organization.

At Athens, two hipparchs exercised overall command of the corps which comprised ten equal-sized tribal squadrons or *phylai*,

[190] Inflexibility: *HMND* 30; *GMAW* 6; *MT* 70–1; see also below 172 ff. Sparta: Lazenby, *Spartan Army*, 4, 26–30; *MT* figs III–VIII (but see Thucy. 5. 71–2 for a Spartan failure in a battlefield manœuvre).

each led by a phylarch.[191] Although there is little evidence that
the *phylai* were also formally divided into sub-units,[192] individual
squadron commanders probably operated with some form of
internal command structure. This is likely because of the way the
hoplite force was structured and because of operational need. The
hoplite *phyle* was subdivided into several *lochoi* (which Siewert
equates with *trittys* contingents)[193] and this may have influenced
the cavalry organization, particularly as the highly respected Spartan army had a well-developed command structure at lower
levels.[194]

In addition to the example of hoplite forces, there was a need
for a network of subordinate leaders. This was required to exploit
to the full the cavalry's mobility and to avoid the inevitable
problems arising from ad hoc command arrangements if a *phyle*
without such a network was divided. Such divisions did occur:
thirty cavalry were sent with the main expedition to Sicily and
someone must have commanded them. Two hundred and fifty
cavalry were also sent there in 414,[195] and this figure presupposes
that one *phyle* was divided in half prior to the campaign. It is
therefore likely that the Athenians were also prepared to sub-
divide squadrons in the field in response to tactical
considerations—perhaps, as Xenophon recommended, when
facing an opposing force of similar size. He also argued that one
of the advantages of having an even number of subordinate
commanders was that the *phyle* could be divided into a number of
equal parts, and advocated appointing file-leaders or *dekadarchoi*,
with an experienced soldier also posted at the rear of each file.[196]

---

[191] Xen. *Hipparch.* 2. 2; *Ath. Pol.* 61. 4–5. For the hipparch *eis Lemnon* see
App. 6.

[192] The use of the term *taxis* at Xen. *Hipparch.* 4. 4 could indicate a division of the
phyle but it is perhaps more likely that Xenophon was using the term (which also
defined an infantry unit of approximately company size) to denote the *phyle* itself.

[193] Siewert, *Trittyen Attikas*, 142 ff.

[194] See Xen. *Lak. Pol.* 11. 4–5 and Thucy. 5. 66. 3–4. For Spartan military
organization in general, see Lazenby, *Spartan Army*, 4–25. I have been unable to
find examples of a similar organization in the Athenian hoplite force but, as
Anderson (*MT* 97) points out, 'our evidence is quite unsystematic'. The lack of
reference to Athenian junior officers therefore may not necessarily prove that they
did not exist.

[195] Thucy. 6. 43, 94. 4.

[196] Xen. *Hipparch.* 8. 17 and 2. 2–9; cf. *Kyrop.* 8. 1. 14 where Cyrus has a
similar scheme for his army. Xenophon's suggestions seem to be modelled on
contemporary Spartan hoplite practice.

It was obviously preferable, as Xenophon's advice implies, for these men to be appointed at the start of each year and therefore to have trained as commanders with the troops they were to lead prior to a real combat situation.

These arrangements would, as Xenophon intended, have imparted considerable operational flexibility to the *phyle*, but it is uncertain whether his system was ever adopted at Athens. From his tone it seems certain that such an organization did not apply at the time he was writing (even though a similar system was already functioning at Sparta) and this is confirmed by the fact that he later describes not how it operated but how it *would* operate.[197] However, whether or not Xenophon's system was ever formally instituted by the Athenians, there was an apparently recognized need for a squadron command structure and its existence in some form or other seems likely—even if only in the shape of informal appointments made for the duration of a campaign or expedition.

At a higher level, the dual hipparchy and the overall division of the cavalry into ten equal-sized tribal squadrons also conferred considerable adaptability. The hipparchs were directly responsible to the *Boule* for the efficiency of the cavalry as a whole, and the phylarchs were there not only to command their *phylai* but also to assist the hipparchs.[198] The administrative chain of command is therefore quite clear and the phylarchs were also subordinate to the hipparchs in operational and training matters too. For example, when describing the relation between his proposed *dekadarchoi* (file-leaders) and the phylarch, Xenophon stated that the former must know where to deploy 'just as the phylarchs are told their position by the hipparch'. Elsewhere, he suggested that the hipparchs could raise the standard of javelin-throwing by making the phylarchs ride to javelin practice at the head of their squadrons.[199]

This relationship between hipparchs and phylarchs is further confirmed by the apparent organization of the cavalry into two groups of five *phylai*, each commanded by a hipparch. If this was

---

[197] Xen. *Hipparch.* 2. 2–7; Martin (*Cavaliers*, 396–7) also believed that this was an hypothetical structure but Kromayer and Veith (*Heerwesen und Kriegführung*, 90) accepted it as real.
[198] Xen. *Hipparch.* 1. 7–8.
[199] Ibid. 1. 21; 2. 7.

a formal division, then each hipparch would presumably have had considerable influence upon and control over his subordinate phylarchs and their squadrons—much more so than if the two hipparchs just exercised a general command over the ten *phylai* with no clear delineation of responsibility. The *Athenaion Politeia* refers to two groupings of five *phylai* in terms which suggest a formal division,[200] and this is supported by Xenophon's accounts of the cavalry displays in the Lykeion and the Hippodrome. On both occasions he describes the horse divided into two equal-sized contingents, each under a hipparch, and in addition describes one of these formations riding 'as if into battle'.[201]

Such a division would obviously impart considerable flexibility to both the general deployment and tactical handling of the *hippeis*. They could, for instance, be sent to two separate theatres of war while still retaining a senior officer in command of each part. On the other hand, if the entire force was deployed to the same theatre the two contingents could operate independently or semi-independently. In fact, Helbig plausibly suggests that the dual nature of the office of hipparch originated from the prevalent and early practice of placing half the cavalry on each wing of the infantry.[202] It would certainly make sense then to place each hipparch formally in command of five *phylai* at the start of his period of office. This would both avoid the need for impromptu command arrangements if the cavalry had to be used in war, and would also make it easier for the hipparchs to exercise the responsibility they had for ensuring the efficiency of the *hippeis*.

However, while this division may have existed in the organization of the force, and in particular for the cavalry displays, there is some doubt that it regularly applied in the field. For example, I can find no military operation during the period 432–279 when the Athenians definitely deployed 1,000 cavalrymen. The largest reliable number specified in our sources is 600,[203] which means that to our knowledge the cavalry force was never actually de-

[200] *Ath. Pol.* 61. 4.
[201] Xen. *Hipparch.* 3. 6, 10 ff.
[202] Helbig, 207.
[203] At Megara in 424, Thucy. 4. 68. 5 and at Corinth/Nemea in 394, Xen. *Hell.* 4. 2. 17; see also below 99–101, esp. n. 237. From at least the mid-4th cent. some cavalry served on Lemnos and *IG* II² 1955 confirms that a contingent was located on Salamis *c.*320. These too should be deducted from the possible totals commanded by the hipparchs at Athens itself.

ployed as two units of 500 men. When fewer than ten *phylai* were used it is quite possible that one hipparch led his contingent of five *phylai* out to battle while the other hipparch and cavalrymen remained in Athens. Even so, most of the cavalry forces recorded in our sources consisted of fewer than 500 men (see Table 3).

The question therefore remains whether it was usual to place a cavalry force of fewer than five *phylai* under the command of a hipparch. If not, then the phylarchs would have had more operational influence than might otherwise be expected. This question also has a wider importance because if the hipparchs did not regularly lead cavalry contingents in the field then what did they do and what influence could they have had on the cavalry? Demosthenes suggests one answer when he criticizes the Athenians for allowing their military officers to spend their time supervising the processions, and in particular for keeping their hipparchs and phylarchs at home while a foreigner was cavalry commander 'of those who are fighting for the city's possessions.' In addition, Demosthenes provides the example of Meidias, a hipparch who evaded active service with the cavalry by equipping a ship for the navy.[204] While this could be an exaggeration, deriving from Demosthenes' personal enmity towards the man, it may indicate that the hipparchs had some discretion in the matter of whether or not they led troops into battle.

However, despite Demosthenes' evidence it seems logical that a force consisting of more than one or two *phylai* would have been commanded by a hipparch. Presumably a contingent consisting of a single tribal squadron would normally have been led by its own phylarch and, in joint operations where the cavalry force was to be split, a contingent of two *phylai* was manageable as each phylarch would lead his own squadron under the overall command of the *strategos*.[205] However, a force of two *phylai* engaged in an independent operation away from the infantry, or a force of three or more *phylai* operating with infantry, would require two or more phylarchs to operate together. Unless an overall cavalry commander was appointed in such cases, there was obviously considerable potential for control problems and for friction be-

[204] Dem. 4. 26–7; 21. 160–6.
[205] It is a reasonably certain assumption that when a *strategos* was present he was also in charge of the cavalry. However, at Tamynai it not only acted on its own initiative but also contrary to the *strategos*' orders (Plut. *Phok.* 13).

tween the phylarchs. While one possibility would be to appoint one of the phylarchs as commander, this might create problems with the other squadron commanders and would also mean finding an acting phylarch for the squadron whose leader was promoted. A more satisfactory solution would be to place one of the hipparchs in command of any cavalry force of two or more squadrons and this deduction is supported by the surviving evidence.

As we have already seen, Xenophon and the *Athenaion Politeia* suggest that in their day hipparchs exercised command over five *phylai* and a story in Pausanias indicates that hipparchs also led smaller contingents in the field.[206] This passage describes the death of the hipparch Kallistratos (Appendix 5.82) in Sicily during the Athenian retreat from Syracuse in 413. Although Pausanias is a late source, his story here does receive circumstantial support from Thucydides, and from a speech ascribed to Lysias.[207] Pausanias' account states that Kallistratos cut his way through the encircling enemy at the River Assinaros, led his cavalry to safety in Katane, and then returned to die on the field of battle. Without mentioning Kallistratos, Thucydides remarks that despite heavy losses many Athenians did in fact escape to Katane from the Assinaros and Lysias' speech confirms that, as might be expected, those who did so included cavalrymen. It therefore seems certain that Kallistratos was present in Sicily as commander of the 250 *hippeis* and the 30 *hippotoxotai* sent to the island in 414 to reinforce Nikias.[208]

We know too that one Kephisodoros (Appendix 5.84) served as hipparch at Mantineia in 362, but the size of the Athenian cavalry contingent here is not recorded. However, given the total allied numbers of 20,000 foot and 2,000 horse,[209] and the effort made by the Athenians to get their troops there in time, it seems highly likely that the Athenian contingent was larger than one *phyle* and

[206] Pausanias, 7. 16. 4–6.

[207] Thucy. 7. 85. 4; [Lysias], 20. 24. The hipparch Kallistratos is also mentioned in Plut. *Mor.* 844b but as P. Levi (*Pausanias: Guide to Greece*, i (Harmondsworth, 1971), 266 n. 69) points out, this confuses the cavalry officer with a politician of the same name.

[208] Thucy. 6. 94. 4. His total command therefore numbered some 250 Athenian cavalry (or possibly 280 if the 30 which sailed with the original force, Thucy. 6. 43, were still there) and 30 *hippotoxotai*. He was perhaps also in at least nominal control of the 400 allied horse recorded in Thucy 6. 98. 1.

[209] Diod. Sic. 15. 84. 4.

may even have been as large as five. In addition to Kephisodoros and Kallistratos, several inscriptions indicate that hipparchs did lead cavalry contingents into battle. One is a dedication by a hipparch whose name has been restored as Pythodoros (Appendix 5.168).[210] As the anaglyph over the inscription portrays cavalry engaged in combat (Plate 12), this suggests that the dedication was of spoils taken in battle. This is definitely the case with another inscription, *IG* I² 400, although this may date from a period (prior to the cavalry reform of *c*.445–438) when there were three hipparchs, each commanding a one hundred man squadron.[211] As a final example, Lysias refers to Alkibiades the Younger attempting to serve with the cavalry on campaign (even though he was not enrolled as a cavalryman in that year) and being deprived of his horse by Pamphilos (presumably a hipparch) and an unnamed phylarch. If this occurred during the campaign, then the Pamphilos (Appendix 5.136) referred to took the field with at least one subordinate phylarch.[212]

These are clear examples of Athenian hipparchs leading cavalry in battle, and the fact that more are not known probably results largely from a deficiency in our sources. Even those literary accounts which take the trouble to list the *strategoi* involved in a campaign usually fail to mention the subordinate commanders. Thucydides, for example, does not record Kallistratos' presence in Sicily, nor the presence of the phylarch Menexenos (5.116) killed at Spartolos in 429. In the second case, he even omits the names of the less important *strategoi* who led the expedition.[213] Similarly, Xenophon's accounts of the battles of Koroneia and Mantineia in 394 and 362 respectively make no mention of the generals leading the Athenian forces, so it is hardly surprising that he neglects to record the death of the phylarch Antiphanes (5.22) in the former campaign, or that Kephisodoros (5.84) commanded the *hippeis* at Mantineia.[214]

Given this, the evidence I have discussed above seems sufficient

---

[210] Relief 30; the restoration is based mainly on his patronymic as only the final letter of his name survives (*IG* I² 816).

[211] See 'Athens', Ch. 1.

[212] Lysias, 15. 5; Alkibiades, however, acquired another horse and served with the *hippotoxotai*.

[213] Thucy. 2. 79. 1 and 7. 82 ff. For Menexenos, see Isaios, 5. 42.

[214] Xen. *Hell.* 4. 2. 13–23, 3. 15–23; 7. 5. 15, 23–7. For Antiphanes see *IG* II² 5222.

to show that Demosthenes' contention that the hipparchs spent their time marshalling processions rather than leading the cavalry[215] was either an exaggeration or, if true in this particular year, was not the case in others. Similarly, even if Meidias was, as Demosthenes claimed, trying to avoid active service while hipparch, the steps he took to do so[216] were elaborate enough to suggest that his presence was expected and that he needed a good reason not to go. These two passages are therefore more likely to have been the product of either enmity or forensic exaggeration than of strict truth. Certainly, Xenophon's treatise on the hipparchy assumes throughout that the hipparch will lead the *hippeis* into battle.

To sum up, I believe that while there were possibly some exceptions it was usual for a cavalry contingent of more than one *phyle* to be led by a hipparch. It also seems to have been the case that the cavalry of the fourth century was divided into two sections, each of five *phylai* and each commanded by a hipparch—although (because of the numbers of cavalry normally deployed) it is less certain that this division regularly applied in battle. However, the relationship between hipparch and phylarch is quite clear, with the phylarchs subordinate in administrative, training, and operational matters. While the precise level of control would have varied according to the personalities of the officers involved, there seems to have been a clear cut chain of command which had the potential to allow a high degree of operational flexibility.

In addition to this, the existence of mounted aides or *hyperetai* apparently attached to the hipparchs (and possibly phylarchs)[217] gave them the capability of disseminating orders much more rapidly than an infantry commander. Although there is some uncertainty as to their exact status and function, a pretty clear idea of their position in the cavalry can be gleaned from a study of the Kerameikos lead tablets and of the way the word *hyperetes* is used by Greek authors. Both of these sources confirm that by the third century the term *hyperetes* had acquired the meaning of 'aide' or 'attendant'. Arrian lists a *hyperetes*, along with other

[215] Dem. 4. 26–7.
[216] Dem. 21. 160–6.
[217] Even without *hyperetai*, a phylarch could use his *prodromoi* or even ordinary *phyle*-members as dispatch riders.

functionaries such as the *stratokerux* (herald) and the *salpingtes* (trumpeter), as part of the normal complement of tactical organizations. Similarly, second century ephebic inscriptions often honour a *hyperetes* (or *hyperetai*) alongside the teachers and *grammateus* (secretary or registrar).[218] In addition, if the Kerameikos tablets 235 and 236 belong to the same year, then the *Higeronos hyperetou* on tablet 236 is not one 'Higeron, attendant' but the 'attendant of Higeron', the man referred to on tablet 235. In this case, Kroll's argument that the *hyperetes* was a special attendant allowed to cavalry officers, and whose horse was also underwritten in case of loss,[219] seems very plausible.

The status of the *hyperetai* in the fifth and fourth centuries seems less certain. None of the small number of fourth-century lead tablets are inscribed with the word *hyperetes*, but the term is used fairly frequently in the literature of the time. However, until it began to acquire the more specialized meaning it held in military contexts in the third century and later, *hyperetes* apparently had a variety of meanings, including that of 'servant'. This is reflected by modern translators of Xenophon, who variously render the word as 'aide', 'quartermaster', 'servant', 'attendant', 'adjutant', 'supporter', 'bodyguard', or (in the plural) even 'henchmen'.[220] In almost all of these cases, though, the original word could be translated by either 'aide' or 'attendant'. These are better in my opinion as they reflect the use of the same Greek word on all these occasions, yet place the emphasis on the person or position rather than on the particular function of the *hyperetai* at specific times.

In a non-military context, the word is usually best rendered as 'servant' and this is also sometimes true for military contexts. Thucydides calls the servants of hoplites *hyperetai* and from other evidence we know that these were normally slaves.[221] Similarly, Xenophon's reference to the *hyperetai* of cavalry strongly suggests that these were the servants of the individual *hippeis*.

---

[218] Arr. *Takt.* 10. 4; 14. 4. Ephebic inscriptions: C. Pélékidis, *Histoire de l'éphébie attique* (Paris, 1962), 207.

[219] Kroll, 125–7.

[220] Xen. *Kyrop.* 2. 1. 21, 31, 4. 4; 4. 6. 1; 5. 3. 52, 4. 18; 6. 2. 13, 3. 14, 29; 7. 1. 38, 5. 18; 8. 5. 13; *Hipparch.* 4. 4; *Anab.* 1. 9. 18, 27; 2. 1. 9; *Mem.* 2. 10. 3; 4. 3. 14; *Hell.* 2. 3. 54–5, 4. 8; 3. 1. 27. For the variety of translations see the relevant Loeb and Penguin editions; cf. LSJ s.v. ὑπηρέτης.

[221] Thucy. 3. 17. 4; cf. Sargent, *CPh* 22 (1927), 202–5.

However, in another work he calls such servants, whose prime function seems to have been that of groom, *hippokomoi*,[222] and the majority of Xenophon's references to *hyperetai* seem to indicate something more than slave attendants or mere grooms. For example, in several passages he uses the term of horsemen engaged in combat or in exposed positions when there was an enemy threat—both of which would seem to rule out slave-attendants.

The *Kyropaideia* describes Persian *hyperetai* siting an ambush and has one of Cyrus' *hyperetai* offering his own horse when Cyrus' was killed in the thick of battle.[223] Elsewhere in the same work, Xenophon portrays some of the *hyperetai* scouting ahead of each squadron to direct the men where to go and in his technical manuals explained that this would prevent whole *taxeis* from becoming lost.[224] Although some refer to Persia, all of these incidents are clearly rather more than one might expect from a slave-groom—particularly given the danger of desertion involved in placing a slave on horseback and sending him on ahead. The strong inference that the *hyperetai* were free men is further supported by another passage in Xenophon. Here Sokrates is made to contrast slaves with a friend acting as an assistant and who is called a *hyperetes* (which Marchant translates in the Loeb edition as 'subordinate'). He argues that 'it is worth many slaves to have an assistant (*hyperetes*) both well-disposed and loyal and competent to do what is ordered—and not only competent to do what is ordered but able to be useful on his own initiative, to plan ahead, and to advise.'[225]

It seems then that the term is one which originally meant servant or assistant but which, particularly in military contexts, gradually acquired the more specialized meaning of 'aide' or 'attendant'. During the fourth century, as Xenophon shows, both meanings still appear, although in many cases its use in a military situation indicates a free man acting as an assistant—as it does in a civilian context. The wide variety of tasks performed by the *hyperetai* in the sources is explicable by modern analogy. A Liaison Officer in the field (or attached to a Headquarters)

---

[222] Xen. *Hell.* 2. 4. 8; *Hipparch.* 5. 6.

[223] Xen. *Kyrop.* 6. 3. 13–14; 7. 1. 38.

[224] Ibid. 7. 5. 18; *Hipparch.* 4. 4. Cf. the ALH use of 'ground scouts', Gullett, *AIF in Sinai and Palestine*, 396.

[225] Xen. *Mem.* 2. 10. 3.

would, for example, be expected to undertake many of the tasks assigned to *hyperetai* in antiquity, but like them, whatever his function at any given moment, he would continue to be referred to as a Liaison Officer.[226]

In a fourth-century cavalry context, the term *hyperetes* almost always denoted an aide attached to the hipparchs (and possibly the phylarchs) and who was available to perform the wide variety of tasks noted by Xenophon. These included reconnaissance, the passing on of orders and the supervision of their execution, and any other tasks which might be required by the officer concerned. Whether they were part of the cavalry establishment, friends or relatives of the officers they attended, or (but much less likely) public slaves as Jordan suggests,[227] is open to debate. However, whatever their precise status, they were available to assist in the sort of tasks which would have enhanced the operational flexibility of the *hippeis* at both *phyle* and corps levels.

The Athenian cavalry, therefore, probably possessed considerable flexibility. Their equipment and organization, aided in part by good training, permitted a high degree of combat flexibility while their command structure and the existence of the *hyperetai* would have facilitated operational flexibility. This last was, in addition, almost certainly improved by what was probably a high standard of skill, and possibly by good leadership and motivation as well.

SIZE

The final characteristic affecting combat potential is that of size. This could be of crucial importance: even a highly skilled and motivated force, well led, mobile, and with excellent firepower and endurance might, under many conditions, be unable to achieve success if too small. This is clearly indicated in the failure of the heavily outnumbered Macedonian cavalry to stem the Thracian invasion of 429/8—despite its high quality.[228] In theory,

[226] Although he would have additional tasks which did not exist in the conditions of ancient warfare, the administrative and logistic tasks mentioned in Xen. *Kyrop.* 2. 1. 21, 31 would today be performed by a specialist staff officer.

[227] B. Jordan, 'The Meaning of the Technical Term Hyperesia in Naval Contexts of the Fifth and Fourth Centuries BC', *CSCA* 2 (1969), 190–3.

[228] Thucy. 2. 100; for another incident see Diod. Sic. 19. 13. 3.

though, the Athenian *hippeis* with a strength of 1,000 was quite a
sizeable unit. By comparison, the entire cavalry force of the
Boiotian League was only 100 men larger and the Spartans did
not even possess any cavalry until *c.*425/4 when a contingent of
400 was raised.[229]

The establishment figure of 1,000 is well attested for the
cavalry of the fifth and fourth centuries; although some sources
do mention 1,200 *hippeis*, this total undoubtedly includes the 200
hippotoxotai.[230] However, it is also clear that the number of
serving cavalrymen did fluctuate from time to time. The evidence
suggests that while it was at full strength, or nearly so, for
approximately the first thirty years after the reform which established it at 1,000, by 410/9 the effective strength of the corps had
dropped to approximately 650. It also seems very likely that the
corps was understrength in the first half of the fourth century,
although it is not possible to estimate the precise figure.[231]

The situation at the commencement of hostilities in 431 is
quite clear, as Thucydides states that there were 1,200 cavalrymen, including mounted archers.[232] There is no reason to doubt
these figures: if the Athenians had, as Thucydides suggests, been
aware of the impending conflict for some time and had taken
precautions to strengthen their military position they would
hardly have allowed any of their defence assets to fall below
strength.[233] In addition, if these numbers were, as Thucydides
claims, cited in one of Perikles' speeches, it is unlikely that the
statesman would have risked a gross exaggeration when those
who knew the true total on the current cavalry rolls could have
corrected him publicly.

The *hippeis* then were almost certainly operating at about their
full establishment of 1,000 men in 431. However, the situation
later in the war is much less certain. Apart from Thucydides'
report of the initial total, there are no statements of the full

[229] *Hell. Oxy.* 11. 3–4; Thucy. 4. 55. 1–2.
[230] Thucy. 2. 13. 8; Ar. *Kn.* 225; Xen. *Hipparch.* 9. 3; Dem. 14. 13; Philo-
choros in Hesychios s.v. ἱππῆς (*FGH* 328 F39). Those which have 1,200 include
Ath. Pol. 24. 3; Andok. 3. 7; Aischines, 2. 174. Thucy. 2. 13. 8 shows that
'*hippeis*' could be used of both cavalry and mounted archers, and it seems
highly likely that the *Ath. Pol.*, Andokides, and Aischines simply included the
hippotoxotai in their total.
[231] See Spence, *ZPE* 67 (1987), 167–75.
[232] Thucy. 2. 13. 8.
[233] Cf. Thucy. 1. 44. 2.

cavalry strength and it is unsafe to assume that the cavalry
remained at or near establishment strength throughout the conflict. Several things in fact suggest that numbers declined as the
hostilities continued. It seems likely that combat losses and plague
casualties (both short- and long-term) would have taken their toll
on the cavalry class, and this is confirmed by Aristotle.[234] Battle
casualties would occur not only in overseas expeditions but also
in the continuous use of cavalry to provide some measure of
defence for Attica. This began with the very first engagement of
431, a cavalry clash at Rheitoi, and continued throughout the
war.[235] The plague too, killed some 300 *hippeis* and no doubt
rendered others permanently unfit for active service. In addition,
the loss of country estates to Peloponnesian ravaging, particularly
severe after the occupation of Dekeleia, would have affected the
financial base of the cavalry class and the ability of at least some
of its members to own and maintain a horse.[236]

That cavalry numbers declined during this period is also supported by an examination of the literary references to cavalry
operations during the war and of the evidence for total numbers
in the fourth century. The largest body of cavalry attested in
action during the war years is a 600-strong contingent at Megara
in 424.[237] While there are some references to *hoi hippeis* ('the
cavalry') in ancient descriptions of engagements it would be
interpreting this phrase far too literally to assume that it denoted
the full establishment of 1,000 men. Instead, this usage seems to
mean either that cavalry (as opposed to infantry) was used, or
that the entire available force was mobilized.[238] No statement of
the number of cavalry actually involved is made on any of these

[234] Arist. *Pol.* 1303ᵃ8–10 (5. 3) stresses the particularly high losses amongst the
upper classes. For hoplite losses, see R. P. Duncan-Jones, 'Metic Numbers in
Periclean Athens', *Chiron*, 10 (1980), 103–8.
[235] Thucy. 2. 19. 2; Table 3.
[236] Plague: Thucy. 3. 87. 1–3. For the long-term ill-effects see Thucy. 2. 49. 6–
7 and the comments on this by B. Baldwin, 'Medical Grounds for Exemptions
from Military Service at Athens', *CPh* 62 (1967), 42–3. Damage to Attica: Thucy.
7. 27–8; *Hell. Oxy.* 12. 3–5.
[237] Thucy. 4. 68. 5. Diod. Sic. 13. 72. 7 does state that the Athenian cavalry
mobilized against Agis in 407 (? see Bugh, *Horsemen*, 84) numbered about the
same as the enemy, who possessed 1,200 (13. 72. 4) but this is highly suspect at
this date. Apart from its inherent unlikeliness (see n. 244 below), his description
of the action may be based on the clash in 411 recorded in Thucy. 8. 71. 2.
[238] For the former see Thucy. 7. 27. 5; for the latter see Thucy. 8. 71. 2; Xen.
Hell. 2. 4. 2, 8, 10.

occasions and on some at least it seems inconceivable that 1,000 were meant.

Thucydides, for example, records that from 413 'the cavalry' rode out every day towards Dekeleia to patrol the countryside.[239] It seems highly unlikely that 1,000 troopers rode out every day of the year, particularly as cavalry contingents were sometimes absent on active service outside Attica. The most logical explanation is that this activity was a purely cavalry task which varying numbers of *hippeis* undertook on a daily basis. The phrase therefore implies nothing about the actual number of horsemen employed and the figure of 600 at Megara remains the highest attested for this period. The fourth century evidence too suggests that the cavalry strength had declined either during or after the war. Xenophon advocated recruiting 200 foreign troopers to raise the total cavalry force to 1,000,[240] which suggests that in about 365 the cavalry was at least 200 men understrength, and is moreover concrete evidence of fluctuating numbers in the *hippeis*, even in peacetime.

The likelihood of a reduction in strength is therefore high, but the evidence of cavalry contingents can show only that a decline took place, not how large it was. This is because the size of cavalry forces mobilized during wartime probably represented only a part of the total available—except for the most major expeditions it is unlikely that all the establishment was mobilized at once. All the evidence can indicate then, is the numbers of cavalry involved in particular campaigns, and that the cavalry size could, and did, fall below 1,000.

It is only for the year 410/409 that more precise figures can be recovered; inscriptional evidence suggests that by then just over 650 *hippeis* was about the most which could be mobilized under normal circumstances.[241] However, this has been challenged by Bugh who argues (quoting Pritchett) that the inscription concerned (*IG* I³ 375 = *IG* I² 304A) 'does not detail "the normal expenditures for maintenance of the military establishment".'[242] However, this inaccurately represents Pritchett's argument, which

---

[239] Thucy. 7. 27. 5.

[240] Xen. *Hipparch.* 9. 3.

[241] Spence, *ZPE* 67 (1987), 167–75; however, this total may well not include the *hippotoxotai*.

[242] Bugh, *Horsemen*, 60–1 n. 86.

specifically excludes the *sitos* payments from the statement quoted. The original reads in full: 'All the loans in the various accounts were made for expeditionary campaigns with the sole exception of fodder for the cavalry in 410/09 BC (*IG* I² 304A). The latter is the only item which may be regarded as part of the regular military budget, and it proves to be a very large expenditure; but it does not recur. Otherwise the records of loans contain no clue to the normal expenditures for the maintenance of the military establishment.'[243] Pritchett is surely correct here, and *IG* I³ 375 can legitimately be used to determine the level of *sitos* for the cavalry.[244]

This evidence for fluctuating numbers, and the likelihood that not all the cavalrymen on the rolls were deployed except on major expeditions, suggest that the cavalry rarely operated at its full strength. If one takes the Peloponnesian War, for example, there is a considerable difference between the largest number of cavalry actually attested in the field, and the theoretical establishment strength of 1,000. This would affect combat potential in several ways. As will be discussed, one of the factors which aided the cavalry in the creation of shock was their intimidating appearance; the fewer the horsemen the less their effect on enemy morale. Similarly, any reduction in numbers would bring about a consequent reduction in firepower. In the pursuit phase, for example, the absence of 350 or more horsemen would significantly reduce the number of casualties the corps could inflict on a fleeing enemy.

It therefore seems that, while in comparison with most other Greek states south of Thessaly the *hippeis* comprised a sizeable force, the disparity between their effective numbers and their establishment figure was such as to reduce their combat potential. The prime reason for this disparity was economic: it was very

[243] W. K. Pritchett, 'Loans of Athena in 407 BC', *AncSoc* 8 (1977), 37.
[244] Bugh's other argument against the inscriptional evidence (*Horsemen*, 85 n. 17) is also untenable. The Aristotle, Thucy., and *Hell. Oxy.* passages cited above confirm the conclusion from *IG* I³ 375 that a fairly major drop in cavalry numbers (just over a third in fact) occurred during the war (cf. Spence, *ZPE* 67 (1987), 174, table 4, but note that the last figure in this table should be 553/4; Bugh himself accepts elsewhere in *Horsemen* (61 n. 86) that the numbers must have fallen to some extent). In addition to this, Alkibiades had 150 *hippeis* with him on the Andrian expedition in 407 (Xen. *Hell.* 1. 4. 21; Plut. *Alk.* 35. 1; Diod. Sic. 13. 69. 4). Given this, the inference from Diod. Sic. 13. 72. 3–9 that the Athenians deployed nearly 1,200 cavalry in that year is clearly incorrect; the difference between the two forces was in fact about 500 men.

expensive to own a horse,[245] the essential prerequisite for membership of the *hippeis*, and this alone would restrict the numbers
available to Athens—particularly in times of economic decline. In
addition to this, the effective strength would undoubtedly be
reduced on specific occasions by the absence of men who were
sick, malingering, or otherwise unable or unwilling to go on
campaign. From time to time, too, attitudes towards the cavalry
(in particular the hostility towards them after the oligarchic revolution), or a general reluctance on the part of the wealthy to
undertake public service (an attitude which seems to emerge in
the fourth century), might have adversely affected recruiting,
although there is no specific evidence to support this suspicion.

COMBAT POTENTIAL

All of the factors discussed above played a major part in determining the combat potential or hitting power of ancient Greek cavalry
in general, and the Athenian *hippeis* in particular. Clearly, some
were more important than others in specific engagements or
campaigns but all are closely interlinked. For example, the amount
of physical damage which could be inflicted on enemy troops
basically derived from the cavalry's firepower and its close-
quarter combat capabilities, which in turn stemmed from its
weaponry. However, the damage could be reduced or even nulli-
fied if the soldiers lacked essential riding or weapon-handling
skills, were poorly led, reluctant to place themselves in danger, or
were greatly outnumbered. Training, leadership, motivation, and
the size of the force, were therefore also crucial. Similarly, its
firepower and close-combat potential would be wasted if the
cavalry was unable to move to the best position to employ its
weapons effectively and this was largely determined by its level of
mobility and protection. Finally, battles are not static affairs and
a force which had sufficient mobility and protection to get to the
enemy and was able to begin the fight effectively because of its
training, weaponry, leadership, motivation, and size, might ultimately fail because it was incapable of adjusting to changing
circumstances during the engagement. Flexibility too was vital.

[245] See App. 4.

These eight major influences on combat potential have been examined separately, but as they are interdependent it remains to show what sort of hitting power they produced. In short, what was the effect a cavalry attack would (or could) have had upon other troops and, as they dominated the battlefield for most of the period in question, upon hoplites in particular?

The short answer is that the hitting power of Greek cavalry was quite considerable. However, its effectiveness derived not from the physical shock action which many believe is the main attribute of cavalry, but from missile-fire and from hand-to-hand combat in the mêlée or the pursuit. This is an important point because for most of the classical period warfare was dominated by heavy infantry and the inability of cavalry to charge into unbroken hoplite formations has persuaded many modern scholars that it was essentially useless in battle.[246] This emphasis on the use of cavalry as a physical shock weapon has obscured the simple fact that cavalry could be quite effective by means other than charging home into a hoplite phalanx. Because of the belief that its inability to engage in physical shock tactics severely limited the hitting power of Greek cavalry, it is important to review the whole question of shock action. It must be determined what the *hippeis* could not do in battle before examining what they could achieve.

It is generally agreed, and quite correctly in my opinion, that Greek cavalry could not normally charge at speed into intact hoplite formations—although several different explanations are offered for this. Modern scholars generally blame deficiencies in equestrian equipment while the ancient writer Arrian believed that it was a result of the tetragonal cavalry formation used by most Greek states south of Thessaly.

Some historians claim that without stirrups it is not possible for horsemen using a rigidly held lance or other weapon to ride into a body of foot at any speed.[247] Their argument is that if a rider attempted to do so, he would almost certainly be pushed over the rear of his horse by the impact. However, Chenevix-Trench, an ex-cavalry officer, argued that using a weapon in this

---

[246] For example, *HMND* 4–5, cf. 53–4; *GMAW* 14; *HCT* i. 15; G. Cawkwell, *Philip of Macedon* (London, 1978), 150–1; cf. *OPW* 372 and Kromayer and Veith, *Heerwesen und Kriegführung*, 93.

[247] *GMAW* 50; cf. *AGH* 129.

way is quite possible without stirrups, as long as the rider has a saddle with a rigid tree and a high cantle.[248] Whichever of these views is correct, though, is immaterial. The ancient Greeks possessed neither stirrups nor saddles with a high cantle and therefore could not use a couched lance in the manner of a medieval knight. Yet, Arrian provides the following discussion of the relative merits of tetragonal and wedge-shaped cavalry formations or *taxeis*:

We hear that the Scythians in particular employed wedge-shaped formations and that the Thracians learned this from the Scythians. Philip of Macedon also trained the Macedonians to use this formation. This formation also seems useful because the leaders are drawn up around the perimeter and the tapering front allows it to cut easily right through the enemy formation and gives the facility to make rapid turns and counter-turns. For four-sided formations are hard to wheel about, but the pointed formation (even if it is deployed in depth while advancing) nevertheless, through wheeling about within a small space around the point, allows the whole formation to manœuvre [*or* 'extend into line'] readily. The Persians in particular employ tetragonal formations as do the natives in Sicily and most of the Greeks, including the most skilled cavalrymen.[249]

As can be seen from this passage, Arrian believed that had Greek cavalry used a wedge-shaped formation they too would have been able to cut through the enemy ranks, and with relative ease at that.[250] This is particularly interesting as Arrian, who had himself served as a cavalry officer, wrote in the pre-stirrup era and must have been aware of what was possible for stirrupless horsemen.[251] Although his testimony seems to contradict the modern theories on this subject, the conflict is more apparent than real and results from a misunderstanding by later writers of how cavalry actually broke an opposing infantry formation.

The popular concept of cavalry as a shock arm seems to have developed in the post-classical period from an erroneous percep-

---

[248] Chenevix-Trench, 58.

[249] Arr. *Takt.* 16. 6–9; I would like to acknowledge the contributions of Colonel A. Treloar and Dr N. V. Sekunda to my translation of this passage.

[250] Epameinondas successfully used a wedge-shaped formation of mixed cavalry and *hamippoi* against the opposing cavalry at Mantineia in 362, Xen. *Hell.* 7. 5. 24.

[251] Markle, 'Macedonian Sarissa', 339; P. A. Rahe, 'The Annihilation of the Sacred Band at Chaeronea', *AJA* 85 (1981), 86 n. 12.

tion of cavalry (and in particular the plate-armoured cavalry of the Middle Ages) as an irresistible force which charged across the battlefield and smashed into the enemy lines using its momentum and mass to ride down the helpless and hapless infantry. It is this sort of view which has led to the assumption underlying many modern assessments of the Greek mounted arm—that the criterion for cavalry effectiveness is its ability to charge into unbroken infantry formations. When it was found wanting in this respect, Greek cavalry was regarded as being only of marginal battlefield use. However, this view grossly exaggerates the ability of any cavalry to charge home into a steady body of infantry.

John Keegan has discussed the mechanics of shock tactics used against infantry by medieval and post-medieval cavalry. He points out that horses do not naturally ride into obstacles, particularly not ones which shout and move, nor do men normally stand still to be ridden down. The most likely consequence is that, while there will inevitably be some individual collisions, on most occasions either the infantry would break before impact or the horses would refuse to charge home.[252] That the latter could and did occur is confirmed by Ensign Gronow's description of a French attack at Waterloo in which 'the horses of the first rank of cuirassiers, in spite of all the efforts of their riders, came to a standstill, shaking and covered with foam, at about twenty yards' distance . . . and generally resisted all attempts to force them to charge the line of serried steel'.[253] Because the success of a charge at a formed body of foot therefore depends on the formation collapsing on or before the point of impact, Keegan maintains that 'the "shock" which cavalry seek to inflict is really moral, not physical in character'.[254]

Keegan's contention is borne out by the history of cavalry in the post-classical era—including the medieval period. Plate-armoured knights are often regarded as the heavy cavalrymen par excellence, but they were often employed only against the opposing cavalry and otherwise generally acquired their reputation

[252] Keegan, *Face of Battle*, 95–7, 154–60. Rahe, *AJA* 85 (1981) reproduces most of his arguments in the context of ancient warfare but is incorrect to argue (at 86) that cavalry could not penetrate an unbroken phalanx using Arrian's tactics quoted above.

[253] Quoted by Keegan, *Face of Battle*, 159; they were of course facing muskets and not spears.

[254] Ibid. 96.

against mass levies of ill-equipped and ill-disciplined footsoldiers. In fact, the view of the medieval horseman as an unstoppable force is contradicted by quite a few engagements where uniformly equipped and well-disciplined infantry repelled even the most determined mounted charge. Courtrai (1302), Bannockburn (1314), and the Swiss victories of the fourteenth and fifteenth centuries spring to mind here, but even the infantry defeats of Hastings (1066), Conway (1295), and Falkirk (1298) illustrate that, without support from archers, heavy cavalry alone could not guarantee success against good infantry.[255] If the hitting power of cavalry really was dependent upon physical shock, then how could the infantry in these cases have withstood the impact of heavily armoured men and horses charging en masse? These battles therefore confirm Keegan's suggestion that cavalry achieved its success not by charging home into infantry formations and shattering them with sheer momentum, but rather caused the formation to break on or before the point of impact was reached. Even the plate-clad horsemen of the high Middle Ages were often stopped by steady spearmen who refused to break when charged.

However, the image of cavalry riding down infantry is so potent that even as late as 1902, long after the introduction and subsequent advances in firearms had really rendered mass cavalry charges against infantry impracticable, Colonel G. F. R. Henderson could claim that 'shock tactics, the charge, and the hand-to-hand encounter are still the one ideal of cavalry action; and the power of manœuvring in great masses, maintaining an absolute uniformity of pace and formation, and moving at the highest speed with accurately dressed ranks, is the criterion of excellence.'[256] The chapter on the tactical employment of cavalry in his book *The Science of War* is largely devoted to persuading his contemporaries away from this concentration on shock tactics. He pointed out that in the nineteenth century 'shock-tactics filled the

---

[255] C. W. C. Oman, *The Art of War in the Middle Ages*, rev. J. H. Beeler (New York, 1968), 64–5 (Courtrai), 119–21 (Conway and Falkirk), 122–4 (Bannockburn) and 73–115 (the Swiss). On the outcome and lessons of Courtrai, see also G. Bruce (ed.), *Harbottle's Dictionary of Battles*, 3rd edn. (New York, 1981), 72. For Hastings, see Oman, *The Art of War*, 26–8 and J. F. C. Fuller, *The Decisive Battles of the Western World*, ed. J. Terraine, i (London, 1970), 270–4.

[256] G. F. R. Henderson, *The Science of War*, ed. N. Malcolm (London, 1912), 51; cf. G. T. Denison, *A History of Cavalry*, 2nd edn. (London, 1913), pp. ix–xv.

entire bill, and the cavalry of Europe, admirably trained to manœuvre and to attack, whether by the squadron of 150 sabres or the
division of 3,000 or 4,000, was practically unfitted for any other
duty.' He then analyses the record of cavalry in the years 1856–
78, a period which includes the Crimean and Franco-Prussian
Wars and the Russo-Turkish conflict of 1877–8, and which in his
eyes represents 'the climax of incompetency' because of the
concentration on shock tactics. He concludes that during these
twenty-two years shock action, or attempted shock action, by
cavalry at regimental level and above produced very limited
results. These comprised 'one great tactical success gained at
Custozza; a retreating army saved from annihilation at König-
grätz; and five minor successes which may or may not have
influenced the ultimate issue.'[257]

Shock tactics rely on moral and not physical shock: infantry in
close order break because of fear and panic, not because their
formation is physically smashed by cavalry. Because of its mobility, and the intimidating appearance of horse and rider (discussed
below), ancient cavalry operating against infantry out of, or in an
unsteady, formation, or against the flank or rear of a formation,
was quite capable of creating moral shock by rapid and intimidating movement and/or surprise. However, what riders without
stirrups could not do with as much chance of success as those
with stirrups, was to ride hard at the front of an enemy formation
to try and cause it to break. If it did not collapse, then the ancient
cavalryman would be more likely to fall off or be thrown immediately in front of the enemy's spears than his stirrup-equipped
successors; this was not only very embarrassing but also highly
dangerous.

However, there were methods of achieving success against
bodies of foot other than by charging at their ranks. The first of
these involved riding up to (but not crashing into) their line and
then creating a gap by engaging and killing some of the men in
the front rank with spear thrusts. These thrusts would be made
with the power of the arm rather than by a combination of a
couched or rigidly held lance and the momentum of a charging
horse. Once a gap was created, the cavalry could then penetrate
the formation and cause it to collapse. It is this tactic which
Arrian is apparently describing in the passage quoted earlier: he

[257] Henderson, *Science of War*, 52–4.

envisages the point of the wedge pushing deep into the enemy
thereby causing an inevitable widening of the gap as the base of
the wedge followed it. The best description of how this might
occur (although referring to *sarissa*-armed Macedonian cavalry) is
that given by M. M. Markle III:

If a squadron of 120 horse in wedge formation charged a hoplite phalanx
eight ranks in depth, the rider at the point of the wedge would slay with
his lance the hoplite facing him, drop his lance, and advance with his
sword against the soldier behind the one whom he had slain. The two
riders stationed to his rear about six feet apart in the second rank of the
wedge would advance with their lances against the foot positioned on
each side of the first one killed, slay them, drop their lances, and advance
with their swords. If, in the meantime, the first lancer had been overpow-
ered and slain by his opponent in the second rank of hoplites, another
lancer in the third rank of the wedge would ride forward into his position
and slay the soldier in the second rank who had killed the first lancer. In
a wedge of 120 lancers, there would be a total of seven lancers, one in
every other rank, in file behind the first lancer. Hence, even on the
unlikely assumption that no rider, after leaving his sarissa in the body of
his first adversary, succeeded with his sword in killing a second opponent,
such a wedge with its sarissae alone could break apart a phalanx of eight
ranks in depth. Moreover, the superior weight and the velocity of the
horses and riders would drive the front rank of foot back against the rear
ranks throwing them into confusion and rendering their weapons useless.[258]

I consider this inaccurate in one minor detail only: the role of
velocity in penetrating the enemy line. For the reasons already
given, it seems more likely that at this stage of the action the
cavalry would be moving fairly slowly and would enter the infantry formation not by hurtling into it but more by pushing forward
like mounted police controlling a crowd. Nevertheless, this would
still force the leading infantry back on to their companions and,
as Markle suggests, create confusion and make resistance more
difficult.

   This too is how a cavalry unit of the post-classical period could
break an infantry line which had failed to collapse on their
approach—if the moral shock failed then the cavalry had to
engage in hand-to-hand combat with the enemy while at a virtual

[258] Markle, 'Macedonian Sarissa', 339.

standstill until they either created a gap or were themselves beaten off. However, penetration against steady troops could only occur by dint of some very hard, and potentially very bloody, fighting by the cavalrymen in the wedge. This type of mêlée combat was presumably much more difficult without stirrups than with them: a stirrupless rider in such a situation would be very prone to being unseated as long as the infantry had sufficient space to use their weapons. Because of this, it seems likely that, as Markle argues, such tactics could only work if the cavalry had numerical superiority at a selected point and longer weapons than their opponents. These advantages were conferred by the wedge formation and the *sarissa*. Therefore, as long as Greek cavalry used a square or rectangular formation and weapons the same length as, or shorter than, the hoplite spear, this method was unlikely to succeed in breaching a determined hoplite phalanx.

Although the Thessalians used a rhomboid or diamond formation and the Macedonians the wedge, most Greek cavalry, including the Athenian arm, used the rectangular formation.[259] If the cavalry of these states could not readily create moral shock against the front of an enemy phalanx, and was unlikely to be successful in creating a gap by the use of thrusting weapons, what sort of combat potential did it possess in the context of hoplite warfare? In fact, cavalry of the Athenian type probably had as much, or nearly as much, potential to destroy formed bodies of hoplites as stirrupped cavalry or *sarissa*-armed cavalry in a wedge formation—it just used different methods to do so.

The flexibility, weaponry, and mobility of the Athenian cavalry (particularly with *hippotoxotai* or *hamippoi* attached) were in theory sufficient to allow it to contain a large infantry army, or a smaller force supported by horse or light troops, and gave it the power to destroy a small or disorganized body of foot. The tactics involved in this were relatively simple and effectively took advantage of the weaknesses of infantry. In the case of hoplites this was their lack of tactical mobility, while for *psiloi* it was their lack of protection. To take the hoplites first; their equipment and formation were primarily suited to fighting other hoplites and one of their main characteristics was the close ordering of the ranks for

---

[259] The wedge does seem to have crept into the tactics of other states in the 4th cent., cf. Epameinondas at Mantineia in 362, Xen. *Hell.* 7. 5. 24 (used against other cavalry).

mutual protection.[260] The co-operative nature of the hoplite
phalanx is well illustrated by the role of the shield or *aspis*. The
Spartan view of 'come back with your shield or on it' was not
unique and most Greek states considered it a disgrace to abandon
one's shield in battle—at Athens it was an indictable offence.[261]
This attitude is explained by Demaratos' statement that it was
disgraceful to lose one's shield, but not one's helmet or breastplate, because the shield was for the safety of the whole line while
the other items benefited only the individual.[262] The fundamental
importance of the *aspis* is further emphasized by the fact that as
the other items in the original hoplite panoply were discarded or
modified it remained unchanged.[263]

The panoply was designed to protect the hoplite while he was
in formation and, because of the deficiencies in cavalry harness,
the nature of the horse, and the use of short spears and tetragonal
formation previously discussed, it was also generally effective
against a frontal cavalry charge. However, because of the rigid
nature of their formation, hoplites were very vulnerable to an
assault on their flanks, particularly the right (or unshielded) one,
or on their rear. In addition, their panoply was probably less
useful in single combat as the large shield with its off-centre grip
would have been rather unwieldy and its weight (along with that
of the other accoutrements) would have handicapped a fleeing or
pursuing hoplite.[264] This explains why the *aspis* was the first
thing discarded in a rout, and not always with the required
feeling of shame—as the following lines from the seventh-century
poet Archilochos show:

Some Saian rejoices in the shield, an unblemished item, which I unwill-

---

[260] Although this has been challenged (Cawkwell, *Philip of Macedon*, 150–3),
A. J. Holladay, 'Hoplites and Heresies', *JHS* 102 (1982), 94–7 adequately disposes
of these arguments. The close-ordering of the ranks was emphasised as late as the
1st cent. AD, Onasander, 27.

[261] A. R. W. Harrison, *The Law of Athens: Procedure* (Oxford, 1971), 32. See
also Aristophanes' jibes at Kleonymos and others: *Peace*, 446, 670–8, 1185–6,
1291–304; *Birds*, 1473–81; *Clouds*, 353–4; *Wasps*, 15–23, 592, 822–3. It was
possibly a source of humour in Attic comedy as late as 300: cf. J. M. Edmonds, 'A
Glimpse of Camp Life in 300 BC', *Mnemosyne*, 2³ (1935), 53.

[262] Plut. *Mor.* 220a.

[263] *MT* 13–42; *AGH* 141–2.

[264] H. L. Lorimer, 'The Hoplite Phalanx with Special Reference to the Poems
of Archilochus and Tyrtaeus', *ABSA* 42 (1947), 76–7; Holladay, *JHS* 102 (1982),
94–5.

ingly abandoned beside a bush—but I saved myself. What do I care for that shield? Sod it. I'll buy another one just as good.[265]

An individual hoplite was therefore vulnerable and needed to stay in formation to derive the maximum protection from his equipment.

This vulnerability was best exploited by attacking the hoplite outside the phalanx—a practice apparently illustrated in Plates 2 and 11–13. This could be done when the phalanx had collapsed or was disrupted either by hostile action or an obstacle. By the fourth century, the efficacy of cavalry used against an enemy crossing an obstacle such as a river was widely recognized in both theory and practice. Aristotle, for example, records it as a well-known fact, and in the middle of the same century the Athenian *hippeis* assisted the Phleiasian horse in just such an action. In 279 they were sent to prevent the Gauls crossing the Spercheios River prior to the battle of Delphi; the Corinthian general Timoleon also used this tactic in 339, at Krimisos in Sicily.[266]

Greek theory stressed two advantages of attacking in this situation. The first was that the hipparch could choose the number of enemy he wished to engage by waiting until the desired portion had crossed over to, or remained on, the bank selected for the action.[267] This was particularly appropriate to independent operations against a superior enemy. The second stressed the disorder caused by such a crossing and the advantage which could be taken of this.[268] In a pitched battle it was this disorder which was probably more important.[269] Alternatively, effective assaults could be launched against hoplites scattered to forage or who had not yet formed their phalanx. It was in these circumstances that cavalry without stirrups could make just as much use of 'moral' shock to create panic and cause a rout as cavalry with stirrups. As Colonel G. F. R. Henderson pointed out, it was the dream of

---

[265] Archilochos 5, M. L. West, *Iambi et Elegi Graeci* (Oxford, 1971); = 6, D. A. Campbell (ed.), *Greek Lyric Poetry* (Bristol, 1982).

[266] Arist. *Pol.* 1303^{b}12–14 (5. 3); Xen. *Hell.* 7. 2. 10; Pausanias, 10. 20. 5–6; Plut. *Timol.* 27. 3–5.

[267] Xen. *Hipparch.* 7. 11; cf. Plut. *Timol.* 27. 3–4.

[268] Cf. Eumenes' successful attack in Diod. Sic. 19. 18. 4–7.

[269] Arr. *Anab.* 1. 13. 4–5. Pyrrhos intended to use his cavalry in this way at the River Siris but changed his mind when the Romans crossed in good order and protected by their own cavalry, Plut. *Pyrr.* 16. 6–7. There is one example of Persian cavalry screening a river crossing (Arr. *Anab.* 2. 8. 5) and one of Carthaginians using chariots to do so (Plut. *Timol.* 27. 3–5), but I can find no Greek examples of this.

cavalry tacticians to catch the enemy out of position, the result in their view being that 'the cavalry, if led with sufficient boldness, and thundering forward in a close succession of steel-tipped lines, will have the supreme satisfaction of riding down a mob of panic-stricken fugitives.'[270]

The creation of this moral shock was no doubt aided by the cavalry's appearance. The sheer bulk of a mounted trooper is impressive to an onlooker or adversary, particularly when the horse is moving at speed. This feature is still exploited today in the deployment of mounted police for crowd-control purposes, and is perhaps best expressed in Sergeant Morris's description of being charged by French cuirassiers at Waterloo:

a considerable number of the French cuirassiers made their appearance, on the rising ground just in our front, took the artillery we had placed there and came at a gallop down upon us. Their appearance, as an enemy, was certainly enough to inspire a feeling of dread—none of them under six feet; defended by steel helmets and breastplates, made pigeon-breasted to throw off the balls. The appearance was of such a formidable nature, that I thought we could not have the slightest chance with them.[271]

Greek riders and horses were smaller, but such impressiveness was recognized in both ancient literature and art. The literary references include Demetrios, who argued that grand subjects like equestrian and naval battles are the most impressive scenes and the most fitting for artists to portray.[272]

This is borne out by late fifth- and fourth-century Attic sculpture which often chose to represent cavalry trampling infantry underfoot. A well-known example of this is Dexileos' funeral monument (Plate 11) which is representative of several reliefs of similar type (see Plates 2, 13).[273] The late fifth-century dedication by Pythodoros (Plate 12), which also shows horsemen riding down infantry, was a larger-scale battle scene of the type which Demetrios recommended (and which Euphranor almost certainly

[270] Henderson, *Science of War*, 64–5. He did not believe this possible (in 1902) because of the use of firearms and because of the level of discipline of most troops. The first of these, and in many cases the second too, did not apply to ancient warfare.

[271] Quoted in Keegan, *Face of Battle*, 156.

[272] Demetrios, *On Style*, 2. 76.

[273] Relief 12; cf. 14, 23, 25–7, 33; 29–30 have similar representations as part of larger scenes.

adopted in his painting, executed in the Stoa of Zeus *c*.360, of the battle of Mantineia).[274]

This general view of the cavalry as impressive, or even awe-inspiring, was probably heightened by the reputation for savagery which the horse possessed in classical Greece. Herodotos, for example, relates the story of a Persian warhorse trained to kill with its hooves, an ability also mentioned by Xenophon.[275] Greek literature also contains several dramatic tales of flesh-eating horses such as those owned by Diomedes and by Glaukos of Potniai.[276] Stories like these may even have had some basis in truth, arising perhaps from the propensity of the Greek horse for biting.[277] This must have been a fairly common habit as Xenophon advocates the use of muzzles to protect grooms and other handlers from injury. On occasion such bites could even prove fatal: Neokles, one of Themistokles' sons, died in infancy from the bite of a horse.[278]

The practice of biting, the associated reputation for savagery, and the impressive bulk and speed of the mounted warrior undoubtedly could create a daunting effect upon opponents on the battlefield. This is confirmed by several recorded instances of Thracian peltast formations (probably composed of peltasts with the longer spears) breaking before a cavalry charge even reached them.[279] However, this was probably much less likely to occur with trained and/or experienced hoplites. While such troops certainly possessed a healthy respect for the dangers posed by cavalry, they would be unlikely to break and run unless nervous,

[274] On the painting, see below 224–5 and cf. Aischines, 3. 164.

[275] Hdtos 5. 111; Xen. *Kyrop.* 2. 3. 9. Although he denies (*Anab.* 3. 2. 18) that any soldier was ever killed by a horse in battle, the fact that Xenophon feels it necessary to reassure the troops on this suggests that it was a reasonably common fear. Horses do fight with their hoofs in the wild and this has sometimes been utilised by man, for example, the old Icelandic horse fights, Chenevix-Trench, 294–6.

[276] The capture of Diomedes' horses was Herakles' eighth labour—see R. Graves, *The Greek Myths*, rev. edn., ii (Harmondsworth, 1974), 123 for the ancient references. It was also occasionally referred to in drama, cf. Eur. *Her.* 380–5; *Alkestis* 481–506, and on vases (see no. 6). Aischylos' play *Glaukos of Potniai* is no longer extant.

[277] See vase 10; but Greek horses were not alone in this, cf. Chenevix-Trench, 275 for a Mughal painting of a horse savaging its groom.

[278] Xen. *PH* 5. 3; for vases depicting muzzles, see Introd. n. 17. Neokles: Plut. *Them.* 32. 1.

[279] Arr. *Anab.* 1. 4. 3; cf. 1. 6. 5–6 (only a small force).

panicked, caught while deploying or otherwise disorganized, or taken in the flank or rear. Nevertheless, such occasions did occur and when they did the horse's bulk, the height of the rider, and the impressiveness of mounted soldiers moving at speed, would have created considerable shock value. Even though this would not have been readily employable in a frontal assault, unless of course the cavalry was fairly certain the enemy would not stand his ground,[280] it was certainly an asset when operating against infantry out of formation or against a phalanx's flank or rear.

This must, on occasion, have contributed to the effectiveness of cavalry operations. For example, it is hard to imagine the Athenian troops at Syracuse in 414/13 remaining unaffected by the continued success of the enemy cavalry and its domination of most of the area. Similarly, Xenophon's remarks after Kounaxa[281] exhibit a real concern to reduce the psychological domination which the large numbers of Persian horse were beginning to exert on the Greek mercenaries. Tarn, too, points out that in the changed circumstances of Hellenistic warfare the 'moral domination of cavalry over infantry ... was one of Alexander's legacies'.[282] The intimidating appearance of cavalry was therefore of some potential importance, although by itself it was probably insufficient to cause Greek armies to cut and run. However, in conjunction with the effects of low enemy morale or of unsteady or disorganized enemy troops, it would have added considerably to the effectiveness of cavalry as a combat arm. This would have been particularly so with infantry already shaken or weakened by a clash with the opposing foot.

However, the *hippeis* did not have to wait around for opportunities to catch infantry out of formation—they themselves possessed sufficient hitting power to break a hoplite phalanx either by charging its flanks or rear or by harassing it with missile-fire. Flank or rear attacks allowed the cavalry to capitalize on the rigidity of a hoplite phalanx and to make full use of moral shock. The confusion and fear generated when a phalanx was charged in its rear or flanks would have been considerable, as some hoplites tried to turn their shields to face the new threat and others tried

---

[280] Experienced soldiers could sometimes predict when this was going to happen, cf. Brasidas at Amphipolis, Thucy. 5. 10. 5.

[281] Quoted above 43.

[282] *HMND* 71.

to run. A phalanx would almost certainly collapse and break under these circumstances—as Cyrus' actions at Kounaxa show. In this case, Cyrus launched the cavalry charge which cost him his life because Artaxerxes had started to wheel his troops to take the Greek mercenaries in the rear and Cyrus feared that he would cut them to pieces.[283] Such attacks could sometimes be avoided by siting the flanks on obstacles or by forming a square. An example of the latter occurred during the battle between Philip II of Macedon and the Illyrian ruler Bardylis. The Illyrians formed a square and engaged Philip's infantry, but were still subject to mounted attack on the left flank and rear. They eventually broke and ran.[284] But, whether a square was formed or not, the close-ordered hoplite ranks provided a good target for projectile weapons—particularly given the fewer items of armour worn from the late fifth century onwards.[285] Apart from retiring to high ground (which ended its usefulness as a military force) the only defence a purely hoplite contingent had against this was to use detachments to charge out to keep the enemy out of range. While this tactic was practised (and even preferred on occasion to the use of *psiloi* to help), the charging troops were vulnerable to individual attack, and often too slow to catch their assailants as the cavalrymen were faster.[286]

Because of its superior mobility, cavalry was much more dangerous in this role than *psiloi*—except in rugged country. Cavalry could harass hoplites with relative impunity until either their movement was curtailed or their formation collapsed, at which point they could be mopped up individually. Even large bodies of hoplites could be contained by aggressive cavalry action—particularly when their own supporting arms were ineffectual or non-existent. This is vividly illustrated by Xenophon's description of an action near Corinth in 369. The cavalry sent by Dionysios of Syracuse numbered only fifty men and was part of an allied

[283] Xen. *Anab*. 1. 8. 24; *katakopto*, the verb used to describe the probable effect on the Greeks, conveys the idea of cutting or mincing up into small pieces.

[284] For a discussion of this action see N. G. L. Hammond, 'The Battle between Philip and Bardylis', *Antichthon*, 23 (1989), 1–9.

[285] In modern American military parlance, a phalanx formed 'a target-rich environment'.

[286] Thucy. 4. 125–7 (used successfully against *psiloi*); Xen. *Hell*. 4. 5. 14–17 and *Anab*. 3. 3. 15. In the first example Brasidas placed his own *psiloi* inside the hoplite square.

Athenian/Corinthian army. The enemy referred to was a Theban invasion force of some 7,000 foot and 600 horse.[287]

As few as they were, Dionysios' cavalrymen scattered here and there, and riding alongside the enemy charged and hurled their javelins at them. When the enemy charged out at them, they would retire and then turn about and hurl their javelins. During this procedure they would dismount from their horses and take a break, and if anyone charged out at them while they were dismounted they would leap on their horses and retire without any trouble. In addition, if any pursued them far from the army, when these retired they would press upon them and wreak havoc with their javelins. So, they forced the whole army to advance or retreat as they themselves wished.[288]

The achievement of the Syracusan cavalry is particularly impressive as the Athenian and Corinthian cavalry had earlier judged the enemy too strong to attack.[289]

Because of their inability to fight in formation, most types of *psiloi* were as vulnerable to cavalry as individual hoplites and although their limited armour did allow them to run faster, this was often insufficient to save them from a mounted enemy. Two Theban successes against Spartan peltasts in 378 illustrate the particular vulnerability of disorganized light troops, but cavalry was also effective against organized *psiloi*. At least once Thracian peltasts fled before a Macedonian cavalry charge even reached them.[290] However, those peltasts equipped with a shield and longer spear and who were able to fight in formation[291] had to be attacked like hoplites. They were therefore not always easy prey for cavalry, as the Dioi proved at Mykalessos. On their way back from Athens, having arrived too late to take part in the Sicilian expedition, they sacked the small town of Mykalessos and massacred many of the inhabitants. During the return to their ships some were cut down by the Theban troopers, but the main body

---

[287] Diod. Sic. 15. 68. 1. These figures applied at the start of the expedition and, as Xenophon's account of the engagement does not mention the Theban cavalry, it might have been elsewhere at the time.

[288] Xen. *Hell.* 7. 1. 21.

[289] Ibid. 7. 1. 20.

[290] Ibid. 5. 4. 39, 44–5; cf. Arr. *Anab.* 1. 2. 5–6 (with infantry support), and the similar (but less successful tactics) in Thucy. 2. 100. 4–5. The Getai fled before contact, although Alexander's rapid and unexpectedly easy crossing of the Ister also contributed to the shock of the attack, Arr. *Anab.* 1. 4. 3.

[291] See J. G. P. Best, *Thracian Peltasts and their Influence on Greek Warfare* (Groningen, 1969), 139–42.

used detachments to charge out against the cavalrymen and prevented them from getting too close.[292] These men charging out
(*ekdromoi*) were probably less likely to suffer casualties than
slower hoplite *ekdromoi*, but it seems likely that the relatively short
distance to the boats also saved them, by denying the Theban
horse sufficient time to pressure their formation into collapse.[293]

Cavalry therefore could be highly successful against infantry,
whether these were in or out of formation. Physical shock action
of the type which is inaccurately assumed to be the way cavalry
achieved success was impossible for the Athenian mounted arm,
as it was for other cavalry, but it none the less had considerable
hitting power. This derived from the moral shock created either
by attacking troops out of formation, or the flanks, rear, or (much
less likely) front, of a phalanx, or from its ability to break up a
formation with missile-fire and to use close-quarter combat
against the fleeing infantry. The characteristics which gave the
potential to accomplish this were flexibility, mobility, weaponry,
and protection. These chiefly arose from the relatively fixed
aspects of the cavalry—the physical nature of the horse, and the
available equipment, weaponry, and organization. These remained basically the same during the fifth and fourth centuries,
but to exploit this potential hitting power to the full also required
the more changeable characteristics of good leadership, training,
motivation, and size.

CONCLUSIONS

In general, Greek cavalry had quite a good combat potential, and
one which was certainly better than many scholars assume. Its
mobility, for example, was far superior to that of infantry, although somewhat more curtailed by steep and/or rough country.
While their lack of stirrups did render ancient riders considerably
less secure than modern ones, their equestrian techniques and

[292] Thucy. 7. 30. 2. He only mentions one item of their equipment, the
machaira (7. 27. 1), but because of their ability to fight in formation they must
also have been armed with a shield and a spear as well. They lost 250 men out of
1,300, mainly stragglers or those who drowned trying to swim out to the boats.
[293] The distance from Mykalessos to the nearest bay is only some 5–7 km., so
allowing for the time it took the Theban cavalry to arrive the pursuit was
probably quite short.

practices made their seat steadier than is often believed. Coupled with this, was the cavalry's capacity for enduring long distance movement over sustained periods, limited only by the need to avoid prolonged periods of overwork and/or under-nourishment. However, these problems were extremely unlikely to occur in normal campaigns in mainland Greece.

Its combat power too was potentially high. Although unable to engage in the physical shock tactics which are widely, but incorrectly, seen as the proper function of cavalry, Greek cavalrymen were still capable of effective action against hoplites. For example, the states which used the wedge formation and *sarissa* (or possibly the *kamax*) could employ the hand-to-hand mêlée technique which Arrian describes used against an unbroken line.[294] However, in most cases, including Athens, the lack of stirrups, the tetragonal formation, and the use of spears the same length as, or shorter than, the hoplite weapon, largely precluded this method. Yet, even in these cases, the combat flexibility conferred by their weaponry gave cavalrymen the potential to disrupt phalanxes with missile-fire and then follow up with close-quarter action against the retiring infantry. Cavalry could also be highly effective against panicked or disorganized troops in formation, or against men caught out of formation. In addition to this, it could also be used to charge at the unprotected flank or rear of a phalanx with a high probability of success. The intimidating appearance of horse and rider, particularly when moving in a group and at speed, was a useful aid to the creation of the moral shock which cavalry uses to scatter the enemy. However, as noted, their appearance was unlikely by itself to cause steady troops to retire. The potential hitting power of the mounted arm was also increased by the level of protection available to the *hippeis*. Despite the uncertainty which hangs over the proportion of cavalry who wore protective dress, it seems likely that breastplate, helmet, and high boots were fairly standard in fourth-century Athens at least, and common in other states too. These would have conferred considerable protection in a mêlée and would therefore have increased confidence and reduced casualties.

The cavalry's flexibility was probably excellent, particularly in comparison to the infantry. At Athens, the command structure

[294] Arr. *Takt.* 16. 6 ff.

permitted the corps to be split into halves, each with a senior officer in command of five phylarchs and their squadrons. It also seems likely that there was some sort of internal command structure within each *phyle* but, if so, it was probably on an informal rather than an institutionalized basis. This created some potential for operational flexibility, a faculty further enhanced by the cavalry's mobility and the existence of the *hyperetai*. Together, these would have allowed cavalry officers to react rapidly in combat by the quick dissemination of orders which the soldiers then had the capacity to execute at some speed.

Several advantages probably accrued to the corps from the levels of leadership, skill, and motivation, although the lack of systematic evidence in most cases precludes us from identifying anything more than general trends. In broad terms, the quality of the Athenian cavalry leadership was probably quite reasonable and certainly no worse than the standard in other states. The level of skill was probably also fairly high as, apart from individual practice, the cavalry corps had a programme of collective training which should have increased the expertise of its members. In this respect the cavalry was better off than the hoplite arm which did not apparently undertake collective training—except in the case of Sparta or, in the fourth century, of those states which created standing bodies of picked troops known as *epilektoi*. It is interesting to note that cavalry and *epilektoi* were often deployed together—perhaps because they were seen as the most professional units in most armies. The Athenian cavalry too possessed a solid sense of corps identity and *esprit de corps* and, while it apparently interfered with military performance in one instance, it would normally have contributed to the cavalry's combat potential by providing positive motivation to do well in front of comrades and the rest of the army. Despite the fluctuations in leadership, skill, and motivation which undoubtedly occurred from time to time, there is no evidence of deficiencies serious enough to reduce the effectiveness of the *hippeis* on campaign. In fact, what evidence survives indicates that the skill, motivation, and leadership of the corps would have enhanced their combat potential—both directly and through the contributions they made to the cavalry's flexibility, firepower, and close-quarter combat capabilities.

So far then, there is nothing in the innate characteristics of the cavalry arm which might reduce its combat potential to the extent that it would be useless in battle. The lack of stirrups certainly diminished its effectiveness in comparison with more modern cavalry, but need not have prevented the mounted arm from making an important contribution in time of war. However, the remaining characteristic, size, did have more potential to affect performance adversely. To harass infantry formations into collapsing would have required considerable missile-fire and I doubt if a small group of horse would have been capable of generating enough to cause a large hoplite force to disintegrate. Similarly, smaller groups of *hippeis* would presumably have been less enthusiastic about attacking sizeable infantry armies, even if these were disorganized or panicked. The establishment figure of 1,000 was quite a good-sized force, particularly with the addition of 200 *hippotoxotai* or the *hamippoi* and, used together, 1,000 horse could have been extremely effective. But any reduction of this number could diminish their hitting power and therefore their combat potential. The evidence in fact indicates that for most of the period under consideration the *hippeis* were understrength, sometimes (although this is probably an extreme example) by as much as 350 or more men. However, a force of even 500–600 cavalry was quite large by Greek standards and still had the capacity to inflict considerable damage upon an enemy—as the small Syracusan cavalry contingent showed near Corinth in 369.[295] It is therefore unlikely that lack of numbers on the scale evident would by itself be sufficient to reduce the cavalry's combat potential to the level where it could not contribute effectively on the battlefield.

With the possible exception of the size of the force, the cavalry's characteristics would probably have produced an effective unit with a high combat potential—even against hoplites. The lack of stirrups did reduce its potential to some degree but not sufficiently to prevent its successful use in the field. It now remains to examine the employment of the cavalry in war, to see how it was used in practice, and whether it lived up to this potential.

[295] Xen. *Hell.* 7. 1. 20–1.

3

The Theory and Practice of
Cavalry Warfare *c*.450–300

THE combat potential of Greek cavalry was relatively high: mounted troops were mobile, flexible, and capable of exerting considerable hitting power, even against heavy infantry, and the course of Greek warfare from *c*.450 to 300 shows that this potential was frequently realized in battle. Cavalry not only achieved some major successes against enemy troops, but there were also solid developments in the theory and practice of cavalry employment; despite this, in most Greek city-states (including Athens) it generally remained subordinate to the hoplite arm. Because of this, and as cavalry was usually employed either in support of or in opposition to hoplites, its military role can only be understood within the framework of hoplite warfare.

HOPLITE WARFARE

The hoplite's dominant position in Greek warfare was not seriously challenged until the introduction of the *sarissa*-armed Macedonian phalanx in the second half of the fourth century and even then hoplite tactics and equipment were retained for many years.[1] Hoplite warfare was a relatively simple affair which essentially involved marching against the agricultural land of the enemy and threatening his crops. He would either accept the challenge and defend his land or would decline and stay within his city walls. If the challenge was accepted and the defender won, his crops would be saved; if he lost, they would be ravaged. If the defender refused to fight, his crops would be ravaged anyway and the invader would return home having gained a moral victory— besides inflicting economic damage on his foe.[2] Limited assault

---

[1] Markle, 'Macedonian Sarissa', 326–31; 'Use of the Sarissa', 486 ff., 491–3.
[2] For the general pattern of hoplite warfare see *HCT* i. 11–15; *MT* 2–3; and most recently V. D. Hanson, *The Western Way of War* (New York, 1989). For the moral victory see Xen. *Hell.* 6. 5. 21.

techniques and the expense of protracted sieges meant that, bar-
ring treachery, a walled city's only vulnerable point was its crops,
orchards, and other fixed assets in the countryside.[3]

Most Greek cities could not afford to lose a harvest without
importing food or starving[4] and this should not be underestimated
as a factor in classical warfare. The Greeks certainly recognized
it, as the mere threat of having its crops ravaged was sometimes
sufficient to make a city capitulate. King Agesilaos of Sparta, for
example, once allowed the Akarnanians to plant their crops unmo-
lested in order to threaten them more effectively once the crop
had matured and was ready to reap. The tactic worked and they
duly came to terms when faced with invasion at the next harvest.[5]
Crops were therefore almost always defended, usually by a positional defence involving a pitched battle between two hoplite
armies supported by cavalry or *psiloi*. This was the normal means
of defending the agricultural hinterland, but there were two other
methods: border defence and mobile defence.[6] It has been argued
that the first of these could be achieved by using light troops to
control the mountain passes and this certainly was attempted
from time to time, particularly in the fourth century.[7] However,
the use of this strategy was limited by several factors.

First, not all states were protected by mountain barriers and
many ranges in fact had passes which could easily be turned or
which were wide enough to require a hoplite defence. Second, the
possibility of an unheralded invasion or the seizure of passes in
advance required that they be guarded for longer than just the
few weeks before the harvest.[8] To do so would rule out the use of
citizen hoplites, but to train, feed, and pay light infantry garrisons

[3] *HCT* i. 16–19; A. W. Lawrence, *Greek Aims in Fortification* (Oxford, 1979),
39–52. The siege of Potidaia cost 2,000 talents, Thucy. 2. 70. 2.

[4] Cf. Xen. *Hell.* 5. 4. 56 and 7. 2. 10, 17–19.

[5] Crops: Thucy. 4. 84. 2, 88; cf. Epameinondas' decision to dispatch his cavalry
against Mantineia, Xen. *Hell.* 7. 5. 14. Agesilaos: Xen. *Hell.* 4. 6. 13, 7. 1; Plut.
Ages. 22. 5.

[6] There was also the offensive option of a pre-emptive strike, J. Ober, *Fortress
Attica* (Leiden, 1985), 70 ff.

[7] P. Cartledge, 'Hoplites and Heroes: Sparta's Contribution to the Technique
of Ancient Warfare', *JHS* 97 (1977), 22–4. For a list of examples see *OPW*
192–4.

[8] Holladay, *JHS* 102 (1982), 98–9.

would have been prohibitively expensive.⁹ Third, there are examples of hoplites forcing their way through defended passes and, as they lived off the land or their own resources, they rarely had vulnerable supply lines which could be cut by border garrisons in their rear.¹⁰ Because of these considerations, this option tended to be neglected in favour of either the positional defence of the plain already mentioned or a mobile defence.¹¹ Mobile defence employed cavalry or *psiloi* to restrict the movement of the enemy army and to prevent it from damaging the crops. Because of its superior mobility, and the lack of trained *psiloi*, it was the cavalry which was normally used in this role in the hoplite areas of Greece. Mobile defence was used in several campaigns,¹² most notably by the Athenians during the Peloponnesian War.

Cavalry could therefore be used either independently or in support of hoplites in the defensive phase of warfare and the same was true of offensive operations. Here, cavalry could mount independent raids or provide support to hoplite invaders. Most other cavalry tasks can similarly be divided into independent or supporting operations, which I define as follows. Independent operations are those operations where either no hoplites were involved, or where they played little or no part in the action. Supporting operations are those where hoplites played the major role in combat and the mounted arm acted in support. While there is obviously some overlap between the two categories (particularly where hoplites were present but not directly involved) they provide a convenient tool for analysing the use of cavalry in combat. Although most Greek cavalry activity falls into the category of supporting operations, (see, for example, Athenian deployments and force compositions, Tables 3–4) I shall deal with the independent operations first as they best illustrate the principles and practice of Greek cavalry in general, and the Athenian corps in particular.

⁹ *HCT* i. 14; *MT* 5. For the daily ration per man and the number of transport animals required to move supplies, see Engels, *Logistics*, 18–19, 123–6.

¹⁰ *MT* 7–8; Holladay, *JHS* 102 (1982), 98–9.

¹¹ A forward frontier defence, based on the Megarid, was possible for Athens, *OPW* 190 ff., but only given an alliance with, or control over, Megara; cf. I. G. Spence, 'Perikles and the Defence of Attika during the Peloponnesian War', *JHS* 110 (1990), 96.

¹² Thucy. 1. 111. 1; 2. 100. 5; Hdtos 5. 63. 3–4; Diod. Sic. 15. 71. 4–5; Xen. *Hell*. 5. 3. 3.

TABLE 4. Athenian force compositions 431–279

Year	Location	Infantry	Cavalry	Ratio[a]	References/Remarks
431	Athens	29,000	1,200	24:1	Thucy. 2. 13. 6–8; total Athenian land-force
430	Peloponnese	4,000	300	13.5:1	Thucy. 2. 56. 2; seaborne force
	Thrace/Potidaia	4,000	300	13.5:1	Thucy. 2. 58. 1
429	Spartolos	2,000	200	10:1	Thucy. 2. 79. 1
425	Corinth/Solygeia	2,000+	200	10+:1	Thucy. 4. 42. 1; allied troops also present
424	Kythera	2,000	'a few'	20:1?	Thucy. 4. 53. 1; the *hippeusi te oligois* seems likely to have been fewer than the 200 specified in the previous two entries
	Megara	4,000	600	6.5:1	Thucy. 4. 68. 5
	Delion	7,000	1,000?	7+:1	Thucy. 4. 94. 1; numbers of cavalry not specified and almost certainly lower than 1,000 because of plague
423	Mende/Skione	1,000	None	—	Thucy. 4. 129. 2; the force also included 600 archers, 1,000 Thracian mercenaries, and some peltasts
422	Amphipolis	1,200+	300	4+:1	Thucy. 5. 2. 1–2; Kleon also collected hoplites from Skione and had other allied troops with him
418	Mantineia	1,000	300	3.5:1	Thucy. 5. 61. 1
416	Melos	2,700	20	135:1	Thucy. 5. 84. 1; the cavalry were *hippotoxotai*; 300 archers also went. The hoplites include 1,500 allied troops
415	Sicily	5,100	30	170:1	Thucy. 6. 43; over half the hoplites were allied troops
414	Sicily	5,100	310	16.5:1	250 cavalry and 30 *hippotoxotai* sent, without horses, (Thucy. 6. 94. 4) as reinforcements to original force (see previous entry)

	Sicily	5,100	650	8:1	Thucy. 6. 98. 8; final figures for Sicilian expedition, including 400 allied cavalry; the 30 *hippotoxotai* are not mentioned but may still have been there (see previous entry)
410	Athens/Ionia	1,000	100	10:1	Xen *Hell.* 1. 1. 34; Diod. Sic. 13. 52. 1
409	Nisaia/Kerata	1,000	400	2.5:1	Diod. Sic. 13. 65. 1–2
407	Ionia	1,500	150	10:1	Xen. *Hell.* 1. 4. 21
394	Nemea	6,000	600	10:1	Xen. *Hell.* 4. 2. 17; numbers are approximate
379/8	Boiotia	5,000	500	10:1	Diod. Sic. 15. 26. 2
378	Athens	20,000	500	40:1	Diod. Sic. 15. 29. 7; response to Sphodrias' raid
	Boiotia	5,000	200	25:1	Diod. Sic. 15. 32. 2
352	Phokis	5,000	400	12.5:1	Diod. Sic. 16. 37. 3; the infantry are called *pezoi*
349/8	Olynthos	4,000	150	27:1	Philochoros, *FGH* 328 F50; infantry were mercenary peltasts
	Olynthos	2,000	300	6.5:1	Philochoros, *FGH* 328 F51
323	Plataia	7,000	500	14:1	Diod. Sic. 18. 11. 3; the infantry are 5,000 Athenians and 2,000 mercenaries
323/2	Lamia	7,000	500	14:1	As for previous entry; two engagements
322	Krannon	?7,000	500?	14:1?	The same force sent out in 323, however, Diod. Sic. 18. 17. 1 records that some of the allied army had gone home so the Athenian numbers may also have been lower
279	Delphi	1,000	500	2:1	Pausanias, 10. 20. 5; they also provided their entire navy

[a] Rounded to the nearest 0.5.

INDEPENDENT OPERATIONS

Greek cavalry was used in a wide variety of independent tasks, and the Athenian arm perhaps more so than the cavalry of most other states (with the exception of Thessaly and Macedon). Independent operations included tasks as disparate as implementing a deception plan or preparing a safe river crossing for the following infantry.[13] However, the major ones were the containment or destruction of enemy soldiers or foragers (especially during mobile defence tasks), reconnaissance, raids, and internal security duties. Of these, the first is the most important, accounting for many of the purely cavalry actions involving the Athenian *hippeis*, but all seem to have determined the character of Athenian cavalry theory in the fourth century. Xenophon's *Hipparchikos*, for example, deals almost exclusively with independent operations; on the two occasions he mentions infantry and cavalry working together, it is the infantry who support the horse.[14]

The previous chapter showed how cavalry was able to contain, or even destroy, enemy infantry, and the theory behind this tactic needs no further discussion here. However, it bears repeating that cavalry was particularly effective against troops either out of formation or whose formation had been disrupted by other hoplites, by harassment from cavalry or *psiloi*, or as a result of obstacle crossing. The use of cavalry against hoplites disrupted by other hoplites will be covered below under the heading of supporting operations, but it is interesting to note that the Greek theory of cavalry use against hoplites involved a sound appreciation of the characteristics of the two arms. Awaiting the disruption of a phalanx by an obstacle or friendly action, or causing this disruption itself, then allowed the cavalry to use its superior mobility to capitalize on the relative weakness of hoplites unprotected by their formation. In fact, Xenophon envisaged even small bodies of cavalry hovering around superior numbers of enemy like a beast or bird of prey until an opportunity to strike presented itself. When it did so, the cavalry would employ its speed and mobility to strike and then retire.[15]

[13] Xen. *Anab.* 6. 3. 19–20; Polyainos, 2. 3. 14; Frontinus, *Strategemata*, 2. 2. 12; Diod. Sic. 18. 35. 1. The Persian cavalry was also used to foul the water supply at Plataia, Hdtos 9. 49. 2; Plut. *Arist.* 16. 6.

[14] Xen. *Hipparch.* 5. 13; 8. 18–20.

[15] Ibid. 4. 17–20; 7. 7–10.

Mobile Defence

Because of the methods used in devastating agricultural areas, the cavalry tactics described above were particularly useful in their defence. Invaders deprived the enemy of agricultural produce by destroying the crops, harvesting them for their own use, or a combination of the two. The Peloponnesians, for example, used the combination method against the Athenians from 431 onwards. Although they brought some supplies with them, they also used local crops—their 425 invasion had to be cut short because the Attic grain was still too green to harvest. However, the devastation of some areas in passing suggests pure destruction rather than harvesting.[16] Long-term damage could be caused by the destruction of vines, trees, and farm-buildings. The precise method of ravaging obviously differed according to local conditions, but burning was probably not the most common medium of destruction.

The verb *temno*, which is frequently used in the context of ravaging, strongly suggests that trees and crops were cut down rather than burned,[17] and fire obviously could not be used where an army was harvesting crops for its own use. It was anyway not a particularly good method of destroying farm-land as the three main objects of destruction: farm-buildings, trees, and crops, were not particularly vulnerable to fire. Ancient Greek country houses were probably difficult to set alight because they were largely constructed of non-flammable materials and the danger could be further reduced by removing woodwork from the houses before an invasion force arrived.[18] Trees could be burned, but the olive in particular would probably have taken some trouble to ignite because of its thick bark.[19] In addition, agricultural theory dictated that olives should be planted a good distance apart, and

[16] Supplies: Thucy. 3. 1. 3; 425 invasion: Thucy. 4. 6; destruction in passing: Thucy. 2. 23.

[17] A. H. Jackson, 'The Original Purpose of the Delian League', *Historia*, 18 (1969), 12–13; cf. Thucy. 2. 21. 2.

[18] J. E. Jones, A. J. Graham, and L. H. Sackett, 'The Dema House in Attica', *ABSA* 57 (1962), 106–8 and 'An Attic Country House below the Cave of Pan at Vari', *ABSA* 68 (1973), 359–69, 424–30, 440–3; cf. Thucy. 2. 14. 1.

[19] Theophrastos, *Enquiry into Plants*, 2. 3. 3; the thicker the bark the smaller the initial heat rise (but there is also a short-term temperature rise after the external heat source is removed), A. J. Kayll, *A Technique for Studying the Fire Tolerance of Living Tree Trunks* (Department of Forestry, Canada, Publication 1012; Ottawa, 1963), 19.

if this was done then it may also have been difficult for the fire to spread easily from tree to tree.[20]

Crops were on occasion burned in ancient warfare but modern experimental tests show that it is often difficult to fire grain (especially wheat) and that the damage is limited to very small areas if the crop is not fully ripe or there has been recent rain.[21] In fact, the scientist who conducted these tests claimed that 'the danger of loss by fire occurs mainly when harvest is delayed beyond the stage when the crop first becomes fit for cutting'.[22] The problem for an invader wishing to use fire would be to arrive when the crop was ripe but not yet harvested—not an easy feat as different crops would ripen at different times. It is clear then that troops destroying or harvesting crops and those destroying vines, trees, and buildings, often used tools to do so and could not therefore operate in close formation.[23] Because of this, unless protected by other troops, they were vulnerable to sudden attack of the type most effectively delivered by cavalry. It was not usual Greek practice to protect foragers and the first examples of this concern Alexander, although in later periods such protection may have been provided as a matter of course.[24]

Most Greek armies had no organized commissariat and there-fore relied on individual foraging or the establishment of markets to feed their soldiers.[25] Constant attacks on their foragers could therefore cause considerable hardship and reduce the military effectiveness of the force. Foragers were especially vulnerable to cavalry attack because they operated as individuals or in small groups and were often encumbered by tools or booty.[26] Two

[20] Theophrastos, *Enquiry into Plants*, 2. 5. 6. This problem has now been rectified by modern ordnance, cf. Fisk's Lebanon report, *The Times* (London), August 11 1983, 4.

[21] Thucy. 6. 94. 3. D. J. Watson, 'Inflammability of Cereal Crops in Relation to Water-content', *EJEA* 18, no. 71 (1950), 150–7 (the experiments relate to the UK and the risk of fire would probably have been greater in the drier Greek condi-tions).

[22] Ibid. 157. However, he also points out that such delays are not infrequent with large crops because of the difficulty of harvesting it all as soon as it ripens.

[23] Cf. H. D. Westlake, *Essays on the Greek Historians and Greek History* (Manchester, 1969), 93 n. 27; *MT* 3.

[24] Arr. *Anab.* 1. 5. 9; 3. 20. 4; cf. Onasander, 10. 8. See Livy, 31. 2 and Caesar, *Civil War*, 1. 40. 3 for Roman practice.

[25] *GSAW* i. 30–52.

[26] Thucy. 7. 4. 6, 13. 2. See Onasander, 10. 7–8 for the defencelessness of foragers—he advocated banning unauthorized foraging and protecting authorized foragers. Equipment: Xen. *Anab.* 6. 4. 23.

incidents involving Greek troops in Asia show that even large bodies of foragers were at risk from horsemen. In the first, 2,000 foragers from the Ten Thousand were attacked by cavalry under Pharnabazos: about 500 were killed and the rest forced to retire to the upland areas. Xenophon also records that in 395 Pharnabazos was again successful under similar circumstances, when he killed 100 of a 700-man group from Agesilaos' army. On this occasion the Greeks managed to form a hasty phalanx when they realized the impending danger, but were nevertheless disrupted by two scythed chariots and then attacked by the cavalry.[27] Another large-scale loss of life occurred in Sicily when over-confident Selinousioi scattered to plunder and were caught in the open by a force including 800 Campanian cavalry; 1,000 of them were killed.[28]

Given the success of these, and other actions, against foragers and even large hoplite forces, it is not surprising that the Persians, and those Greeks from traditional cavalry areas such as Thessaly and Sicily, regularly and successfully used their mounted arm against invaders.[29] It was such a natural tactic for the Macedonians that, when a large army of Thracians invaded in 429/8, they did not even consider engaging it with infantry but restricted themselves to a mounted resistance.[30] However, the defence of Attica during the Peloponnesian War represents the most sustained use of cavalry in the mobile defence role and it is instructive to examine how and why it was adopted.[31]

The Spartan strategy here was initially limited to the traditional one of forcing an enemy to submit by ravaging his crops. To achieve this, Attica was invaded annually by two-thirds of the Peloponnesian League forces. The theory behind the Athenian counter strategy is presented by Thucydides in Perikles' famous policy speech of 432/1. This argued that as Athens could not afford a major defeat she should not deploy her hoplites in

---

[27] Xen. *Anab.* 6. 4. 24; *Hell.* 4. 1. 17–19.

[28] Diod. Sic. 13. 44. 1–4.

[29] Thucy. 1. 111. 1; Diod. Sic. 15. 71. 4–5 (Thessaly); Thucy. 7. 4. 6; Plut. *Nik.* 19. 6; Diod. Sic. 11. 21. 2; 13. 44. 1–4, 88. 1 (Sicily). Although the Syracusans also used their infantry, it was the cavalry which normally played the most effective part.

[30] Thucy. 2. 100.

[31] For a more detailed discussion, see Spence, *JHS* 110 (1990), 91–109.

defence of Attica; the consequent food loss was to be replaced by imports.[32]

However, because of the risk of damage to his own political position, and to the Athenian will to resist, Perikles could not afford to abandon Attica entirely to the enemy. Instead, he chose to employ the *hippeis* to provide some protection to the Athenian *chora*, and to retaliate in kind with attacks on the Megarid and seaborne raids on the Peloponnese.[33] The factor of morale was initially very important because of the prominence of the hoplite ethos in Greek thinking. Perikles' problem was that in traditional hoplite warfare a state which did not mobilize its hoplites to defend its farmland was considered to have suffered a moral defeat.[34] This view lasted throughout the classical period and there is considerable evidence from both the fifth and fourth centuries to show that a refusal to fight was regarded as dishonourable.[35]

A prime example of this is the Athenian reaction to the first invasion of the Peloponnesian War:

when they saw the army at Acharnai, only sixty stades from the city, they could no longer tolerate the situation. Their land was being ravaged right in front of them, something which the young men had never seen, nor the old men—except at the time of the Persian invasion. It was terrible and they (especially the young) wanted to march out and put up with it no longer.[36]

Perikles was in fact accused of cowardice (*ekakizon*) for not leading them out to defend their land and, significantly, Diodorus Siculus notes that, when he did lead the first retaliatory raid, Perikles was praised by the Athenians 'on the grounds that he was

[32] Thucy. 1. 143. 4–5.

[33] Thucy. 2. 23–31, 56. If de Ste. Croix's interpretation of the Megarian decrees (*OPW* 261–7) is correct then the invasions of the Megarid may have been influenced by religious considerations. See also Westlake, *Essays*, 91 ff., although he is not entirely convinced that the morale factor was the sole motive.

[34] Garlan, *War in the Ancient World*, 60. Cf. Thucy. 1. 140. 5; 2. 21. 3; Diod. Sic. 12. 61. 2.

[35] This was expressed as late as 355 in Isok. 8. 77. Cf. Xen. *Hell.* 6. 5. 20–1; Plut. *Nik.* 20. 4–5; Thucy. 8. 27. Although the last two of these involve naval engagements, the *strategoi* involved were all of hoplite class and the reaction of the Argive hoplites in Thucy. 8. 27. 6 shows that the principle was the same.

[36] Thucy. 2. 21. 2. See also Hermippos in Plut. *Per.* 33. 7 for a similar quotation. *HCT* ii. 75–6 cites two fragments of comedy which may also refer to this incident.

acting as a general and waging war on the Peloponnesians'.[37]
Perikles remained apparently unmoved by the accusations of
cowardice and the demands to march against the enemy but he
nevertheless refrained from calling an assembly, checked the
city's defences, and tried to keep things calm. In addition, he also
continually sent the cavalry out to prevent the enemy from
ravaging the area close to the city.[38]

Perikles was bound to provide some sort of defence for Attica
and—as he quite sensibly did not want to risk the losses involved
in a pitched battle against superior numbers—the only viable
alternative was to use the cavalry in the mobile defence role. Even
before the main Peloponnesian army reached the outskirts of
Athens in 431, and while the Athenians were still hoping that it
would withdraw (as it had under Pleistoanax in 446), the Athenian
cavalry was engaging the enemy at a place called Rheitoi on the
Thriasian Plain.[39] Then, when the Peloponnesians moved north-
wards and began ravaging Acharnai in view of the city, Perikles,
as noted, continually (*aiei*) used the cavalry to protect the countryside close to the city. However, it was unrealistic to expect that
the cavalry could protect the whole of Attica or could be used to
attack the main body of enemy hoplites, which was defended by
its own cavalry, drawn from Boiotia, Phokis, and Lokris. But, as
we have already seen, the Athenian *hippeis* were prepared to
operate as far afield as the Thriasian Plain and in 430 they, and
some Thessalian cavalry, are attested at a place called Phrygia,
which is apparently in the deme Athmonon, north-east of
Athens.[40]

After their initial reverse at Rheitoi, which took place in unspecified circumstances, and their success against the Boiotian horse at
Phrygia, the *hippeis* seem to have perfected their tactics and by
428, according to Thucydides, 'they were able to prevent the
majority of the light troops from leaving their camp to harm the
areas near the city.'[41] As Thucydides also states here that this

[37] Diod. Sic. 12. 42. 8.
[38] Thucy. 2. 22. 2.
[39] Ibid. 2. 19. 2.
[40] Ibid. 2. 22. 2; for its location see J. S. Traill, *Demos and Trittys* (Toronto,
1986), 135 and map.
[41] Thucy. 3. 1. 2; for the possible extent of the secure area see the map in
Spence, *JHS* 110 (1990), 103. As much of the local food supply was probably
grown near to the city, the preservation of these areas would also aid the war
effort.

had been the practice on previous occasions, it is quite clear that
the cavalry was used to protect as much of Attica as possible
during the first four years of the Archidamian War. This was also
the case for the whole of the Dekeleian War. With the Peloponnesian occupation of Dekeleia in 413, the ravaging became much
more extensive and Thucydides records that from this point
onwards the cavalry rode out every day to harass the enemy and
protect the countryside.[42] This phase of the war lasted from 413
to 404. The evidence for the remaining period of hostilities, that
is from 427–421, is rather sketchy. This is not least because the
invasions ceased after the Athenians threatened to execute the
Spartans captured on Sphakteria in 425.[43] However, as the cavalry
was used in mobile defence for two-thirds of the war (including
the periods at both the start and end of the conflict), it does seem
highly likely that this was also true of the two invasions (427 and
425) recorded during the middle third.

Additional support for this view is lent by Hippokrates' speech
before Delion in 424. Thucydides portrayed him as encouraging
the troops to fight by pointing out that if the Athenians were
victorious the Peloponnesians, thereby deprived of the Boiotian
horse, would never again attack Attica.[44] This statement has been
dismissed, unfairly in my view, by de Ste. Croix,[45] but it makes
eminent sense if Attica was being protected by cavalry in a
mobile defence role. I have already demonstrated that an infantry
force operating alone was vulnerable to good cavalry and, as the
Boiotians provided the bulk of the Peloponnesian League's
mounted arm,[46] their loss would render League operations in
Attica difficult in the face of mobile defence. Hippokrates' remark
then seems to show that the cavalry was still active in its normal
role in the years preceding 424, and that it was therefore used in
the defence of Attica throughout the war. As a further piece of
minor circumstantial evidence, the whole of Xenophon's *Hipparchikos* is heavily influenced by the hit and run tactics employed
against a superior enemy,[47] and I consider that this represents

---

[42] Thucy. 7. 27. 5.
[43] Ibid. 4. 41. 1.
[44] Ibid. 4. 95. 2.
[45] *OPW* 194.
[46] Thucy. 2. 9. 3.
[47] See esp. 4. 13–20 and 7. 5–14.

the lasting effect which nearly twenty years of such activities in defence of Attica had left upon Athenian cavalry tactics.

Athens therefore adopted mobile defence to protect Attica during the Peloponnesian War but this could never be more than partially successful because of the numbers of enemy horsemen. However, although Perikles' decision to use the *hippeis* in this role was influenced by the need to maintain morale, it also reveals a sound grasp of their military characteristics and their potential against infantry engaged in ravaging.

Reconnaissance

With the development of military techniques in the post-classical period, reconnaissance became increasingly important. Until the advent of motor vehicles and aircraft this was usually the province of cavalry, whose mobility and endurance particularly suited it to this role. Its employment in such tasks in classical Greek warfare, however, was limited because reconnaissance itself was often a neglected practice. Nevertheless, the use of cavalry is attested for three different types of reconnaissance tasks in ancient Greece. As two of these, scouting ahead of a moving force and observing a static enemy camp, were almost always part of supporting operations, they will be dealt with in that section. The other task, reconnoitring an area to locate the enemy or to report on the topography, did feature in independent operations or was conducted by purely cavalry forces operating away from the main army.

Although reconnaissance was by no means universally practised, its need was stressed by Xenophon[48] and some examples do occur in classical warfare. In 370/69, for instance, cavalry was used to conduct area reconnaissance to locate the enemy during the first Theban invasion of Lakonia. According to Xenophon, Iphikrates dispatched Athenian and Corinthian cavalry to Oneion to ascertain whether the Thebans had already passed there.[49] The recording of such a specific operation to locate the enemy is rare, but it does accord with the principles espoused in Xenophon's military treatises. Because literary accounts tend to

[48] Xen. *Hipparch.* 4. 4 ff.
[49] Xen. *Hell.* 6. 5. 52.

concentrate on the hoplites, it is quite possible that the practice was not as infrequent as the lack of evidence suggests. Despite his particular interest in the cavalry, even the Oneion mission might not have been recorded if it had not provided the opportunity for Xenophon to illustrate the principle of using the right size force for reconnaissance.[50]

There are more frequent examples of area reconnaissance aimed at securing topographical information such as routes, sources of supply, or even sites for forts and anchorages. However, most of these are fairly late and all refer to Asian campaigns—probably because in Greece itself there was a better chance of relying on local knowledge. Apart from Xenophon's fictional account of Cyrus and his cavalry checking part of Armenia for suitable fort sites,[51] all the extant examples concern Alexander. In two of these cases, the inspection of Gaugamela before the battle and the reconnaissance of the coastline near the Indus, the cavalrymen can perhaps be regarded primarily as escorting their leader, but this was not always the case. Arrian, for example, states that while traversing the Gedrosian desert Alexander sent some cavalry under Thoas son of Mandrodoros to check the coast for food and water for the army and anchorages for the accompanying fleet.[52] Because the army was suffering hardship, the cavalry was undoubtedly chosen for its speed and Alexander presumably did not accompany it because the sight of their leader disappearing over the horizon might well have had a detrimental effect on the morale of those left behind.

I have argued below that Greek neglect of reconnaissance resulted from a reliance on alternative sources of information and from the general nature of hoplite warfare,[53] but Alexander's presence on many scouting missions suggests an additional reason—a lack of confidence in the quality of reported information. Today, reconnaissance is rightly regarded as a task best performed by specialist troops, but Greece almost certainly had no cavalry whose main role was reconnaissance until the creation of the *prodromoi* in the fourth century. Even though warfare was less complicated then than it is now, the lack of specialized

---

[50] Xen. *Hell.* 6. 5. 52; cf. *Hipparch.* 7. 9 and 8. 12–14.
[51] Xen. *Kyrop.* 3. 2. 1.
[52] Arr. *Anab.* 3. 9. 5; 6. 20. 4, 23. 2.
[53] See 'the influence of hoplite warfare and the hoplite ethos', Ch. 4.

reconnaissance troops probably reduced the overall quality of information gathered. Xenophon's remarks praising the unusually accurate reports of one Demokrates of Temnos certainly suggest that the general standard of intelligence reporting was fairly low, and this is confirmed by Aineias Taktikos. He advised choosing scouts from experienced soldiers who would be less likely to cause unnecessary alarms by ignorant reports—but even so recommended posting them in groups of three.[54]

Raids

Raiding was a common tactic, familiar to most Greek states, and cavalry was particularly suited to this role because its mobility and endurance allowed it to penetrate and damage the enemy's territory with relative impunity. This was recognized in practice by most *poleis* and at least one, Athens, had developed a solid theory of raiding by the mid-fourth century. Xenophon discussed the techniques involved, quite rightly stressing the need for rapid movement and/or stealth to attack, inflict damage, and retire before the enemy could react.[55] The Athenians probably acquired the solid basis for raiding operations reflected in this advice during the Peloponnesian War—many of the basic skills and techniques required for successful raids were the same as those needed in the mobile defence role. Here too, quick attacks against targets of opportunity and rapid withdrawals in the face of superior numbers were essential. Practical experience in large scale raiding was also gained from the fairly regular cavalry incursions into the Megarid down to 424.[56]

While large scale raids might have had the additional intent of inflicting casualties upon enemy troops sent out to meet them, most raids were aimed at depriving the enemy of their property. This was achieved by either damaging it, destroying it, or removing it. The last was presumably fairly popular with cavalryman and state alike as both could benefit financially from looting—although in what proportion depended upon the booty-sharing arrangements.[57] In fact, the profit motive occasionally

[54] Xen. *Anab.* 4. 4. 15; Ain. Takt. 6. 1.
[55] Xen. *Hipparch.* 7. 7–10, 14–15.
[56] Thucy. 2. 31. 3.
[57] On the division of spoils see *GSAW* i, chs. 3–5.

became uppermost, particularly with mercenary or tribal cavalry whose raids were sometimes, at least as far as they were concerned, little more than business ventures. For example, the cavalry of the Thracian Odrysai which served with Derkylidas in Bithynia acquired large quantities of booty (including slaves) from their regular raids. However, the frequency of these attacks undoubtedly caused considerable damage to the Bithynian countryside and disrupted its agricultural and commercial routine; so here, as must have been the case on many occasions, private interests coincided with the general's main aim. Derkylidas certainly thought the Odrysian contribution valuable enough to provide guards for the booty which they rather coyly stored some distance from his camp—rather too coyly in fact as the unfortunate guards were later massacred and most of the property recovered by irate Bithynians seeking revenge and restitution.[58]

A variant on this type of raid was to extort money by mounting a large-scale cavalry incursion and threatening to plunder the countryside. Alkibiades, for example, used this tactic to raise money for his army during the final stages of the Peloponnesian War.[59] Cavalry was excellent in this role because it was quick enough to surprise the enemy before stock and portable property could be moved inside the city walls—as Epameinondas' cavalry swoop on Mantineia intended.[60] Finally, cavalry raids were also planned for other very specific purposes—Gelon, tyrant of Syracuse, for instance, launched one in 480 to kill Hamilcar, the opposing Carthaginian general. In 317, Eumenes of Kardia dispatched his horse to seize the baggage belonging to Sibyrtios, satrap of Arachosia.[61]

Internal Security

Greek history is replete with examples of betrayals, traitors, and fifth columns. This is reflected in Aineias Taktikos' treatise on besieged cities, much of which concentrates on the internal rather

---

[58] Xen. *Hell*. 3. 2. 2–5.
[59] Ibid. 1. 3. 3; the force also included a few hoplites.
[60] Ibid. 7. 5. 14.
[61] Diod. Sic. 11. 21. 5; 19. 23. 4.

than the external threat.[62] Cavalry, though, is not particularly suited to military operations in an urban environment,[63] as the undignified death of King Pyrrhos in Argos shows. Although initially successful in breaking into the city at night, when day dawned he realized his position was untenable and began to withdraw his force. While fighting his way back out through the narrow streets, Pyrrhos was knocked senseless by a roof tile hurled by the aged mother of an Argive he was trying to kill. As he lay in the road stunned (always embarrassing for a cavalryman) he was recognized by an opponent, dragged into a doorway, and beheaded.[64] Perhaps because of such limitations, the use of cavalry in internal security operations is attested only outside the main built-up areas. While its speed and mobility were probably a factor here, in at least one case, and possibly in two, it was the cavalry's political reliability which determined its use.

This is certain in the Athenian use of the *hippeis* to forcibly evacuate Eleusis in 404, in order to provide a suitable place of refuge for the oligarchic government known as the Thirty, and it may also apply to a Spartan operation in 398. In this case, the government separated a suspected revolutionary named Kinadon from his co-conspirators by sending him away on a spurious mission; a *mora* of cavalrymen was used to assist the officers who arrested him.[65] Presumably their mobility was an asset here, but it is just possible that they were mercenaries chosen because of their likely innocence of the plot. Xenophon states that the Spartan cavalry only collected its mounts and equipment after mobilization, but elsewhere remarks that they did have a good quality force of mercenary cavalry.[66] If both these passages apply to 398, and if the mercenary cavalry was a permanent or semi-permanent force, then it seems likely that it performed this mission.

[62] Ain. Takt. *passim.*, esp. 1, 2, 4 and 5. See also A. H. Chroust, 'Treason and Patriotism in Ancient Greece', *JHI* 15 (1954), 280–8 and L. A. Losada, 'The Fifth Column in the Peloponnesian War', *Mnemosyne*, supp. 21 (1972), *passim*. Ain. Takt. 11. 3 ff. lists some examples famous in antiquity.

[63] Cavalry can be quite effective for crowd control in limited police actions in cities (as mounted police are used today) but cannot normally be used as true cavalry in streets, particularly narrow ones.

[64] Plut. *Pyrr.* 32–4.

[65] Xen. *Hell.* 2. 4. 8 (Eleusis); 3. 3. 8–11 (Kinadon).

[66] Ibid. 6. 4. 10–11; *Hipparch.* 9. 4.

TABLE 5. Battles involving the Athenian *Hippeis* 429–279

Year	Battle	No.	Command	Result	References/Remarks
429	Spartolos	200	Athens	Lost	Thucy. 2. 79; Isaios, 5. 42
425	Solygeia	200	Athens	Won	Thucy. 4. 42–3; landed by sea
424	Delion	all?	Athens	Lost	Thucy. 4. 93–4; Plut. *Alk*. 7. 4; Diod. Sic. 13. 69–70
422	Amphipolis	300	Athens	Lost	Thucy. 5. 2, 7–10
418	Mantineia	300	Allied	Lost	Thucy. 5. 61–73; Diod. Sic. 12. 79
414	Syracuse	250	Athens	Lost	Thucy. 7. 6
409	Ephesos	100	Athens	Lost	Xen. *Hell*. 1. 2. 7 ff.; landed by sea
	Abydos	100?	Athens	Won	Xen. *Hell*. 1. 2. 16
	Kerata	400	Athens	Won	Diod. Sic. 13. 65. 1–2
404	Mounychia	all?	The Thirty	Lost	Xen. *Hell*. 2. 4. 10–19; the democrats had no cavalry
394	Nemea	600	Allied?	Lost	Xen. *Hell*. 4. 2. 16–23; Diod. Sic. 14. 83. 1; *IG* II² 5222; 6217
	Koroneia		Allied?	Lost	Xen. *Hell*. 4. 3. 15–20; *IG* II² 5222
364	Olympia	400	Allied	Lost	Xen. *Hell*. 7. 4. 28 ff.
362	Mantineia		Allied?	Lost	Xen. *Hell*. 7. 5. 15–17, 23–4; Diod. Sic. 15. 84–7
348	Tamynai		Athens	Won	Plut. *Phok*. 12–13; Aischines, 3. 88; Dem. 21. 132–4, 162
338	Chaironeia	all?	Allied	Lost	Diod. Sic. 16. 85–6
323	Plataia	500	Athens	Won	Diod. Sic. 18. 11. 5
	Lamia	500	Allied	Won	Diod. Sic. 18. 12. 4
322	Lamia	500?	Allied	Won	Diod. Sic. 18. 15
	Krannon	500?	Allied	Lost	Diod. Sic. 18. 17
279	Delphi	500	Allied	Won	Pausanias, 10. 20. 3 ff.

Notes to Table 5: This table includes only major engagements—minor actions are shown in Table 3. In many cases the command arrangements of allied forces are unknown and, even when Athens was in charge of a joint army, the considerations of inter-state relations may have affected the deployment of the troops.

Delion (424): Hippokrates placed 300 cavalry at Delion and deployed the rest on the wings (Thucy. 4. 93–4). As he was aware of the importance of the Theban *hippeis* (4. 95. 2) he probably took as many cavalry as possible. However, Athens' cavalry was almost certainly understrength because of the plague; cf. Gomme, *HCT* iii. 564.

Mantineia (418): Thucy. 5. 61. 1 gives the number as 300, Diod. Sic. 12. 79. 1 has 200. Although in general (and here) I prefer Thucydides' account, it is always possible that Diodorus could be correct in a particular instance. The command was a joint one (Thucy. 5. 47. 7).

Syracuse (414): Although Thucydides makes no mention of them, the cavalry sent out earlier (Thucy. 6. 94. 4) were presumably present and may even have been supported by the 400 Sicilian cavalry allied to Athens (Thucy. 6. 98. 1). However, if this was the case they were unable to protect their own hoplites from the more numerous Syracusan cavalry.

Abydos (409): Thrasyllos had started with 100 *hippeis* (Xen. *Hell*. 1. 1. 34), but some may have been killed at Ephesos. It is also possible that Alkibiades had some cavalry with him.

Nemea (394): That the Thebans were on the right (Xen. *Hell*. 4. 2. 18) suggests they held the command.

Koroneia (394): The command is uncertain but, as the Thebans were again posted on the right (Xen. *Hell*. 4. 3. 16), they quite possibly held it.

Olympia (364): As the *hippeis* were there without Athenian hoplites the Arkadians presumably commanded.

Mantineia (362): The command was possibly held by each in turn for 5 days, as in the 369 agreement (Xen. *Hell*. 7. 1. 14).

Chaironeia (338): Athens marched out *pandemei* (Diod. Sic. 16. 85. 2), but even if they took all the cavalry the numbers may well have been below the traditional 1,000 (see Kroll, 95–6 and 97–8 n. 36). The Athenians seem to have exercised overall command (Diod. Sic. 16. 86. 2).

Lamia (323): Leosthenes, an Athenian, was in command (Diod. Sic. 18. 11. 5).

Lamia (322): The original contingent was 500 (Diod. Sic. 18. 11. 3), but (like the soldiers of other states) some could have returned home after the initial successes (Diod. Sic. 18. 13. 4, 15. 2, 17. 1). Another Athenian, Antiphilos, had replaced Leosthenes as commander and a Thessalian, Menon, led the cavalry (18. 13. 6, 15. 4).

Krannon (322): As the total cavalry numbers remained around 3,500 (Diod. Sic. 18. 15. 2, 17. 2) the Athenian contingent could have continued at 500. The commanders were the same as for Lamia (322).

Delphi (279): The Athenians held the command (Pausanias, 10. 20. 3). The cavalry was used to try to prevent the Gauls from crossing the river Spercheios prior to the battle but could not be used in the main engagement itself because of the terrain.

SUPPORTING OPERATIONS

For most of the fifth and fourth centuries heavy infantry was the dominant force on the Greek battlefield and the cavalry was usually employed in its support. The exceptions to this were Thessaly, Macedonia, and the less developed areas of Greece where cavalry and light infantry respectively predominated. As outlined in the previous section, Athens too made frequent use of her cavalry in the independent role and, during the Peloponnesian War, relied on it and not her hoplites to provide some measure of protection to Attica. However, despite the concentration on purely cavalry operations in Xenophon's manual on the hipparch's duties, most of the activities of the Athenian cavalry were in support of hoplites (see Tables 3–5). This is typical of most hoplite states in classical Greece.

Although the hoplite panoply became progressively lighter and hoplite tactics more sophisticated during the two centuries in question, for the most part the basic military action remained a head-on clash between infantry phalanxes.[67] At its simplest level, and certainly far more applicable to the fifth than to the fourth century, this was not entirely removed from the famous statement attributed to Mardonios to the effect that hoplite warfare basically involved two armies finding a flat piece of ground on which to kill each other.[68]

However, while the hoplite battle was the real tactical expression of the age, this period saw an increasing use of supporting arms such as cavalry or *psiloi*. In the mid-fourth century, Demosthenes summed this up (with some exaggeration) when referring to Philip II 'marching wherever he wishes, not leading a phalanx of hoplites but accompanied by an army of *psiloi*, cavalry, archers, and mercenaries'.[69] Cavalry was employed in a variety of support tasks and it is convenient to discuss these under the two broad categories of hoplite operations: the march and the battle.

---

[67] Cf. *AAG* 109–13; *MT* 13 ff., 40–2; *AGH* 141–2.
[68] Hdtos 7. 9 (quoted on 172 below).
[69] Dem. 9. 49.

The March

The march phase of war encompasses the movement of formed bodies of hoplites in the advance, and in the withdrawal conducted over a long distance (the immediate withdrawal from the battle-field forms part of the battle proper and is dealt with in that section). In this phase, cavalry was employed in two major tasks: reconnaissance and the provision of security to the hoplite forma-tion. Today, both of these tasks are regarded as crucial to the safety of a moving body of troops, but this was not always so in Greece.[70] However, as a result of growing military professional-ism and of experience gained in Asia, the fourth century saw an increasing emphasis on march security.[71] This led to a recognition that the two main dangers to a hoplite column—meeting an enemy army already deployed for battle and harassment, or attack, by cavalry and/or *psiloi*—could best be countered by the intelligent use of cavalry.

Other measures were theoretically possible, and were tried in practice, but at best only provided partial protection. Xenophon mentioned one when advocating that wherever possible advancing troops should move in battle formation to avoid the dangers of unexpected contact with the enemy.[72] However, he also accepted that this was not always feasible. For example, hoplites were often restricted to a column by roads or tracks which passed through defiles. This tactic also suffered from other deficiencies such as a reduced march rate and, more importantly, did not confer much protection against the other main danger to hoplites on the march—enemy cavalry and *psiloi*.

The threat from these types of troops could in theory be overcome by marching in a square formation, as the Ten Thou-sand did during their withdrawal after Kounaxa. By using a set drill to contract and then expand their frontage on the move they were even able to traverse defiles while maintaining a protective formation.[73] Nevertheless, this approach to march security also had its defects. The Ten Thousand were very experienced soldiers

[70] Cf. Xen. *Hipparch*. 4. 5 and *Oik*. 20. 6–9.

[71] Cf. A. Ferrill, *The Origins of War* (London, 1985), 149 ff.

[72] Xen. *Hipparch*. 4. 3. Although this refers to cavalry it is clear from the tactics described elsewhere (*Anab*. 3. 4. 19–23; *Oik*. 20. 6–7; *Kyrop*. 6. 3. 2–3) that he also believed this for infantry.

[73] Xen. *Anab*. 3. 4. 19–23.

and their technique was probably beyond the average citizen army. In addition, march rates would be reduced and, more importantly, a square formation was particularly vulnerable to attack by other hoplites already deployed for battle. Finally, over an extended distance determined cavalry or *psiloi* probably had the capacity to destroy a square formation by continual harassment. This is clear from Xenophon's account of the same withdrawal which shows that, despite their expertise in advancing in formation, the Ten Thousand still had to raise a body of cavalry and slingers in order to make any progress at all.[74]

Marching in battle formation therefore provided security against meeting an enemy army, but not against enemy cavalry or *psiloi*, while a square formation gave some protection against the latter, but not the former. In short, no formation conferred protection against both the main threats to a moving body of hoplites. However, the proper use of cavalry and/or light infantry could achieve precisely this. Deployed as scouts some distance ahead of the moving force, they could provide sufficient advance warning of an enemy army deployed for action. Used on the flanks and rear of the main body, they could protect against attacks by enemy cavalry and/or *psiloi*. However, the superior mobility of cavalry best suited it to this role, and only it could provide proper protection against the threat from other cavalry; light infantrymen were too slow. A further advantage lay in the faster rate of movement possible: hoplites protected by cavalry could move in a column rather than in the slower battle or square formations. It is not surprising then that the use of cavalry as a protective screen on the march became relatively common, at least with the more professional generals.

The tactics used when a hoplite column was attacked (whether in the advance or the sustained withdrawal) involved keeping enemy troops outside arrow or javelin range by charging out, or threatening to charge out, at them.[75] There seems to have been considerable flexibility in the positioning of cavalry to achieve this, but, as might be expected, the deciding factor was the

[74] Ibid. 3. 3. 16–20.
[75] On the ranges of ancient bows and javelins see Lawrence, *Fortification*, 39–40; Gardiner, *JHS* 27 (1907), 249–73; Harris, *G&R* 10 (1963), 26–36; W. McLeod, 'The Range of the Ancient Bow', *Phoenix*, 19 (1965), 1–14, esp. 8 and 'The Range of the Ancient Bow: Addenda', *Phoenix*, 26 (1972), 78–82.

perceived enemy threat. During their withdrawal from Kounaxa, for example, the cavalry of the Ten Thousand (commanded by the Athenian Lykios), is recorded only at the rear of the column. However, once Thrace was reached and the threat to the rear had passed, it was apparently switched to the van.[76] In other cases the cavalry appears only in the van, but if the direction of the threat was uncertain and an army possessed sufficient cavalry (unlike the Ten Thousand whose force of fifty was too small to divide), then it could be split to protect both the front and rear.[77] This was possible because the cavalry's mobility allowed it to be moved rapidly from one end of a column to the other in response to a changing threat.

The split organization and the facility for rapid redeployment are well illustrated by Agesilaos' return to Greece in 394. Fresh from a victorious Asian campaign, and accompanied by a cavalry force which had been trained to a high standard,[78] the Spartan King made an opposed crossing of Thessaly. This was always a difficult operation because the Thessalian cavalry was both skilled and numerous.[79] When, inevitably, the local cavalry attacked, Agesilaos' infantry was marching in a square formation with the cavalry equally divided between the van and the rear. As the Thessalian threat to the rear became pressing, Agesilaos redeployed most of the cavalry from the front of his army to reinforce his rearguard. Shortly afterwards, with a little prodding from him and with the arrival of the remainder of the horse, the rearguard successfully attacked the enemy cavalry and drove it from the field. Agesilaos was particularly pleased by this success as the Thessalian cavalry had the reputation of being the best in Greece.[80]

However, many advances were unopposed and more numerous examples of cavalry protecting a marching column can be found when armies were withdrawing. The classic example, discussed above, is the retreat of the Ten Thousand across Asia Minor, but on another occasion Olynthian cavalry serving with Agesilaos

[76] Xen. *Anab.* 6. 3. 10, 22. When the famous shout was raised on reaching the sea the cavalry was in the rear (4. 7. 22–4).

[77] The van: Xen. *Hell.* 3. 4. 13; *Anab.* 6. 3. 10, 22; 7. 3. 43; *Kyrop.* 6. 3. 2. Split: *Hell.* 4. 3. 4.

[78] Xen. *Hell.* 3. 4. 15–16.

[79] Cf. Thucy. 4. 78–9, explaining how Brasidas tricked his way through in 424.

[80] Xen. *Hell.* 4. 3. 4–9; cf. *Ages.* 2. 2–4 and Plut. *Ages.* 16. 5.

beat off peltasts in the pay of Thebes. In 368/7 Epameinondas achieved the same result against the harassing attacks of Alexander of Pherai.[81] However, if cavalry was to be successful in this it had to be used aggressively and this did not always occur. Even Agesilaos' cavalry needed some prompting before it engaged the enemy during the Thessalian march mentioned earlier and, in the second case just cited, the Thebans were in considerable difficulty until Epameinondas was promoted in the field and changed their tactics. An Argive attempt to discourage Phleiasian attacks by posting their entire cavalry (with supporting infantry) as the rearguard, failed miserably when sixty Phleiasian cavalry routed it with a charge,[82] apparently because the Argives remained static instead of using their mobility to keep the enemy at a distance.

These incidents highlight the need for a skilfully led and determined cavalry if a column of hoplites was to be protected adequately and this is confirmed by the action at Lechaion.[83] Here, a *mora* of Spartan infantry was ambushed by peltasts on its way back from escorting other hoplites part of the way home to Sparta for a festival. The *mora* had turned back just short of Sikyon but their mounted troops had continued with the festival contingent. As the *mora* passed Lechaion they were attacked by Athenians based in Corinth who thought, correctly, that Iphikrates' peltasts would make short work of hoplites without cavalry protection. Although the Spartan hoplites were in serious trouble, their cavalry returned to their aid and, if it had been properly handled, the situation could well have been retrieved. But instead of charging the enemy and forcing them to keep their distance from the infantry, the cavalry 'kept level with the men charging out (*ekdromoi*), both in the pursuit and when turning back again'. Although the presence of Athenian hoplites nearby may have been an inhibiting factor, Xenophon bluntly describes the charge as mismanaged.[84] By restricting its pace to that of the infantry, the Spartan cavalry here completely wasted its advantage of mobility and so allowed the peltasts to keep up the pressure on the *mora* until it broke.

The evidence for Athenian practice in the advance is limited

[81] Xen. *Hell.* 5. 4. 54; Diod. Sic. 15. 71. 4–6.
[82] Xen. *Hell.* 7. 2. 4.
[83] Ibid. 4. 5. 11–17.
[84] Ibid. 4. 5. 16; cf. *MT* 124–6.

during this period, mainly because they tended not to move armies any great distance overland, and when they did so no details are recorded. However, the actions of Athenian officers during the march of the Ten Thousand suggest that they knew of, and used, the standard tactics to protect a column on the move.[85] In addition, the assessment of the situation at Lechaion by Kallias and Iphikrates showed that Athenian commanders were well aware of the vulnerability of hoplites moving without the protection of cavalry or *psiloi*.[86]

As suggested above, in more open terrain a hoplite army could lessen the danger resulting from surprise by marching in battle formation rather than in a column. If it could not do so, advance warning of the enemy's presence was necessary to compensate for the time it took to deploy the army. Because of its mobility, such early warning should logically have been provided by cavalry. In practice however, reconnaissance was often neglected,[87] even though its theoretical need had been accepted by the fourth century. Xenophon, for instance, stated that it was desirable to locate the enemy at some distance whether one were attacking or defending. He also added that a knowledge of the area of operations was important and that a hipparch who knew the routes through it was at a considerable advantage.[88] His writings therefore identified the two essential objects of reconnaissance: information about the enemy and about the terrain.

Despite this, there were several disasters or near disasters in the early fourth century when armies were moved either with no reconnaissance, or with reconnaissance elements insufficiently far forward to give adequate warning. In 391 a column under Thibron, the Spartan commander in Asia, was decimated near Ephesos when surprised by Persian cavalry under Struthas. At the time Thibron seems to have been marching without any properly constituted vanguard or reconnaissance group and was amusing

[85] Apart from Xenophon himself, the first commander of the cavalry contingent was an Athenian, Lykios (App. 5.102; Xen. *Anab.* 3. 3. 20), who remained in charge at least until they reached the Euxine (ibid. 4. 7. 22–4). Other members of the cavalry may also have been Athenian as it chose to stay with Xenophon when the army split up in Thrace (ibid. 6. 2. 16), although by then it was commanded by Timasion (ibid. 6. 3. 14).
[86] Xen. *Hell.* 4. 5. 13.
[87] See *GSAW* i. 127–8 for a list of examples.
[88] Xen. *Hipparch.* 4. 5–6.

himself by throwing the discus. Struthas noted Thibron's general overconfidence and took advantage of his lack of reconnaissance to launch a mounted attack before he could react.[89]

Several years prior to this, Derkylidas, Thibron's predecessor, was rather more fortunate in similar circumstances. During a march from Caria to Ionia in 398/7, and while convinced that the enemy was elsewhere, he unexpectedly met a Persian army already deployed for battle. Sensing disaster, many of his Ionian troops simply ran, but Derkylidas was able to deploy the rest of his army. This was due in part to the good discipline of his Peloponnesian troops (and to an apparent lack of discus-throwing), but I suspect also because the Persians were divided over whether or not to attack. This suspicion is reinforced by the fact that a fight was avoided by negotiation and both armies marched away intact.[90]

In more recent times, great emphasis has been placed upon reconnaissance as a means of acquiring that necessary information about the enemy which Major General Fuller has described as 'the foundation of battle'.[91] If this is so, then why did the Greeks often neglect it? One reason is a reliance on other methods of obtaining intelligence. In antiquity, prisoners, spies, deserters, and traitors, were all regarded as prime sources of tactical information, whereas in modern mobile operations information from such sources rapidly loses its value.[92]

Xenophon, for example, advocated enlisting spies before the outbreak of war and both Ephialtes, the traitor at Thermopylai, and later the exiled Athenian general Alkibiades, provided important military and topographical information to an enemy state.[93] The importance of such sources is reflected in the emphasis placed on the spy Araspas in Xenophon's fictional account of the planning for the battle of Thymbrara.[94] Details of the terrain

---

[89] Xen. *Hell.* 4. 8. 18–19. Although Xenophon's account mentions τοὺς πρώτους (which Warner translates as 'advance party', Penguin (1979), 235) the discus-throwing, the general disorder of the army, and the associated lack of orders all suggest that this phrase refers simply to the leading elements of the army rather than to a true vanguard.

[90] Xen. *Hell.* 3. 2. 14–20.

[91] J. F. C. Fuller, *Armoured Warfare* (London, 1943), 54.

[92] Ibid. 62.

[93] Xen. *Hipparch.* 4. 7. Ephialtes: Hdtos 7. 213–18; Akibiades: Thucy. 6. 74. 1, 88. 10 ff.

[94] Xen. *Kyrop.* 6. 3. 14 ff.

could also be gained from personal knowledge—Xenophon suggests that the hipparch should familiarize himself with both friendly and potentially hostile countries even in times of peace.[95] Xenophon's emphasis on reconnaissance or personal knowledge in both his personal practice and in his writings shows that he did not regard other sources as a substitute for reconnaissance,[96] but other commanders may well have done so.

However, apart from personal knowledge of the terrain (which is not always available or up to date) there are considerable disadvantages involved in neglecting reconnaissance and securing military intelligence by means of spies, deserters, or traitors. All could be unreliable and Xenophon mentions the usefulness of sham deserters,[97] presumably amongst other things to spread misinformation. Sinon's classic role at Troy must have been a prominent reminder of this stratagem and a variant of this occurred in 413, during the Sicilian campaign, when Hermokrates delayed Nikias' withdrawal overnight by a false message.[98] In addition, as Xenophon points out, spies and traitors could not always communicate information in time for it to be acted upon.[99]

Reconnaissance would seem at the very least necessary to supplement these alternative methods, and would often be the only available source of information about the countryside or the enemy. The use of other information sources then is insufficient by itself to explain why armies moved without scouts. Another possible factor is a distrust of their reports, but the main reason for the lack of reconnaissance was probably the nature of hoplite warfare and the conservatism it tended to engender in its generals.[100]

---

[95] Xen. *Hipparch.* 4. 6. This practice was followed by von Moltke, who toured France two years prior to the Franco-Prussian War of 1870, Denison, *History of Cavalry*, 37. It was also regularly adopted by post-war Russian armoured commanders who rode as 'co-drivers' in lorries travelling around Western Europe, M. G. Welham and B. Quarrie, *Operation Spetsnaz* (Wellingborough, 1989), 94–5.

[96] See Xen. *Anab.* 6. 3. 10–11; *Hipparch.* 4. 4–5, 16.

[97] Xen. *Hipparch.* 4. 7; see also Frontinus, *Strategemata*, 2. 5. 18.

[98] Thucy. 7. 73. 3–74. 1. *GSAW* i. 127 unfairly criticizes Nikias' failure to test this by reconnaissance—this was unlikely to have occurred to many Greek generals and, even if it had, the circumstances here would have made it seem suicidal to the generals and, more importantly, to the soldiers who had to be persuaded to go. This may be the sort of ruse Xenophon has in mind at *Hipparch.* 5. 8.

[99] Xen. *Hipparch.* 4. 8.

[100] On the effect of hoplite predominance on the use of other arms, see Ch. 4; *GSAW* i. 132–3; P. Green, *The Shadow of the Parthenon* (London, 1972), 32.

The most dangerous threat to an army marching in column was an encounter with hostile forces already deployed. Because of the relative slowness of communicating orders by runner, or even by dispatch rider, and because of the length of marching columns, deployment times could be long.[101] It was apparently not unknown for less experienced commanders who had descended on to a plain, to look back and mistake the rear of their column, still in the hills, for the enemy. This sometimes resulted in the commander launching the head of the column against his own troops in the rear![102] A good example of the time it took to deploy an ancient army is Kounaxa, where Cyrus' army needed several hours to manœuvre from the line of march. The Persian commander was first informed of the enemy's approach 'about mid-morning' (ἀμφὶ ἀγορὰν πλήθουσαν) but by the time the army had deployed it was about 'midday' (μέσον ἡμέρας)—even though the manœuvre was carried out 'with all speed' (σὺν πολλῇ σπουδῇ).[103] However, as most hoplite engagements in Greece were restricted to the plains, encounter battles of the type discussed above were comparatively rare. The main likelihood of being surprised therefore probably lay more with two marching columns running into each other, as the Thebans and Spartans did at Tegyra in 375.[104] If this did occur, then in theory the slow march rate and lengthy deployment time would be equally disadvantageous to both sides.

So, as long as wars consisted of hoplite clashes on plains and surprise would normally affect both sides equally, the practice of reconnaissance may well have seemed unnecessary. If any solution was sought to this problem it was probably initially in the area of modifying march formations (as was the case with the Ten

[101] F. Maurice, 'The Size of the Army of Xerxes in the Invasion of Greece 480 BC', *JHS* 50 (1930), 229 estimates that 10,000 spearmen with good march discipline would form a column (excluding baggage) about 6 miles long. The 3rd ALH Brigade took 3 hours to pass a fixed point according to an observer in Palestine in 1918, C. Falls, *Military Operations Egypt and Palestine from June 1917 to the end of the War*, i (London, 1930), 373.
[102] Onasander, 6. 5.
[103] Xen. *Anab*. 1. 8. 1–8.
[104] Plut. *Pelop*. 17. 1 ff. For the date of the battle see Diod. Sic. 15. 37. See also *MT* 164, 312 n. 46—although the man who first reported the enemy's approach need not necessarily have been a scout as stated there. Plutarch's account does not specify this and he could perhaps have been a member of the front rank of the column.

Thousand) rather than by providing advance warning. Until commanders became convinced of its utility, the theory and practice of reconnaissance was bound to remain undeveloped. The examples of Thibron and Derkylidas, and the battle of Tegyra, show that the old habits lasted well into the fourth century, despite an apparent increase in the use of reconnaissance in this period.

This increase is illustrated by the actions of several commanders from different states. At the end of the fifth century, for example, Xenophon used cavalry to scout ahead of his section of the Ten Thousand in Thrace—even before he learned of the attack on the Arkadian contingent. He also continued this practice until the army was reunited, at which time Seuthes' Thracian cavalry took over this role.[105] The Spartan King Agesilaos too used scouts while campaigning in Asia at the start of the fourth century, and the evidence suggests that this was Alexander's usual practice.[106] Unfortunately, the number of examples which mention cavalry scouts is relatively small. This is partly because in some instances the terrain precluded their use,[107] but it mainly results from a lack of detailed march descriptions in our sources. However, their existence is confirmed by Onasander and by several passages in Xenophon, all of which mention προ(δι)ερευνώμενοι or διερευνώμενοι cavalrymen.[108]

The Greek here means 'searching out before' and 'searching' respectively, which strongly suggests that the troops described had a reconnaissance function—despite Pritchett's contention that they were a vanguard not a scouting force.[109] In modern usage, the main function of a vanguard is to provide physical security to the main body, but it is debatable whether the troops described by Onasander were actually intended to destroy enemy ambushers. First, they are described as 'searching the road' (διερευνωμένους τὰς ὁδούς) and second, Onasander's discussion centres around

---

[105] Xen. *Anab.* 6. 3. 10–11; for Seuthes see 7. 3. 40–4.
[106] Agesilaos: Xen. *Hell.* 3. 4. 13; Alexander: Arr. *Anab.* 1. 12. 7; 3. 7. 7.
[107] Xen. *Anab.* 6. 3. 15; *Hell.* 3. 2. 15; *Kyrop.* 6. 3. 2.
[108] Onasander, 6. 7–8. Xen. *Kyrop.* 5. 4. 4; *Lak. Pol.* 13. 6; *Hipparch.* 4. 5.
[109] *GSAW* i. 128–9. His argument is based on a very rigid definition of the word 'scout' which is at variance with modern military practice and terminology. Today a scout is someone who moves at the head of a force and who is tasked with providing advance warning of enemy activities or of any aspects of the terrain which will affect the move.

the detection not the destruction of enemy ambuscades. Cavalry would in any case be unsuitable for attacking infantry in ambush positions in the type of broken or wooded terrain in which Onasander suggests these scouts be used. In addition, Xenophon uses the terms προδιερευνησομένους and διερευνωμένους to describe cavalry patently operating in the reconnaissance role.[110] The phrase προ(δι)ερευνώμενοι or διερευνώμενοι ἱππεῖς therefore probably refers to cavalry acting as scouts.

The existence of *prodromoi*, attested around 365, certainly suggests that the principle of scouting ahead was recognized and applied within the Athenian cavalry itself.[111] By analogy with the role of their Macedonian namesakes, and as they were equipped with javelins and not *kamakes* (and therefore perhaps more suited to reconnaissance than close-quarter combat), these troops were highly likely to have been scouts. Their function, if this was the case, was presumably to provide the phylarch with his own integral scouting force to ride ahead of the squadron on the march.[112]

The development of reconnaissance as a cavalry task during this period can best be explained by Greek involvement in Asia Minor, and by the different conditions pertaining there. Modern sources rightly stress the particular need for intelligence gathering in more mobile operations,[113] and this was the type of warfare which was the norm in Asia. Here, larger distances and the associated emphasis on cavalry increased the need for advance knowledge of both terrain and enemy. This was particularly important for Greeks, who presumably often lacked local knowledge (or perhaps even access to local knowledge); such information was best provided by reconnaissance.

The evidence therefore suggests that, while generals still occasionally neglected the basic precautions of route reconnaissance and of protecting a body of hoplites on the march, there was an increasing use of cavalry in these roles in the fourth

---

[110] Xen. *Kyrop*. 5. 4. 4 (MSS D and F have προερευνησομένους, E. C. Marchant, OCT) and *Hipparch*. 4. 5.

[111] Xen. *Hipparch*. 1. 25.

[112] On the *prodromoi* see *GSAW* i. 130–1; there may have been five from each *phyle*, cf. Sekunda, *AG* 44. For the Macedonian *prodromoi* see Hammond and Griffith, 411–13.

[113] Luttwak, *Dictionary of Modern War*, 163, s.v. reconnaissance; Fuller, *Armoured Warfare*, 54–63.

century—particularly by experienced commanders. Additionally, although there are few direct examples of Athenian usage, it seems likely that Athens also adopted those techniques (especially march security) which were fairly commonly used by other states. The theoretical knowledge was available in Xenophon's writing and there was a pool of men experienced in these tasks among Athenian veterans of the anabasis and other Asian campaigns. Finally, as noted above, the existence of *prodromoi* within the Athenian cavalry shows that, at that level at least, the principle of scouting ahead of a moving body of troops was well understood and catered for by the structure of the cavalry corps.

The Battle

A Greek battle of the classical period normally had three parts: the deployment, the infantry clash, and the pursuit/withdrawal. Cavalry had the potential to perform several tasks during all three. Its involvement in the first of these phases could include reconnoitring the battlefield, observing the enemy's camp, and covering the deployment of friendly troops. During the infantry clash, the cavalry's main role was protecting their own infantry and attacking the enemy foot. In the pursuit/withdrawal phase the cavalry could either exploit a victory by pursuing the enemy or, if on the losing side, could attempt to minimize casualties among friendly troops by protecting their withdrawal.

Although cavalry had the potential to play an important part in the preliminaries to a battle, this phase is often neglected by our sources, which tend to concentrate on what happened once the opposing armies were deployed to fight. For example, the only recorded battlefield reconnaissance by Greek cavalry is the inspection of Gaugamela by the Macedonians[114] and, as noted, even here the cavalry should probably be regarded more as an escort to Alexander. There is better evidence, however, for the use of horsemen to observe an enemy encampment. Although armies in close proximity were often unaware of each other's activities,[115] on other occasions a close watch was kept on the enemy. This was frequently done by infantry, particularly when a high vantage

[114] Arr. *Anab*. 3. 9. 5.
[115] *GSAW* i. 127–8.

point was used or where concealing horses was a problem,[116] but there are cases where cavalry were employed. At Katane in 415 the Syracusan cavalry conducted regular missions to check on (and insult) the Athenians, and presumably did the same outside their own city in 413.[117] Xenophon also suggested that the hipparch should personally watch the enemy so he could exploit any errors, and advocated the use of observation posts for the purpose.[118]

The evidence is much better for the employment of cavalry during the infantry clash which formed the main part of the battle. Its main task here was the provision of security to the hoplites. The phalanx was basically designed to resist a frontal attack and protection from this direction was good—except for the unfortunate man on the extreme right of the front rank whose body was partially exposed.[119] The phalanx was therefore mainly vulnerable to attack from the flank or rear, and particularly on the unshielded right flank.[120]

The Spartans capitalized on this at Nemea in 394, at Corinth in 392, and (perhaps unintentionally) at Mantineia in 418.[121] They may also have intended to do so at Leuktra in 371 but were outmanœuvred by Epameinondas.[122] However, for much of the hoplite era Sparta was the only state whose hoplite army was drilled to a level where tactical movement was practicable on the battlefield. They alone are described as turning part of their formation through ninety degrees in order to take an enemy in the flank.[123]

---

[116] Vantage points: *GSAW* i. 129–30; hidden observation posts: Xen. *Hipparch.* 4. 10–11. As Xenophon pointed out, concealment could be important—what little warning Derkylidas received at Daskylion came from the sighting of the Persian scouts prominently posted on burial mounds, Xen. *Hell.* 3. 2. 14–15.

[117] Thucy. 6. 63. 3; 7. 4. 6. The Persians did the same at Thermopylai, Hdtos 7. 208.

[118] Xen. *Hipparch.* 4. 10–12, 16.

[119] Thucy. 5. 71. 1.

[120] This was a contributing factor in the Athenian defeat at Amphipolis, Thucy. 5. 10. 3–8 and formed part of the Athenian plan at Lechaion, Xen. *Hell.* 4. 5. 13; see also Onasander, 19. 2. This vulnerability had been exploited in fortress design from very early times, Lawrence, *Fortification*, 304–9.

[121] *MT* 141 ff., 398–9.

[122] Ibid. 198–218, esp. 216.

[123] *MT* 398–9 has a clear diagram of how this may have been executed at Nemea. The *epilektoi* of other states may have been capable of similar manoeuvres, but not whole armies, and the Theban oblique attack was less complicated in terms of the drill required.

Although most armies were incapable of such manœuvres close to the enemy, a flank attack by a separate body of troops was always possible. Any such attack, though, was more likely to employ cavalry (whose mobility and flexibility particularly suited them for this task) than hoplites, all of whom were normally placed in the phalanx to give it more weight. This is exemplified by the second battle at Syracuse in 414 where the Spartan commander Gylippos routed the Athenians with a mounted assault on their exposed left flank. They had already been on the receiving end of a similar attack at Delion ten years earlier.[124]

Therefore, whenever possible, and particularly when outnumbered in cavalry, Greek practice was to protect the flanks by means of natural or man-made obstacles.[125] The latter included the placing of cavalry or (less effectively) light troops on the wings. These could deal with enemy cavalry, *psiloi*, or even hoplites engaged in a flank attack. Although not intended as a solid physical barrier to hoplites, by striking at the flank or rear of the attacking force cavalry could discourage or even prevent a flank attack. Sometimes the mere presence of a force positioned to threaten the enemy in this way was sufficient to inhibit any tactical manœuvring. Xenophon states that at Mantineia Epameinondas specifically placed a body of cavalry (supported by hoplites) to prevent the Athenians from aiding their allies on the right. This is the only explicit statement of such a motive, but similar blocking forces are mentioned at Potidaia in 432 and at Delion in 424.[126]

Positioning the cavalry on the wings could therefore provide a high level of flank protection, but horsemen could also be used more aggressively to eliminate the threat by driving the enemy cavalry from the field. With this tactic, the cavalry was sometimes drawn up in front of the foot rather than on the wings, in order to ensure that the enemy horse was neutralized before the hoplites met. This was normally done when one side wished to capitalize on their cavalry superiority by destroying the enemy horse and thus isolating its infantry. This is the reason given for the deployment of the cavalry in front of the army by the Athenian com-

[124] Thucy. 4. 96; 7. 6. 2–3.
[125] Cf. Thucy. 6. 66. 1; Xen. *Anab*. 1. 8. 13.
[126] Xen. *Hell*. 7. 5. 24; Thucy. 1. 62. 3–4; 4. 93. 2–3.

mander of the Greek forces at Krannon.[127] Pelopidas also took advantage of the size and quality of his horse to do the same at Kynoskephalai in 364.[128]

In addition, as some generals realized, defeating the enemy cavalry in front of its own army before the infantry engaged could have other benefits. Xenophon states that the Theban general Epameinondas chose this disposition at Mantineia precisely because he expected the enemy cavalry to lose and thought that the sight of this would cause the hoplites to flee as well.[129] There was also the possibility, of which Leuktra provides an instance, that cavalry defeated in front of its infantry might be forced back on to them, thereby disrupting the phalanx before the battle proper began.[130] The theory here was sound and the rewards for success high, but so were the risks involved in failure. Deploying the cavalry on the wings on the other hand not only provided flank protection but allowed it to happily engage the enemy's cavalry without getting in the way of the hoplites. In short, the traditional tactic of deploying the cavalry on the wings was easier, probably safer, and required less thought from the commander. Not surprisingly, it was the preferred option for most generals.[131] Athenian *strategoi* were no exception to this; they deployed their cavalry on the wings at Delion and had it with them on the left wing at Mantineia (418).[132] They almost certainly did the same at Spartolos, Syracuse, and Nemea,[133] and probably also at Solygeia.

However, there were occasional exceptions to this, and in at least one engagement, and possibly in two, cavalry under Athenian command was placed in front of the infantry. This is attested for

[127] Diod. Sic. 18. 17. 2–4; unfortunately for the allies the Macedonian general, Antipater, successfully countered by leading his infantry against the Greek foot while the cavalry was still engaged.
[128] Plut. *Pelop.* 32. 2.
[129] Xen. *Hell.* 7. 5. 24. Note the alternative explanation in Frontinus, *Strategemata*, 2. 2. 12; cf. Polyainos, 2. 3. 14.
[130] Xen. *Hell.* 6. 4. 13. Cf. Plut. *Arat.* 37. 2–3 and the battle of Issos, *HMND* 65–6.
[131] See *GSAW* ii. 193–9, table 8, for a list of examples.
[132] Thucy. 4. 94. 1; 5. 67. 2.
[133] Thucy. 2. 79. 3 suggests that the cavalry and infantry engaged simultaneously at Spartolos and if so the horse cannot have been in front of the foot. At Syracuse the enemy cavalry was on the flank (Thucy. 7. 6. 2) so presumably any Athenian cavalry was also positioned there. At Nemea the infantry apparently opened the fighting, Xen. *Hell.* 4. 2. 20.

PLATE 1. Cavalry training: mounting with spear. *Munich 2639 (vase 28, exterior - A). Courtesy, Staatliche Antikensammlungen und Glyptothek, Munich.*

PLATE 2. Cavalryman in combat. *Athens, NM 3708 (relief 27). Courtesy, TAPA.*

PLATE 3. Cavalry inspection (*dokimasia*). *Berlin F 2296 (vase 32, exterior). Courtesy, Antikenmuseum Berlin, Staatliche Museen Preußischer Kulturbesitz.*

PLATE 4. Cavalry inspection (*dokimasia*). *Berlin F 2296 (vase 32, exterior). Courtesy, Antikenmuseum Berlin, Staatliche Museen Preußischer Kulturbesitz.*

PLATE 5. Mounted archer (*hippotoxotes*). *Berlin F 2296 (vase 32, interior). Courtesy, Antikenmuseum Berlin, Staatliche Museen Preußischer Kulturbesitz.*

PLATE 6. 'Gina', Ypres Salient, AD 1917. *Courtesy, The Tank Museum, Royal Armoured Corps Centre, Bovington.*

PLATE 7. Chair seat. *London, BM E 3 (vase 11, interior). Courtesy, Trustees of the British Museum.*

PLATE 8. Mounted javelin event (Panathenaic Games). *Panathenaic Prize-amphora, first half of the fourth century. London, BM 1903.2-17.1. Courtesy, Trustees of the British Museum.*

PLATE 9. Panaitios relief. *Athens, NM 884 (relief 20). Courtesy, TAPA.*

PLATE 10. *Hamippos* and cavalryman. *Louvre 744 (relief 32). Courtesy, Réunion des musées nationaux, Paris.*

PLATE 11. Dexileos relief.
*Kerameikos P 1130 (relief
12). Courtesy, DAI
Athens (neg. Ker. 5976).*

PLATE 12. Pythodoros
relief. *Eleusis 5101 (relief
30). Courtesy, DAI
Athens (neg. Eleusis 534).*

PLATE 13. State monument, Corinthian campaign, 394/3. *Athens, NM 2744 (relief 25). Courtesy, TAPA.*

PLATE 14. Dismounted hipparch. *Leiden PC 93 (vase 42, interior). Courtesy, Rijksmuseum van Oudheden, Leiden.*

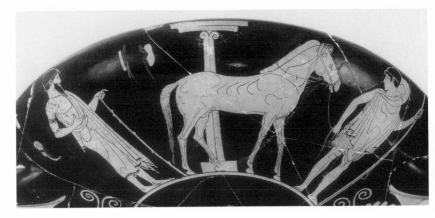

PLATE 15. Young cavalryman. *Leiden PC 93 (vase 42, exterior - A). Courtesy, Rijksmuseum van Oudheden, Leiden.*

PLATE 16. Negro groom relief. *Athens, NM 4464 (relief 28). Courtesy, TAPA.*

Krannon in 322 and may also have occurred at the second battle of Lamia in the same year.[134] Here too the allied forces were apparently relying on their cavalry and as the mounted engagement began the action, the horse may well have been in front of the army and not on the flanks. Unfortunately, it is impossible to know whether these dispositions originated from Antiphilos, the Athenian in supreme command, or from Menon, the Thessalian, who led the cavalry,[135] although the former is perhaps more likely.

The evidence strongly suggests that the *hippeis* were posted in the rear at Mounychia. They cannot have been on the wings because of the built-up terrain, they did not open the battle and so were not in front of the foot, and, as the victorious democrats abandoned their pursuit on reaching level ground, the cavalry was probably deployed there.[136] Because of the special conditions pertaining to Mounychia, and to Lamia and Krannon (where the cavalry was three thousand five hundred strong),[137] they are most probably atypical. However, along with the non-Athenian examples discussed earlier, they do show that Greek commanders sometimes varied the disposition of their cavalry according to circumstance and did not always follow the normal practice of deploying them on the wings.

The offensive use of cavalry against the enemy infantry was less common than the defensive use just examined, but could have a profound effect on the outcome of a battle. I have already discussed the vulnerability of a hoplite phalanx's flanks and there are at least four occasions where cavalry was used to mount a flank attack—Delion, Syracuse, Mantineia (362), and an action in Illyria (against peltasts operating in formation) c.359. At Delion in 424, the Theban commander dispatched two squadrons of horse around the back of a hill to take the Athenians in the left flank. When these appeared unexpectedly, the Athenians, fearing they were the advance guard of another army, panicked and fled. A decade later at Syracuse the local cavalry put the Athenians to

[134] Diod. Sic. 18. 15, 17.

[135] Ibid. 18. 13. 6, 15. 4, 17. 6. For Antiphilos' career see *PA* 1264.

[136] Xen. *Hell*. 2. 4. 10–19. This seems a much more plausible explanation for the lack of a real pursuit than the literary motive suggested in V. Gray, *The Character of Xenophon's* Hellenica (London, 1989), 100–3.

[137] Diod. Sic. 18. 15. 2.

flight by means of a direct charge against the left flank.[138] The Thebans also used their cavalry against the flanks of the enemy at Mantineia in 362, after they had driven the opposing cavalry from the field, and Philip II of Macedon ordered his cavalry against the flanks and rear of an Illyrian army about three years later.[139] All these actions involved non-Athenian troops but the Athenians were aware of these tactics (particularly, and no doubt painfully so, after Delion and Syracuse) and possibly made use of them on occasion. For example, Hippokrates deployed his cavalry on the wings at Delion, but left three hundred *hippeis* at the temple both as a guard 'and to look out for the opportunity to attack the Boiotians during the battle'. While this could allow several courses of action, it could easily include attacking the enemy flank. At any rate, the Thebans considered this force so threatening that they posted a contingent to prevent its moving against them.[140]

Although the details of the battle are rather sketchy, another possible example is Solygeia. Here the Athenians were landed by sea and almost immediately engaged by the Corinthians. The cavalry did not apparently open the battle and so was not placed in front of the hoplites and, as the Corinthians had no cavalry, the 200 *hippeis* can only have been used against the enemy foot. Because it decided the outcome, it seems highly likely that the Athenian cavalry was used against the enemy flanks, or perhaps solely against the right (unshielded) flank which suffered the heaviest casualties in the engagement.[141]

Cavalry could also be used to disrupt the enemy formation with missile-fire, particularly when it was negotiating an obstacle. In addition, on several occasions cavalry destroyed the cohesion of phalanxes which had successfully resisted attacks by other hoplites. The Athenians twice fell victim to such tactics in the Chalkidike in the latter half of the fifth century. At Spartolos in 429, the two thousand Athenian hoplites who had beaten the opposing foot were defeated by the enemy cavalry and *psiloi* who had turned on them after neutralizing the 200 Athenian *hippeis* present. Thucydides remarks that it was the enemy horse which

[138] Thucy. 4. 96. 5–6 (Delion); 7. 6. 2–3 (Syracuse).
[139] Diod. Sic. 15. 85. 7; 16. 4. 5.
[140] Thucy. 4. 93. 2–3.
[141] Ibid. 4. 42–4.

was largely responsible for the ensuing rout, in which the Athenians lost 430 men, all the *strategoi* present, and the phylarch Menexenos (Appendix 5.116).[142] In a similar situation in 422, the Athenian right wing at Amphipolis managed to beat off several of Klearidas' infantry attacks before succumbing to the enemy cavalry and *psiloi*.[143] Pelopidas too won the battle of Kynoskephalai in 364 with a cavalry charge against the enemy foot which was withdrawing step by step under heavy pressure from his infantry. Later still, at Siris in Italy, Pyrrhos finished off the Romans with a cavalry attack when they wavered under the onslaught of his infantry and elephants.[144] A similar, but less bloody, result was achieved by Seleukos at the battle of Ipsos in 301. He exploited the absence of the enemy horse (which was still in hot pursuit of part of his own army) by repeatedly sending his cavalry around his opponent's phalanx and threatening to attack, until part of it deserted to him and ended the battle.[145]

These are excellent examples of the ability of cavalry to achieve victory even when their own heavy infantry had failed to break the enemy formation. However, the overriding impression given by contemporary descriptions of hoplite battles is that cavalry generally fought cavalry and/or provided the infantry with flank protection. It is also interesting that nearly half of the examples of the offensive use of cavalry in battle are from the fifth century. Excluding the developments under Philip and Alexander of Macedon, the fourth century apparently saw no major innovations in the battlefield support of hoplites other than deploying cavalry in front of the foot.

One of the most important tasks of the cavalry when the pursuit/withdrawal phase succeeded the infantry clash was the exploitation of victory. As outlined earlier, hoplites were vulnerable out of formation and in a rout their heavier equipment slowed them down making them fairly easy prey for cavalry.[146] Although referring to a much later period, perhaps the most graphic expression of the vulnerability of fleeing troops to cavalry is Cromwell's comment after the battle of Gainsborough in AD

[142] Ibid. 2. 79; Isaios, 5. 42.

[143] Thucy. 5. 10. 9–10.

[144] Plut. *Pelop.* 32. 3–7; *Pyrr.* 17. 3.

[145] Plut. *Dem.* 29. 3. This incident aptly demonstrates the moral dominance of cavalry in the period of Alexander and the *diadochoi* mentioned earlier.

[146] See 'combat potential', Ch. 2.

1643. Having described how the enemy horse was routed and fled, he adds 'our (cavalry) men pursuing them, had chase and execution about five or six miles';[147] the 'execution' would presumably have been far greater against a dismounted foe. The use of *hippeis* in the pursuit became increasingly important with the growing tendency to try to inflict maximum casualties rather than simply to drive the enemy from the field. A purely hoplite force could only engage in a limited pursuit as its members were hampered by their equipment, and by the need to retain some semblance of formation.

Infantry pursuits then were of limited value and, even though hoplite clashes could produce heavy casualties, it was still basically true of Greece that, as General Marmont remarked, 'a battle won without cavalry does not afford a decisive result'.[148] It is also quite clear from Xenophon that this concept was familiar to Greek soldiers. He points out that the Greek survivors of Kounaxa believed that the enemy's cavalry superiority meant that, even if the Greeks won, they would not kill many Persians, whereas if they lost they would be slaughtered to a man.[149]

Whether success during the main clash was achieved by the infantry or by the cavalry, it was frequently exploited by a mounted pursuit. Xenophon's comment about the lack of a determined follow-up at Mantineia in 362[150] suggests that by that date pursuit was a standard procedure, the omission of which required explanation. Cavalry pursuits were used by the Spartans, Thebans, Thessalians, Timoleon, and Demetrios Poliorketes ('the Besieger').[151] These pursuits, however, were of short duration and should not be confused with the sustained ones made by Alexander or by more modern cavalry forces. As Hammond points out, such pursuits (which in modern times were designed to effect the disintegration of the enemy's military structure) were 'alien to earlier Greek warfare'.[152] The normal conditions of

[147] Quoted in P. Young, *The Fighting Man* (London, 1981), 100.
[148] Cited in *GMAW* 52.
[149] Xen. *Anab*. 3. 1. 2; Klearchos, their general, believed this too, ibid. 2. 4. 6.
[150] Xen. *Hell*. 7. 5. 25.
[151] Spartans: *Hell. Oxy*. 6. 4; Xen. *Hell*. 7. 1. 31. Thebans (and Thessalians): Plut. *Pelop*. 32. 7. Thessalians: Hdtos 5. 63. Timoleon: Diod. Sic. 16. 79. 5–80. 2. Demetrios Poliorketes: Plut. *Dem*. 29. 3. Other examples of cavalry involved, or probably involved, in a pursuit by the entire army include Xen. *Hell*. 3. 4. 24; 4. 6. 10–11; Diod. Sic. 16. 4. 6–7.
[152] N. G. L. Hammond, 'A Note on "Pursuit" in Arrian', *CQ* 28 (1978), 138.

Greek hoplite combat did not permit sustained chases lasting several days and covering hundreds of miles, simply because most battles were fought fairly near to walled cities which could serve as a refuge for the beaten troops. Cavalry pursuits in a hoplite context were probably designed to keep the enemy quiet for as long as possible by inflicting maximum casualties upon him with minimum losses to the pursuing force. Alexander, on the other hand, was trying to win a kingdom by removing the occupant of the throne. This could best be effected by securing his person rather than by simply beating his army, and Alexander was therefore prepared to press the chase for long distances and at some cost to his men and horses.[153]

There are only two recorded instances of the Athenian cavalry engaging in a pursuit, but this is hardly surprising as they had little opportunity to do so for most of the period in question. Of the twenty-one battles listed in Table 5, the Athenian cavalry were on the victorious side only eight times. For two of these (Delphi and the second battle of Lamia), the cavalry could not be used because of the terrain,[154] no details are known for three others (Tamynai, Plataia, and the first battle of Lamia), and they did pursue at Abydos and at Kerata, both in 409.[155] There was no determined pursuit for the last battle, Solygeia in 425, but there were valid reasons for this. With the exception of the right wing, the Corinthian army retired in good order and as the Athenian horses had been landed by sea they may not have been up to a vigorous pursuit. In addition, the men certainly would not have wished to stray too far from their ships—especially as they had only faced half of the Corinthian army, the rest of which was nearby at Kenchreiai.[156]

While cavalry was deadly in the pursuit, it could also be used to protect defeated hoplites who were trying to extricate themselves from the battlefield. In fact, mounted troops were often the only means available to minimize casualties during a rout. Although there are isolated instances of a defeated phalanx re-forming and successfully turning on its pursuers (as the Mantineians

[153] Arr. *Anab.* 3. 15. 6, 21. 3 ff.
[154] Pausanias, 10. 21. 2.
[155] Xen. *Hell.* 1. 2. 16 (Abydos); Diod. Sic. 13. 65. 1–2 (Kerata; the pursuit was directed at only part of the enemy).
[156] Thucy. 4. 42. 4, 44. 1–2.

did at Orchomenos in 370),[157] once a phalanx lost cohesion the situation was extremely difficult to retrieve. Xenophon implies that it was only possible to do so in broken country and recommends hunting regularly to develop the requisite skills, but I doubt whether most armies possessed enough men of sufficient ability to perform this feat. The best a resolute hoplite could probably expect in a retreat was perhaps to preserve both honour and life by emulating Sokrates' calm withdrawal at Delion in 424.[158]

The only realistic method of protecting fleeing hoplites was the use of cavalry, but even this was not always possible as the cavalry needed considerable self-discipline not to join in the initial retreat. As Xenophon points out, 'it is very difficult to find men who are willing to stand their ground when they see some of their own (troops) fleeing.'[159] This may explain why the protection of defeated hoplites is recorded less frequently than their pursuit, but it was certainly known and practised by the Greeks. For example, some of the Spartans who escaped the disaster at Lechaion did so by attaching themselves to their cavalry. At Mantineia in 418 the Athenian hoplites were left in a desperate position when their allies collapsed and Thucydides states that if the cavalry had not been there to assist them they would have fared even worse. Some fifty-six years later, at the second battle of Mantineia, the Eleian cavalry commander's timely attack on the Theban horse again saved the Athenian foot from disaster.[160]

The battle of Delion in 424 may provide evidence of Athenian intentions to protect themselves in this way if they lost the infantry clash. Hippokrates' orders to the cavalry at the temple to intervene in the battle as necessary may also have encompassed assisting the hoplites to withdraw if they were worsted. This was certainly the case at Gela in 405 when the Syracusan cavalry was given pre-battle orders to attack the enemy if its own infantry proved victorious, or to protect its own hoplites in the event of defeat.[161] Although the contingent at Delion was unable to

[157] Xen. *Hell.* 6. 5. 13–14; cf. Onasander, 27.
[158] Xen. *On Hunting*, 12. 4–5; Pl. *Symp.* 221a–b.
[159] Xen. *Hell.* 7. 5. 24.
[160] Lechaion: Xen. *Hell.* 4. 5. 17. Mantineia (418): Thucy. 5. 73. 1 (their casualties were also reduced because Agis withdrew his troops to assist his left wing, ibid. 5. 73. 2). Mantineia (362): Diod. Sic. 15. 85. 7.
[161] Diod. Sic. 13. 109. 5.

intervene because of the Theban force assigned to cover it,
Plutarch describes how Alkibiades refused to ride off and stayed
to protect Sokrates' withdrawal.[162] This shows that individual
hippeis at least did assist the infantry during the retreat.

In most cases where the details are available, the cavalry did
not prevent pursuit by interposing itself between the two forces
involved, but instead mounted an attack against the flank or rear
of the pursuers.[163] Xenophon records two such cases in the
Hellenika, the first at Olynthos and the second in the Peloponnese.
In 382 the Olynthian cavalry defeated the Spartan and Boiotian
cavalry on the right wing, causing the infantry there to turn tail
as well. Xenophon claims that the whole army could easily have
been worsted if Derdas' cavalry had not charged for the gates of
Olynthos. Apparently fearing that their line of retreat might be
severed, the Olynthians relinquished the victory and hastily retired to the city. In 370 the Phleiasian cavalry saved some of
Polytropos' mercenary infantry from the Mantineians by threatening the rear of the enemy and forcing them to abandon the
chase.[164]

However, as the battle outside Syracuse in 415 illustrates, a
more direct approach was possible. According to Thucydides,
when the Syracusan hoplite formation was cut in two and fled,
the Athenians could not pursue them far because of the local
cavalry.[165] It charged at any Athenians who were pressing ahead
of the main body, forcing them to follow up in compact formations
and therefore too slowly to kill large numbers of their opponents.
Such tactics were possible because to pursue the enemy successfully a hoplite phalanx also had to abandon its formation. Keeping
in line while running after men who were scattering at some
speed was presumably not only difficult, but would also reduce
the pursuit to the pace of the slowest man.[166] Therefore, breaking
formation to allow for effective exploitation rendered the infantry
vulnerable to mounted attack. Light troops in pursuit were always
at risk from this as they did not often operate in close formation

[162] Plut. *Alk.* 7. 4.
[163] Xen. *Hipparch.* 4. 15 recommends this tactic; see also 8. 15.
[164] Xen. *Hell.* 5. 2. 41–2; 6. 5. 14.
[165] Thucy. 6. 70. 2–3; cf. Plut. *Nik.* 16. 4–5.
[166] Apart from the differences in speed, the excitement of a pursuit would
probably cause any but the most disciplined hoplite to break ranks and charge.

anyway. These examples fully justify the fear of the Ten Thousand that, even if they defeated the Persians in a pitched battle, they could not exploit their victory because of the enemy cavalry.[167] However, like the protection of a marching column, the use of cavalry to protect fleeing hoplites required a disciplined body of horse which was intelligently and aggressively handled. This was not always the case.

CONCLUSIONS

An examination of the ancient evidence shows that cavalry could perform well against even large hoplite formations, but that its full potential was often not realized. The reasons for this (discussed in detail in the next chapter) were not really military in origin. For example, while deficiencies in equestrian equipment made a frontal charge against a hoplite formation extremely difficult, this was not a fatal weakness. As noted in Chapter 2, few, if any, cavalry forces have been able to achieve such charges against disciplined and well-equipped heavy infantry and there were other, more efficient, methods for *hippeis* to deal with a hoplite phalanx. As the examples collected in this chapter show, all the tactics discussed in Chapter 2—flank or rear attack, harassment, and charging a disorganized formation, were effectively used by Greek cavalry at one time or another.

The successful use of cavalry in all phases of hoplite warfare strongly supports the idea that the lack of emphasis on the mounted arm does not result from any inherent deficiency on its part. However, a lack of cavalry numbers sometimes inhibited its full use. This is illustrated by an incident from the struggle for power which followed Alexander the Great's death. The Macedonian Seleukos apparently decided not to attack the troops of Eumenes of Kardia while they crossed a river (normally an excellent time to attack because of the disruption caused during this operation) because he had insufficient cavalry.[168] Even good cavalry could be rendered largely (but not completely) ineffective when greatly outnumbered.[169] Although lack of numbers could,

---

[167] Xen. *Anab.* 3. 1. 2.
[168] Diod. Sic. 19. 13. 3.
[169] Thucy. 2. 100. 5.

in theory at least, be partly compensated for by the use of *psiloi* to perform some of the cavalry functions discussed above, they could not wholly replace cavalry. Cavalry was highly effective against light troops and, because of its superior mobility and endurance, was more useful than *psiloi* except in broken or steep terrain. Athens, for one, anyway possessed no proper *psiloi* prior to 424.[170]

In summary then, the history of Greek cavalry use between *c*.450 and 300 supports the conclusions arising from the discussion of its combat potential: the mounted arm could be extremely useful in all phases of war, whether acting alone or operating in support of hoplites. This also applied to the Athenian cavalry. During the fourth century in particular, Greek cavalry in general was increasingly used in both reconnaissance and combat and, despite gaps in the literary evidence, it appears extremely likely that this was also the case at Athens. In addition, Athens was more likely than most other hoplite states to use her *hippeis* in independent operations, a very noticeable feature of the Peloponnesian War. Athenian cavalry theory, as exemplified by Xenophon's *Hipparchikos*, was heavily influenced by the use of cavalry in independent operations, and yet their main employment, even in the fourth century, continued to be in a subordinate role (see Tables 3–5).

[170] Thucy. 4. 94. 1. See also *HCT* iii. 564–5.

4

The *Hippeis* and Society

So far it has been shown that the combat potential of classical Greek cavalry (including that of the Athenian *hippeis*) was quite high, and that this potential was periodically realized in wartime. The adverse effects deriving from the lack of stirrups and, perhaps more seriously, from fluctuating numbers, are not sufficient to account for cavalry's relatively minor role in fifth- and fourth-century warfare. What does explain this are the principal remaining social influences upon the *hippeis*. In the case of most states, the hoplite domination of Greek military theory and practice held back the development of the cavalry, and this was compounded at Athens by the attitudes of the rest of the citizens towards the cavalry arm and those who served in it.

The domination of Greek military theory and practice by the hoplite arm was a fairly widespread phenomenon, particularly in the developed states south of Thessaly, and caused the cavalry to be regarded as less important than the heavy infantry. There were exceptions, especially Macedonia, Thessaly, and the Greek cities of Sicily and Italy, where there were fewer hoplites, aristocracies tended to dominate, and/or geographical conditions particularly favoured horse-breeding. However, in most states (including democratic Athens) the emphasis on the heavy infantryman hindered the employment and ultimately the development of cavalry. This is not surprising; the hoplite ethos emphasized the virtues of solid dependability and endurance while mounted warfare required its practitioners to possess the rather different attributes of flexibility and speed of thought and reaction.

Apart from the influence of hoplite views, other attitudes which the rest of society held towards the cavalry and cavalrymen also had the potential to exercise a considerable impact upon their efficiency and employment. However, because of the lack of suitable evidence from most states, this can only be identified as an important factor in the case of Athens, and from the early fifth century she was in many ways atypical because of her naval orientation. Despite the fact that this increased the confidence and political influence of the non-hoplite classes there, the hoplite ethos continued to exert considerable influence on those sections of Athenian society which provided the land forces and the bulk of the military leadership. Ironically, although the democratic system and beliefs at Athens had the clear potential to weaken this hoplite domination of military thought, they also ensured that the cavalry arm would not benefit if this occurred. Athens' naval emphasis meant that if the hoplite's position as defender of the state was to be challenged, it was not the *hippeis* but naval power, and the non-hoplite naval personnel, which were likely to be put forward as the alternative. This likelihood was rendered a certainty by Athenian attitudes towards their cavalry. These generally had an adverse impact, and the prevailing view of the mounted arm was particularly hostile at the very time when its importance was otherwise most likely to be recognized. This presumably brought about a reduction in morale and efficiency and helped to prevent the recognition of its military virtue—with a consequent impairment of the combat ability of the corps.

THE INFLUENCE OF HOPLITE WARFARE AND THE HOPLITE ETHOS

From the mid-seventh century onwards, the hoplite was the most important offensive and defensive land arm of the *polis* and, despite some changes in the way war was waged, this remained so in most of Greece until the late fourth century.[1] It was the hoplites, for example, who protected the city's agricultural land in the classic positional defence outlined in the previous chapter. This predominance on the battlefield led to the development of attitudes and beliefs which affected not only general military thought but also moral and political opinion—or at least its literary expression.[2] As far as the effect upon the cavalry is concerned, the most important aspect of the hoplite influence was

[1] Cf. *HCT* i. 10–15; Best, *Thracian Peltasts*, 139. The main changes were the increased use of peltasts and the introduction of the Macedonian phalanx.

[2] While most of the literature originated from the hoplite or cavalry classes and therefore did not necessarily represent popular thinking, it does represent the views of the most militarily influential sections of society.

its stultifying effect upon the development of other arms. This derived from a belief in the moral and physical superiority of the hoplite, and hoplite combat, and from the relatively slow pace of hoplite operations.

Despite the fairly frequent successes of cavalry and light troops, particularly in the fourth century, the general pattern of fifth- and fourth-century warfare clearly illustrates the hoplite domination of the battlefield. Although innovations like Perikles' mobile defence of Attica did occur, most issues continued to be settled by means of a hoplite clash on an agricultural plain. It is also clear that well into the fourth century the defence of the state was still seen predominantly in terms of the heavy infantryman. Both Aristotle and Plato, for example, assumed that the ideal state would be defended primarily by hoplites. Plato used the hoplite and his equipment as examples in a discussion of the need for a professional military class, and the hoplite nature of his *polis* is later confirmed by his stated preference for the hoplite victories of Marathon and Plataia over the naval victory of Salamis. The latter, he believed, elevated the less respectable elements of society.[3] Aristotle also argued that a military class was indispensable to the survival of a state and subsequently revealed that the class envisaged was composed of hoplites. He apparently thought that some military personnel, which we would regard as essential for a state's defence (such as sailors), should not even be included as full citizens of the ideal state.[4]

Despite the general problems associated with seeing Plato and Aristotle as representative of fourth-century thought (or even as an 'intellectual systematization' of ordinary fourth-century thinking)[5] their typicality in this particular case is confirmed by the frequency with which other contemporary authors express, or assume, hoplite primacy. A good illustration of the hoplite emphasis in the literature is the fact that for eight of the battles included in Table 5 (Amphipolis, Syracuse, Mounychia, Nemea, Koroneia, Olympia, Plataia (323), and Chaironeia) we have no details of the cavalry participation apart from a simple statement of their

---

[3] Pl. *Repub.* 347b–d; *Laws*, 707a–d; cf. 706b–d (quoted below 170).

[4] Arist. *Pol.* 1290^{b}38–1291^{a}34 (4. 4); 1327^{b}9–15 (7. 6); at 1297^{b}12 ff. (4. 13) he refers to contemporary states with purely hoplite citizen bodies.

[5] Dover, *Greek Popular Morality*, 1–2, esp. n. 1.

presence. In the majority of cases our sources do not even tell us
where the cavalry was stationed during the action.[6]

This literary emphasis stemmed partly from the hoplite's important role in battle, but was also influenced by the associated belief
that only the hoplite really defended the *polis* and therefore was
most qualified as a citizen; the hoplite and the concept of the
agathos or good man were strongly linked. In conventional
thought the defence of the *chora* was an important aspect of *arete*
(virtue or excellence), a concept which dates at least as far back as
Homer and which lasted throughout the fifth century.[7] The
possession of *arete* was in turn a key part of defining the *agathos*,
and other hoplite virtues such as steadfastness and co-operation
also figured in contemporary ideas about the ideal citizen.[8] However, arguments could be raised against linking the heavy infantryman with military excellence (and hence with *arete*),[9] and this
view was particularly under challenge at Athens in the hey-day of
her naval power. On the other hand, the extant literature
suggests that the conventional view survived well into the fourth
century—even at Athens. But, more important than mere survival,
was that the traditional perception survived among the middle
and upper echelons of society which provided the vast majority of
the state's military commanders. Even as a minority view in
democratic Athens, the hoplite ethos could be very influential in
determining military theory and practice.

The conventional view of the hoplite as the defender of the
state and therefore possessor of *arete* occurs in Athenian oratory,
philosophy, drama, and in the operation of the state training
system, the *ephebeia*. For example, the whole of Lykourgos'
speech delivered against Leokrates in 330 is based on this premise
and the accused is described in section 43 as 'neither taking up
arms on behalf of his fatherland nor presenting his body to the
generals to place in formation, but fleeing and betraying the
safety of the people'.[10] The phrase 'presenting his body to the
generals to place in formation' (τὸ σῶμα παρασχόντα τάξαι τοῖς
στρατηγοῖς) confirms that Lykourgos is thinking in hoplite terms.

---

[6] The exceptions are Delion, both battles of Mantineia, and Krannon.
[7] A. W. H. Adkins, *Merit and Responsibility* (Oxford, 1960), 31–6, 164–8.
[8] Ibid. 236–7; cf. Soph. *Antigone*, 661 ff.; Ar. *Frogs*, 1009–17.
[9] Adkins, *Merit and Responsibility*, 215 n. 6, 236–7.
[10] Lyk. *Against Leokrates*, 43, cf. 57.

Later in the same speech he asks 'what should a man suffer who
does not repay his country for his nurture?' (i.e. by defending
it).[11] Aischines too, (and again employing hoplite terminology)
cites amongst those disbarred from speaking in the assembly the
man who 'either has not performed his required service in the
army or who has thrown away his shield (*aspis*)'. He adds that
this is quite proper treatment for anyone who fails to bear arms in
defence of his city.[12]

The state military training organization, the *ephebeia*, was also
seen primarily in hoplite terms. The pediment of a fourth-century
ephebic oath found at Acharnai depicts hoplite armour, and
another ephebic oath recorded by Lykourgos was couched in
hoplite language and involved swearing 'neither to disgrace the
sacred arms nor to leave the ranks, but to defend the fatherland
and to hand it over in an improved state'.[13] In addition, the
graduation of ephebes to full citizen status seems to have emphasized the hoplite arm,[14] and this would have reinforced further the
tendency to see the defence of Attica in terms of heavy infantry.

The belief in the superiority of hoplite troops arose primarily
from the fact that, in most of Greece, light troops and cavalry
generally played little part in winning pitched battles until at least
the Peloponnesian War. The understandable conclusion was that
the hoplites were not only the most important members of the
land forces but also the best troops. Aristotle, for example, stated
that a city was deemed great because of the number of its citizen-
soldiers, but that this did not apply to any *polis* 'which can
mobilize a large number of inferior types (*banausoi*) but only a
few hoplites'.[15]

The view of the hoplites as superior was particularly reinforced
by the associated idea that true courage was found only in their
ranks, an opinion fairly frequently voiced in Athenian literature
of the late fifth and early fourth centuries. The co-operative

[11] Ibid. 53; cf. 77 and Pl. *Repub.* 429a–430c, where the true definition of
bravery is seen as a military one (429a–b) and is the bravery of a citizen (430c).
[12] Aischines, 1. 28–9.
[13] Lyk. *Against Leokrates*, 76: μήτε τὰ ἱερὰ ὅπλα καταισχυνεῖν μήτε τὴν τάξιν
λείψειν, ἀμυνεῖν δὲ τῇ πατρίδι καὶ ἀμείνω παραδώσειν. M. N. Tod, *Greek
Historical Inscriptions*, ii (Oxford, 1948), no. 204. See N. C. Conomis, 'On the
Oath of the Athenian Epheboi', *Athena*, 63 (1959), 119–31 for the various texts.
[14] *Ath. Pol.* 42. 4.
[15] Arist. *Pol.* 1326ᵃ21–5 (7. 4).

nature of hoplite warfare outlined in Chapter 2 heavily influenced this concept of courage; as one of Euripides' characters pointed out, 'a hoplite is a slave of his weapons and if those alongside him are not brave then he will die through his neighbours' coward-ice.'[16] Because of this, hoplite warfare called for a particular type of *andreia* or courage—the ability to stand fast in the ranks (*en te taxei*), and to meet the enemy head on in a situation where there was little room for personal manœuvre and where one's ultimate fate depended upon the integrity of the line as a whole. The importance of this concept is reflected in the transference of the phrase to denote sticking to one's post (*en te taxei*) from a purely hoplite context to a wide variety of non-hoplite or even non-military situations.[17]

As Lykos, another Euripidean character, put it: 'the measure of a man's bravery is not archery; rather he who stands fast in his rank and gazes unflinchingly at the swift gash of the spear (is a brave man).'[18] This contains a clear criticism of the value and courage of archers and, although his opponent in this debate produces counter arguments,[19] other evidence suggests that Lykos' views of the hoplite's superiority were fairly common. Sophokles' *Ajax* and Plato's *Laches* contain similar sentiments, and the latter also shows that cavalry was seen by some as requiring a different, and inferior, brand of courage. When asked what courage was in the dialogue which bears his name, the general Laches confidently replied: 'by the gods, Sokrates, that's not hard to answer! For if a man is willing to remain in the ranks and to resist the enemy without fleeing, you know for certain he is brave.'[20] This definition, as Sokrates is quick to point out, can only apply to hoplites: cavalrymen and other soldiers are excluded by their method of fighting. But, when Sokrates described mounted combat as involving fighting while fleeing, Laches con-firmed the strictly hoplite nature of his definition with the rather dismissive comment: 'cavalry do fight in this way, but for hoplites it is as I say.'[21]

The same contempt for non-hoplite warfare and troops is even

[16] Eur. *Her*. 190–2.
[17] Aischines, 3. 7; Dem. 21. 166; 18. 320 (quoted below 227–8).
[18] Eur. *Her*. 162–4. See also Lazenby, *Spartan Army*, 4, 25–6, 37–8.
[19] Eur. *Her*. 188 ff.
[20] Pl. *Laches*, 190d–191e; cf. Soph. *Ajax*, 1120–2.
[21] Pl. *Laches*, 191b.

more forcefully expressed in Plato's *Laws*, which argues that the Athenians ought to have preferred to pay Minos' tribute seventy times over rather than:

becoming, instead of steadfast hoplites, sailors who often charge forward and then rapidly retreat at a run back to their ships. They think it no disgrace to fear to stand and die when the enemy attacks, but have plausible pretexts so readily produced when they throw away their weapons and then flee what they call 'the flight without dishonour'. This is the sort of saying which will occur from amphibious soldiers—not 'beyond praise' but just the opposite. For men should never become accustomed to bad habits, least of all the best part of the citizen body.[22]

For 'Laches' and the unnamed Athenian in the *Laws*, courage and true fighting are defined not by the *hippeus* or *psilos* but by the hoplite and by hoplite warfare. Despite Perikles' defensive tactics and the use of mobile defence elsewhere in Greece, the idea that anything other than a phalanx versus phalanx engagement was somehow dishonourable persisted into the Peloponnesian War and beyond. Thucydides portrays the Athenians trying to persuade the Melians that there is no disgrace involved if they capitulate because 'for you it is not an equal contest, concerning bravery or avoiding shame, but rather a decision concerning safety and not resisting those who are far stronger.'[23]

In the *Rhesos*, the title character expresses revulsion at Odysseus' tactics of ambush and trickery in the following terms:

the man who goes against his enemy face to face is worth the epithet brave, not he who kills his enemy by stealth. I shall take alive this man, whom you say goes like a thief and weaves ambushes, and shall place him at the exits of your gates, impaled through the back as a feast for the winged vultures. For the robber and despoiler of the gods' temples should die this death.[24]

This seems to be a relatively common attitude, at least in literature, to ambush and ruse[25]—the mainstays of cavalry operations

---

[22] Pl. *Laws*, 706b–d.   [23] Thucy. 5. 101.   [24] [Eur.] *Rh*. 510–17.

[25] Although in Homer ambush was regarded as one of the greatest tests of one's *arete*, Adkins, *Merit and Responsibility*, 32 (cf. *GSAW* ii. 178 for a list of Homeric examples of the special courage required in ambush). The change in values may help explain the largely unsympathetic treatment of Odysseus in 5th-cent. Attic drama. For a fairly recent discussion of trickery in warfare and the ambivalent attitude of the ancient Greeks towards it, see D. Whitehead, 'Κλοπὴ Πολέμου: "Theft" in Ancient Greek Warfare', *C&M* 39 (1988), 45–53, esp. 47 ff.

in Xenophon's *Hipparchikos*. Even Polybios, writing in the mid-
to late second century, links the practice of ambush with deceit
and trickery on no fewer than four occasions.[26]

Although there are examples of Athenian ambushes during the
Peloponnesian War and the years immediately following it (Thucydides records four cases and Xenophon a further five between
400 and 388), significantly only two of the examples, Ellomenos
and Olpai in 426, involve hoplites.[27] All of the others apparently
involve *psiloi* and all of the Thucydidean examples, including
Ellomenos and Olpai, are the work of one *strategos*: Demosthenes.
Surprise attacks by the Athenians during this period are similarly
rare, with only one recorded example each of a dawn or major
night attack, again both under the leadership of Demosthenes.[28]
The lack of surprise attacks and ambuscades suggests that, with
the notable exception of Demosthenes, there may have been some
diffidence on the part of Athenian *strategoi* to win by anything
other than a straightforward hoplite contest.[29] Demosthenes
gained first-hand experience of the value of *psiloi* with his defeat
in Aitolia, and this may explain why he had an unusually good
grasp of the more mobile warfare involved in utilizing them to
their full potential.

The beliefs that the only true courage was hoplite courage and
that hoplite warfare was the only proper military activity also
survived into the fourth century. The discussion in Plato's *Laches*
certainly suggests that both were current at the time and their
unequivocal expression in the *Laws*, one of his later works,
indicates that this was still the case in the mid-fourth century. In
addition, there was an apparently widespread view at Athens, at
least at the time of the Corinthian War, that cavalry service was
considerably safer than being in the hoplite phalanx.[30] Despite
the particular circumstances which may have influenced public

[26] Polybios, 3. 81. 9; 4. 8. 11; 13. 3. 2–7; 18. 3. 1–4.

[27] Thucy. 3. 94. 1, 107. 3, 110. 1–112. 6; 4. 67. Xen. *Anab.* 4. 1. 22, 6. 17, 7. 22;
Hell. 4. 4. 15, 8. 35–9; 5. 1. 10–13. The *Anab.* examples (except possibly 4. 6. 17)
involve troops commanded by Xenophon; the *Hell.* examples concern peltasts
under Iphikrates or Chabrias.

[28] Thucy. 3. 112. 2–6; 7. 43–4. For dawn attacks see *GSAW* ii. 161, table 3.

[29] Cf. Q. Curtius Rufus, 4. 13. 3–9 and Arr. *Anab.* 1. 13. 2–7 describing
Alexander's angry reaction to the 'dishonourable' suggestion he mount a night or
dawn attack. The difficulties of moving large bodies of hoplites at night might
also have discouraged such operations.

[30] Below 219–22.

opinion on this occasion, the idea of the hoplite as the prime military arm, and the associated belief in its superiority over other troops, undoubtedly contributed to early fourth century views about the relative safety of cavalry service. Finally, as late as 341 and having just described the good old days of honourable hoplite campaigns fought without bribery or trickery, Demosthenes could still rather contemptuously state that 'now you doubtless see that traitors destroy most (cities) and battle array or battle none. Instead, you hear of Philip marching wherever he wishes, not leading a phalanx of hoplites, but accompanied by an army of *psiloi*, cavalry, archers, and mercenaries.'[31]

As will be seen, such beliefs dovetailed neatly with, and undoubtedly reinforced, the unpopularity of the Athenian *hippeis* in the first part of the fourth century. But in addition to their influence here, the nature of hoplite warfare also posed a real problem for both the employment and development of the mounted arm. In the well-known speech of Mardonios, Greek hoplite warfare is described as follows:

whenever they declare war on each other they find the best-looking and most level ground and go there to fight. As a result, the victors come off with great losses and I will say nothing about the losers for they are utterly destroyed. . . . if it is absolutely necessary to wage war against each other, they each ought to find the most defensible spot and make their stand there.[32]

Although this is an oversimplification (the choice of terrain at Thermopylai and Plataia alone challenges the accuracy of the last part of the statement), hoplite casualty rates show that it did contain an element of truth.[33] The defeated army usually lost 10–20 per cent of its total force, the victorious army about 3–10 per cent,[34] quite heavy losses for actions before the effective employment of gunpowder.

As the general neglect of reconnaissance discussed in Chapter 3 shows, hoplite operations were normally conducted at a relatively slow tempo. All things being equal, two armies on the march had the same chance of deploying in time, and once the battle com-

---

[31] Dem. 9. 49.
[32] Hdtos 7. 9.
[33] See P. Krentz, 'Casualties in Hoplite Battles', *GRBS* 26 (1985), 13–20.
[34] Ibid. 18.

menced there was little that any individual, whether soldier or
strategos, could do to affect the outcome, except to fight to the
best of his ability. This was so familiar a concept that Plutarch
recorded its use in the third century to discredit the Achaian
general Aratos. He claimed that 'flatterers of tyrants' used to say
that, in addition to displaying physical signs of fear, Aratos 'after
deploying his force, disseminating the password, and asking his
lieutenants and *lochagoi* whether he needed to be present (as the
die had been cast), would withdraw to a distance and await the
outcome'.[35] Even if this were untrue of Aratos himself, it is still
an excellent indication that, despite the more fluid and mobile
operations of the third century, it was assumed that as soon as the
phalanxes clashed there was nothing much the general could do
to influence events. But this had never been true if an army
possessed cavalry, as it could be manœuvred on the battlefield to
influence the outcome—as happened at Delion (424) and Olynthos
(382), and as Philip II and Alexander of Macedon definitively
proved in their campaigns. Even in those engagements which
only involved hoplites, Spartan and Theban successes showed
that the assumption that once battle began nothing further could
be done was not based on reality but arose from the conservative
way in which hoplite warfare was normally conducted. The theories and assumptions associated with this conduct encouraged a
slow and fairly static approach to tactics and had the clear potential to affect the development of arms with different characteristics.

   This general slowness particularly restricted the proper utiliza-
tion of the most important cavalry characteristic: mobility. At the
tactical level this is particularly well exemplified by the action of
the Spartan cavalry at Lechaion. Instead of exploiting its advantage of mobility to drive off Iphikrates' peltasts, it conformed
entirely to the movement of the hoplites and thus conceded the
engagement.[36] Later on, the Thebans must have been committing
a similar error while withdrawing under pressure from the Thessalian cavalry until Epameinondas was promoted in the field and
changed their tactics.[37] Indeed, the effect of this aspect of the
hoplite ascendancy in warfare was similar to the concentration on

---

[35] Plut. *Arat.* 29. 5–6.
[36] See above 144.
[37] Diod. Sic. 15. 71. 5–7.

the infantry tank concept in Britain, and other countries, between the two world wars: it precluded the effective development of a truly mobile arm at a time when mobility was becoming increasingly important.

The general effect of the emphasis on the heavy infantry is also apparent in specific incidents during, and the overall pattern of, Athenian military operations from c.450–300. Despite the use of the *hippeis* as the mainstay of the defence of Attica, it is clear that many *strategoi* of the Peloponnesian War continued to think in terms of hoplite rather than combined arms operations. The expedition to the Chalkidike in 429 foundered at Spartolos because the Athenians dispatched insufficient cavalry and light troops to support their hoplites against a foe which possessed them in abundance.[38] Because of the long Athenian presence in the region, lack of local knowledge probably does not account for this oversight, which seems more likely to have occurred because of the belief, either that the hoplites could deal with any situation, or that the only engagements would be traditional hoplite clashes on the plain.

This sort of thinking probably played a large part in Demosthenes' Aitolian defeat in 426. Either ignorant of the circumstances of the defeat at Spartolos three years before, or having failed to learn from them, he chose to advance inland without waiting for his Lokrian allies who were equipped in the same way as the enemy. This proved to be a major error, but one which is easily understood when the hoplite influence is taken into account. Up to that point Demosthenes had encountered no resistance and his hoplites were first-rate troops.[39] Furthermore, he had been told that the enemy would be easily subdued as they lived in scattered villages and were only 'lightly equipped'.[40]

The Sicilian expedition shows that the Athenians were still making the same mistakes later in the war. Their enemy here was traditionally cavalry orientated and, if Thucydides' account of Nikias' speech is accurate, this was discussed at Athens before the

[38] See Thucy. 2. 79.

[39] Thucy. 3. 97–8. Demosthenes may not have been fully aware of the details of the defeat at Spartolos because he certainly took to heart the lessons of his Aitolian reverse. From this point on, he alone of contemporary *strategoi* seems to have grasped the potential of *psiloi* in the right circumstances—as he showed at Olpai and Pylos.

[40] καὶ σκευῇ ψιλῇ χρώμενον, Thucy. 3. 94. 4.

expedition was dispatched. However, whether or not Nikias actually raised the question of enemy *psiloi* and cavalry numbers, and recommended embarking a large contingent of light infantry to counter this, the Athenian cavalry and *psiloi* which were sent were clearly insufficient, particularly in proportion to the number of hoplites in the force. The expedition originally comprised 5,100 hoplites, 480 bowmen, 700 slingers, 120 *psiloi*, and 30 cavalry. Even when reinforcements of 250 cavalrymen and 30 *hippotoxotai* were sent out (without horses),[41] the ratio was still worse than one cavalryman to sixteen hoplites. The lack of cavalry ultimately played a major part in the destruction of the Athenian expeditionary force.

The extent to which the Athenians at this time believed in the efficacy of hoplites is confirmed by their complete lack of regularly armed light troops as late as 424. Although this deficiency was sometimes partly compensated for by the use of mercenaries,[42] the lack of proper Athenian light troops displays a marked lack of interest in developing a balanced force. The small numbers of cavalry and light infantry often deployed in support of hoplites, and their generally stereotyped and restricted use on such occasions, also demonstrate the predominance of the hoplite in both fifth and fourth century military thinking. The ratio of hoplites to cavalry in Athenian forces in the period 431–279 ranges from 170:1 to 2.5:1; of the twenty-four cases where we have good information, five are at the ratio of 10 hoplites to 1 cavalryman, twelve are greater than 10:1 (six of these involving ratios of 20:1 or higher), and only seven are below 10:1 (see Table 4). Although in some cases the number of cavalry available may have affected the proportion of cavalry to hoplites, the impression gained from these figures is that on many occasions far fewer cavalrymen were deployed than was possible. The most likely reason for this is the concentration on the hoplite component of the force and this explanation is confirmed by a similar emphasis on the hoplite in the tactical employment of Athenian armies.

As can be seen from the discussion in Chapter 3, the main use for cavalry in supporting operations was to protect the hoplite phalanx. This is why the Athenian cavalry was deployed on the wings at Delion, at Mantineia in 418, and most probably at

---

[41] Thucy. 6. 21–2, 43, 94. 4; their mounts were to be purchased locally.
[42] See Thucy. 4. 94. 1, 129. 2; 6. 43; 7. 27. 1–2, 29. 1.

Spartolos, Solygeia, Syracuse, and Nemea. The extant evidence strongly indicates that the standard disposition of the Athenian *hippeis* was in a flank protection role on the wings, although the different deployment dictated by the special circumstances at Mounychia and Krannon shows that this was not an immutable rule.[43] The role of the hoplite influence in determining this subordinate position is brought even more sharply into focus when the pattern of military development in Macedonia and Thessaly is considered.

Like other peoples in the same region, the Macedonians retained a strong cavalry tradition.[44] Thucydides records that it was cavalry which they supplied to aid the Peloponnesians in 432, and in sufficient numbers for Perdikkas to be appointed overall cavalry commander of the allied forces at Olynthos.[45] When Sitalkes invaded with superior forces in 429 the Macedonians resisted only with their cavalry arm and, according to Thucydides, their cavalrymen were quite effective (except when vastly outnumbered) because they were 'good horsemen and protected by armour'.[46] Their hoplite tradition on the other hand was apparently non-existent. In 423, for example, the only hoplites in Perdikkas' army seem to have been provided by Greeks living in Macedonia and not by native Macedonians.[47] In terms of hoplites the Macedonians, as Hammond points out, possessed 'no infantry worthy of the name'.[48]

This relationship between the cavalry and infantry arms remained essentially the same in the fourth century, with the cavalry regarded as the more important of the two under Philip II and Alexander. Although the new infantry arm (quite probably created by Philip himself) was of vastly increased importance, it was not used as the decisive striking force in battle. The members of this new foot levy were not primarily hoplites, either in equipment or tradition. They were more lightly equipped than conven-

[43] The Athenians may have determined the deployment at Krannon.

[44] See Hammond and Griffith, 147–8.

[45] Thucy. 1. 62. 2–3; Perdikkas apparently had 200 cavalrymen with him (loc. cit.) and Philip and Pausanias had supplied 600 to the Athenians (1. 61. 4).

[46] ἄνδρας ἱππέας τε ἀγαθοὺς καὶ τεθωρακισμένους, Thucy. 2. 100. 5.

[47] Thucy. 4. 124. 1. That the Macedonians were not hoplites is also implied by the composition of the force which Perdikkas requested from his allies, 4. 78. 1, 79, and perhaps too by the vulnerability of the Macedonians in retreat when compared to Brasidas' hoplites, 4. 125–7.

[48] Hammond and Griffith, 148; cf. *AAG* 116.

tional hoplites, carrying a smaller shield and wearing less body
armour, but armed with a longer spear.[49] Unlike their fifth-
century predecessors, these infantrymen were able to challenge
hoplites on their own terms and were indispensable to the success
of Macedonian expansion. This was because, as Tarn notes, if
cavalry is to be used decisively in a pitched battle it needs a
steady infantry force to engage and hold the enemy.[50] However,
the important point about Macedonian military history under
Philip II, Alexander, and their successors, is that it was the
cavalry and not the infantry which was used as the battle-winning
arm; it was mounted charges which were used to shatter the
enemy's formations.[51]

The Thessalians placed a similar emphasis on their cavalry.
From an early period, the feudal aristocracy could mobilize relatively large numbers of horsemen from their own estates and by
375 the *Tagos*, or leader, of Thessaly could muster as many as
6,000 local horse.[52] The Thessalians also regularly made use of
mobile defence to protect their country from the effects of invasion, and performed well in such major battles as Krannon
(322), the Crocus Plain (353), and Gaugamela (331).[53]

The importance the Macedonians and Thessalians placed on
the offensive use of the *arme blanche* is illustrated by their use of a
wedge- or diamond-shaped cavalry formation.[54] Philip II, who
may have borrowed the idea from the Thracians (who in turn had
got it from the Scythians), trained the Macedonians in the wedge
formation. Arrian points out that this formation is greatly superior
to an oblong one 'because the leaders are drawn up around the

[49] For a general discussion of their equipment see Hammond and Griffith, 421–
4 and, for more detailed treatments, Markle, 'Macedonian Sarissa', 323–39 and
'Macedonian Arms', 87–111. Dr Markle, however, argues that the phalangites
were sometimes equipped as hoplites when terrain and mission required.

[50] *HMND* 18, 60–1.

[51] On the general importance of cavalry in this role see *HMND* 11, 61–71. The
best evidence is for Alexander's battles: Arr. *Anab.* 1. 14. 6 ff.; Diod. Sic. 17. 19.
6 ff. (Granikos). Arr. *Anab.* 2. 9 ff.; Diod. Sic. 17. 33. 5 ff.; cf. Q. Curtius Rufus,
3. 11. 2 ff. (Issos). Arr. *Anab.* 3. 11 ff.; Diod. Sic. 17. 60. 1–4; Q. Curtius Rufus, 4.
15–16 (Gaugamela).

[52] Dem. 23. 199; [Dem.] 13. 23; Xen. *Hell.* 6. 1. 8, 19; the 8,000 of the latter
includes allies.

[53] Mobile defence: Thucy. 1. 111. 1; Diod. Sic. 15. 71. 4–5. Diod. Sic. 18. 17.
1–5 (Krannon). Diod. Sic. 16. 35. 5 (Crocus Plain). Arr. *Anab.* 3. 15. 3; Diod. Sic.
17. 60. 5–8; Q. Curtius Rufus, 3. 11. 14–15 (Gaugamela). See also 'Thessaly', Ch. 1.

[54] See also 'combat potential', Ch. 2.

perimeter and the tapering front allows it to cut easily right through the enemy formation and gives the facility to make rapid turns and counter-turns.'[55] This particular formation may have been used by Alexander at the Hydaspes and quite possibly by Philip against Bardylis and at Chaironeia.[56] The Thessalians also used a similar formation, although in the shape of a rhomboid or diamond.[57] The whole point of such a formation, as the passage quoted from Arrian suggests, was to aid the penetration of an enemy formation. As discussed in Chapter 2, though, the practice in most Greek states (including Athens)[58] was to use a square or oblong formation. This was basically the same as the hoplite formation and was designed to allow the maximum number of horsemen to engage the enemy at once, whether with missiles or hand-to-hand weapons, rather than to facilitate penetration at a given point.[59] The wedge is entirely absent from Xenophon's technical treatises, throughout which he talks in terms of the square or oblong formation.[60]

The difference in formation used is indicative of the different approach to cavalry tactics in the hoplite states and in the traditional cavalry states like Macedonia and Thessaly. The Macedonian and Thessalian cavalry played the decisive role in warfare and this continued to be the case with the former—even after the creation of the redoubtable Macedonian phalanx. The most likely explanation for this is the prominence of the cavalry tradition, and the absence of a hoplite tradition in these regions. Just the opposite situation prevailed at Athens, which had a fairly strong hoplite tradition and, until sometime between 445 and 438, only a

[55] Arr. *Takt.* 16. 6–7. Aelian, *Takt.* 18. 3 also credits Philip II with adopting this and Asklepiodotos, 7. 3 mentions the Macedonians using this formation but does not mention Philip by name. On the wedge under Alexander see E. W. Marsden, *The Campaign of Gaugamela* (Liverpool, 1964), 68–73. See also Markle, 'Macedonian Sarissa', 339. The whole of the Arrian passage is quoted above 104.

[56] Hydaspes: Arr. *Anab.* 5. 15. 2; against Bardylis and at Chaironeia: Hammond and Griffith, 414, see also Markle, 'Use of the Sarissa', 486, 488 ff. Markle's arguments, however, have not been without criticism, see Rahe, *AJA* 85 (1981), 84–7 and, on the *sarissa*, P.A. Manti, 'The Macedonian Sarissa, Again', *AncW* 25 (1994) 77–91.

[57] Asklepiodotos, 7. 2; for the method of drawing it up see 7. 5–9 and Marsden, *Gaugamela*, 68–70.

[58] Asklepiodotos, 7. 4; Arr. *Takt.* 16. 9.

[59] In this respect the oblong formation could perhaps be likened to Wellington's line formations in the Napoleonic Wars and the wedge to Napoleon's columns.

[60] See, for example, Xen. *Hipparch.* 2. 2 ff.

small cavalry force. The situation was even more marked at Sparta, and in other Peloponnesian states, where the hoplite tradition was stronger than at Athens. The Spartans, for example, had no cavalry prior to 425/4 and in the fourth century what they did have was of poor quality.[61] The discomfort the Spartans felt with a mounted role is exemplified by their cavalry under Pasimachos at Corinth; instead of utilizing their mobility the men dismounted and fought on foot as hoplites.[62] The influence of the hoplite ethos was unfortunate for balanced military development, particularly for Athens at the end of the Peloponnesian War, when it probably had a better opportunity than most hoplite states to develop the true potential of its mounted arm.

At the outbreak of this war, Perikles decided to defend Attica with the cavalry and this policy was continued by his successors. In the light of the prevailing military theory this was an unusual and rather bold decision, and one which met with opposition from the hoplites who were confined in Athens watching their rural property being ravaged.[63] Apart from this activity, the *hippeis* were involved in regular attacks on the Megarid, raids on the Peloponnese, and overseas expeditions (see Table 3). During over twenty years of this sort of campaigning, the *hippeis* must have built up a considerable body of experience and expertise in mounted warfare.[64] This is confirmed by the apparently speedy development of tactics to cope with the annual invasions and is mirrored in the soundness of the advice contained in Xenophon's *Hipparchikos*. Although this work was presumably also influenced by his Asian experiences, it concentrates on the type of tactics involved in the defence of Attica and his recommendations are almost certainly based upon, or influenced by, his service in the cavalry at the end of the Peloponnesian War. However, this experience never really bore fruit because of the attitude of the rest of the Athenians towards their cavalry.

[61] Thucy. 4. 55. 2; Xen. *Hell*. 6. 4. 10–11.

[62] Xen. *Hell*. 4. 4. 10.

[63] However, Hippias used allied Thessalian cavalry against Spartan invasions in 510, Hdtos 5. 63–4 (probably also influenced by doubts concerning the loyalty of his subjects).

[64] Cf. Diod. Sic. 14. 23. 3–4 on how experienced Cyrus' Greek hoplites were because of the Peloponnesian War.

ATTITUDES TO THE CAVALRY CLASS

In the discussion which follows, I have used the term 'cavalry class' to denote the group which consisted of those Athenians wealthy enough to maintain a horse, and from which the cavalry was recruited. The term is a convenient way of referring to this group but it should not be taken to imply that the other citizens always perceived this group as a class of cavalrymen. Unlike Sparta, Athenian society was not dominated by its military aspects; the city possessed no standing army and all military service was part-time. As a result, even though this section of society provided all the state's cavalry, a contemporary would have considered this only one of its attributes and perhaps not even the most important. A modern analogy is provided by the use of the term 'officer-class' to denote the social group which provided the officers of the British army in the first half of this century.[65] Although accurate enough in a socio-military context, in a more general context 'the upper classes' might better convey the way the rest of society perceived this group. In the same way, the Athenians undoubtedly considered what I refer to as the 'cavalry class' simply as *hoi plousioi* or 'the wealthy'. Nevertheless, the two groups are in fact the same and, as one of the most prominent symbols of wealth was the owning or breeding of horses, the cavalry and the wealthy were inextricably linked in the views of their fellow citizens.

At first glance, this class would seem to be the same as the Solonic census classification of *hippeis* and this term was used interchangeably in antiquity to denote both the cavalry corps itself and the census class whose military function was to provide it. Solon's reforms divided Athenian society into four groups with different political rights and military obligations, and whose membership was determined according to landed wealth. In descending order, these groups were the *pentakosiomedimnoi* (those with a minimum annual agricultural production of 500 measures or *medimnoi*), the *hippeis* (those producing 300–500 *medimnoi*), the *zeugitai* (200–300 *medimnoi*), and the *thetes* (those who produced fewer than 200 *medimnoi*). Although the name '*hippeis*' continued in use, the cavalry class of the late fifth and the fourth

---

[65] Or even later, cf. Keegan, *Face of Battle*, 323, which refers to a contemporary Western European 'officer-class'.

centuries did not correspond exactly with the Solonic class of the same name.

The first difference was that, in Solonic terms, the cavalry class of the period *c*.450–320 was composed of both the *hippeis* and the *pentakosiomedimnoi*. Members of the latter could be required to serve one year in every three as a trierarch, or ship's captain, but were eligible for cavalry service in the other two.[66] Another difference was that by this time membership of the cavalry class almost certainly did not depend upon a fixed financial assessment of one's annual produce. By the end of the fifth century the Solonic requirement for membership of the cavalry (owning sufficient agricultural property to produce between 300 and 500 *medimnoi*) had fallen into disuse, or had been replaced by either a simple monetary equivalent or the possession of a specified capital sum or property.[67] Whichever is correct, Lysias could publicly claim in 403 that large numbers of hoplites and cavalrymen owned no landed property at all.[68]

The original function of Solon's system was to determine eligibility for political office and the level of a man's military obligation. However, by the fourth century the Solonic classifications seem to have become an archaic survival of little or no practical use in Athenian political or military life. Because there was apparently no simple way of determining to what Solonic class an individual belonged, citizens could claim to be a member of whichever class suited them. The *Ath. Pol.*, for example, states that when candidates for offices technically restricted to the higher classes were formally asked their status, 'nobody would say he was a member of the thetic class'.[69]

The same was presumably true in the military sphere. There

[66] Meidias (App. 5.112) apparently managed to do both in the same year, Dem. 21. 161–6; Alkibiades (5.10), who was clearly of pentakosiomedimnic status also served in the cavalry, Pl. *Symp.* 221a. Other cavalrymen who held trierarchies are the anonymous no. 5.197, Demochares (5.47), Philoktemon (5.154), and Philomelos (5.155). Isaios, 7. 38 shows that in the 4th cent. a man should only hold the trierarchy once in any 3 years; for the 5th cent. see P. J. Rhodes, 'Problems in Athenian *Eisphora* and Liturgies', *AJAH* 7 (1982), 2–3.

[67] See G. E. M. de Ste. Croix, 'Demosthenes' *Τίμημα* and the Athenian Eisphora in the Fourth Century BC', *C&M* 14 (1953), 41 ff. and A. H. M. Jones, *Athenian Democracy* (Oxford, 1964), 142 n. 50.

[68] Lysias, 34. 4 (with Dion. Hal.'s introduction); the financial hardships of the recent war presumably helped to bring this about.

[69] *Ath. Pol.* 7. 4. Isaios, 7. 39 has an example of a man understating his class to avoid his state obligations.

was almost certainly no fixed assessment according to which citizens were allocated to the hoplite, cavalry, or trierarchic lists, and while *antidosis* cases, or legal pressure from generals and hipparchs, could force the financially qualified to serve, the system must in effect largely have been one of self-assessment.[70] In short, a man's choice of arm arose from his ability and willingness to pay, and not from formal membership of a specific Solonic class. To be eligible for cavalry service therefore required only the ability to keep a horse. The feasibility of such a system is supported by the pre-Solonic situation—considerable evidence exists that the *hippeis* as a class pre-dated Solon and that, as Cichorius argued, they constituted the highest level of society, 'der eupatridische Reiteradel'.[71] At this time, it was certainly composed of those who could both afford to buy the horse and equipment necessary for mounted service and who were also prepared to do so. In effect, this is what it had returned to in the fifth and fourth centuries.

Therefore, the cavalry class to which I refer is not the same as the Solonic census class of *hippeis*, but consists of those financially able to maintain a horse. It encompassed past, present, and future members of the cavalry corps, and their families, and even those wealthy enough to keep a horse but who for various reasons might not have done so. Because of its wealth, its relatively small numbers, and its prominence in public and private life, the cavalry class was a distinctive part of Athenian society.

According to Davies, the richest, or as he terms it the 'propertied', class was a small section of society which comprised some 1–2 per cent of the fifth- and fourth-century population.[72] However, Rhodes has more recently, and quite plausibly, argued that this underestimates the numbers,[73] but, even without the additional members apparent from Rhodes's arguments, Davies's register of the 'propertied' class is already too small. He did not use horse-ownership or cavalry service as a criterion for

[70] Legal sanctions: Xen. *Hipparch*. 1. 9–10. On the *eisphora* as a self-assessed tax, see de Ste. Croix, *C&M* 14 (1953), 33–4.

[71] C. Cichorius, 'Zu den Namen der attischen Steuerklassen', *Griechische Studien: Hermann Lipsius zum sechzigsten Geburtstag dargebracht* (Leipzig, 1894), 136.

[72] J. K. Davies, *Wealth and the Power of Wealth in Classical Athens* (Salem, 1981), 6.

[73] Rhodes, *AJAH* 7 (1982), 1–19.

inclusion—an omission he has since acknowledged as a mistake.[74] Because of the expense of keeping a horse, he is certainly correct to think that cavalrymen should have been included in his original classification; had he done so the expanded group would exactly equate with the cavalry class discussed here.

It is in fact possible to estimate the cost of keeping a horse and to obtain some indication of the monetary expenditure required for membership of the *hippeis*. This is discussed in detail in Appendix 4, but the picture which emerges confirms the impression conveyed by the contemporary literature—belonging to the equestrian milieu was sufficiently costly to place a man in a financially exclusive group.[75] Not all the the costs associated with cavalry service can be recovered but in the fourth century at least the following applied (see Appendix 4). A cavalry mount would have cost a minimum of 100 drachmas, with most cavalrymen paying around 500. The minimum was equivalent to ten months' wages for a skilled craftsman (or over two years' fairly generous wheat ration for an adult male) while the average would have bought nearly twenty months' wheat supply for a family of six. Although the state *katastasis* or establishment grant assisted the cavalryman with the initial purchase, most cavalrymen would have ended up repaying most or all of the cost of their horse themselves. Feeding a horse was similarly expensive and, for at least part of each year, the cavalryman's two mounts would together cost him upwards of 2 obols a day over and above the state *sitos* or feed grant. In times of extreme shortage it could have cost up to 14 obols a day more than the *sitos* payment. The cost of only one javelin (most *hippeis* carried two) would have paid for between 24 and 48 days' wheat supply for an active adult male.

So, even with his state allowances, a cavalryman had to possess substantial financial resources and this, as will be seen, was clearly recognized by Athenian society in general. The horse was quite rightly regarded as a sign of wealth and a particularly obvious sign at that. It was this rather than, for example, a distinctive form of dress which served to differentiate rich from

---

[74] The register is contained in *APF*, the error is acknowledged in *Wealth*, p. vi.

[75] See e.g. Ar. *Peace*, 135–9 and *Clouds*, 12–35; Arist. *Pol.* 1289[b]33–7 (4. 3); 1321[a]5–13 (6. 7); Thucy. 6. 12. 2; Isaios, 5. 43; Isok. 6. 55 and 16. 33; Hyper. 1. 16; Xen. *Hipparch.* 1. 11–12 and *Agesilaos,* 9. 6. It also perhaps has a more universal truth – in 1990 I saw a car-sticker in Brisbane which read: 'POVERTY is owning a horse.'

poor.[76] In addition, the prominence of the horse as a symbol of wealth was accentuated by the frequent public appearance of the cavalry class, whether as individuals or in a group as the cavalry corps.

Firstly, there was the private use of the horse as a means of transport around the city or Attica. How common this was is a little difficult to ascertain, but there are several attested examples of men riding around Athens and her environs on purely civilian business. Lysias wrote a speech for an invalid who used to ride around the city and Xenophon records the end to a party when, inspired by the performance of 'Ariadne' and 'Dionysos', 'the unmarried vowed to marry, and the married men mounted their horses and rode off to be with their own wives.'[77] The dinner was held in the Peiraieus and, although it was on the occasion of the equestrian events of the Great Panathenaia, Kallias, the host, invited Sokrates and his companions, saying that he would rather have them than *strategoi*, *hipparchoi*, and office-seekers.[78] This event cannot be explained simply as a gathering of serving cavalrymen and yet some guests had ridden to it.[79]

On another occasion, Demosthenes escorted Macedonian ambassadors out of Attica on horseback[80] and Xenophon confirms that Athenians did stable their horses within the city limits. He informs us that each day Ischomachos had his groom lead his horse out to the farm and back for its daily exercise session.[81] The exemplary Ischomachos walked out to his estate to improve his own fitness and so did not actually ride his horse through the streets on these occasions, but many, if not most, members of the cavalry class would probably have ridden home in the same circumstances. The phylarch in *Lysistrata*, for example, remained mounted even while buying porridge in the market place.[82]

[76] Thucy. 1. 6. 3; Xenophon the Orator, *Ath. Pol.* 1. 10. However, it is likely that, even if the garments were basically the same, the rich would have had better quality clothes; Ar. *Kn.* 1331 suggests that the cicada clasp and linen undergarments may still occasionally have been worn in Athens.

[77] Lysias, 24. 11; Xen. *Symp.* 9. 7. [78] Xen. *Symp.* 1. 2, 4.

[79] Even if the guests had attended the equestrian games on horseback they could, like Ischomachos in Xen. *Oik.* 11. 18, Pheidippides in Ar. *Clouds*, 32, or Antimachos in Ar. *Acharn.* 1164–8, have sent the horse home with a groom and walked to their destination.

[80] Aischines, 2. 111; cf. 3. 76.

[81] Xen. *Oik.* 11. 15–18.

[82] Ar. *Lysis.* 561–2.

Some members of the cavalry class seem to have gone one further than this and used chariots instead of riding horses. Demosthenes describes Meidias as 'conveying his wife to the Mysteries and wherever else he wishes with a white chariot team from Sikyon', and another speech attributed to him accuses Phainippos of giving up riding, selling his war-horse, and adopting a chariot as his mode of transport.[83] Even if only a few members of the cavalry class did this, it would have been a forceful reminder to their less wealthy compatriots of their privileged financial position within Athenian society.

Horses as a simple means of private transport were therefore likely to have been a frequent sight in Athens. In addition to this, the general public would have been accustomed to seeing cavalrymen training or exercising either as a corps, in small groups, or as individuals. As outlined in Chapter 2, collective cavalry training occurred from time to time and, although its frequency depended to some extent on the hipparchs and on the willingness of the men to attend, the *Boule* did have the power to determine the amount of exercise required.[84] Such collective training would have been a very vivid reminder of their existence as a group within society, especially when reinforced by the regular sight of people simply riding around Athens or exercising their horses. Horses need daily exercise, and riders, especially military ones, need practice, and the vase paintings show numerous scenes of equestrian activity ranging from boys and youths being taught to ride to grooms or owners exercising their animals (see Plate 1, and the sample of vases in Appendix 1).

The vase-paintings also suggest that young men of the cavalry class congregated for informal group-practice sessions, although not always with the desired result. Andokides for example records the unhappy conclusion to what was probably a riding session of this type: 'I fell from my horse in Kynosarges, breaking both my collarbone and skull and was taken home on a litter.'[85] Kynosarges was located on the outskirts of the city,[86] but other sessions

---

[83] Dem. 21. 158; [Dem.] 42. 24.

[84] Xen. *Hipparch.* 1. 13.

[85] Andok. 1. 61. On the gymnasium there see S. C. Humphreys, 'The Nothoi of Kynosarges', *JHS* 94 (1974), 90–1.

[86] See J. Travlos, *A Pictorial Dictionary of Ancient Athens* (New York, 1980), 340, figs. 219 and 379.

probably took place nearer the centre of Athens. The *Hipparcheion*, or cavalry headquarters, was very probably located in or near the Stoa of the *Hermai* and several vases portray equestrian scenes and *hermai* together. This suggests that riders exercised near the Hipparcheion, on the open area called the Herms in the north-eastern corner of the Agora.[87] This would have been a very prominent location indeed.

The perception of the cavalry class as a distinct group within society would also have been reinforced by their involvement as a body in public displays, religious festivals, and processions. According to Xenophon, the *hippeis* were involved in displays in the Academy, in the Lykeion, at Phaleron, and in the Hippodrome.[88] These mass displays would presumably have been amongst the most memorable manifestations of the cavalry's corporate and social identity. Their sheer impressiveness is well documented, particularly by Xenophon. He concluded his recommendations on the staging of the Hippodrome display with the remark 'what an awe-inspiring sight when they charge front to front against each other, how majestic when they stand facing each other again after riding across the Hippodrome, and how noble when, on the sound of a trumpet, they charge back again a second time more quickly.'[89] Several other sources show that this was not merely the opinion of an old cavalryman. In Aristophanes' *Frogs*, 'Dionysos' covers up a yelp of pain by pretending that it was a cry of joy and excitement at seeing the cavalry.[90] Similarly, prancing and rearing steeds in battle (which the Hippodrome display was designed to simulate) were regarded by Demetrios as the best subject for a painter; Poseidon too is pictured by Aristophanes as rejoicing in the brazen clash of steeds.[91]

As the Parthenon frieze attests, the cavalcades which were included in the public processions or *pompai*, must also have been spectacular, although, as Martin notes, direct statements of cavalry involvement in specific festivals are rare.[92] However, a variety

[87] On the Hipparcheion and the Herms see Kroll, 83–4, esp. n. 2 and Bugh, *Horsemen*, app. C. For the vases see *PP* 137–8. Athenaios, 4. 64 (167), quoted on next page, also demonstrates a link between the cavalry and the Herms.

[88] Xen. *Hipparch*. 3. 1.

[89] Ibid. 3. 11.

[90] Ar. *Frogs*, 653.

[91] Demetrios, *On Style*, 2. 76; Ar. *Kn*. 551–3.

[92] Martin, *Cavaliers*, 149–50.

of sources attests its participation in processions in general. For example, Xenophon includes among the hipparch's civic duties making the state festivals 'worthy spectacles'.[93] In his speech against Meidias, Demosthenes describes cavalry involvement in the processions through the Agora; elsewhere he complains to the assembly that the phylarchs and hipparchs (among other officers) 'conduct your processions along with the *hieropoioi* (overseers of the sacrifices)', instead of attending to their military duties.[94]

Other evidence supports their involvement at particular festivals and suggests that Martin was correct to argue that the cavalry had a greater role in festal processions than other parts of the army.[95] For example, Plutarch records that the cavalrymen riding in procession in the Olympeia (a festival to Zeus which also involved equestrian games) placed their wreaths on the prison where the condemned general Phokion was held.[96] Their presence in the Panathenaic festival is not explicitly stated by any ancient writer, but is rendered certain by the weight of supporting evidence, especially the Parthenon frieze itself. The theories that the mounted participants are the heroized dead from Marathon or mounted *epheboi* are unlikely for the reasons given in Appendix 3, and their presence in the Panathenaic procession, the most important celebration in the Athenian festal calendar, is confirmed by other sources.

The first of these is a remark by Hegesandros that when Demetrios of Phaleron (Appendix 5.46) 'was hipparch for the Panathenaia he set up a grandstand for Aristagora in front of, and higher than, the Herms.'[97] The Panathenaia, and particularly the Great Panathenaia held every four years, was the largest and greatest Athenian religious festival and it is difficult to imagine that it was not included in Xenophon's and Demosthenes' general references to cavalry participation in *pompai* or processions.[98] This is particularly so as equestrian games had been part of the

---

[93] Xen. *Hipparch.* 3. 1.
[94] Dem. 21. 171, 174; 4. 26.
[95] Martin, *Cavaliers*, 146–7.
[96] Plut. *Phok.* 37. 1.
[97] Athenaios, 4. 64 (167).
[98] Xen. *Hipparch.* 3. 1 and Dem. 4. 26. On the size and importance of the Panathenaia see E. Simon, *Festivals of Attica* (Madison, Wis., 1983), ch. 4; H. W. Parke, *Festivals of the Athenians* (London, 1977), 33.

competitions associated with this festival since the mid-sixth century.[99]

It also seems likely that the cavalry participated in the procession of *mystai* during the Great Eleusinia. I have argued in Appendix 3 that the rider on the Little Metropolis frieze in Athens is a cavalryman and represents a cavalry escort, and Martin also cites Polybios in support of cavalry participation.[100] The Eleusinian procession is described as a *hypapantesis* and the Polybios passage describes Attalos' entry into Athens (called an *apantesis*) in terms which suggest that the cavalry was a normal part of such processions.[101] The cumulative effect of all this evidence is therefore sufficient to sustain the view that the *hippeis* participated as a matter of course in many Athenian *pompai*, and almost certainly in the major ones like the Panathenaia.

In addition to their high public profile arising from private horse usage, public cavalry displays, collective and individual training, and cavalry participation in festal processions, the cavalry class was also identified with the cult of Poseidon *Hippios* and its temple at Kolonos. Sophokles, himself a native of Kolonos, describes the area as *euhippos*, or 'famed for horses', and later in the same play states that the most prized gifts to the city were the horse and power over the sea.[102] There may have been an equestrian statue of the hero Kolonos at the site,[103] and Euripides confirms the strong equestrian nature of the area with his description of it as 'Sacred Kolonos, home of the god of horses.'[104] An inventory, made by the *neokoroi*, or temple-wardens, of Poseidon *Hippios* at Kolonos (probably in 413/12 when the offerings were removed to Athens for safe keeping),[105] contains some items of equestrian equipment. The first of these is the [*kekry*]*phaleio*,

[99] J. A. Davison, 'Notes on the Panathenaea', *JHS* 78 (1958), 26–9.

[100] Martin, *Cavaliers*, 155–6, citing Polybios, 16. 25. 3 ff. In addition to the above evidence there are some indications of cavalry association with the Eleusinion during this period, cf. *IG* II² 1542, l. 25 and the Pythodoros relief, Eleusis 5101 (no. 30; Pl. 12).

[101] 'For not only the archons along with the *hippeis*, but also all the citizens with their wives and children, went out to meet them.' Polybios, 16. 25. 5.

[102] Soph. *OC* 668–9, 707–11. The term *euhippos* was also used of the King of Kyrene, Pindar, *Pythian*, 4, l. 2.

[103] Soph. *OC* 58–60 includes the phrase 'this rider Kolonos'.

[104] Eur. *Phoin.* 1707.

[105] *IG* I³ 405; for the date see W. E. Thompson, 'The Neokoroi of Poseidon Hippios', *Hesperia*, 40 (1971), 232–4.

most probably a pair of headbands from a horse's bridle.[106] The
second is the *macha[ira]* at lines 11–12 (although, despite Xenophon's suggestion that all cavalrymen should use this weapon,
not all dedications of *machairai* necessarily support a cavalry
link).[107]

The cavalry was also heavily involved in the oligarchic movements at the end of the fifth century and it is interesting to note
that the assembly which dissolved the democracy in 411 was held
not only at Kolonos but on ground sacred to Poseidon[108]—presumably the sanctuary of Poseidon *Hippios*. Further to this, the
Chairelaos of Kikynna mentioned as one of the wardens in line 2
of the temple inventory just discussed may well have been the
man of that name included in Xenophon's list of the Thirty
Tyrants.[109]

Finally, Aristophanes also records the close relationship between the god and the equestrian class. In one play the chorus of
cavalrymen invoke 'Poseidon Lord of Horses' while in the *Clouds*
Pheidippides swears not only by Poseidon *Hippios* but 'by *this*
Poseidon *Hippios*',[110] which suggests that he had a statuette of
the god in the room with him. Although none of these points is
by itself conclusive, together they are sufficient to show that there
was a close link between Poseidon *Hippios* and the cavalry class.
This too would have strengthened its identity as a group within
Athenian society.

A final reinforcement of this group or class identity in the eyes
of the city, and in some cases a reinforcement intended by the
hippeis themselves, would have arisen from cavalry dedications,
and from monuments depicting the cavalry. These include Dexileos' gravestone and the state monument to the citizens killed at

[106] Line 5, cf. A. M. Woodward, 'Financial Documents from the Athenian
Agora', *Hesperia*, 32 (1963), 159. Although this could be a woman's headdress,
dedications of riding tackle were made (Plut. *Kim.* 5. 2; *IG* II² 1542, l. 25; see
also Woodward, n. 19) and given the nature of the shrine this seems a much more
likely interpretation.

[107] Xen. *PH* 12. 11. For other dedications of *machairai*, see *IG* II² 1380, l. 8 (*c.*
400); *IG* II² 1415, ll. 16–17; 1421, ll. 84–6; 1423, ll. 11–13 (ranging from *c.*385/4 to
*c.*370, and all recording the same weapon); and *IG* II² 1424, l. 20 (*c.*368/7).
However, the weapon in *IG* II² 1415–23 was dedicated by the *Boule*, and Ar.
Thes. 693–5 and *Peace*, 948–9 have a *machaira* used as a sacrificial knife.

[108] Thucy. 8. 67. 2.

[109] Woodward, *Hesperia*, 32 (1963), 157–8, citing Xen. *Hell.* 2. 3. 2.

[110] Ar. *Kn.* 551; *Clouds*, 83 νὴ τὸν Ποσειδῶ τουτονὶ τὸν ἵππιον.

Corinth (Plates 11, 13), both with large cavalry reliefs, and a cavalry funerary inscription from the same campaign which was presumably also once attached to an equestrian relief.[111] Together with the statue of Anthemion on the Akropolis and Euphranor's painting in the Stoa of Zeus of the cavalry action at Mantineia, these would have been solid reminders of hippic activity and identity.[112]

By virtue of their wealth and their prominence in Athenian life, the cavalry class in general, and the serving cavalry in particular, therefore formed a distinct and readily identifiable group within Athenian society. As might be expected, this was reflected in their portrayal in Athenian literature and art. The opinions expressed there can conveniently be divided into two: the basic perception of the cavalry and the specific attitudes arising from this. While the basic perception remained essentially constant, the frequency and force of the more specific attitudes, and their distribution within the population, varied considerably over time. In addition, (and although it always had more potential to generate hostile rather than favourable attitudes) the base perception was essentially neutral, whereas the more specific attitudes to the *hippeis* were often quite partisan.

Before examining both the specific attitudes to the hippeis and the fundamental perception which underpinned them, the identification of the serving cavalrymen with the wider cavalry class should be reiterated. Although, as will be seen, some of the critical views expressed about members of the cavalry class are not explicit criticisms of those on the cavalry rolls, there was rarely any real distinction drawn between the two.[113] In essence, criticism of the general equestrian milieu, of which the cavalry corps itself was the most prominent and frequent public reminder, does seem to have affected the attitude towards the serving cavalryman. The opinions expressed about the cavalry class, and in particular about the wealth and display of its richest members, also affected the less wealthy members of the cavalry corps; both were regarded as part of one and the same group by Athenians in general.

[111] *IG* II² 5222.

[112] Anthemion: *Ath. Pol.* 7. 4. On Euphranor's painting see R. Vasić, 'Some Observations on Euphranor's Cavalry Battle', *AJA* 83 (1979), 345–9; see also 224–5 below. Other equestrian paintings of impressive appearance included Mikon's painting of mounted Amazons referred to in Ar. *Lysis.* 678–9.

[113] Dem. 21 is an exception.

The Basic Perception of the Cavalry

The basic perception of the Athenian cavalry can be recovered quite readily from fifth- and fourth-century literature and art. An analysis of these reveals that the *hippeis* were basically seen as forming a wealthy, aristocratic, and youthful section of society. This general perception of the cavalry and cavalry class was apparently universal within Athens, being expressed at all levels and in all literary genres throughout the fifth and fourth centuries.

Wealth

As we have seen earlier in this chapter, owning a horse (and in particular breeding horses) was an expensive business, and it is not surprising that wealth was seen by the Athenians as one of the main characteristics of the *hippeis*. However, the importance of this view is not so much that it was true but that it, rather than say public service or military effectiveness, was seen as a characteristic, and possibly the most dominant characteristic, of the class and also the corps. In fact, it is one of the most commonly expressed or implied views of the cavalry and occurs in all types of Athenian literature.

In comedy for example, the expense of horsekeeping is usually portrayed as a burden, the comic potential of which is most fully exploited in Aristophanes' *Clouds*. The basis for Strepsiades' actions throughout this play is his complaint at lines 12–35 that his son's equestrian interests are bankrupting him. This motif recurs in other plays: in the *Peace*, Trygaios rejects his daughter's suggestion to ascend to heaven on Pegasos and not a dung-beetle on simple economic grounds—he cannot afford to buy feed for a horse, whereas a dung-beetle recycles his master's food.[114] Similarly, it is revealed in the *Birds* that one common topic of conversation in barbers' shops was the perfidy of those who persuaded one's sons to become interested in chariot-racing. This makes even more heartfelt the battered Strepsiades' cry in the *Clouds* that he would prefer his son to maintain a four-horse chariot team (where before it had only been a two-horse team) than to continue beating him.[115]

[114] Ar. *Peace*, 135–9.
[115] Ar. *Birds*, 1439–43; *Clouds*, 1406–7.

In tragedy, horses are consistently connected with the wealthy and powerful; the expense required to keep them manifests itself in gorgeous display, not in complaints. In Aischylos' *Prometheus Bound* the eponymous hero claims proudly that it was he who first tamed horses and harnessed them to chariots 'as an adornment of very wealthy luxury' (ἄγαλμα τῆς ὑπερπλούτου χλιδῆς.[116] This is also a nice illustration of the ambivalent attitudes which could derive from such display. The word χλιδή (appearing in the genitive, χλιδῆς), translated here as 'luxury', can mean 'insolence', and is in fact used in this way earlier in the same speech (line 436). It is unlikely that the Prometheus character intended χλιδή to mean 'insolence' in the section just quoted, as he is listing there the benefits he has conferred on mankind, but even so the word undoubtedly suggested something of the unacceptable face of pride and luxury to the audience.

Prose and oratory too present horse-owning as an expensive pastime. Xenophon claimed that the keeping of chariot horses marked one out as wealthy, and Aristotle believed that the number of horses a man owned indicated the degree of his wealth because 'horse-breeding requires the ownership of large resources'.[117] Plato's *Meno* linked wealth and riding as the two main things for which the Thessalians were previously renowned, and one of Isokrates' works used the feeding of a hungry team to represent luxurious extravagance.[118] A speech of Hypereides complained that Lykophron continually overstretched his financial resources by breeding horses for the glory of the city.[119] Finally, Xenophon advised hipparchs to increase recruiting by telling fathers that, under their command, young men would be discouraged from making extravagant equine purchases.[120]

The breeding of race-horses and participation in chariot-racing was the most potent symbol of the cavalry class. However, despite some acknowledgement that chariot-horses were more of a luxury item than war-horses, it is clear that in general terms the stereotype of the rich *hippeus* also applied to the cavalryman of more

[116] Aisch. *Prom.* 462–6.
[117] Xen. *Ages.* 9. 6; Arist. *Pol.* 1289ᵇ33–6 (4. 3); 1321ᵃ5–13 (6. 7); the quotation is l. 11 of the latter reference.
[118] Pl. *Meno*, 70a–b; Isok. 6. 55.
[119] Hyper. 1. 16.
[120] Xen. *Hipparch.* 1. 11–12.

modest means.[121] Aristophanes, for example, linked one horse
with expense, and Lysias shows it could be associated with
arrogance and insolence.[122] However, the evidence for horse
values discussed in Appendix 4 shows that in reality there was
considerable variation in the sum each cavalryman was able or
willing to spend on his mount and it might have been fairer to
regard only the larger *hippotrophoi*, or horse-breeders, as truly
rich. Even so, owning just one horse apparently marked an
Athenian as possessing considerably larger financial resources
than those of the average citizen. It is therefore not surprising
that the class as a whole, and not just the large-scale breeders,
was regarded as wealthy.

Aristocracy

Closely linked with the view of the *hippeis* as wealthy was their
association with aristocracy or aristocratic tendencies. This was
especially prevalent in tragedy but occurs in all Athenian literary
genres. For example, the idea that equestrianism was a suitable
medium for educating royalty, and the upper echelons of society,
frequently surfaces during the classical period. In the fifth century
both Perikles and Themistokles had their sons trained as expert
horsemen and the latter's son, Kleophantos, could apparently
even ride and throw a javelin while standing up on horseback.[123]
Somewhat later, Aristotle's *Politics* records the existence of a
contemporary belief that the sons of kings ought to be educated
in 'riding and the art of war'.[124] All this is rather reminiscent of
Herodotos' claim that the Persian education system was based on
teaching children three things: 'to ride, to use the bow, and to tell
the truth' (ἱππεύειν καὶ τοξεύειν καὶ ἀληθίζεσθαι).[125] However, the
attitude was not without its critics. In the *Politics* passage just
mentioned, Aristotle was careful to note that he was putting
forward the opinion of others and not his own views. Similarly,
Plato's judgement of the children of Themistokles and Perikles
was that, despite their training, each was not as good (*agathos*) or

[121] Chariot horses: Xen. *Ages.* 9. 6; [Dem.] 42. 24; 'more modest means' is
relative to the richest members of the hippic class and not to society as a whole.
[122] Ar. *Peace*, 135–9; Lysias, 24. 11.
[123] Pl. *Meno*, 93d, 94a–b.
[124] Arist. *Pol.* 1277ª16–18 (3. 4).
[125] Hdtos 1. 136; cf. Aisch. *Pers.* 21–32. Judging by the Behistun inscription,
Herodotos may well be right.

wise (*sophos*) as his father, nor possessed of as much virtue or excellence (*arete*).[126]

Riding was therefore associated with the education of rulers and aristocrats and this must have been reinforced by the sight of young men of the leisured classes exercising their horses or practising their riding at the exercise grounds. The link between the equestrian class and the aristocracy (or an aristocratic way of life) was also prominent in the general literary treatment of the horse, and in particular of the chariot—the symbol of the richest members of the class. In the *Erotic Essay*, ascribed rather doubtfully to Demosthenes, it is claimed that Athenian *apobatai* (equestrian competitors who leaped in and out of moving chariots) were drawn not just exclusively from citizens but also from the best (*hoi beltistoi*).[127] When Peisistratos gained his second tyranny he considered it appropriate for Phye, his bogus Athena, to ride in a chariot. This was presumably to impress the people as a mark of her supposed divinity—although it failed with the later writer Herodotos who described it as the silliest trick he had ever come across.[128] The link between aristocracy and horses or chariots is particularly commonplace in Attic tragedy which uses equestrian imagery to help create an atmosphere of nobility, wealth, and opulence.

Aischylos, for instance, pictures the Persian aristocracy of Xerxes' invasion as either mounted or chariot-borne, and the great King himself is described in Homeric style as 'flashing from his eyes the dark glare of a murderous dragon, with hosts of soldiers and sailors; he urges on his Syrian chariot.'[129] Sophokles too has the occasional reference: Laios rides in a horse-drawn vehicle when travelling abroad[130] and elsewhere there are firm links between horses and both gods and heroes. The hero Kolonos himself is portrayed as a rider and Aphrodite is later described as *chrusanios* or 'golden-reined'.[131] Euripides in particular uses

[126] Pl. *Meno*, 93e and 94a–b. Interestingly, Plut. *Them*. 32. 1 interprets the remarks about Kleophantos rather more strongly than this, claiming that 'Plato the philosopher records that he was a good horseman but not worth much else.'
[127] [Dem.] 61. 23.   [128] Hdtos 1. 60.
[129] Aisch. *Pers*. 21–32, 40–8, 81–4.
[130] Soph. *Oedipus the King*, 752–3, 800–4.
[131] Sophokles *OC* 58–60, 693. The epithet *chrusanios* or *chrusenios* was also applied to Artemis: *Il*. 6. 205, to Ares: *Od*. 8. 285, and to Thesmophore (Demeter) in Pindar fr. 37 = Hymn 3 in A. Peuch (ed.), *Pindar*, 3rd edn., iv (Paris, 1961), 92.

equestrian imagery to establish an atmosphere of aristocracy, wealth, and even royalty, and does so more frequently than either Sophokles or Aischylos. It is interesting to note that Aischylos, who wrote entirely before the institution of the cavalry as a corps of 1,000 men, has fewest references while Sophokles and Euripides, most of whose plays post-date the reform, have a far higher proportion of equestrian images. As was perhaps the case for the Parthenon frieze,[132] their work may have been influenced by the prominence of the cavalry in public life. However, if this is true, Euripides' particularly frequent use of this device must also have been influenced by personal preference.

Apart from the stock references to the sun's chariot,[133] horses and chariots are associated with many gods and heroes in Euripides' plays. Athena is chariot-borne twice, once against the giants and once on the blazon of the Athenian contingent at Aulis. She is also once graced with the epithet *ambrotopolou*, 'of the immortal steeds'.[134] Poseidon too is portrayed riding his grey steeds across the waves, and a whole host of heroes and demigods, ranging from Herakles through Zethus and Amphion to Kastor and Polydeukes, ride or drive their way through various plays.[135] Pelops' chariot race against Myrtiles is also a popular image and Amphiaraos, Iolaos, and Hyllos all appear mounted, the last two in battle.[136] Perhaps most impressive of all is the Thracian prince Rhesos, described as follows:

> I saw Rhesos, like a God,
> Towering upon his Thracian battle-chariot.
> Golden the yoke-beam was that linked the necks
> Of chariot-steeds gleaming whiter than the snow.
> Upon his shoulders his gold-blazoned shield
> Flashed: a bronze Gorgon, as on Pallas' shield,
> Upon the frontlet of his horses bound,
> Clanging with many a bell clashed forth dismay.[137]

[132] Martin, *Cavaliers*, 134.

[133] For example, *IA* 156–9; *Or.* 1001–2; *Phoin.* 1–3, 1562–3; *IT* 192–3, 1138–9.

[134] *Hek.* 466–71; *IA* 247–52; *Trojan Women*, 535–6.

[135] Poseidon: *Andromache*, 1010; Herakles: *Her.* 174–80; Zethus and Amphion: ibid. 26–30; Kastor and Polydeukes: *Helen*, 636–45.

[136] Pelops: *Or.* 987–94, 1547–8; *IT* 1–3. Amphiaraos: *Phoin.* 171–3. Iolaos and Hyllos: *Children of Herakles*, 800–3, 843 ff.

[137] [Eur.] *Rh.* 301–8, slightly adapted from A. S. Way's translation, *Euripides' Plays* (London, 1956), 328.

Such a figure clearly inspired awe and admiration in the shep-
herd who delivered this speech and this is a common aspect of the
association of horses with divine, semi-divine, or aristocratic
figures in tragedy. One can compare this with the close association
between horses and heroes in Attic votive reliefs. Mitropoulou has
plausibly argued that in these contexts the inclusion of a horse's
head is intended to show 'that the reclining figure or figures are
heroes and not gods'. She even provides one example of a second
century Rhodian relief where the horse is apparently a substitute
for the hero.[138]

In tragedy, as in art, the horse itself is often treated as a
majestic or awe-inspiring beast, particularly in battle scenes.
Aischylos' imagery here is particularly effective, with descriptions
like 'the Argive host in full array is already near at hand, advancing, filling the air with dust; white foam stains the plain with
drops from the chargers' breath.'[139] Another is of Eteokles' team
eager for battle: 'as he wheels them around, his horses champ at
the bit in their eagerness to fall upon the gates. Their piped nose-
bands, filled with blasts of air from their nostrils, produce an
outlandish roaring sound.'[140] A large part of the description of
war in Sophokles' OC is devoted to the picture of cavalry charging
across the plain, and [Euripides]' Rhesos contains the exhortation
'come, appear, raising up your gold-rich shield aslant the split
chariot rail into the eyes of Achilles, urging on your colts and
brandishing your two-pronged javelin.'[141] Finally, in the same
play even two stalwarts like Odysseus and Diomedes were initially
alarmed by the noise of the horse chains from the parked chariots.[142] This imagery is reminiscent of the portrayal of horses in
monumental sculpture—especially the type which shows infantry
ridden down by cavalry (Plates 2, 11–13), but also in others; see
Plate 16 for a particularly impressive depiction of a horse in a
non-combat scene.

The power and majesty of the horse and of the chariot are also

---

[138] E. Mitropoulou, Horses' Heads and Snake (sic) in Banquet Reliefs and their
Meaning (Athens, 1976), 70.

[139] Aisch. Seven Against Thebes, 59–61. It is even more impressive in the
original: ἐγγὺς γὰρ ἤδη πάνοπλος Ἀργείων στρατὸς | χωρεῖ, κονίει, πεδία δ' ἀργηστὴς
ἀφρὸς | χραίνει σταλαγμοῖς ἱππικῶν ἐκ πλευμόνων.

[140] Ibid. 461–4. See also 121–3, 150–4, 203–7, 391–4, 475–6, and Pers. 45–8.

[141] Soph. OC 1059 ff.; [Eur.] Rh. 370–5.

[142] Rh. 565 ff.

evident in non-battle scenes. The use of equestrian imagery or
epithets like 'golden-reined' (*chrusanios*), 'of the immortal steeds'
(*ambrotopolou*), or 'driver (or rider) of horses' (*hippotas*)[143] seems
intended to conjure up an heroic or Homeric atmosphere suitable
for the subject matter of tragedy. This would certainly accord
with Aristotle's theory that the manner of depiction was very
important in ensuring the success of a tragic play. He claimed
that tragedy 'is a representation of an action that is worth serious
attention . . . in language enriched by a variety of artistic devices
appropriate to the several parts of the play'.[144] Therefore, he
suggested, the best plots are those drawn from the histories of a
few famous families and the language involved should be varied
and enriched with metaphors rather than commonplace.[145]

The use of horses and equestrian imagery to achieve this in
tragedy is confirmed by three passages in Aristophanes which
suggest that equestrian imagery was typical of that genre. In the
first, the Euripides character in the *Frogs* accuses Aischylos of
introducing the adjective *kodonophalaropolous* ('with jingling
harness') purely for effect.[146] In the *Peace*, Trygaios' daughter
believes that a dung-beetle is an inappropriate mount for a hero
and asks her father 'shouldn't you have harnessed winged Pegasos
in order to seem more of a tragic hero to the gods?' Finally, the
wandering poet who tries to peddle his wares to Peisthetairos in
the *Birds* sprinkles his conversation with overblown phrases,
including an equine metaphor comparing a saying of the Muses
with 'the flashing hooves of horses'.[147]

Euripides and, to a slightly lesser extent, Aischylos and Sophokles used equestrian metaphor, analogy, and imagery, to help
create their desired effect and in doing so undoubtedly contributed to the contemporary perception of the *hippeis*. The influence,

[143] For *hippotas* see Eur. *El.* 448–9 and *Hek.* 710. For the power and majesty
of horses in non-battle scenes, see Soph. *Elektra*, 690 ff.; Eur. *Hipp.* 228–31,
1218 ff.

[144] Arist. *Poetics*, 1449b24–8 (6), T. S. Dorsch's translation, *Aristotle/Horace/
Longinus: Classical Literary Criticism* (Harmondsworth, 1986), 38–9.

[145] Arist. *Poetics*, 1453a7–22 (13) and 1458a18–1459a16 (22).

[146] Ar. *Frogs*, 961–3. The only extant tragedy with horses actually outfitted like
this (although *kodonophalaropolous* is not used) is [Eur.] *Rh.* 307–8 (quoted, 195
above). It is therefore possible that this is an ironical accusation reflecting upon
Euripides himself, but as so few of Aischylos' plays are extant it is not possible to
be certain that he never used this word.

[147] Ar. *Peace*, 135–6; *Birds*, 924 ff.

however, was reciprocal: equestrian imagery was exploited by the tragedians to emphasize the wealth, power, and nobility of their subjects because this fitted with the common perception of the equestrian class. Their continuing use of this imagery in turn undoubtedly reinforced this perception and therefore contributed to contemporary views of the *hippeis*.

Youth

Another commonly held view of the cavalry, both in literature and art, was that its members were predominantly young. However, and this is an important part of the concept, they were fairly distinctive young men—wealthy, aristocratic, and long-haired. This view of the cavalry occurs frequently in both comedy and prose, and also makes an occasional appearance in tragedy. There must have been some truth in it as riding bareback in combat must have required a fairly high level of fitness and Xenophon certainly sees rich young men as a prime source of recruits for the corps.[148] However, it cannot have been entirely correct as Lysias, for example, describes some *hippeis*, who had never served in the infantry as men who 'had always been cavalrymen and had done much harm to the enemy'.[149] This suggests fairly long-term service with the mounted arm and Xenophon too talks of older *hippeis* as well as of young ones; Meidias apparently served with the cavalry when aged 50.[150] Nevertheless, the stock cavalryman of literature and art was youthful and, in addition, usually aristocratic and long-haired.

This is particularly so in Aristophanic comedy, with the *Knights* naturally providing some of the more obvious examples. For instance, the chorus of cavalrymen, later described by Paphlagon as being composed of 'youths', make a plea to the audience 'not to envy our flowing locks nor our well-groomed look'. 'Demos' too, when suggesting that he is not as simple as the chorus and others believe, retorts to their criticism with the remark 'you have no brains under your long hair'.[151] The word for long hair used here, *kome*, is also used elsewhere in Aristophanes' depiction of cavalrymen. The *hippomanes* or 'horse-mad' Pheidippides in

---

[148] Xen. *Hipparch.* 1. 11–12.
[149] Lysias, 14. 10.
[150] Xen. *PH* 2. 1; Dem. 21. 154, 162.
[151] Ar. *Kn.* 580, 730–1, 1121–2.

the *Clouds* is described at line 14 as 'having long hair' (ὁ δὲ κόμην
ἔχων) and elsewhere as being spawned of Koesyra, a byword for
opulence and luxurious living.[152] The phylarch buying porridge
in the market-place in *Lysistrata* is also described as long-haired,
although in this case there is no indication of his age.[153]

The direct association of youths and the Athenian cavalry
corps is infrequent in tragedy because of its preference for mythical subject matter,[154] but there is some linking of youths and the
equestrian milieu. For example, Euripides' portrayal of Hippolytos in the play of that name produced in 428 may be based on
observation of contemporary well-to-do youths. Hippolytos lived
to ride and hunt, character traits which eventually caused his
downfall at the hands of Aphrodite. His death was, ironically,
encompassed through his favourite chariot team, which he used
to hand-feed, and one of his regrets at dying was that no one
would look after Artemis' hounds or horses, nor serve her, nor
tend her images.[155] Hippomedon, one of the seven who marched
against Thebes, and whom Sophokles describes as being sent off
to war by his father,[156] displays a similarly keen interest in both
riding and hunting. He is described in another play as eschewing
the easy life in favour of 'going into the countryside, rejoicing in
horses, and bending the bow with his hands'.[157]

The sculpture and vase-painting also present this view of the
cavalry and cavalry class, although in the case of grave stelae this
picture may have been influenced almost as much by the self-
perception of the class as by the attitude of the painter or sculptor.
Most cavalrymen in art are portrayed as young—only two of the
horsemen on the Parthenon frieze are portrayed as bearded, the
others are youths. This pattern is repeated on grave stelae and
other sculpture where bearded, and hence older, cavalrymen are
much less common than beardless youths.

In fact, many of the existing examples of older cavalrymen in

[152] *Clouds*, 799–800; cf. 48 and *Acharn.* 614. See also Sommerstein's note on l.
48 *Aristophanes: Clouds* (Warminster, 1982), 161 and Dover's note, *Aristophanes:
Clouds* (Oxford, 1968), 99–100; cf. W. J. W. Koster (ed.), *Scholia in Aristophanem*
i. 3. 2; *In Nubis* (Groningen, 1974), 202–3.
[153] Ar. *Lysis.* 561–2; Moschion, the phylarch in Menander's *Samia* is clearly
young.
[154] An exception is the eulogy of the cavalry, Soph. *OC* 1059 ff.
[155] Eur. *Hipp.* 10–22, 108–13, 1132–9, 1355–7, 1397, 1399.
[156] *OC* 1317–18.
[157] Eur. *Suppliants*, 885–6.

sculpture are representations of either phylarchs or hipparchs, whose age, seniority, and position were reflected in the wearing of a beard. This is certainly true of the three phylarchs on the Bryaxis monument (relief 21), the Pythodoros relief at Eleusis (Plate 12), and probably also of the Leontis dedication and the two bearded riders on the Parthenon frieze.[158] This leaves only a few monuments with bearded horsemen whose status as hipparchs or phylarchs cannot be determined (for example, the four funeral lekythoi of Menyllos—probably set up *c.*340–330, and the rider on the Moscow stela);[159] the majority of the other extant reliefs portray beardless riders.[160]

The vase-paintings too present a similar picture and suggest that this image of the youthful cavalryman pre-dated the formal institution of the 1,000-strong corps in the second half of the fifth century (see Plates 1–2, 3–4, 7, 15). Only ten Greeks depicted with horses on those vases in Appendix 1 for which I have seen illustrations are bearded,[161] and, like the reliefs, some of these may represent cavalry officers. This seems to be the case with the bearded man in a chiton, chlamys, and petasos, and carrying two spears (Plate 14) illustrated on the inside of a cup by the Painter of Acropolis 356.[162] Although he is not in fact mounted or holding a horse, the other scenes on this kylix (see Plate 15 for one) strongly suggest cavalry training and it seems probable that, like the two bearded riders on the Parthenon frieze, he too represents a hipparch.

This is supported by the existence of two other cups where the

---

[158] Parthenon frieze figures: West IV 8 and VIII 15. The Eleusis relief (no. 30), although incomplete, probably represents Pythodoros himself as the bearded cavalryman in the upper central portion of the stone (Pl. 12). The Bryaxis relief depicts three different phylarchs from the same family, all victorious in the *anthippasia*; the Leontis relief (no. 36; Bugh, *Horsemen*, fig. 7) almost certainly depicts the same event. See also the probable hipparch on vase no. 42 (Pl. 14).

[159] Menyllos lekythoi (reliefs 18–19, 34–5): D. Peppas-Delmousou, "«'Επιστήματα» τοῦ Τάφου τοῦ Μενύλλου 'Αλαιέως. 'Η Βάση EM 13451", *AAA* 10 (1977), 228–30, 235, 240; Moscow stela (relief 4): J. Frel and B. M. Kingsley, 'Three Attic Sculpture Workshops of the Early Fourth Century BC', *GRBS* 11 (1970), pl. 24. There are also seven other examples in App. 2: nos. 3, 8, 9(?), 15, 17, 24, 29.

[160] Reliefs 1, 6, 7, 10–13, 16, 20, 22, 25–6, 27 (3 riders), 33, 36 (at least 2 riders), 37.

[161] Vases: 20 (at least two figures), 25, 34, 41, 46–7, 109, 156, 166. Vase 31 has 3 bearded horsemen who may be either Greek or Thracian but the quality of the available illustration makes it difficult to distinguish.

[162] Vase 42.

pictures on the inside are closely linked with an exterior equestrian design. The first, by the Dokimasia Painter,[163] provides excellent evidence for this. It shows an inspection of cavalrymen as a continuous scene on both A and B; the interior depicts a dismounted *hippotoxotes*, accompanied by his horse and in the process of checking an arrow for straightness (Plates 3–5). An earlier cup by Onesimos (vase 28) also contributes some support: side A portrays youths involved in equestrian training (Plate 1) and side B youths training or exercising a horse. The interior has a naked youth in a petasos, carrying a spear in his right hand, with an animal (leopard?) skin draped over his left arm. In this case, the youth, like the bearded man in Plate 14, probably represents a dismounted cavalryman; the animal skin appears to be a saddle-cloth (see Plate 16) pressed into service as a make-shift shield, just as the youth on slab VII of the West frieze of the Parthenon uses his as a garment.[164] Although the figure on this second vase and the bearded man on the cup in Plate 14 are without horses, this is explained by the medium.

The problem of fitting a horse and a man into the centre of a kylix is illustrated by Plate 5. Here, the archer could only be fitted in as a dismounted figure and, compared with the horses and men on the exterior, his horse is portrayed slightly underscale in relation to him. Even so, the horse's right rear leg disappears outside the edge of the circle. The solution Onesimos and the Painter of Acropolis 356 adopted for this problem was to omit the horse altogether and to show the connection with the cavalry or cavalry class by the figure's dress and equipment and the subject of the exterior scenes. Including the three figures of ambiguous nationality on vase 31 and our bearded hipparch without horse in Plate 14, this gives a total of fourteen bearded cavalrymen on the vases—a minute number when compared with the number of beardless riders depicted on the other pots. The conclusion must be that the painters, and presumably their prospective buyers, essentially saw the cavalry in terms of youths rather than older men.

However, as the reliefs, and possibly some of the vase-paintings

---

[163] Vase 32.

[164] The youth (figure no. 14) wears it over his chest and shoulders. For animal skin saddles see also vases 157 (Persian), 159, 193 (Amazon), 198, and relief no. 28 (Plate 16).

too, were commissioned by members of the cavalry class, they
may have had some influence on the execution of the figures. In
this case both grave stelae and ceramic items would be slightly
more likely to represent the cavalry class' perception of itself
rather than the perception of Athenian society as a whole. Despite
this, the influence of the buyer presumably did not entirely
determine the artists' treatment of their subjects, especially as
these are in accord with the basic view of the cavalry held by
other Athenians—the literary evidence shows that the basic view
of the cavalry class included the idea that it was a predominantly
youthful group. In addition, the Parthenon frieze has a similar
treatment of the *hippeis* and it was a public commission, rather
than one designed for wealthy patrons.

The Perception

The Athenians, therefore, basically perceived their cavalry and
cavalry class as a group of wealthy aristocratic youths. At its
simplest level, which is reflected in most of the examples given
above, this perception is essentially neutral—by itself it neither
suggests hostility nor goodwill towards the *hippeis*. But people
reacted differently to the *hippeis*, and to their perceived characteristics; depending upon their view of wealth, aristocracy, and youth,
this could produce either favourable or unfavourable attitudes to
the cavalry.

For example, Athenian public art, public practices, and literature confirm that the cavalry's basic attributes could excite (or at
least did not hinder) a favourable response. The prominence of
the riders and the *apobatai* in the Parthenon frieze points to
collective pride in the equestrian side of Athenian society, as does
an inscription which is roughly contemporary with the frieze.
This lists those who are entitled to dine at the state's expense in
the Prytaneion (the building where the currently presiding section
of the Council was housed) and includes, among such worthies as
the descendants of the tyrant-slayers Harmodios and Aristogeiton,
'victors in the races for horses and chariots at the Olympic,
Pythian, Nemean, and other games'.[165]

Victors in equestrian games, which represented the most expensive and aristocratic pursuit in fifth- and fourth-century Greece,

[165] *IG* I³ 131, ll. 15–17.

were therefore amongst those honoured by free meals in the
Prytaneion. This practice seems to have continued for some time
since, when asked to nominate his own punishment for corrupting
the youth and introducing new deities, Sokrates suggested he
should be similarly honoured (the jury was unamused by this and
sentenced him to death instead).[166] However, it is possible that
the victorious horsemen and chariot-owners in this inscription
were singled out for an additional and special honour. W. E.
Thompson argues that as the equestrian victors should logically
have been encompassed by the earlier general reference to victors
at the Olympic, Pythian, Isthmian, and Nemean games (lines 11–
15), their later specific mention for these same games (lines 15–
17) most probably refers to a different privilege which the other,
non-equestrian, victors did not receive. He plausibly suggests
that this involved the provision of fodder for the horses involved
in the victory.[167] In addition to the strong reasons Thompson
adduces for this, it is clear that winning teams sometimes did
receive special treatment, if only at the hands of their owners.
Aelian records that Kimon's grandfather Miltiades (nicknamed
Koalemos or 'the thick') buried his famous thrice-victorious team
in the Kerameikos when they eventually died; Euagoras of Sparta
apparently accorded one of his teams similar treatment.[168] If
Thompson's theory is correct, it serves to emphasize further the
esteem in which equestrian victors could be held at Athens.

The popularity which could accrue to such men is also attested
in the literature. Thucydides, for example, has Alkibiades talk of
the honour the city gained from his entering seven chariots at
Olympia and carrying off the first, second, and fourth prizes—a
financial and equestrian display which was still remembered in
the fourth century.[169] Xenophon too talked of the desirability of
a city possessing the greatest number of horse-breeders and
competitors at equestrian festivals, and of the admiration which
accrued to private competitors in such events.[170] Victories could

[166] Pl. *Apology*, 36b ff.
[167] W. E. Thompson, 'More on the Prytaneion Decree', *GRBS* 20 (1979), 326–
9.
[168] Aelian, *On Animals*, 12. 40.
[169] Thucy. 6. 16. 1–2; cf. Isok. 16. 32–4 (dating to 397). Dem. 21. 144–5 (dating
to 351/50) included these equestrian victories on the credit side of Alkibiades'
rather chequered career.
[170] Xen. *Hiero*, 11. 5.

also bring forms of public recognition other than free meals—
Lysias states of an unnamed cavalryman (5.195), that 'he not
only bought magnificent horses but also won horse races at the
Isthmian and Nemean games so that the city was extolled in
public and he was crowned.'[171]

The *Erotic Essay* gives some inkling of why chariot-racing in
particular was so popular with all sections of society. In sections
24–5 the author dwells on its brilliancy, contrasting it favourably
with boxing and athletics and describing it as an event which

in the magnificence and majesty of the equipment resembles the power
of the gods, moreover provides the most pleasant spectacle comprised of
the greatest number and largest variety of features, and is considered
worthy of the greatest prizes. For, in addition to those prizes offered,
exercising and practising such skills in itself offers a worthy prize to
those who even moderately desire excellence (*arete*).

It is not surprising then that the fictional young cavalryman
Pheidippides found his mother's vision of the future (riding in a
chariot to the Akropolis like his uncle Megakles) much more
attractive than his father's picture of a life herding goats.[172]
Finally, good horse teams are portrayed in the *Rhesos* as so
worthy of admiration that they are seen as very valuable spoils of
war.[173]

Race-horses and chariots, the most potent symbols of the
cavalry class' wealth and aristocratic nature, could therefore
arouse feelings of admiration and a favourable response from the
citizenry on both a public and private level. However, the perceived characteristics of the *hippeis* could also excite hostility of
the type which could not only damage the cavalry's morale but
also overshadow its military virtues. The potential for this
reaction developed as Athenian society became increasingly democratic, and aristocratic values became less acceptable. This hostility was partially associated with the general criticism of the rich
which Isokrates complained about in a case involving levels of
property ownership. He contrasts the happy days of his childhood,
when people exaggerated their wealth because of the standing and
reputation it gave, with the present day (354/3), when

---

[171] Lysias, 19. 63.
[172] Ar. *Clouds*, 66–74.
[173] [Eur.] *Rh.* 164–94, 613–21.

a wealthy man must be prepared to defend himself, as if being rich was one of the greatest crimes, and keep a sharp look-out if he intends to ensure his safety. This is because it has become far more dangerous to seem to be rich than to be patently committing a crime—the latter are pardoned or given small penalties while the former are completely destroyed. You will see that more men have been deprived of their property than those who have paid the penalty for their wrongdoings.[174]

Although there is undoubtedly a degree of personal bitterness running through this speech, Hypereides too complains that the possession of wealth can be used to smear a man in court, and there are numerous examples of this in other speeches.[175]

However, such hostility often focused on the evidence of wealth provided by cavalry service or equestrian sports, and especially on the type of ostentatious display which chariot-racing typified. Thucydides, for example, has Alkibiades refer to this as an apparently normal hazard of performing liturgies, stating 'whenever I am distinguished by providing choruses, or in any other way, I am naturally envied by the citizens'.[176] This is confirmed by several of the examples of the admiration for equestrian victors and horse-breeders just discussed which also contain references to the likelihood of envy (*phthonos*) arising instead of admiration. In fact, there seems to be a very fine line between these two reactions to the attributes of the cavalry class. In the *Hiero*, after pointing out the admiration generated by equestrian victors in general, Xenophon is careful to caution the despot of the title not to compete against private citizens in chariot races, as victory in these circumstances 'will not arouse admiration but envy'.[177] In the *Rhesos*, horses are admired but their owners envied, to the extent that, having extracted the promise of Achilles' chariot team as a reward for spying, Dolon feels constrained to say to Hektor 'but do not be envious; you, who are the noblest in the land, have a thousand possessions to gladden you.' Later in the same play, Rhesos' groom automatically assumes that Hektor

[174] Isok. 15. 160.
[175] Cf. Isokr. 7. 31–5; Hyper. 4. 32. Other examples are Dem. 21. 158–9; Isok. 20. 19–22; [Lysias], 6. 48; Lysias, 28. 6–7; [Andok.] 4. 30–2; Lyk. *Against Leokrates*, 139–40; cf. Xen. *Oik.* 2. 6.
[176] Thucy. 6. 16. 3. But see Rhodes, 'Political Activity in Classical Athens', *JHS* 106 (1986), 137–8 on the political value of chariot-racing to the wealthy Athenian.
[177] Xen. *Hiero*, 11. 5–6.

has murdered Rhesos for the sake of his chariot team, praised by Athena herself with the words 'no such chariot-team as this exists anywhere else on earth'.[178]

Envy or hostility of this type was especially likely to occur when someone was thought to be putting on a display of wealth inappropriate to their station. As a young man in the early fifth century, Themistokles was heavily criticized for trying to rival Kimon's establishment at the Olympic games. Kimon's display was accepted because he was young, and from an illustrious family, and so thought entitled to such ostentation whereas Themistokles 'had not yet become well-known, but in appearing to try to rise above his station without any real means he acquired the additional reputation of boastfulness.'[179]

For the poorer sections of society, though, the actual level of wealth behind the display was probably immaterial, and something of this general attitude is apparent in Aristophanes' work of the last quarter of the fifth century. In the *Clouds*, a rich creditor limps on stage having suffered an accident while driving a chariot and Strepsiades eventually drives him off with a *kentron*, or goad, proclaiming; 'I'll poke you up your thoroughbred (*seiraphoron*) arse'.[180] The use of the word *seiraphoron* is interesting here—I have used A. H. Sommerstein's rather neat translation of 'thoroughbred' but, as he points out, it literally means 'trace-horse' and conveys the sense of 'pampered'.[181] Although Strepsiades is ultimately punished for his behaviour towards his creditors, his treatment of the limping charioteer on this occasion probably appealed to many in the audience. The same contempt is expressed in the *Wasps*, although this time of the rich in general rather than of someone explicitly connected with horses. When describing the pleasures of jury service, Philokleon asks 'but isn't this (being a juror) great power and a flouting of wealth?'[182]

In all this, the cavalry class was envied not so much for its possession of horses *per se* but for the financial resources which this required. However, closely associated with the view of the cavalry as wealthy, and the hostility this often elicited, was the

---

[178] [Eur.] *Rh.* 193–4, 620–1, 837–40; cf. 859–60.
[179] Plut. *Them.* 5. 3.
[180] Ar. *Clouds*, 1259–72, 1299–1300.
[181] Sommerstein, *Aristophanes: Clouds*, 223.
[182] Ar. *Wasps*, 575.

common linking of equestrian symbols with arrogance. An excellent example of this is in the *Wasps*, where Bdelykleon is described
as *phruagmosemnakous* or 'having a very proud manner like a
whinnying thoroughbred'.[183] The word is apparently an Aristophanic coinage, derived from *phruagma* or a 'violent snorting,
especially neighing or whinnying of a spirited horse' and Sommerstein reconstructs the meaning of the word as 'very (*ak*) proud
(*semnos*) like a whinnying thoroughbred (*phruattesthai*
"whinny")'.[184]

This linking of horses and horsemen with arrogance is confirmed by the fourth-century orators. In a speech Lysias wrote
for a client trying to get a disability pension restored, the speaker
claims that he rides a horse around Athens 'through necessity and
not through arrogance (*hubris*)'—as his opponent has apparently
claimed.[185] The use of the highly pejorative *hubris* here is particularly significant. Elsewhere, a speech ascribed to Demosthenes
suggests that luxury and arrogance lie behind Phainippos' decision
to give up riding a horse and to buy a chariot. In another speech
he smears each of Aischines' associates with the phrase 'great and
glittering horse-breeder'.[186]

Similar sentiments occur in tragedy. In the play of the same title,
Aischylos has the *Eumenides* or Furies use the verb *kathippazomai* (to
ride down) to conjure up an image of the youthful Apollo riding
down the elderly with arrogant disregard for their rights[187]—
although the audience presumably had little sympathy for this
particular group of senior citizens. The use of *kathippazomai* here
has the ring of a stock usage, but this cannot be confirmed.[188]
Finally, Euripides occasionally uses horses and chariots to convey a
sense of pride as well as the sense of majesty and power previously
discussed. Elektra says of her hated mother 'how glittering she is
with her chariots and attire', and elsewhere Teiresias advises
Kadmos against going to see Dionysos in a chariot because this
would unduly elevate them in the presence of the god.[189]

[183] Ibid. 134–5.
[184] LSJ s.v. φρύαγμα; A. H. Sommerstein (ed.), *Aristophanes: Wasps* (Warminster, 1983), p. 164. He also points out a similar derivative in Menander fr. 333. 13.
[185] Lysias, 24. 11.
[186] [Dem.] 42. 24; Dem. 18. 320.
[187] Aisch. *Eumenides*, 149–50, 731; cf. 778–9.
[188] It appears nowhere else in Aischylos and is not used by Sophokles or Euripides.
[189] Eur. *Elektra*, 966; *Bakchai*, 191–2.

The linking of the *hippeis* with arrogance was partly determined by their image as wealthy and aristocratic, but is also tied in with the perception of them as an essentially youthful organization. We have already seen how Kimon's Olympic display early in the fifth century was excused because of his youth and social status, but later Athenians were not usually so forgiving. Demosthenes' speech for Ariston to use against Konon in an assault case depicts wealthy Athenian youths as a rowdy and arrogant lot interested solely in their own pleasure. At the start of the speech he accuses Konon's sons of being perpetually drunk and abusive while on garrison duty at Panakton, and towards the end gives a graphic account of the misdeeds of Konon while a member of a society of youths called the Triballi.[190] His description of how he believes Konon will argue young men behave is particularly interesting:

he will say that there are many in the city, sons of the noble and virtuous (*kaloi k' agathoi*) who, as young men do, have given themselves joke nicknames like *Ithyphalloi* ('the hard-ons') or *Autolekythoi*[191] and that some are in love with courtesans. He will say indeed that his own son is one of those who has often given and received blows over courtesans, and that these things are the custom for young men.[192]

Although later on in the same speech he makes a plea for some allowance to be made for youthful folly,[193] it is clear from the work as a whole that he is highly critical of the behaviour of Konon's sons, as well as of Konon himself.

The same portrait of aristocratic youth occurs in Plato's *Republic*. Here the timocratic, or oligarchic, constitution is described as vulnerable because the rulers 'do not wish to constrain the intemperance of youth by law and prevent them from spending and using up their estate'. Further to this remark is the portrayal of the subsequent degeneration when a youth, brought up 'thriftily and in an untutored fashion', is exposed to the society of those who think of nothing but self-indulgence and their own pleasure.[194]

Antiphon presents two opposing views of youth in his third

[190] Dem. 54. 3–5, 39.

[191] This is very difficult to translate, it literally means those who carry their own lekythoi (oil-flasks), rather than having a slave carry it for them. It could perhaps signify poverty or, more probably, engaging in activities which they did not wish a slave attendant to witness.

[192] Dem. 54. 14.

[193] Ibid. 21.

[194] Pl. *Repub.* 555c and 559c–e.

Tetralogy. The *Tetralogies* are a series of speeches designed, as a teaching guide, to illustrate both sides of a case. This one gives both the prosecution and defence speeches in a case of homicide against a young man who had allegedly killed an older companion during a drunken brawl. The prosecution speech understandably capitalizes on the youth of the assailant, claiming that 'you should first understand that young men are more likely to behave badly while drunk than the old. This is because they are incited to vent their anger by youthful arrogance (ἡ μεγαλοφροσύνη τοῦ γένους), physical exuberance, and their unfamiliarity with wine'.[195] The defence speech of course argues differently, claiming that youth does not have a monopoly on drunken violence and that many young men are self-controlled (*sophronountes*) and many old men are drunkenly violent (*paroinountes*).[196] While the defence viewpoint seems entirely logical and reasonable to the modern reader, the ancient evidence suggests that the prosecution view of the young drunken lout was widespread, certainly to the extent that the young drunken idler may have been a fairly stock character in new comedy, and features in other literature too.[197]

Suspicion of the young *hippeis* and their life-style may also have been strengthened in the latter part of the fifth century by the association of long hair with anti-democratic and pro-Spartan sympathies. This is very clear in the attitude of the chorus in Aristophanes' *Wasps*, which declaims, in its initial argument with the apparently long-haired Bdelykleon, that

> is it not now patent
> to the poor, how dictatorship has stealthily
> crept up and tried to seize me,

---

[195] Antiphon, 3. 3. 2. As K. Maidment points out, *Minor Attic Orators*, i (London, 1960), 130–1, 'ἡ μεγαλοφροσύνη τοῦ γένους ought to mean "pride of birth"'. However, he argues that here it means 'type' or 'class' as 'the speaker is not limiting his remarks to young aristocrats'. While this is true, the use of this particular phrase would have suggested the image of the arrogant young aristocrat to the audience and provides another example of characteristics strongly associated with the cavalry being used to create an unfavourable impression in court.

[196] Antiphon, 3. 4. 2.

[197] The chorus in Menander's *Perikeiromene* was probably composed of a gang of drunken youths; Aristophanes also used similar characters in the closing part of *Lysis.* (1216 ff.) and these are described as long-haired. A similar picture of arrogant youth emerges in the *Wasps* (1249 ff.), where Bdelykleon explains to his father how one can carouse and upset people with impunity if one can then charm them with a funny story. Cf. Dem. 54. 3–5, 14, 39.

> when you, you villainous villain, you long-haired Amynias,
> seek to shut us off from the laws the city has made
> without offering any justification
> or any quick-witted argument,
> but like a sole autocrat?[198]

Later in the same debate Bdelykleon is accused of pro-Spartan views, and long hair is also linked with anti-democratic beliefs or philo-Lakonism in other works.[199] Some further support for this view, although long hair is not specifically mentioned, is given in Demosthenes' speech against Konon which links the general's drinking partners with pro-Spartan views and immoral practices.[200]

The general or base view of the cavalry, therefore, was as a wealthy and aristocratic body primarily composed of young men. Although this perception could arouse a favourable or positive attitude to the *hippeis*, from the mid-fifth century onwards it always had more potential to evoke an unfavourable or negative response. This unfavourable response mainly involved viewing the cavalry as arrogant and out of step with the democratic ideal, but important variants arose in response to specific events or incidents involving the cavalry or cavalry class. The occurrence and development of specific Athenian attitudes towards their cavalry arm and class form the basis of the next section.

Specific attitudes to the cavalry

The specific attitudes which arose from, or were associated with, the base perception of the *hippeis* show an interesting pattern of development. Down to its participation in the oligarchic coup of 404, the cavalry was generally regarded favourably. After the coup, and the subsequent restoration of democracy, the Athenians were quite hostile towards the *hippeis* and remained so for some time. Although the hostility gradually diminished, the cavalry may not have been fully rehabilitated until their excellent performance in the Mantineian campaign of 362. From this point on they were generally seen as an important part of the state's resources, but traces of the suspicion that they held anti-democratic tenden-

---

[198] Ar. *Wasps*, 463–70; Sommerstein's translation, *Aristophanes: Wasps*, 49.
[199] Ar. *Wasps*, 474–6; *Birds*, 1280 ff.; Lysias, 16. 18.
[200] Dem. 54. 34.

cies nevertheless remained until at least the last quarter of the fourth century.

Attitudes to the cavalry c.445–405

From their institution as a corps of 1,000 men *c.*445–438 to about the end of the Peloponnesian war, the attitude to the cavalry seems to have been primarily positive—the democracy was fairly young and aristocratic values were still largely tolerated. I have already mentioned the cavalry's prominence on the Parthenon frieze and the privileges accorded to equestrian victors in the pre-war period, but the cavalry was also favourably treated in Aristophanes' two earliest extant plays: the *Acharnians* and the *Knights*. Both of these date from the period of the Archidamian War (431–421) and took first prize at the Lenaian festival in 425 and 424 respectively. The first play has several favourable references to the *hippeis* and in particular to their hostility towards Kleon. The main character, Dikaiopolis, records his love for the cavalry when recalling some action on their part which apparently resulted in Kleon being forced to hand over five talents. Later in the same play the chorus expresses its hatred of Kleon and its favourable attitude to the cavalry with the jibe 'I hate you even more than I do Kleon—whom I'm going to chop up into shoe soles for the *hippeis*.'[201]

The *Knights* (or *Hippeis* in the original), as one might expect from the title, contains even more favourable references to the mounted arm. The chorus of cavalrymen celebrate their recent military service through their horses, which they believe 'are worth eulogizing as they bore along with us many exploits, raids, and battles'. In addition, the humorous panegyric which follows dwells at some length upon their deeds at Solygeia the year before the play was produced. This is hardly surprising as Thucydides states that the battle was decided by the cavalry. The chorus members also criticize the current *strategoi* for being more interested in public banquets than fighting, claiming that 'we consider it proper to fight for the city and her gods for free'.[202]

However, in some of these cases, it is uncertain exactly how far the bulk of the audience would have agreed with Aristophanes' views—he himself has the chorus in the *Knights* announce that no

[201] Ar. *Acharn.* 5–8, 300–1.
[202] Ar. *Kn.* 573–7, 595–610; Thucy. 4. 44. 1.

other comic poet could have secured their services, and that they
only agreed to help 'because you (i.e. Aristophanes) hate the same
men as we do'.[203] On the other hand, even if the audience might
not have agreed with every line in either the *Acharnians* or the
Knights, Aristophanes obviously felt that the climate of opinion
was generally favourable to the cavalry. This is particularly so
with the *Knights* and the correctness of his judgement is confirmed by the fact that it won first prize.

After the *Knights*, though, cavalrymen are nowhere near as
prominent in Aristophanes' work and their presence is restricted
to an occasional short reference.[204] The other literature of the
same period tended to mention the cavalry class or the general
equestrian milieu rather than the cavalry itself, and expressed, in
approximately equal proportions, both the admiration and envy
previously discussed.[205] Their generally good reputation during
the pre-war period probably stemmed initially from the novelty
of their establishment and from their prominence in the public
life of the city. The apparent popularity of cavalrymen recorded
in the early work of Aristophanes presumably resulted from their
continuous service, both in the defence of Attica and in raids on
the Peloponnese, during the Peloponnesian War.[206] There are
indications, however, of their involvement as a body in politics
and, in particular, of some sort of clash between them and Kleon
in the first part of this war, although it is not certain how far this
affected their popularity.

The hostility between Kleon and the cavalry is clear from the
Acharnians and the *Knights*,[207] and must therefore have existed
fairly early on in the war, most probably after the death of

[203] Ar. *Kn.* 507–11.

[204] *Lysis.* 561–2 does mention a long-haired phylarch in an unflattering light
but this section is directed at the military domination of life in general and also
complains about other soldiers.

[205] Admiration: Thucy. 6. 16. 2; [Eur.] *Rh.* 613–21; Ar. *Frogs*, 653; *Clouds*, 69–
70. Envy: Thucy. 6. 16. 2–3; [Eur.] *Rh.* 181–94 (also expressing admiration); Ar.
Clouds, 1299–1300; *Wasps*, 1427–32. These illustrate the ambivalent attitude
which could arise from the basic perception of the cavalry—both views could be
expressed in the same work and, presumably, coexist in the same person at
different times, or even at the same time.

[206] On their employment at this time see 'mobile defence', Ch. 3 and Spence,
JHS 110 (1990), 91–109. Ar. *Kn.* 595–610 confirms that their military contribution
was noticed and appreciated, with 573–80 perhaps suggesting that they were the
only group really involved in military (as opposed to naval) activities of the time.

[207] Esp. *Acharn.* 5–8 and *Kn.* 225–6.

Perikles and the subsequent increase in Kleon's prominence.
Later commentators, or scholiasts, to these plays cited a fourth-
century historian, Theopompos, to explain the mutual hatred
existing between the *hippeis* and Kleon. Unfortunately, Theopompos' work is no longer extant and the scholiast's accounts are not
always clear. For example, they claim that the 5-talent payout
mentioned in the *Acharnians*, 5–8 arose from Kleon's bad treatment of the *hippeis*. They got their own back when they discovered
he had been bribed by the islanders to persuade the assembly to
reduce their war-tax (*eisphora*), by accusing him and having the
money confiscated.[208] However, the *eisphora* is not otherwise
known to have been applied to members of the empire so the
details of this affair are rather obscure.[209]

Similarly, the scholiast to *Knights*, 225 states that the *hippeis*
hated Kleon because 'he had treated them badly' in that he had
'attacked the constitution (*politeia*) . . . and had accused them of
desertion'.[210] Again, though, there are problems and C. W.
Fornara believes that Kleon actually attacked the *katastasis* (or
establishment money) of the cavalry and not, as the scholiast
claims, the *politeia* or constitution (confusion arising because
both *katastasis* and *politeia* can mean 'constitution').[211] This
makes more sense and, in addition to the arguments Fornara
adduces, it receives some confirmation from later remarks in the
Knights. The Kleon figure, Paphlagon, is called a *taraxippostratos*
or 'troubler of the cavalry corps' and the Demosthenes character
later remarks that Paphlagon will burst into the Bouleuterion, or
Council Chamber, and 'lie against us all'.[212] These may be
allusions to a real attack made upon them by Kleon, as the
cavalrymen were presumably included in the 'us all' of the last
comment. There may be a similar reflection of reality in the

[208] *Acharn.* 5–8; N. G. Wilson (ed.), *Scholia in Aristophanem* i. 1. B; *In
Acharnenses* (Groningen, 1975), 5, no. 6a.

[209] A. H. Sommerstein (ed.), *Aristophanes: Acharnians* (Warminster, 1980), p.
158. The suggested emendation of τὰς εἰσφοράς (war-tax) to τοὺς φόρους
(tribute) or the possibility that *eisphora* was used here to mean *phoros* would
remove the difficulty (Wilson (ed.), *Scholia in Aristophanem* i. 1. B; *In Acharnenses*,
app. crit. 5).

[210] D. M. Jones and N. G. Wilson (ed.), *Scholia in Aristophanem* i. 2; *In Equites*
(Groningen, 1969), 56, no. 226b.

[211] C. W. Fornara, 'Cleon's Attack Against the Cavalry', *CQ* NS 23 (1973), 24.

[212] *Kn.* 247, 485–7. For a possible personal reference in line 247 see A. H.
Sommerstein (ed.), *Aristophanes: Knights* (Warminster, 1981), 156.

sausage-seller's description of Kleon's actions in the Council
Chamber: 'he was inside, crashing, talking up a storm, dashing
words hurled like thunder at the *hippeis*; crashing great rocks and
calling them, most persuasively, conspirators'.[213]

Therefore, although precise details are difficult to recover, it is
fairly safe to say that there was conflict between Kleon and the
cavalry in the period following the death of Perikles. It has also
been argued that this hostility continued until the very moment
of Kleon's death. According to J. McInnes, the cavalry broke and
ran at Amphipolis in 422, leaving the unpopular general to his
fate.[214] As a consequence of this, he believes 'that the Athenian
democracy, indignant at the insubordination and cowardice of the
hippeis, avoided using them afterwards unless in operations very
near Athens, as against Decelea, or in conjuction with a democracy
such as Argos.'[215] Although McInnes's argument would nicely
suit my contention that the Athenian attitude towards the cavalry
affected its military use, there are in fact several problems with
his theory.

The first is that it is not certain that the cavalry was in fact
posted on the left wing which broke and fled at Amphipolis.
McInnes cites Solygeia and Mantineia as two examples of Athenian cavalry positioned in this location[216] but both of these are
open to objection. Thucydides' account of Solygeia does not state
where the cavalry was posted. Although the larger number of
Corinthian casualties occurred on their right wing, suggesting the
cavalry was used against them, this does not preclude a cavalry
presence or attack on both wings. Casualties were inflicted on
both wings and one would expect more casualties from a cavalry
attack on the right, or unshielded, flank of a phalanx than on its
left, or shielded, side. It was more usual for the cavalry to be
placed on both wings, and this was almost certainly the case for
the entire army at Mantineia. It was a joint expedition and

[213] *Kn.* 626–9.
[214] J. MacInnes, 'The Athenian Cavalry in the Peloponnesian War and at
Amphipolis', *CR* 25 (1911), 194.
[215] Ibid. 195.
[216] Ibid. 194. His argument elsewhere gives few grounds for confidence, esp.
his suggestion that the Athenians could perhaps spare no cavalry for the battle of
Delion (ibid. 193): Thucy. 4. 93. 2, 94. 1 records (as MacInnes acknowledges)
that 300 cavalrymen were left at the temple at Delion but adds (at 4. 94. 1) that
the remainder was posted on both wings.

Thucydides implies that the cavalry contingents were located with their own hoplites.[217] So, although the Athenian cavalry was posted next to its hoplites on the left wing, any allied cavalry was presumably deployed on the right. The second problem with McInnes's theory is that the evidence for Athenian cavalry use in the remainder of the war shows that whenever it was necessary they did continue to use it—even if not always initially in sufficient force (see Tables 3–4). The lower numbers employed in the Dekeleian War are best explained by the decline in cavalry numbers during the course of the protracted hostilities to a little over 650,[218] and the need for the cavalry to constantly defend Attica against raids from Dekeleia. McInnes's case therefore remains unproven.

The evidence so far then suggests that the pre-war popularity of the cavalry lasted for most of the Archidamian War, although there was some sort of conflict between the *hippeis* and Kleon which may have affected their standing with some sections of society.[219] There is no detailed evidence of attitudes towards them during the rest of the war, but, because of their continued military activity in defence of Attica, their popularity most probably continued, although it may have been adversely affected by the involvement of some cavalrymen in the revolution of the Four Hundred in 411. The link between the cavalry as a group and the Four Hundred, though, is not overwhelming: some, if not all, of the main conspirators were of cavalry class but no evidence survives that any of the ringleaders were serving *hippeis* at the time.[220] The major links are that the assembly which voted the democracy out of existence was held at the precinct of Poseidon *Hippios* at Kolonos—a cult particularly associated with the cavalry—and that young *hippeis* were there to reinforce Aristarchos in his attempt to halt the fortification of the Peiraieus.[221]

[217] At 5. 67. 2, Thucy. records that the Athenians were on the left wing 'and with them were their own cavalry' (καὶ ἱππῆς μετ' αὐτῶν οἱ οἰκεῖοι).

[218] See Spence, *ZPE* 67 (1987), 167–75.

[219] Although enhancing it with those who held the same views as Aristophanes.

[220] Of the main conspirators, Theramenes and an Aristarchos (but possibly not the same man as the oligarch of this name) were wealthy enough to qualify for inclusion in *APF* (nos. 7234 and 1663 respectively). A Dieitrephes (App. 5.52), and most probably the general sent to Chios by the oligarchs to abolish the democracy there, had been both a phylarch and a hipparch; *PA* 3755 at any rate identifies the general with the cavalry officer.

[221] Thucy. 8. 67. 2, 92. 6.

However, even if there was cavalry involvement in the anti-democratic movement in 411, it was nowhere near as great as in 404/3
and seems to have been on an individual rather than on a corps
basis. Because of this, it may well have gone unnoticed amongst
the participation of so many middle-order citizens of hoplite
status. The propaganda of the conspirators certainly stressed the
hoplite nature of the new government of Five Thousand and, if
the speech in defence of Polystratos is to be believed, the actual
number enrolled was 9,000.[222]

Attitudes to the cavalry c.404–363

The cavalry was therefore not collectively prominent in the revolution of 411, but the same cannot be said for the coup staged by
the Thirty in 404. The specific identification of the cavalry corps,
and not simply the cavalry class, with this oligarchic movement
caused a major shift in the attitude of other Athenians towards it.
This had long-term effects upon its status and upon its military
effectiveness and employment.

The cavalry played a very active part in both the revolution
and in the post-revolution internal security duties. Theramenes'
publicly stated basis for the oligarchy was that the hoplites and
cavalry should rule, and some cavalrymen were indeed amongst
the most active supporters of the oligarchy—even in its dying
stages.[223] This involvement of the *hippeis* as a group is particularly clear in the military activities arising from Thrasyboulos'
counter-revolution. The cavalry was heavily involved in the initial
excursion against Thrasyboulos at Phyle, and when this failed it
was the *hippeis* which, as in the time of the Peloponnesian invasions, were most active in the defence of Attica. Not only did
the cavalry mount raids and conduct patrols against the democrats
at Phyle and later at Peiraieus, but it was also used to forcibly
evacuate Eleusis to allow its use as a potential refuge for the
Thirty Tyrants. After the Thirty retired to their cavalry-secured
safety at Eleusis, their successors, the Ten, and the hipparchs
were in charge of the city, and the cavalry patrolled on horseback
by day and guarded the walls as hoplites by night.[224]

It was not just the political and military prominence of the

[222] [Lysias], 20. 13.
[223] Xen. *Hell*. 2. 3. 48; *Ath. Pol*. 38. 2.
[224] Xen. *Hell*. 2. 4. 2–8, 24–6.

cavalry in the revolution which branded its members as committed oligarchs, though, but also the corps' involvement in several
atrocities. The operation at Eleusis was a particularly nasty task
as it involved the subsequent execution of all the male Eleusin-
ians.[225] In addition, Xenophon records that a body of cavalrymen
under the command of the hipparch Lysimachos summarily executed some of the inhabitants of Aixone who were going to their
own farms for provisions—despite their pleas for mercy and the
views of some of the cavalry present.[226]

As might be expected, this cavalry participation led to a rapid
decline in its popularity and in fact tainted the cavalry with an
anti-democratic reputation for much of the first part of the
following century. This is apparent in the abundant anti-*hippeis*
sentiments expressed in the literature of the post-oligarchic
period. These sentiments are far more vitriolic than the adverse
views generated by the association of the cavalry with youth,
wealth, and aristocracy, identified earlier (although these undoubtedly helped strengthen the particular animosity aroused by hippic
involvement in the oligarchic coup). This animosity clearly survived the final and formal reconciliation of 401 between the last
oligarchs in Eleusis and the restored democracy.

In 399, Thibron, the Spartan commander in Asia, asked Athens
for 300 cavalrymen, and Xenophon states that the Athenians 'sent
those who had served as cavalrymen under the Thirty, considering
it a gain to the people (*demos*) if they were to go abroad and die
there'.[227] Financial sanctions were also applied against those
hippeis who had served under the oligarchy. Lysias' defence
speech for Mantitheos states that the restored democracy voted
'that the phylarchs should hand over the names of those who had
served in the cavalry, so that the *katastasis* could be recovered
from them'. Later in the same speech he makes it clear that
katastasis money was repaid, although it is not clear exactly how
many *hippeis* were affected by this measure.[228] In addition to
this, around 403/2 the campaign pay of the cavalry was reduced
from one drachma (= six obols) per day to four obols while that
of the mounted archers, the *hippotoxotai*, was raised from two

[225] Ibid. 2. 4. 8–10.
[226] Ibid. 2. 4. 26.
[227] Ibid. 3. 1. 4.
[228] Lysias, 16. 6–7.

obols to eight.[229] As Grenfell and Hunt point out in their commentary to the papyrus which records this law, it was 'evidently a democratic measure'.[230] In addition to these financial measures and the sending of politically suspect cavalry to fight in Asia, those who served in the cavalry under the Thirty and the Ten may also have suffered in civic life. Lysias claims in a prosecution speech that

if he (Euandros) were now under scrutiny for entry to the *Boule*, and his name had been recorded on the lists as a serving cavalryman under the Thirty, you would reject him—even without a formal accuser. But now, when it is clear that he not only served as a cavalryman and *Bouleutes* (Councillor) at that time, but also committed crimes against the people, wouldn't it be contradictory if you failed to show the same reaction to him?[231]

However, Lysias may be exaggerating here. He argues just the opposite in one of his defence speeches, suggesting that mere membership of the cavalry was insufficient to disbar a man from civic office—he must also have committed a crime. He continues 'and I see you too have the same view and that many of those who served in the cavalry then (i.e. under the Thirty) are currently serving in the *Boule*, while many others have been elected as generals and hipparchs.'[232] Determining the exact truth is therefore rather difficult as Lysias clearly adjusted his descriptions of Athenian practice to fit his clients' cases. However, on balance it seems more likely here that each case was judged on its merits and that cavalry service was not automatic grounds for exclusion from public office. Some men (but possibly not all) had managed to overcome the stigma of cavalry service under the Thirty and were participating in government.

This may even have been the case with Euandros as it seems that he was appointed for the archon year following this speech. However, the speech against him was apparently delivered the very day before the archons were due to take office and the

[229] Lysias, fr. 6 *Against Theozotides* = B. P. Grenfell and A. S. Hunt, *The Hibeh Papyri*, part 1 (London, 1906), 51–2, no. 14, ll. 70 ff.
[230] Grenfell and Hunt, *Hibeh Papyri*, part 1, 55. For rather more up-to-date discussions see R. S. Stroud 'Greek Inscriptions, Theozotides and the Athenian Orphans', *Hesperia*, 40 (1971), 297–9 and Kroll, 97–8 n. 36.
[231] Lysias, 26. 10.
[232] Lysias, 16. 8.

timing of the case may have proved a stronger influence on the verdict than his cavalry service. If Euandros were rejected there would have been one too few archons for the festival of Zeus *Soter* the next day.[233] Because of the problem this would have caused with the civic administration, even the best arguments against him may not have been sufficient to sway the jury against his appointment. But, whatever the real truth of the matter, we can at least say that as late as 382, some twenty years after the restoration of democracy, Lysias clearly thought that the case against Euandros would benefit from the inclusion of anti-cavalry sentiments.

Other indications of hostility to the *hippeis* are perhaps reflected in the funerary monuments of the time. The well-known Dexileos relief (Plate 11), for example, is a rarity amongst Attic gravestones as the inscription records the deceased's date of birth and death. It has been suggested, very plausibly in my view, that the dating formula was intended to show passers-by that Dexileos had been too young to serve in the cavalry under the Thirty, and was therefore free of any oligarchical taint.[234] In addition, it is likely that the monument to the cavalrymen (including Dexileos) killed at Corinth and Koroneia in 394 was set up by the cavalry corps and was designed to draw attention to their military contribution.[235] The survival of this inscription is particularly interesting as the Athenians who died in this campaign were already commemorated on a state casualty list organized on the usual tribal basis.[236] The most plausible explanation for this apparent duplication is that, like the family of Dexileos, the *hippeis* collectively felt their unpopularity and decided to publicize their contribution to the city's war effort.

This is particularly understandable, as a new variant of the envy which the cavalry could attract first appears in Athenian literature around the same time. This was the view that cavalry

---

[233] W. R. M. Lamb (ed.), *Lysias* (London, 1960), 558.

[234] Edmonson, cited in Bugh, *Horsemen*, 138–9.

[235] *IG* II² 5222; G. Smith, 'Athenian Casualty Lists', *CPh* 14 (1919), 357. Bugh, *Horsemen*, 139 reaches the same conclusion.

[236] *IG* II² 5221 (relief 25); its equestrian combat scene (Pl. 13) suggests that the *hippeis* may have performed well enough to override—at least temporarily—the general hostility towards them, or that the state may have been generous enough not to carry the ill-feeling across the grave. However, an equally likely explanation is simply that the sculptor decided upon the more impressive (and by this date almost standard) equestrian scene.

service not only ensured a more comfortable life on campaign[237] but was also much safer than serving on foot. There is some truth in this view—it is a simple fact of warfare that a mounted man can usually escape a defeat more readily than an infantryman. As Field Marshal von der Glötz commented, 'the possession of a horse furnishes a man in the hour of his greatest danger with the means of saving himself and it cannot be expected of him that he should not avail of it.'[238] However, this facility need not necessarily reflect badly on the mounted arm, and there is no evidence that its existence was used as a criticism of the cavalry prior to the restoration of the democracy at the end of the fifth century.

One of the key passages for identifying this concept is in Lysias' speech in defence of Mantitheos, which addressed the jury as follows.

At first, when you had allied with the Boiotians and we had to relieve Haliartos, I had been enrolled in the cavalry by Orthoboulos. But when I saw everyone thought that the *hippeis* would be safe, while the hoplites would be at risk (and although others illegally mounted their horses for cavalry service without passing the scrutiny), I went to Orthoboulos and told him to remove me from the roll. I considered it shameful to go on campaign after organizing my own safety while the majority would be facing danger.[239]

This expedition was made in 395/4 and is also referred to in the speech against Alkibiades the Younger who was charged with desertion. In this work, Lysias accused Alkibiades (who was enrolled as a hoplite) of a variety of things, including 'cowardice, since he chose to serve with the *hippeis* when he should have shared the danger with the hoplites'. He also adds that others, who had been cavalrymen for some time and had never before served in the infantry, did so now because 'they did not dare mount their horses through fear of you (i.e. the people) and of the law'. Later on, he expressed wonder that anyone could think it right to convict of desertion a man who retired from the front hoplite rank to the second when the enemy approached and then

[237] Cf. Dem. 21. 133, quoted below 226.
[238] Quoted in Liddell-Hart, *Sword and the Pen*, 8. Plato's recommendation, *Republic*, 467b–e, that the children of his guardian class should observe battles from a safe distance while mounted is a neutral recognition of the opportunity a horse offered for escape.
[239] Lysias, 16. 13.

acquit another who, although a hoplite, appeared in the cavalry ranks.[240] While he did concede later that there was some risk attached to cavalry service,[241] the whole thrust of the early part of this speech was that being in the cavalry was far less dangerous than being in the infantry.

It is interesting that most of our evidence for this particular attitude is concentrated in the first few years of the Corinthian War and that it was at precisely this time that the cavalry apparently chose to set up private and public monuments to their war dead. The two facts may be unconnected, the result of chance in the survival of the evidence, but it is very tempting to see the hippic grave-reliefs from the Corinthian War as being, at least in part, a response to the criticism that cavalry service was safe. A similar reaction is described in I. L. Idriess's diary of the Palestine campaign of World War I. This describes how an Australian Light Horseman

got a parcel addressed to 'a lonely soldier'. Enclosed was a note from the lady expressing the pious wish that a brave soldier in France should get the parcel and not a cold-footed squib in Egypt. The chap who received the parcel sent the lady some photos of our desert graves, with compliments from a cold-footed squib in Egypt.[242]

However, this particular variant of the widespread anti-*hippeis* attitude apparent in the years immediately following the overthrow of the oligarchy may have been fairly short-lived. It was expressed almost entirely in 395/4 and may have been a product of this one campaign rather than a consistently held belief.[243] Included in the allied forces of this expedition were 1,100 Boiotian cavalrymen and it is possible that the availability of so much friendly cavalry and the paucity of the Spartan cavalry[244] was

[240] Lysias, 14. 7, 10–11.

[241] Ibid. 14; the truth of this is of course supported by the dead recorded in *IG* II² 5222.

[242] Idriess, *Desert Column*, 228.

[243] The only other expression of this is the neutral Pl. *Repub.* 467b–e, but cf. Pl. *Laches*, 191a–b where 'Laches' seems to believe that the cavalry's mobility, with its potential for retreat and then a rapid advance again, is a rather dubious quality which sets it apart from the hoplites.

[244] See S. Hornblower, *The Greek World 479–323* (London, 1983), 196–7 on the alliance and its effects and *Hell. Oxy.* 11. 3–4 on the Boiotian forces. The Boiotians supplied most of the Peloponnesian League's mounted troops during the Peloponnesian War (Thucy. 2. 9. 3, 12. 5). In 395 Agesilaos had not yet returned with the cavalry he had raised in Asia.

thought to guarantee the safety of the Athenian *hippeis* involved. However, whether this attitude towards the cavalry resulted from the particular circumstances of this campaign, from the more deep-seated dislike of the cavalry already identified, or from a combination of the two, it was very forcefully expressed at this time. The cavalry certainly considered itself under considerable pressure if Mantitheos and other long-serving cavalrymen felt obliged to serve as hoplites during this campaign.[245]

The remainder of the forensic evidence from the early fourth century is less clear, although there are possible indications of hostility in some defence speeches. In these, while detailing their contributions to public life, several men of trierarchic qualification (and therefore of cavalry class) fail to list the cavalry service which might have been expected.[246] On the other hand, in prosecution speeches of the same period where one might have expected cavalry service to be used against the accused this either does not happen or is not pressed at all.[247] Unfortunately, in most of these cases it is impossible to tell if this reflects attitudes to the cavalry because we do not know whether the cavalry class litigants involved had actually served as cavalrymen or not.

The overriding tenor of Athenian attitudes to their cavalry in the post-oligarchic period was therefore one of criticism. However, despite the depth of hostility apparent in the actions over pay, the *katastasis*, Thibron's request for troops, and in the speeches, the city generally seems to have respected the amnesty accorded to the participants in the oligarchic movement.[248] One of Lysias' speeches also suggests that, as far as overt punitive action went, the cavalry was not always adjudged collectively guilty but according to each individual's involvement.[249] A study of the later fourth-century evidence also reveals that, while the anti-democratic taint did affect its reputation to the extent that its efficiency and development were probably retarded, the cavalry was at least partially if not fully rehabilitated towards the end of the first half of this century. Although the quantity of surviving evidence, particularly from *c.*380–370, is insufficient to allow one

[245] Lysias, 16. 13; 14. 10.

[246] Lysias, 21. 1–10; 25. 12; Isok. 18. 58 ff.; Isaios, 6. 60–1.

[247] Cf. Lysias, 12 and 14 *passim*.

[248] On the terms of this see Andok. 1. 90–1; cf. [Dem.] 40. 32, 46; *Ath. Pol.* 39–40.

[249] Lysias, 16. 8.

to trace the course of events, or changes of attitude, with any real precision, it seems that time (and success in battle) helped heal the wounds to its reputation caused by cavalry involvement with the Thirty.

By the early fourth century the useful dramatic evidence has finished. Neither Aristophanes' *Ekklesiazousai* nor *Wealth* mention the cavalry at all,[250] and Menander's rather patchy extant works from the end of the century tell us virtually nothing about the position of cavalry in Athenian society. Menander's soldiers represent character-types, although possibly more sympathetically portrayed than may have been the case with the stock soldiers of his contemporaries, and are often poorer men trying to make their fortune through military service overseas. As such they provide no help for identifying attitudes to Athenian cavalry.[251] The evidence of the orators is also less important for the years between *c.*380 and 360 as no pieces survive from this period, except some works of Isokrates and Isaios which add little or nothing to our knowledge of the *hippeis*.

The best evidence, and evidence which in fact indicates the survival of some hostility to the mounted arm, comes from Xenophon's *Hipparchikos*. He mentions the need for hipparchs to have friends on the *Boule* in order to deflect any ill-timed anger, and later refers to a period 'when the hipparchs were sufficiently influential to get what they wanted'.[252] These passages suggest that the hipparchs had to overcome some resistance to ensure the smooth running of the cavalry and other sections imply that there

[250] Although this could possibly reflect the hostility to the cavalry of this period, Aristophanes' work at this time seems to be more concerned with the wider problems of society. The *Wealth* with its embryonic stock characters and its lack of a *parabasis* is already part of the way towards new comedy; as such there is not much scope for the appearance of the cavalry.

[251] The one exception is Moschion in *Samia*, 15, a young man who describes himself as a phylarch while listing his social status and achievements. On stock-characters in Menander and other 4th-cent. comedians see T. B. L. Webster, *Introduction to Menander* (Manchester, 1974), 22, cf. 29 and W. G. Arnott (ed.), *Menander* i (London, 1979), pp. xxxii–xxxiv. On military service overseas: Kleostratos in *Aspis*, 1–15, and quite probably the youth in the *Xenologos*, T. Kock, *Comicorum Atticorum Fragmenta* (Leipzig, 1880), 354, 355. Even Moschion, the young phylarch in *Samia*, threatens to go off and become a mercenary if his father blames him unfairly (616 ff.). For a real-life example cf. Aischines, 2. 147.

[252] Xen. *Hipparch*. 1. 8 and 3. 5 (although the latter could refer to influence with the cavalrymen rather than the *Boule*). Cf. 5. 13 which also implies that the hipparchs had to be good politicians to get what they wanted.

were some problems in recruiting.[253] If this was true, then it seems likely, given the evidence for anti-cavalry views in the early part of the century, that these were a contributory factor.

It is probable then that some of the anti-cavalry opinion of the immediate post-oligarchic period persisted until around 365, the approximate date of the *Hipparchikos*, but the view may have started to decrease in strength from *c*.380 and there is evidence to suggest that by *c*.362 or shortly before the cavalry was to a large extent rehabilitated. For example, a speech by Isaios, which dates from 364, argues that the childless Philoktemon decided to make a will 'because it was wartime and he was exposed to danger through his cavalry service and his frequent sailings as a trierarch'.[254] This admission that cavalry service could be dangerous is a far cry from the first decade of the century, when Lysias attacked Alkibiades the Younger using the argument that cavalry service was a safe option, and felt unable to contradict this view in his defence of Mantitheos the following year.[255]

Attitudes to the cavalry c.362–300

However, our first major indication of a real change in the hostile attitude to the *hippeis* comes with the reaction to the battle of Mantineia in 362. In an engagement which preceded the main battle the Athenian cavalry (which included Xenophon's sons) defeated the Theban and Thessalian horse. Xenophon devotes considerable attention to this and praises the Athenians highly. He notes that they had travelled all night, their horses were not rested, and their opponents were reputed to be the best cavalry in Greece, but the cavalrymen did not shirk the battle, fought bravely, and won.[256] While this could conceivably be dismissed as the description of a proud father (his son Gryllos probably died in this action rather than in the following battle), the cavalry's victory over the Thessalians and Thebans was the only success of the campaign and apparently had a marked impact in Athens. This is evident from Euphranor's painting of the battle in the Stoa of Zeus in the Agora.

The mere existence of this painting is indicative of the impact

---

[253] Ibid. 1. 9–12; 9. 3–6.
[254] Isaios, 6. 5.
[255] Lysias, 14. 7 ff.; 16. 13.
[256] Xen. *Hell.* 7. 5. 15–17.

of the battle and of the cavalry engagement which preceded it. As Rastko Vasić notes, the depiction of a contemporary battle between Greeks 'was, towards the middle of the fourth century BC, still an exceptional and unusual theme'. In addition to this, it is highly likely that the most prominent aspect of the painting was individual combat between cavalrymen—again a rare subject for fourth-century painting.[257] The work itself was probably executed *c.*360 and has been reconstructed by Vasić from the numerous ancient literary references which describe it.[258] Although Gryllos and Epameinondas almost certainly did not meet in the main battle, which is the subject of the painting, it seems that the two cavalrymen in the centre of the picture were popularly identified as them shortly after the painting was completed.[259] Vasić's reconstruction of the central part of this work is of course conjectural, but the literary evidence for the picture is sufficiently good to allow us to believe that the cavalry clash was the most eye-catching and prominent part of it. The cavalry engagement, and the subsequent depiction of the triumphant cavalry in the Stoa of Zeus, seem to have caught the imagination of the Athenians and undoubtedly helped in the process of restoring the cavalry to a better standing with their fellow citizens.

The forensic and political speeches of the period following Mantineia also illustrate this. There are no criticisms of the *hippeis*, with the exception of an occasional swipe at the ostentation and luxury of major *hippotrophoi*[260] (which shows that the basic perception of the cavalry class remained unchanged). The change in attitude from the start of the century is fairly pronounced.

For example, those speeches which survive from the years between Mantineia and the 320s portray the cavalry as a necessary, or even indispensable, part of the Athenian armed forces whose administration was a legitimate concern for the public

---

[257] Vasić, *AJA* 83 (1979), 347–8.

[258] Date: R. Vasić, 'Grylus and Epaminondas in Euphranor's "Cavalry Battle"', *ŽA* 29 (1979), 261. References: Vasić, *AJA* 83 (1979), 345 n. 1 and *ŽA* 29 (1979), 262. For his reconstruction, including a diagram of the central combat between 'Gryllos' and 'Epameinondas', see *ŽA* 29 (1979), 264–8.

[259] Vasić, *ŽA* 29 (1979), 263–4; this identification could also originate from Pausanias' guides (ibid. 263).

[260] [Dem.] 42. 24; Dem. 18. 320, both dated to 330. Aischines, 2. 111 criticizes Demosthenes for acting as a mounted escort to Macedonian envoys.

arena. This is certainly the case with Demosthenes who talked of
the cavalry as an important state asset, the care of which was
clearly an area of public interest and concern.[261] On one occasion,
he attacked the defendant stating that 'having annulled the present
penalty for abstaining from public service, he destroys all our
affairs—the assembly, the cavalry, the Council, and the sacred
and civic property.' Elsewhere, he criticized Meidias for passing
laws as hipparch which actually weakened the cavalry.[262] Deinarchos, in a speech which probably dates to 323, in turn attacked
Demosthenes' political record, asking 'what triremes did he add
to the city as Euboulos did? What shipyards were built under his
administration? When did this man strengthen the cavalry either
through law or decree?'[263] When recalling military exploits,
Aischines always seems careful to mention the cavalry as well as
the infantry and, in a speech delivered in 330, publicly praised its
performance at the battle of Tamynai.[264]

However, perhaps the best examples of how attitudes to the
cavalry had changed by this period are Demosthenes' attack on
Meidias and Hypereides' speech written on behalf of Lykophron.
The former, written around 351 but never delivered in court,
attacked Meidias by concentrating on his luxury, arrogance, and
insolence. Part of this attack was along the traditional lines of
using the possession of horses and chariots as symbols of wealth
and luxury.[265] But, rather than emphasizing Meidias' cavalry
service to damage his reputation (as he might well have done if
writing in the early fourth century), Demosthenes was very careful
not to include, even by implication, the rest of the cavalry in the
attack. Throughout the speech Meidias is contrasted with his
fellow cavalrymen. At section 133, for example, he is asked who
is the greater scandal to the city—the *hippeis* who crossed to
Euboia in proper order, 'or you, who prayed not to draw a lot for
this expedition, who never put on his breastplate, and who rode
on a silver-embossed Euboian saddle, with your shawls and drinking vessels and jars which the excisemen confiscated?' Demosthenes stressed that Meidias' fellow troopers were disgusted by

[261] Dem. 4. 21, 26–7; 14. 13; 18. 299, 311; 24. 216; [Dem.] 13. 9 and 10. 19.
[262] Dem. 21. 173; 24. 101.
[263] Dein. 1. 96. Demosthenes asks a very similar question of Aischines in 18.
311.
[264] Aischines, 3. 88; cf. 140.
[265] Dem. 21. 158.

this and, as previously mentioned, he also criticized him for the harm he did to the cavalry while hipparch.[266]

A speech of Hypereides, dating to around 333, stressed Lyko-phron's contributions to Athens. In it, Lykophron argued that he has never before been in court, and claimed that 'I have continu-ally been a zealous horse-breeder, often exceeding my strength or financial resources. I have been decorated for bravery by the entire cavalry and by my fellow archons. For you, gentlemen of the jury, elected me first phylarch and then hipparch to Lemnos'. He then outlines his public-spirited actions while *hipparchos eis Lemnon* and adds that he was crowned three times there by the local communities of Hephaistia and Myrina.[267] Here cavalry service and chariot-racing are used to try to sway the audience in the defendant's favour—a ploy which was only once attempted in the 390s, by Isokrates, and probably only then because it would have been rather difficult to avoid the issue in a case concerning a team of chariot-horses.[268]

Despite the changes in attitude during the fourth century, the basic perception of the cavalry as a wealthy and essentially aristo-cratic body still remained, and with it an associated distrust of their political reliability. This stemmed initially from doubt about the strength of the democratic views of the rich and was brought sharply into focus by the oligarchic activities of the cavalry at the end of the fifth century. Although the open hostility generated by these seems to have dissipated after a time, it is likely that a fairly general belief in the cavalry's lack of deep commitment to the democracy continued to exist throughout most of the fourth century. There is no direct expression of this distrust in the sources, but there are some hints that this was the case.

Demosthenes certainly links the major *hippotrophoi*, who were of course the upper echelons of the cavalry class, with anti-democratic sentiments and activities, addressing one opponent in front of the jury as follows:

when events had taken an unfortunate turn and there was a call, not for advisers, but for men who would follow orders, who would work against

[266] Ibid. 134, 173–4, 197.
[267] Hyper. 1. 16–18.
[268] Isok. 16. 25, 32–5. The remarks concern the elder Alkibiades, who was dead before the Thirty came to power, but Isokrates is careful to point out that, despite frequent invitations, Alkibiades declined to join the Four Hundred, ibid. 5.

their homeland for pay, and who were willing to fawn upon foreigners, at that moment you and each of them—a great and glittering horse-breeder—was at his post (*en taxei*). I was helpless, I agree, but I had your (i.e. the jury's) interests more at heart than they did.[269]

In addition, much of the blame for the fall of Olynthos to Philip II in 348 was attributed to the Olynthian cavalry officers, including the hipparchs, whose act of betrayal was seen by both Demosthenes and Hypereides as the major cause of the Olynthian collapse. This must have been a reminder of the oligarchic tendencies and activities of the Athenian cavalry at the turn of the century, which may help explain the prominence of this incident in the speeches of the time. Hypereides refers to it in a speech against Demades, and Demosthenes mentions it several times in different speeches.[270] The association between the cavalry class and anti-democratic ideas was apparently still there, and perhaps not too far below the surface either.

It is clear that, while the fundamental perception of the hippic class in general remained the same, the popularity of the class did fluctuate in response to events. Its membership was always associated with wealth (which according to the individual view could be cause for admiration, or envy, or even both), and the serving cavalrymen were further stereotyped as aristocratic youngsters. As a group, they seem generally to have been regarded in a favourable light from the time of the cavalry's institution until its involvement in the oligarchic coup of 404. For some years after this, cavalry service was associated with the oligarchy and the cavalry was correspondingly quite unpopular. It is possible that the public expression of hostility over its oligarchic activities had started to abate by about 380, but our evidence is insufficient to accurately identify attitudes from about 380 to 365. Xenophon's *Hipparchikos*, however, contains hints that the cavalry was still suffering from some residual hostility from its fellow citizens during these years. Although the cavalry seems to have enjoyed some popularity again after the battle of Mantineia, and was treated in debates as an integral part of the state's defences, the suspicion that the cavalry class was not quite politically reliable

[269] Dem. 18. 320.
[270] Dem. 9. 56; Hyper. fr. 76 (OCT) *Against Demades*, 1. The two Olynthian hipparchs mentioned here were Euthykrates and Lasthenes: Hyper. loc. cit.; Dem. 8. 40; 9. 66. See also Dem. 19. 266–7.

probably persisted for the remainder of the fourth century. In fact, it seems likely that the inherent potential for hostility towards the *hippeis* present in Athenian society's basic perception of them was so aroused by the cavalry involvement in the oligarchic movements that it never quite managed to regain its pre-oligarchic status—at least in the period down to the end of the fourth century.

CONCLUSIONS

At the end of the fifth century, the Athenian cavalry was likely to have been one of the most experienced mounted corps in the whole of Greece proper and had proved fairly successful at minimizing the damage to Attica during the Peloponnesian invasions. However, as outlined at the beginning of this chapter, the hoplite influence had still affected the cavalry's employment during the war, and fourth-century Athenian theory and practice continued to see cavalry in a subordinate role. This subordination, which occurred despite its relative success, its enhanced expertise, and its undoubted potential, stemmed from both its unpopularity after the restoration of democracy and also from over 200 years of hoplite supremacy. Despite the role of Lysander's navy, Athens' final defeat in the Peloponnesian War presumably reinforced the belief in the hoplite arm. The Spartans' fame as the hoplites *par excellence* and their identification with hoplite warfare would have caused many observers to consider the victory in terms of a hoplite power defeating a naval power. This is perhaps why the defeat of the Spartan *mora* at Lechaion came as such a shock,[271] and perhaps too helps to explain the emphasis on the heavy infantryman in the political theory of Plato and Aristotle. At the same time, the Athenian cavalry had become the least popular arm of service because of its involvement in the oligarchic movements at the end of the war. Because of this, it laboured under financial and civic penalties in the early part of the fourth century, and even had 300 experienced members of the corps sent overseas with the idea that their deaths would be no great loss to the democracy.[272] Quite apart from the absence (temporary or other-

[271] Xen. *Hell.* 4. 5. 10; cf. the renewed heart this put into the opposition, ibid. 4. 5. 18; Diod. Sic. 14. 91. 2–92. 1.
[272] Xen. *Hell.* 3. 1. 4.

wise) of these veterans, the level of hostility expressed towards the *hippeis* at this time must have affected morale and recruiting.[273]

There were no overwhelming military reasons why the Athenian cavalry should have occupied such an apparently inferior role in the warfare of the period *c*.450–300, a role which failed to develop much of its potential. However, a variety of factors did contribute to this. For example, the economics of horse-keeping certainly limited the number of cavalrymen available, but at full strength the Athenian cavalry corps had only 100 fewer men than that of the entire Boiotian League,[274] and was large enough to give a good account of itself against most other *poleis*. The lack of stirrups too had some effect on the value of the *hippeis* as a fighting arm but, as discussed above, this was nowhere near as grave a handicap as has commonly been assumed. Similarly, while its training and the system of appointing commanders might seem inadequate by modern standards, the cavalry trained far more frequently than the hoplites and its command structure was determined by exactly the same procedure. Apart from the Spartans, who Aristotle states were distinguished not so much by their training methods as by the fact that they trained at all,[275] and later the Theban Sacred Band and the Macedonians, the Athenian military system was probably little different in this respect from most of her potential foes in the fifth and fourth centuries.

The explanation for the failure to develop the mounted arm or even fully exploit its existing potential largely lies elsewhere, and almost certainly with Athenian attitudes to the cavalry, particularly the influence of the hoplite ethos and tradition and the hostility towards the *hippeis* in the period after the restoration of the democracy in 403/2.

---

[273] Cf. the concern with recruiting in Xen. *Hipparch*. 1. 2, 9–12; 9. 3–6. However, what prosopographical evidence remains indicates that at least some families continued to maintain a tradition of cavalry service; see the start of App. 5.

[274] The League's cavalry comprised 1,100 men, *Hell. Oxy*. 11. 3–4.

[275] Arist. *Pol*. 1338[b]24–9 (8. 4).

APPENDIX I

Attic Red- and White-Figure Vases with Equestrian Scenes *c*.530–300

THE main aim of this appendix is to provide a representative and reasonably comprehensive sample of those red- and white-figure vases which are useful for the study of the Athenian *hippeis*. My original intention was to provide a list of all such vases with cavalry, equestrian, and equine scenes, partly because the only other list (in Webster's *Potter and Patron*) is occasionally taken as complete—despite its brevity.[1] The resulting catalogue consisted of nearly 630 entries and was obviously far too large for inclusion in a book of this size. Because of this, subjects of marginal interest (for example chariot scenes or vases portraying horses' heads) have been excluded, as have many vases for which illustrations are not fairly readily available. The vases which are included portray the Athenian cavalry class engaged in combat or other, more peaceful, equestrian activities. Some examples of more exotic scenes such as grypomachies and amazonomachies are also listed because of the information they provide about cavalry weapons and their use.

The catalogue concentrates on those vases post-dating the mid-fifth-century reform which established the cavalry corps as a body of 1,000 men. However, as it also seemed useful for the appendix to provide a simple method of referring to vases in the main part of the book, it also includes those vases mentioned there and which pre-date 450. To facilitate easy reference, Beazley's practice of numbering the vases in a series for each painter has been replaced by a continuous number sequence for all entries.

However, the method of numbering is the only real departure from Beazley's scheme; his format proved most appropriate for my purposes, particularly as it was important to allow rapid cross-checking with his works. This is because it was impractical, and to a large extent unnecessary, to reproduce the listings of published illustrations cited for the vases in Beazley's *ARV*[2] and *Paralipomena*, and in the *Beazley Addenda*. Although it would obviously be useful to collect all these references together in one place, this was not my first priority as the information already existed—albeit in a rather scattered fashion. To have included it would also have reduced the space available for the detailed descriptions

[1] *PP* 179–95; cf. Bugh, *Horsemen*, 4 n. 5.

inserted, wherever possible, to supplement Beazley's short accounts of the scenes. The list in this appendix therefore complements rather than replaces Beazley and the entries are divided, as is Beazley's work, into periods. The vases are arranged according to painter within these. The list of artists in a particular period is roughly chronological but this consideration is subordinated to a policy of placing associated painters in close proximity to each other.[2]

This practice has one disadvantage—as Beazley himself admits, it can sometimes give a misleading impression of the relative date of an individual vase.[3] However, providing an accurate date for each pot and then listing them chronologically is far too large a task for anyone other than a specialist, or for anything other than a specialist work on the subject. It would also have required a radical departure from Beazley's format without many tangible gains—particularly as the possibility of chronological confusion can be reduced by providing extra guidelines.

First, wherever possible, I have indicated when a vase has been dated by any of the various scholars working in the field. Second, as outlined in the Introduction, T. B. L. Webster's dates are applied to all the periods listed in ARV^2 except the last two. Here, Richter is followed and the lower date for the 'Classic' (Richter's 'Free Style') and 'Late Fifth Century' periods are extended downwards by five and ten years respectively.[4] Nevertheless, it should still be stressed that the general periods into which this appendix is divided are only approximate and that many potters and painters were active over more than one period.[5]

The entries follow much of Beazley's usage and, if in doubt, the reader should refer to the 'Instructions for Use' in volume 1 of ARV^2 for the detailed procedures adopted.[6] The format of each entry is as follows: my reference number, location and museum number (if known), type of pot, and Beazley's references (listed in order: ARV^2, *Para.*, *Add.*, and *Add.*[2]; a bracketed entry for ARV^2 means that the vase first appears in its addenda or in one of the later works). This is followed by a description of the relevant scenes. The following conventions also apply unless otherwise specified: all Amazons in my vase descriptions can be assumed to be wearing anaxyrides (although this may not be the case for descriptions attributed to someone else); the name of a town or city signifies the major collection in that place. Note that in the case of 'St Petersburg' the relevant Beazley entries will have 'Leningrad'.

[2] ARV^2 p. xliii.
[3] Loc. cit.
[4] *PP* 27–41; Richter, *Attic Red-figured Vases*, 115–17, 139–53.
[5] Cf. ARV^2 p. xliii.
[6] Ibid. pp. xliii–xlvii. In particular note the method adopted for referring to the vases from Spina, now in Ferrara, and for the Akropolis fragments in the National Museum in Athens.

The following terms and their definitions apply in the descriptions of each scene:

hoplite signifies that the figure is armed with an *aspis* and either a sword or spear. He may or may not be carrying or wearing other items of hoplite equipment;

long hair describes hair which is shoulder length or longer. Hair resting between the nape and the base of the neck is described as *longish*. If the hair is not mentioned at all it is either short or not visible;

alongside (behind) signifies that a figure is standing alongside a horse portrayed from the side and that from the observer's point of view the figure is on the far side of the horse, as for the *hippotoxotes* in Plate 5;

alongside (in front of) means the figure is on the observer's side of a horse portrayed from the side, as for Panaitios in Plate 9;

to the rear or *front of* the horse denotes that the figure is clear of the fore or hindquarters of the animal in question, as for the youth in Plate 15;

right or *left* denote the observer's right or left.

The abbreviations 'fr.' and 'frr.' denote 'fragment' and 'fragments' respectively. As vases often had more than one painted scene I have followed the usual convention of referring to those on the outside of the vase as either 'A' or 'B' and any on the interior as 'I'.

The authorship of any descriptions or datings other than my own is indicated by the use of square brackets, as are attributions (with the exception of Beazley's) of vases to painters. Many of the attributions and dates are those of other scholars cited in *ARV*². While I have checked these for accuracy (where the work was available), they are not listed in my bibliography as they can be easily located in *ARV*². Because Beazley has supplied the basic classification according to artist, any attribution of pot to painter not otherwise indicated can be assumed to be his. I have had to rely fairly heavily on published sources for these areas as, with the exception of vases in the UK and in Athens, I have been restricted to an examination of illustrations of the vases rather than of the items themselves. Because of this, I have been reluctant to produce my own attributions or datings for vases not in Beazley. Such pots are therefore placed in sections entitled 'Unattributed, Miscellaneous' at the end of the appropriate general period. Apart from this, and the heading 'Europa Painter' from the fourth century (derived from Schefold),[7] all headings within the list of vases are from Beazley.

[7] K. Schefold, *Untersuchungen zu den Kertscher Vasen* (Berlin and Leipzig, 1934), 158.

EARLY RED-FIGURE (*c*.530–500)

The Andokides Painter

1. Leipzig T. 635, frr. Amphora. *ARV*² 3.3; *Para.* 320; *Add.* 71; *Add.*² 147. B. Mounted youth in chiton, chlamys, and boots, holding two spears; hoplite and part of archer.

2. Paris F 203. Amphora. *ARV*² 4.13; *Add.* 71; *Add.*² 150. A. Three Amazons preparing: one, dressed in a tunic and with a bow at her left side, is mounted on a stallion, beneath which is a crested helmet. *c*.530 [C. T. Seltman, *Attic Vase-painting* (Cambridge, Mass., 1933), pl. 9].

3. Philadelphia 5399. Amphora. *ARV*² 7.3. B. Youth in alopekis, chiton, chlamys, and boots, carrying two spears; he is turning to the rear to look at two horses (one a muzzled stallion) which he is leading by the reins. *c*.510–500 [W. N. Bates, 'A Signed Amphora of Meno', *AJA* 9 (1905), 178].

Psiax

4. London 1900.6–11–1. Alabastron. *ARV*² 8.13, 1589, 1608; *Para.* 321; *Add.* 72; *Add.*² 151. Naked youth with staff facing a muzzled stallion which he holds on a long rein; a second naked youth similarly holding a rearing white stallion. Behind the first horse a tree.

Euphronios

5. Munich 2620. Cup. *ARV*² 16.17, 1591, 1619; *Para.* 322; *Add.* 73; *Add.*² 153. I. Mounted youth in chiton, short zeira, petasos, and boots.

Oltos

6. Florence 1 B 32, frr. (part ex Villa Giulia). Cup. *ARV*² 58.47; *Add.* 80; *Add.*² 164. A. Herakles and the horses of Diomedes: what remains is the head of a horse with a human arm in its mouth, and a male head and shoulders, including an arm with a club.

7. London E 41. Cup. *ARV*² 58.51, 1622; *Add.* 80; *Add.*² 164. B. Male and woman (heads missing) conversing, flanked by two naked youths (the one on the left with a wreathed head) mounted on stallions and facing inwards. *c*.520 (Theseus and Helen with the Dioskouroi?) [J. Neils, 'The Loves of Theseus: An Early Cup by Oltos', *AJA* 85 (1981), 177–8].

8. Florence 3923. Cup. *ARV*² 61.72, 1622. I. Naked youth with wreathed head mounted on a stallion, riding to left; inscribed [M]emno[n] *kalos*. *c*.520–510 [*CVA* Italy, xxx (Florence 3), 3].

9. Copenhagen 3877. Cup. *ARV*² 63.87, 1573; *Para.* 327. A. Theseus

fighting the Minotaur. B. Achilles fighting Chiron. Each of these
scenes is flanked on both sides by a naked horseman who has a void
horse alongside (behind).

10. Florence (V) from Chiusi. Cup. *ARV*² 64.97, 1600. A. Youth
    attacked by horses [Beazley].

Epiktetos

11. London E 3. Cup. *ARV*² 70.3, 1623; *Para*. 328; *Add*. 82; *Add*.²
    166–7. I. (black-figure). Youth in chiton, zeira, and with wreathed
    head, mounted on a stallion, carrying two spears (points down-
    wards) diagonally across the horse's shoulder; (see Pl. 7).
12. Berlin 2262. Cup. *ARV*² 72.15, 1623; *Para*. 328; *Add*. 82; *Add*.²
    167. B. Youth in chiton and boots standing between, and holding
    the reins of, two left-facing muzzled horses.
13. London E 136. Plate. *ARV*² 78.94; *Add*. 83; *Add*.² 169. I. Warrior
    in crested Corinthian helmet, chlamys, and greaves, carrying a
    spear and standing alongside (behind) a muzzled stallion.

Near the Thalia Painter

14. Basle, Cahn 133. Cup. *ARV*² (115), 1626, 1707 (incorrectly as-
    cribed to the Splanchnopt Painter, 894.40 *ter*), 1708; *Para*. 332. A–
    B. Inspection: A. Legs and arms of male in chiton, short zeira(?),
    and boots with a writing tablet, towards whom three horses are
    each being led by a youth in chiton, cloak, alopekis, and boots and
    carrying two spears. B. As for A except the youths are wearing
    chlamydes and slung petasoi. *c*.510–500 [Cahn, *RA* (1973), 8].

The Epileios Painter

15. Munich, 2 frr. Cup. *ARV*² 147.21. Outside. Youths and horses,
    including part of a horse tethered to a pillar [Beazley].

Manner of the Epileios Painter

16. East Lansing, Michigan State Univ. 65.57. Cup. (*ARV*² 151); *Para*
    335; *Add*. 89; *Add*.² 180. A. Two horses facing right in single file,
    each held by a naked youth in a crested Chalkidian helmet standing
    alongside (behind); a *pelte* hangs on the wall (? or is possibly slung
    on the back of the left hand youth). A third naked youth in a high
    crested Chalkidian helmet and a *pelte* on his left arm stands along-
    side (behind) a stallion facing left. B. Two horses moving to right
    in single file, each held by a naked youth in a crested Chalkidian
    helmet standing alongside (behind); a third naked youth (with a
    bare head) moving to right but looking to left is alongside (behind)
    a horse moving to left. *c*.510–500 [J. T. Cummings, 'The Michigan
    State University Kylix and its Painter', *AJA* 73 (1969), 69].

The Hischylos Painter

17. Munich 2588. Cup. *ARV*² 162.2; *Para.* 337; *Add.* 90; *Add.*² 182.
B. Youth in chlamys and carrying two spears, leading a muzzled
stallion from the front on a long rein; he has his right hand on his
mount's forehead.

The Bowdoin-eye Painter

18. Basle, Ant. Mus. Lu 34 (was Aachen, Ludwig). Cup. (*ARV*² 166.3
quater); *Para.* 325, 337; *Add.* 91; *Add.*² 183. I. (black-figure).
Naked youth with wreathed head riding to the right.

LATE ARCHAIC (c.500–475)

The Kleophrades Painter (Epiktetos II)

19. Munich 2305. Amphora. *ARV*² 182.4, 1631; *Para.* 340; *Add.* 93;
*Add.*² 186. Mouth (black-figure). A. Chariot; horsemen, each carrying two spears; youths. B. Deer hunt: six mounted hunters, some in
zeirai others in chlamydes, some in alopekides. Each carries a spear,
although four others have already been cast at the deer; the position
of their fingers suggests the use of javelin loops. c.500 [*CVA*
Germany, xii (Munich 4), 19].
20. Paris CA 453. Loutrophoros. *ARV*² 184.22, 1632; *Para.* 340; *Add.* 93;
*Add.*² 187. Prothesis, youth. Below (black-figure), valediction: six
horsemen, four in file to right, two in file to left; each is in a zeira and
carries two spears; two wear petasoi, two alopekides, one is bareheaded, and the head of the last is missing; at least two are bearded.

The Nikoxenos Painter

21. Athens, NM Acr. 727, frr. Calyx-krater. *ARV*² 221.17. B. One fr.
has a youth in himation with staff seated on a chair, facing him is a
horse, alongside (behind) which stands a male in chiton, chlamys,
and greaves carrying two spears; part of a hoof and male leg. A
further fr. has a youth in a cloak(?) and greaves with two spears
standing alongside (behind) a horse.

The Eucharides Painter

22. Eleusis, from Eleusis. Column-krater. *ARV*² 228.25; *Add.* 99;
*Add.*² 199. A. Male in helmet, corselet, and chiton, with a spear
resting on his shoulder, leading a horse.

Group of Acropolis 787

23. Athens, NM Acr. 787, frr. Column-krater. *ARV*² 233.1. B. Horses,
males in chitones with one spear each (one may have two spears);
one figure may be wearing a helmet.

Myson

24. Boston, Alpers and Shulman (was Philadelphia market). Column-krater. *ARV*² (239.23 *bis*), 1638; *Para.* 349; *Add.*² 201. A. Two youths, the first naked with two practice spears, the second in a chiton with one practice spear; each is standing alongside (behind) a stallion whose reins he holds.

The Syriskos Painter

25. Taranto 4553 (3799). Round aryballos. *ARV*² 264.57, 1573, 1585 (last two cited under 3799); *Add.* 101; *Add.*² 205. B. Bearded man in chiton, chlamys, slung petasos, and boots, leading a horse on a long rein.

Side-palmette Lekythoi (Fashioned by the Diosphos Potter)

26. Boston 99.528. White lekythos. *ARV*² 301.2, 1643; *Add.* 105; *Add.*² 211. Naked warrior in a crested Corinthian helmet and greaves, with two spears and a sword on a baldric, moving alongside (in front of) a stallion. (He is either running beside it or, more likely, is trying to bring it to a halt).

Onesimos

27. Paris G 105. Cup. *ARV*² 324.60, 1579, 1595, 1645; *Para.* 359; *Add.* 107; *Add.*² 215. I. Mounted youth in chiton, chlamys, petasos, and boots, carrying two spears. A. Youth in chiton, chlamys, boots, and alopekis-style cap controlling a horse by means of long reins; a naked youth with long hair, carrying a stick and two spears stands alongside (behind) the horse; watching this is a mounted small youth or boy in a chlamys, carrying two spears. B. Three mounted youths in chlamydes and boots, two with slung petasoi, the other bareheaded, each with a spear, riding in single file.

28. Munich 2639 (J 515). Cup. *ARV*² 324.61, 1645; *Add.*² 215. I. Dismounted cavalryman(?): naked youth with long hair (in a bun), wearing a petasos; he is moving to the right but looking to the left and has an animal-skin saddlecloth over his left arm as a shield; he holds a spear in his right hand, pointing left. A. Naked youth on horseback holding a stallion while another naked youth attempts to mount it with the aid of a practice spear; a bearded man in himation with staff watches. B. Naked youth with forked stick leading a horse, watched by a youth in himation with staff; (see Plate 1 for A).

29. Bryn Mawr P-246, P-931, P-935, and P-986 (not 984 as stated in *ARV*² 324.72), frr. Cup. *ARV*² 324.71, 72; *Para.* 359; *Add.* 107; *Add.*² 215. A. Two men with a horse: P-935, legs and waist of man

in chlamys, sandals and stockings, forelegs of a horse, behind which, a tree; P-986, hindquarters of horse with right arm holding reins, two javelins with loops(?) held in left hand. B. Man and horse: P-246, raised head of whinnying horse in bridle, behind it, a tree; P-931, left leg of man in sandals, stockings, and bordered cloak. 490 [*CVA* USA, xiii (Bryn Mawr 1), 12]. Despite Beazley's reservations in *ARV²* 324.72, I accept Ashmead and Phillips's arguments (*CVA* 11) that all the frr. are from the same cup.

The Bonn Painter

30. Bologna 363. Cup. *ARV²* 351.5; *Add.²* 221. A. Two groups of three hoplites fighting, separated by a youth mounted on a stallion with its hind legs collected beneath it and its forelegs raised. The youth wears a chiton and cloak. B. Two groups of fighting hoplites separated by a youth mounted on a stallion in the same posture as on A; this youth wears a chiton and carries an *aspis* (device a swastika).

The Foundry Painter

31. Rome, Villa Giulia 50407. Cup. *ARV²* 402.24, 1651; *Para.* 370; *Add.* 114; *Add.²* 231. I. Bearded horseman in chiton, zeira, alopekis, and boots, with reins and two spears held horizontally in right hand; chair seat. A. Hoplite flanked by two dismounted horsemen. Each of the latter stands alongside (behind) a stallion which faces left. Both men are dressed in a chiton, long zeira, alopekis, and embades, and carry two spears. The one on the right is bearded and possibly non-Athenian, the one on the left is probably the same but the photograph in Mingazzini, *Catalogo*, pl. cxxii is not clear here. B. Youth in petasos, long zeira, chiton, and embades, leaning on a spear. He is flanked by two inwards facing stallions each of which stands alongside (in front of) a column [Beazley].

The Dokimasia Painter

32. Berlin F 2296. Cup. *ARV²* 412.1; *Add.* 115; *Add.²* 233. I. Bearded archer in anaxyrides and alopekis, standing alongside (behind) a stallion and examining an arrow. A–B. *Dokimasia*: bearded man in himation seated with writing tablet, male in himation standing in front; three youths in chlamydes and petasoi, each carrying two spears and leading a stallion towards the two men; two other himation-clad figures with staffs (one a youth? the other a bearded man); olive tree. *c.*480–470 [Cahn, *RA* (1973), 10]; (see Pls. 3–5).

EARLY CLASSIC (*c*.475–450)

The Boreas Painter

33. Syracuse, from Syracuse. Column-krater. *ARV*² 537.18. A. Two riders mounted on stallions in single file. Each wears a chiton, chlamys, crested helmet, and possibly a corselet, one is carrying two spears; (parts missing).

The Painter of London E 489

34. Once Syracuse, Gargallo (later in the Italian market), from Syracuse. Column-krater. *ARV*² 546.12. A. Fight: bearded cavalryman in chlamys and petasos, thrusting underarm with a spear (with butt-spike) at a light armed foot-soldier to his front. Behind the infantryman is a hoplite, while to the rear of the cavalryman are the forequarters of a horse with a rider.

35. Ferrara 3175 (T 722). Column-krater. *ARV*² 547.16; *Para.* 385; *Add.* 125; *Add.*² 256. A. Two warriors mounted on stallions in single file to the right, to their rear the forepart of a third horse. The first rider wears a crested Corinthian(?) helmet, chiton, and a linen/leather corselet with pteryges, and carries two spears in his left hand. The second rider wears a crested Corinthian helmet, chiton, and a leather(?) cuirass without pteryges, he carries two spears in his right hand. *c*.460 [N. Alfieri, *Spina: museo archeologico nazionale di Ferrara* (Bologna, 1979), 28, no. 68].

The Niobid Painter

36. Izmir 3361, frr. Volute-krater. *ARV*² 599.7; *Add.*² 266. Warriors, some in cuirasses but no helmets, making ready; hoof of horse. Beazley suggests that the horse is part of a chariot team but there is no evidence for this in the photographs of these frr.

37. Bologna 278. Volute-krater. Von Bothmer, *Amazons*, 162, no. 9, pl. 76.1; H. C. Ackerman and J. R. Gisler (eds.), *Lexicon Iconographicum Mythologiae Classicae,* i (Zurich, 1981), 606, no. 300 and pl. 479. A.(?) Amazon, bow at left side, thrusting underarm with a spear (with butt-spike) at a fleeing infantryman; to her rear an Amazon archer. *c*.460 [*LIMC* loc. cit.].

38. Paris G 165. Calyx-krater. *ARV*² 601.21; *Add.* 130; *Add.*² 266. B. Dismounted youth in chiton, zeira, and alopekis, carrying two spears, shaking hands with a seated male; to the right a female stands next to his horse. Mid-5th cent. [Cahn, *RA* (1973), 22].

39. Paris G 341. Calyx-krater. *ARV*² 601.22, 1661; *Para.* 395; *Add.* 130; *Add.*² 266. A. Herakles and Athena with a group of warriors: one naked male with a Boiotian(?) helmet, chlamys(?) wrapped around right arm, a sheathed sword on a baldric, and holding two

spears, stands longside (behind) a stallion; to his front is a bearded man in chiton and petasos holding a spear with a butt-spike. On the far side of the scene is another youth, dressed identically to the first (except his helmet is slung) but without the horse; all the other figures are equipped as hoplites. *c.*460–450 [J. P. Barron, 'New Light on Old Walls: Murals of the Theseion', *JHS* 92 (1972), 23].

The Painter of Bologna 279

40. Bologna 279. Volute-krater. *ARV*² 612.3; *Add.*² 268. Amazonomachy: includes three mounted Amazons, one an archer in alopekis and chiton(?), a second bareheaded archer in chiton, and the third, in crested Ionian helmet and chiton(?), thrusting underarm with a spear at a hoplite. *c.*450 [*CVA* Italy, xxvii (Bologna 4), 10].

The Villa Giulia Painter

41. London E 240. Hydria. *ARV*² 623.68. Bearded man in cloak, petasos, and stockings, carrying two spears and standing alongside (behind) a stallion with a broad noseband (*phorbeia*). He is taking his leave from a woman and a male(?) with sceptre(?).

The Painter of Acropolis 356

42. Leiden PC 93 (xviii a 3). Cup. *ARV*² 816.2. I. Bearded man in chiton, chlamys, and petasos, with two spears in his left hand (dismounted hipparch?). A. Youth in chiton, chlamys, and slung petasos with two practice javelins (no points, but with throwing loops) holding a stallion by its reins; bearded man in himation and with staff, column; sandals etc. hanging from wall. B. Identically clad youth (but no loops on javelins), flanked by two bearded men in himatia with staffs; column, sandals etc. on wall; (see Pls. 14–15).

The Pistoxenos Painter

43. Florence 75770. Cup. *ARV*² 861.15; *Add.*² 298. I. Male with an alopekis-style helmet, chlamys, chiton, and boots, carrying two spears, mounted on a stallion; inscribed *ho pais kalos*. *c.*470–460 [*CVA* Italy, xxx (Florence 3), 17].

The Penthesilea Painter

44. Hamburg 1900.164. Cup. *ARV*² 880.4, 1673; *Para.* 428; *Add.*² 301. A. Two youths in chlamydes and petasoi; the one on the left holds two practice javelins (loops but no points), the other has long hair and holds a practice spear and the reins of a stallion, behind which is a column and a youth in himation with a crooked staff pointing to left. B. Two youths in chlamydes; the one on the right has his hair in a bun, holds two practice javelins (loops but no

points) and stands with his stallion, to the rear of which is a column. The other youth has long hair and a slung petasos, holds two spears and stands alongside (behind) his stallion. *c*.460 [E. Pfuhl, *Masterpieces of Greek Drawing and Painting* (London, 1955), 55, pl. 73].

45. Ferrara 44885 (T 18 C VP). Cup. *ARV*² 882.35, 1673; *Para*. 428; *Add*. 148; *Add*.² 301. I. Two youths with long hair, head-bands, a garment draped over their shoulders and under their arms, and each carrying two spears approaching an altar. The first youth is riding a stallion with a patterned chest girth and leads a void horse alongside, the second youth walks beside him. They have been variously identified as Kastor and Polydeukes [N. Alfieri, P. E. Arias, and M. Hirmer, *Spina: die neuentdeckte Etruskerstadt und die griechischen Vasen ihrer Gräber* (Munich, 1958), pl. 29], and Theseus and Perithöos [Alfieri, *Spina*, 53]. For a nearly identical chest girth see St Petersburg 663 (*ARV*² 403.25). *c*.460–450 [Alfieri, *Spina*, 54].

The Painter of Brussels R 330

46. Birmingham 1621.1885. Stamnos. *ARV*² 930.102, 1675; *Para*. 431. B. Bearded man in chiton, linen/leather corselet, and pilos, carrying a spear, standing alongside (behind) a stallion with a woman; a bearded man in himation with staff stands at the horse's head.

The Painter of London D 12

47. Karlsruhe 245 (B 42). Cup. *ARV*² 960.24. A. Bearded male in a himation holding the reins of two stallions, to the rear of which sits a himation-clad youth. B. Two youths in himatia, one with staff; both face inwards and flank a stallion facing right. *c*.460 [*CVA* Germany, vii (Karlsruhe 1), 31].

CLASSIC PERIOD (*c*.450–420)

The Achilles Painter

48. London E 300. Neck-amphora. *ARV*² 988.15, 1590. A. Youth in fillet, with garment draped across his back and over his forearms, carrying a spear and riding a stallion. The woman on B is possibly waiting to greet him. 'Early' [Beazley].

49. Philadelphia 30.51.2. Lekythos. *ARV*² 993.95; *Para*. 437. Youth in chlamys and slung petasos, carrying spear, riding a stallion. *c*.460 [C. Vermeule, 'Young Man on Horseback (500 BC)', *Boston Museum Bulletin*, 64 (1966), 128, fig. 6].

Manner of the Achilles Painter

50. Athens, NM 12133. Lekythos. *ARV*² 1003.20; *Add.* 153; *Add.*²
313. Youth, in chiton and slung petasos, sheathed sword in his belt,
holding two spears and the reins of a stallion, standing at a tomb
decorated with fillets. *c.*470–450 [R. C. McMahon, 'A Doryphorus
on a Red-figured Lecythus', *AJA* 10 (1906), 406].

The Waterkeyn Painter

51. Berkeley 8.3375. Neck-amphora. *ARV*² 1005.1; *Add.*² 314. A.
Youth in chiton with a garment wrapped around his arms and a
slung petasos; he is mounted on a stallion and carries two spears.

The Westreenen Painter

52. Maplewood, Noble. Small Pelike. *ARV*² 1006.2; *Para.* 439; *Add.*²
314. A. Youth in chlamys and petasos, carrying a spear and riding a
stallion.

53. Paris, Cab. Méd. 377. Neck-amphora. *ARV*² 1006.4. A. Youth in
chlamys and petasos, mounted on a rearing stallion, holding a spear
(with butt-spike) at shoulder height in his right hand. Beazley
describes him as throwing the spear, but the position of the arm
could equally well suggest a preparation for an overarm thrust or
even represent a heavy spear carried, ready for action, at the point
of balance rather than underarm.

Loosely Connected with the Achilles Painter

54. Athens, NM 1856 (CC 1843). White lekythos. *ARV*² 1008.1.
Mounted youth, in chiton(?), slung petasos and boots, carrying two
spears. *c.*440–430 [R. C. McMahon, 'The Technical History of
White Lecythi', *AJA* 11 (1907), 29].

The Persephone Painter

55. Paris, Cab. Méd. 388. Stamnos. *ARV*² 1012.5. A. Kastor and
Polydeukes: Kastor, dressed in chlamys and petasos, has the reins
in his left hand and [A. de Ridder, *Catalogue des vases peints de la
Bibliothèque Nationale* (Paris, 1902), 282] two spears in his right;
Polydeukes is semi-naked (garment draped over his shoulder), with
the reins in his right hand and two spears in his left. Both are
mounted on stallions and ride with a very straight-legged seat.

Polygnotos

56. Ferrara 3089 (T 411). Bell-krater. *ARV*² 1029.21; *Para.* 442; *Add.*
155; *Add.*² 317. A. Two mounted Amazons, moving to right in
single file, separated by an Amazon on foot. Both are riding stallions

and wear crested Ionian helmets; the first, dressed in a chiton and a leather or metal cuirass, is unarmed and holds the reins in both hands; the second, dressed in a patterned chiton(?) and with a sheathed sword at her waist, carries two spears. *c.*450 [*LIMC* i. 631, no. 724]; *c.*430 [Alfieri, *Spina*, 64, no. 46].

57. London E 280. Neck-amphora. *ARV*² 1030.35; *Add.* 155; *Add.*² 317. A. Achilles and Penthesilea fighting on foot; she is alongside (in front of) the hindquarters of a void horse facing left.

58. London E 337. Neck-amphora. *ARV*² 1031.47. A. Naked youth on stallion, two thonged whip in right hand, reins in left.

59. Syracuse 23507. Pelike. *ARV*² 1032.53; *Add.*² 317. A. Amazon, mounted on a stallion, thrusting a spear underarm at the head of a hoplite (shield device a lion).

The Group of Brussels A 3096 (By/close to Polygnotos)

60. Warsaw 142261 (was Czartoryski 40). Hydria. *ARV*² 1033.6; *Para.* 443; *Add.*² 318. Above. Youth in chlamys, slung petasos, and carrying two spears, standing at altar with a woman; to his rear an unarmed youth in chlamys and petasos holds a stallion.

Near the Peleus and Hector Painters

61. St Petersburg 769 (St 1680). Calyx-krater. *ARV*² 1037.3; *Para.* 517; *Add.*² 319. A. Theseus and the Amazons: includes an Amazon mounted on a stallion, with a *pelte* slung on her back, bow at her left side, thrusting a spear overarm at a hoplite to her front.

The Curti Painter

62. Syracuse 22833. Bell-krater. *ARV*² 1042.4. A. Mounted Amazon with *pelte* slung on her back, thrusting a spear underarm at a light-armed infantryman and a hoplite to her front.

The Guglielmi Painter

63. Vatican, from Vulci. Stamnos. *ARV*² 1043.1, 1679. A. Amazonomachy: includes an Amazon, mounted on a stallion, sword at her waist, thrusting a spear overarm at a retreating infantryman.

64. Naples 1768. Bell-krater. *ARV*² 1043.3. A. Amazonomachy: includes a mounted Amazon, *pelte* slung on her back, carrying a spear(?) in her right hand.

The Christie Painter

65. Ischia, from Ischia, fr. Calyx- or Bell-krater. *ARV*² (1046.8 *bis*), 1679. A. Amazonomachy: one foreleg of Amazon's horse and parts of the legs of the two Greeks [Beazley, citing Shefton].

66. London 1898.7–15.1. Stamnos. *ARV*² 1048.35. A. Rider (Amazon?), in crested Ionian helmet, linen/leather corselet with

pteryges, chiton, and shoes, bow slung on her back, mounted on a stallion. She is thrusting a spear overarm to her front at a hoplite (shield device a snake) who has his boot on a rock; to his rear stands a light-armed soldier. Note that the no. of this vase is misprinted as 1898.7–16.1 in *CVA*.

67. Copenhagen, Ny Carlsberg 2694. Stamnos. *ARV*² 1048.36. A. Amazon, with bow at her waist, mounted on a stallion, striking overarm to her front with a spear at a hoplite, to the rear of which is a light-armed footsoldier.

Close to the Christie Painter

68. London Market, Christie (was London market, Edwards). Bell-krater. *ARV*² 1049.1; *Add*. 157; *Add*.² 321. A. Amazonomachy. Probably by the painter himself [von Bothmer, *Amazons*, 229, no. 39 *bis*].

Group of Polygnotos—Undetermined

69. Vatican, from Vulci. Stamnos. *ARV*² 1051.13, 1680. A. Amazon with bow at her left side, sliding down the shoulder of a horse, while thrusting a spear overarm at a hoplite and light-armed soldier to her front.

70. Bologna 176. Stamnos. *ARV*² 1051.14, 1680. A. Amazon, sheathed sword at left side, mounted on a stallion, with right arm raised for an overarm spear thrust at a hoplite and light-armed soldier to her front; a fallen Amazon lies in the foreground. 'Outskirts of the Group' [Beazley].

71. London 1899.7–21.5. Dinos. *ARV*² 1052.29; *Add*. 157; *Add*.² 322. Amazonomachy: includes three mounted Amazons riding up in support of a foot mêlée. The first, mounted on a rearing horse, is in chiton, linen/leather corselet with pteryges, and an oriental-style helmet, and carries her spear ready for an underarm thrust. The second, also mounted on a stallion, carries her spear underarm in her right hand. The third, mounted on a stallion, has a bow at her left side and carries an axe.

72. Naples RC 148. Bell-krater. *ARV*² 1054.50; *Add*. 157; *Add*.² 322. A. Amazon, mounted on a rearing stallion, bow at left side, spear poised for close range throw at a hoplite (shield device a star), who stands on rocky ground to her front.

73. Bologna 319. Bell-krater. *ARV*² 1054.56; *Add*.² 322. A. Two naked boys or youths, with riding crops, riding past a column, in the background is a large cauldron, lying on its side.

74. Madrid? from Tútugi. Bell-krater. *ARV*² 1054.56 *bis*. A. Naked jockey on a stallion; Nike. *c*.mid-4th cent. [Garcia y Bellido, *Hispania Graeca*, ii (Madrid, 1948), 182, no. 1].

75. Naples RC 161. Bell-krater. *ARV*² 1055.74. A. Amazon, mounted on a stallion, thrusting a spear overarm at a hoplite, to the rear of which is a light-armed soldier.
76. Oxford 1924.929. Calyx-krater. *ARV*² 1056.88; *Add.* 157; *Add.*² 322. A. Dismounted youth (head missing), in chiton, cloak and boots, holding two spears and standing alongside (in front of) a stallion; to his front sits a bearded man in himation, with staff (behind the chair stands a young man in a himation, leaning on a staff). c.450–440 [*CVA* GB, iii (Oxford 1), 19].
77. Geneva 15 038. Neck-amphora. *ARV*² 1058.112; *Para.* 445. A. Youth in chlamys, slung petasos, and high sandals, carrying two spears and riding to right on a stallion, preceded by a woman; to his rear is a male in himation with a staff. c.450–440 [*CVA* Switzerland, i (Geneva 1), 22].
78. Syracuse 9317. Pelike. *ARV*² 1059.132; *Add.* 158; *Add.*² 323. Amazonomachy: includes an Amazon with slung *pelte*, mounted on a stallion, thrusting a spear underarm at a hoplite (shield device a lion's hindquarters) standing on rocky ground. c.440–430 [P. E. Arias, M. Hirmer, and B. Shefton, *A History of Greek Vase Painting* (London, 1962), pl. 191].

The Biscoe Painter

79. Fayetteville, University of Arkansas 57–24–21. Pelike. *ARV*² 1063.1; *Add.* 158; *Add.*² 324. A. Two Amazons, each in chiton, linen/leather corselet, and crested Ionian helmets, carrying two spears, and riding a stallion.

The Barclay Painter

80. Paris G 537. Pelike. *ARV*² 1067.10. A. Youth in chlamys, petasos, and boots, carrying a spear and leading a stallion from alongside (in front).
81. Paris, Mus. Rodin 1052. Bell-krater. *ARV*² 1068.1. A. Two men with van Dyck beards, wearing zeirai, alopekides, and shoes, each carrying one spear and facing the other; the left hand man is standing alongside (behind) a stallion. May be by the Barclay Painter [Beazley].

The Polydektes Painter

82. New York 06.1021.187. Bell-krater. *ARV*² 1069.1. A. Youth in chlamys, petasos, and boots, holding two spears, standing alongside a stallion and bidding farewell to a man. c.440 [G. M. A. Richter and L. F. Hall, *Red-figured Athenian Vases in the Metropolitan Museum of Art* (New Haven, 1936), 167, no. 133].

The Eupolis Painter

83. Leipzig T 647, fr. Bell-krater. *ARV*² 1073.5. Youth with horse leaving home: what remains is an old man and the hindquarters of a horse [Beazley].

84. Ferrara 3108 (T 203). Bell-krater. *ARV*² 1073.7, 1681; *Add.* 159; *Add.*² 325. A. Amazon with downcast head, bow at waist, axe in left hand, leading a stallion; behind the horse, a column. *c.*450–400 [S. Aurigemma, *Il reale museo di Spina*, 2nd edn. (Ferrara, 1936), 278].

85. Syracuse 21475. Calyx-krater. *ARV*² 1074.5. A. Two Amazons setting out, one on foot, the other on a stallion. The rider is equipped with an *aspis* (device a fox), crested helmet and spear, and wears a sword at her waist. Probably by the Eupolis Painter [Beazley].

The Clio Painter

86. Munich 2331. Neck-amphora. *ARV*² 1081.12, 1682. A. Amazon, mounted on a stallion, with spear and *aspis* (device a snake).

87. St Petersburg 717 (St 1632). Neck-amphora. *ARV*² 1081.13; *Para.* 517. Amazon, mounted on stallion, carrying spear and *aspis* (device an alpha). Almost identical to previous entry.

The Cassel Painter

88. Vienna 786. Bell-krater. *ARV*² 1083.4; *Add.* 160; *Add.*² 327. A. Riding lesson: naked boy on stallion with long reins riding to right towards a bearded man in himation with staff. *c.*450 [*CVA* Austria, iii (Vienna 3), 18].

89. Brooklyn 09.3. Stamnos. *ARV*² 1084.15, 1682; *Add.* 160; *Add.*² 327. A. Amazon, mounted on a stallion, thrusting a spear underarm at a hoplite on rocky ground to her front.

90. Rhodes 12016. Neck-amphora. *ARV*² 1085.20. A. Amazon in crested Ionian helmet, chiton, and boots, with sword at left side, riding a stallion and thrusting a spear underarm at a retreating hoplite.

The Painter of the Louvre Centauromachy

91. Paris G 361. Column-krater. *ARV*² 1088.3; *Add.*² 327. A. Naked rider mounted on a stallion; a woman and a king.

92. Warsaw 147955. Column-krater. *ARV*² (1090.34 *bis*), 1683; *Para.* 449. A. Youth in zeira and alopekis, carrying two spears, standing alongside (behind) stallion and facing a woman.

93. Paris, Cab. Méd. 413. Column-krater. *ARV*² 1090.39. A. Two naked riders with crops, mounted on stallions, racing past a column; a large cauldron lies on its side in the background.

94. Bologna 246 *bis*. Column-krater. *ARV*² 1095.3. Two men with van Dyck beards, wearing zeirai and alopekides; each carries two spears and stands alongside (behind) a horse. Near to or by the painter [Beazley].

The Naples Painter

95. Vienna 647. Column-krater. *ARV*² 1097.18. A. Horseman in chlamys and slung petasos, spear ready to throw in right hand and two more in the left, riding a stallion after a woman running to right. *c.*450 [*CVA* Austria, ii (Vienna 2), 31].

96. London E 485. Column-krater. *ARV*² 1098.32, 1683; *Add.* 161; *Add.*² 328. A. Riding lesson: naked boy climbing on to stallion, assisted by a man, watched by a youth in himation.

The Ariana Painter

97. Munich 2376. Column-krater. *ARV*² 1101.1; *Para.* 451. A. Amazon in chiton, alopekis, and shoes, bow at left side, mounted on a stallion, thrusting a spear overarm at two hoplites on rocky ground to her front; to her rear, the forequarters of a second horse.

98. Geneva 14990 (ex Ariana). Column-krater. *ARV*² 1101.2; *Add.*² 329. A. Amazon in chiton, alopekis, and leather (or metal?) cuirass, bow at left side, mounted on a stallion. She is thrusting underarm with a spear at two hoplites to her front; to her rear, the forepart of another horse.

The Orpheus Painter

99. Syracuse 37175. Column-krater. *ARV*² 1104.2; *Add.* 161; *Add.*² 329. A. Mounted Amazon either thrusting a spear underarm at a hoplite to her front or merely carrying the spear underarm as she rides towards him; behind the hoplite is a light-armed infantryman and a tree. *c.*430 [P. E. Arias, M. Hirmer, and B. Shefton, *A History of Greek Vase Painting* (London, 1962), pl. 192].

The Nausicaa Painter

100. Lucerne Market (A.A.) Column-krater. *ARV*² 1108.21. A. Man, mounted youth in chlamys and petasos, carrying two spears; woman running to right [Beazley].

101. Cracow, University 152. Column-krater. *ARV*² 1108.22. A. Two long-haired riders in chlamydes, petasoi, and each carrying two spears; the first, mounted on a stallion, also wears stockings.

102. Corinth C 34.372 and 373, 2 frr. Column-krater. *ARV*² 1108.24. A. Male in chiton, chlamys, and alopekis, riding a branded stallion. *c.*460 [M. Z. Pease, 'A Well of the Late Fifth Century at Corinth', *Hesperia*, 6 (1937), 271, no. 19].

103. Bologna 179. Column-krater. ARV^2 1109.29. A. Naked youth in stockings and sandals(?) grooming a stallion; naked, bearded man in stockings, sandals(?) and pilos grooming a stallion. Both horses have their tails tied up off the floor and are muzzled.

The Orestes Painter

104. Paris, Niarchos (ex Hirsch). Column-krater. ARV^2 1113.7. A. Two youths, each in chlamys, slung petasos, stockings and sandals, and carrying two spears, riding in single file, the first on a stallion.

The Painter of Oxford 529

105. (?), from Al Mina. Bell-krater. ARV^2 1119 bottom. Long-haired youth with wreathed head, chlamys, slung petasos, sandals and stockings, mounted on a stallion; to his rear a bearded male in himation, to his front, a running woman. To be compared with the work of the Painter of Oxford 529 [Beazley].

The Academy Painter

106. Ferrara 2794 (T 200). Column-krater. ARV^2 1124.6; *Para.* 453; *Add.* 163; *Add.*^{2} 332. A. Two mounted youths with longish hair and wreathed heads, both in chlamydes and carrying a spear; one is mounted on a stallion.

Manner of the Washing Painter

107. Berlin 2357. Pelike. ARV^2 1134.8. A. Unarmed youth in patterned chlamys and slung petasos mounting a horse which appears to be crouching to aid him. 'Later than 430' [Richter, *Attic Red-figured Vases*, 191 n. 3].

The Hasselmann Painter

108. Reading 51.7.1. Oinochoe. ARV^2 1138.45; *Para.* 454. Naked boy/youth on horseback, holding reins in both hands.

The Kleophon Painter

109. Tour la Reine, Serpieri. Pelike. ARV^2 1146.41. A. Fight (youth to right, bearded horseman to left) [Beazley].
110. Athens, NM 1700 (CC 1477), frr. Loutrophoros. ARV^2 1146.50; *Para.* 456; *Add.* 164; *Add.*^{2} 335. Hoplite and attendant and bearded man at tomb with male in chlamys and petasos who carries two spears and holds a horse. c.450–425 [D. C. Kurtz, *Athenian White Lekythoi* (Oxford, 1975), 219, no. 45.1].

The Dinos Painter

111. Brunswick, Maine, Bowdoin College 1895.2. Pelike. ARV^2 1155.41; *Para.* 457; *Add.* 165; *Add.*^{2} 335. A. Youth with wreathed head,

chlamys, and slung petasos, carrying two spears and riding a stallion towards a seated man, a standing woman, and a youth. *c*.425–420 [K. Herbert, *Ancient Art in Bowdoin College* (Cambridge, Mass., 1964), 73, no. 202].

The Painter of Munich 2335

112. Ferrara T 857. Bell-krater. *ARV*² 1163.46; *Para.* 458. A. Horseman in chlamys, slung petasos, sandals and stockings, carrying two spears horizontally, riding a stallion in pursuit(?) of a woman running to right; to his rear a second woman runs to the left while looking back to right.

The Painter of Bologna 322 (?)

113. Once Deepdene, Hope 135 (bought by Cory). Column-krater. *ARV*² (1171), 1685; *Add.*² 338. A. Amazon with axe, riding a stallion in pursuit of a hoplite; to her rear another Amazon on foot. To be compared with his work [Beazley]. *c*.435 [E. M. W. Tillyard, *A Catalogue and a Discussion of the Hope Collection of Greek Vases* (Cambridge, 1923), 79, no. 135].

Polion

114. Nikosia C 765. Oinochoe. *ARV*² 1173 top. Naked boy on branded stallion. 'Not far from Polion' [Beazley].

Aison

115. Chantilly, from Nola. Neck-amphora. *ARV*² 1176.25. A. Amazon, mounted on stallion, thrusting a spear overarm at a hoplite to her front; to her rear an Amazon archer.

The Painter of Ferrara T 300 A

116. Ferrara 2687 (T 566). Column-krater. *ARV*² 1183.4; *Add.* 167; *Add.*² 340. A. Amazon in patterned chiton, zeira, and alopekis, carrying two spears and leading a horse from alongside (in front); a tree. B. The like [Beazley, who identifies the figure on A as a 'youth']. *c*.430 [Alfieri, *Spina*, 84, no. 189].

Near the Klügmann Painter

117. Athens, NM 12738 (N.985). White lekythos. *ARV*² 1200.3. Amazon, with *pelte* on left arm and spear in left hand, blowing a trumpet while galloping on a stallion. She is wearing a metal cuirass according to W. Riezler, *Weißgrundige attische Lekythen* (Munich, 1914), 97. *c*.460 [C. Zervos, *L'Art en Grèce* (Paris, 1934), fig. 276].

The Alexandre Group

118. Athens, NM 1236 (CC 1596). Kantharos (sessile). *ARV*² 1213; *Add.* 172; *Add.*² 348. A. Andromache on horseback, another

Amazon on foot. Andromache wears a chiton and crested helmet, is armed with a bow (at her waist), and carries a spear. B. Theseus (as hoplite), lower part of mounted archer in boots and chiton with a bow at the waist. 'Not too far from London E 157 ($=ARV^2$ 1213.2) in style and date' [von Bothmer, cited in Beazley].

The Group of the Perseus Dance

119. Providence 25.090. Oinochoe. ARV^2 1215.2. Youth in chlamys and slung petasos with two spears talking to seated man while his horse grazes near a stela.

The Painter of Athens 17191

120. Athens, NM 17191. Pyxis. ARV^2 1222.1. Youth with wreathed head, chlamys, slung petasos, sandals and stockings, mounted on a stallion; three other youths (two similarly clad to first, the other in himation), woman, two columns with fillets.

The Eretria Painter

121. Boston 95.48. Squat lekythos. ARV^2 1248.2, 1688; *Para.* 522; *Add.* 176; *Add.²* 353. A. Amazon in crested helmet, scale corselet with pteryges, and a chiton, bow at left side, mounted on a stallion. She is thrusting upwards with a spear at a hoplite standing on a hill to her front; to the rear of the hoplite is a light-armed man and, to the rear of the mounted Amazon, a Greek and an Amazon fight on foot.

The Codrus Painter

122. Altenburg 232. Cup. ARV^2 1270.14. A. At left, youth in chlamys, high sandals, and petasos, facing right and holding a stallion while a hoplite and man shake hands. B. Herakles driving off two horses (the horses of Diomedes?). *c.*430 [*CVA* Germany, xviii (Altenburg 2), 22].

Manner of the Codrus Painter

123. Godalming, Charterhouse. Cup. ARV^2 1274 top. I. Boy on horseback and youth. A. Youth on horseback and youths. B. Mounted youth and youth; youth and man. 'May perhaps be compared to London 1948.10–15.3' ($=ARV^2$ 1274) [Beazley].
124. Florence 21 B 268 (part ex Rome, Villa Giulia); Leipzig T 591; Chicago, Univ.; Naples, Astarita 263, frr. Cup. ARV^2 1274 (i). A–B. Amazonomachy: includes parts of two mounted Amazons. The first, in a linen/leather corselet, sword at her side and riding a rearing horse, is thrusting a spear underarm at a hoplite; the second, in a linen/leather corselet and carrying a *pelte*, is falling

backwards wounded or dying from her rearing mount. Resembles
the early work of the painter [Beazley].

The Marlay Painter

125. Cambridge 4.12 (ex Marlay). Calyx-krater. *ARV*² 1276.3. A. Bareheaded youth in chlamys and high laced sandals mounted on a
stallion, moving to right towards a dismounted youth in chlamys,
slung petasos, and high laced sandals, holding two spears. *c*.430
[*CVA* GB, vi (Cambridge 1), 37].

126. Roman Market (Depoletti). Cup. *ARV*² 1280.66. A. Youth on
horseback pursuing (or preceded by) a woman. B. The like; (rape of
the Leukippids?) [Beazley].

127. Naples, Astarita 7. Cup. *ARV*² 1281.74. A. Bareheaded Amazon in
patterned chiton and sandals, mounted on a rearing stallion and
thrusting a spear underarm at a hoplite to her front (shield device a
lion). B. Similarly clad and mounted Amazon, with a spear in right
hand, poised either for a close range throw or overarm stab at a
hoplite like the one on A.

The Lid Painter

128. Athens, NM 1569 (CC 1206). Cup. *ARV*² 1284.31. I. Amazon
with sword at left side and carrying two spears, horse to her rear
with lowered head.

The Painter of London E 105

129. Once Roman Market, Castellani, from Tarquinia. Cup. *ARV*²
1293.5; *Add*. 179; *Add*.² 359. B. Youth in chlamys and petasos
carrying a spear and leading a horse [Beazley].

Unattributed, Miscellaneous

130. Rhodes 11974, from Jalysos, tomb 471. Oinochoe. *CVA* Italy, x
(Rodi 2), Group III Ic, p. 2 and pl. 8.5; G. Jacopi, 'Scavi nella
Necropoli di Jalisso', *Clara Rhodos*, 3 (1929), 248. Naked youth
riding a colt or small horse to right.

131. London E 482. Column-krater. A. Youth in patterned chlamys (or
zeira), boots, chiton, alopekis, and carrying two spears, mounted on
galloping stallion, following similarly clad but dismounted youth
with *pelte* and spear. *c*.440–430 [BM].

132. Boston 01.8147. White lekythos. Fairbanks, *AWL* ii. 116–17, class
XI, series 5, no. 1 and pl. 17.1; von Bothmer, *Amazons* 193, no. 107
and pl. 81.8. Youth in chiton, zeira, slung petasos, and boots
mounted on a stallion, holding a spear underarm and pursuing a
fleeing Amazon hoplite. Both her spear and that of the rider have a
butt-spike. 450–425 [Fairbanks, *AWL* 122].

133. London 1897.3–17.4. White lekythos. Fairbanks, *AWL* ii. 119, class xi, series 5, no. 8. Young cavalryman in chiton, chlamys, and petasos, mounted on a rearing horse, thrusting a spear underarm at a hoplite in a pilos to his front. 450–425 [ibid. 122].

LATE FIFTH CENTURY (*c.*420–390)

The Manner of the Meidias Painter

134. Boston 13.171. Oinochoe. *ARV*² 1324.41. Horse race: two naked boys riding past a column with a cauldron on top. They both have crops and the leading rider is turned to the rear and appears to be striking at his opponent's mount with his crop.

Near the Pronomos Painter

135. Athens, NM 1333 (CC 1259). Pelike. *ARV*² 1337.8; *Add.*² 366. A. Gigantomachy, including a horseman in petasos and chlamys, mounted on a stallion and thrusting a spear with butt-spike at a fallen opponent.

The Talos Painter

136. Amsterdam 2474, frr. Loutrophoros. *ARV*² 1339.4; *Add.*² 367. Fight, including two cavalrymen. The first, mounted on a white horse, is in a patterned chiton, petasos, and footwear, sheathed sword on baldric at left side, striking overarm with a spear (with butt-spike?) at a hoplite to his front. To the rear of the first rider is a second in chiton, chlamys, and high sandals, carrying a spear and mounted on a stallion.

Near the Talos Painter

137. Tübingen E 160, frr. Loutrophoros. *ARV*² 1339.1; *Add.*² 367. Fight, including two cavalrymen. The first wears a chiton, the second carries a spear in position for an overarm blow.

The Painter of Louvre G 433

138. Athens, NM 2396. Pelike. *ARV*² 1342.2. A. Mounted Amazon with bow at left side thrusting a spear underarm into the side of a light-armed man to her front; a second infantryman grabs her hair from behind. The whole occurs on rocky/broken ground.

Near the Painter of Louvre G 433 (?)

139. Warsaw 198559 (198556 in *Add.*² 367). Pelike. *ARV*² 1343 middle; *Para.* 482; *Add.*² 367. A. Amazon, mounted on branded white stallion, thrusting a spear (with a butt-spike) at a hoplite, behind

which is a light-armed soldier. To be compared with his work [Beazley].

The Suessula Painter

140. New York 17.46.1. Neck-amphora. *ARV*² 1344.2; *Add.*² 368. A. Long-haired youth in chlamys, boots, and petasos with two spears and a white stallion. *c.*400 [G. M. A. Richter and M. J. Milne, *Shapes and Names of Athenian Vases* (New York, 1935), fig. 23]; 400–375 [G. M. A. Richter and L. F. Hall, *Red-figured Athenian Vases in the Metropolitan Museum of Art* (New Haven, 1936), 210–11, no. 165].

The Reed Painter

141. Oxford 263. White lekythos. *ARV*² 1377.17. Youth in chiton, chlamys, and petasos, a spear in his left hand, the right resting on his stallion; tomb. 4th cent. [P. Gardner, *Catalogue of the Greek Vases in the Ashmolean Museum* (Oxford, 1893), pl. 20, no. 263].

142. Athens, NM 14521. White lekythos. *ARV*² 1377.18; *Para.* 485. Youth in himation, chlamys, and petasos, carrying two spears and standing alongside (in front of) his horse. *c.*425–400 [P. Devambez, *Greek Painting* (London, 1962), no. 142].

143. London D 63. White lekythos. *ARV*² 1378.34. Youth in chlamys and slung petasos, holding two spears and sitting at tomb, on the far side of which a stallion stands in front of a tree. Not later than end of 5th/start of 4th cent. [Fairbanks, *AWL* ii. 161].

144. Munich 7620. White lekythos. *ARV*² 1382.129; *Add.*² 371. Youth standing alongside his horse, facing left.

145. Paris S 1161. White lekythos. *ARV*² 1382.134; *Add.* 186; *Add.*² 371. Youth in chiton, short cloak, cap, and boots, sword at waist, mounted on a stallion, spear in right hand raised for downward thrust or close range throw at hoplite to his front.

146. Hobart 30*a*. White lekythos. *ARV*² 1382.135; *Para.* 486; *Add.*² 371. Bareheaded youth in chiton and cloak, mounted on a stallion below which is a petasos. He holds a spear at head height for an overarm thrust or throw at a hoplite to his front; to his rear a light-armed soldier runs to the right. Late 5th cent. [R. G. Hood, *Greek Vases in the University of Tasmania*, 3rd edn. (Hobart, 1982), 35, no. 30*a*].

147. Hobart 30*b*. White lekythos. *ARV*² 1382.136; *Para.* 486; *Add.*² 371. Mounted warrior in petasos(?), boots, and cloak, with a spear held overarm at head height, fighting an infantryman in a pilos [Hood, *Greek Vases*, 35, no. 30*b*]. Late 5th cent. [loc. cit.].

Inferior, but Hardly to be Separated from Group R

148. New York 41.162.11. White lekythos. *ARV*² 1384.2; *Add.*² 372. Fight, hoplite at right versus rider at left (only the hooves of the

horse are visible in D. C. Kurtz, *Athenian White Lekythoi* (Oxford, 1975), pl. 48.2. Related to the three preceding entries [Hood, *Greek Vases*, 35].

The Painter of Todi 474

149. Ferrara T 308. Cup. *ARV*² 1403.3. I. Horseman [Beazley].

The Painter of London E 130

150. Boston 1903.819. Cup. *ARV*² 1404.2; *Para.* 488; *Add.*² 374. I. Eros with wreathed head and sandals riding a stallion.

Unattributed, Miscellaneous

151. Syracuse 19846, from Gela. Calyx-krater. *CVA* Italy, xvii (Syracuse 1), Group III Ic, p. 7 and pl. 11.2–3. Upper zone. Horse race: six naked youths, some with riding crops, gallop past a column; most, if not all, are mounted on stallions.

152. Paris CA 2316. Pelike. *CVA* France, xii (Louvre 8), 33–4 and pl. 47.1, 4, 5. A. Naked boy with right arm raised galloping on a horse. The himation-clad youth leaning on a staff on B may well be watching him; if so, the scene is a riding lesson or exercise session. Second half of 5th cent., start of 4th [loc. cit.].

153. Madrid 11126. Hydria. *ARV*² 1564 bottom; *Add.*² 338. Amazono-machy: includes a mounted Amazon in chiton, cap, and boots, thrusting a spear underarm at a fleeing hoplite.

154. Baltimore, Walters Art Gallery 48.231. White lekythos. Von Both-mer, *Amazons* 199, no. 143 and pl. 83.5. Mounted Amazon (? no face remains, but the arms and legs are painted white) in chiton and carrying a spear.

155. Berlin (Furtwängler 2677), from Athens. White lekythos. Fair-banks, *AWL* ii. 173, class XIV, no. 23, pl. 30.2. Youth riding a stallion towards a stela. He carries a spear in his right hand and, according to Fairbanks, his chlamys is blue and his shoes and slung petasos are red. Late 5th/early 4th cent. [ibid. 203].

156. Berlin (Furtwängler 2683). White lekythos. Fairbanks, *AWL* ii. 204–5, class XVI, no. 1. Youth seated at tomb, man, bearded man in chiton holding two spears upright in his left hand; (alongside) a prancing horse [Fairbanks]. *c.*400 [ibid. 215].

FOURTH CENTURY (*c.*390–300)

The Xenophantos Painter

157. St Petersburg (St 1790). Squat lekythos. *ARV*² 1407.1; *Para.* 488; *Add.* 187(? the *Add.* entry seems to be a combination of this vase and that of the Painter of the New York Centauromachy, 1408.1).

Body. Persians hunting (relief): includes one in tunic, trousers, cap, and cloak, mounted on a horse with a saddle-cloth secured by a chest girth, and about to thrust a spear overarm at an animal. He is the only beardless male in the picture.

The Meleager Painter

158. Florence PD 363–4, frr. Cup. *ARV*² 1413.62; *Para*. 490. I. Male(?) on a horse: rear of rider's body, chlamys, and part of horse's hindquarters remain. Start of 4th cent. [*CVA* Italy, xxxviii (Florence 4), 21].

Manner of the Erbach Painter

159. Munich (was Lugano, Schoen). Oinochoe. *ARV*² 1419.2; *Para*. 490; *Add*.² 375. Three youths on horseback throwing javelins at a target. The centre youth, who is being crowned by a winged Nike, is in boots and patterned chiton and mounted on a white stallion with an animal skin secured by a chest girth as a saddle-cloth. The position of his forefinger suggests the use of a javelin loop. In the background is a column with a Panathenaic amphora depicting this event. Start of the fourth century [Metzger, *Représentations*, 358, no. 29, citing Beazley; R. Lullies, *Eine Sammlung griechischer Kleinkunst* (Munich, 1955), 33, no. 72].

The Painter of Louvre G 521

160. Vatican 9102. Bell-krater. *ARV*² 1441.5. A. Youth with wide fillet, chiton(?), chlamys, and slung petasos, mounted on a stallion, thrusting a spear underarm at a hoplite to his front on rocky ground; to the rear of the rider is a light-armed soldier.

161. Ferrara T 35 A VP. Bell-krater. *ARV*² 1441.6. A. Three youths on horseback casting javelins at a shield [Beazley].

The Toya Painter

162. Florence 4051. Bell-krater. *ARV*² 1448.12; *Add*.² 379. A. Initiates (two youths on horseback—Dioskouroi(?)—and two on foot, all holding *bakchoi*) [Beazley].

The Filottrano Painter

163. Cambridge 43.6 (GR 6.1943). Bell-krater. *ARV*² 1454.23; *Add*.² 379. A. Kastor and Polydeukes riding with Nike; both are clad in chiton, petasos, and boots, and are mounted on stallions.

164. Athens, Agora P 25587, fr. Bell-krater. *ARV*² 1454.24. A. Horseman: raised right hand, petasos, and part of the head remain; as the second Dioskouros on the last [Beazley].

165. Oxford 1956.319, 3 frr. Bell-krater. *ARV*² 1454.25. A. Kastor and Polydeukes riding [Beazley].

166. Antioch HM 6462, fr. Bell-krater. *ARV²* 1454.34. A. Horseman: a bearded man wearing a chlamys over his left shoulder riding to right, looking back. Early 4th cent. [C. Clairmont, 'Greek Pottery from the Near East', *Berytus*, 11 (1954/5), 122, no. 212].

Group G

167. Geneva I 680. Pelike. *ARV²* 1462.1; *Para.* 494. A. Arimasp on rearing stallion slashing overarm with a sword at a gryphon to his rear; second Arimasp on foot fighting a gryphon.

168. Naples 2892. Pelike. *ARV²* 1462.4. A. Arimasp(?) on rearing horse, slashing overarm with a sword at a gryphon to his rear.

169. Naples 147320. Pelike. *ARV²* 1462.5. A. Arimasp in anaxyrides riding a rearing stallion, thrusting a spear underarm at a gryphon to his front.

170. Paris, Cab. Méd. 406. Pelike. *ARV²* 1462.7. A. Rider in anaxyrides and mounted on a stallion, thrusting a spear underarm at a gryphon to his front.

171. New York X.21.21 (GR 625). Pelike. *ARV²* 1462.8. Arimasp on rearing stallion, arm positioned for underarm blow (no weapon visible).

172. Warsaw 31978(?) (ex Choynowski 253). Pelike. *ARV²* 1462.9. A. Arimasp on a stallion fighting a gryphon to his front (no weapon visible).

173. Moscow, Pushkin Mus. 377. Pelike. *ARV²* 1463.14. A. Arimasp on a rearing stallion, right arm in position for an underarm thrust at gryphon to his front (no weapon visible).

174. Once Mylasa, Metaxas, from Mylasa. Pelike. *ARV²* 1463.19. A. Bearded rider in anaxyrides and cap, mounted on a stallion, thrusting a spear (with butt-spike?) underarm at a gryphon to his front.

175. St Petersburg (St 2173). Pelike. *ARV²* 1463.23. A. Mounted Arimasp thrusting a spear underarm at gryphon to his front.

176. Würzburg 633, fr. Pelike. *ARV²* 1463.26. A. Horse's head and neck and rider's head and shoulders. The rider has long hair and may be wearing a crested helmet. *c.*360 [E. Langlotz, *Griechische Vasen in Würzburg* (Munich, 1932), 121, no. 633].

177. Altenburg 318. Pelike. *ARV²* 1463.29. A. At left, a long-haired rider in anaxyrides, alopekis, and shoes, mounted on a stallion, thrusting a spear underarm at a gryphon to the right. 350–325 [*CVA* Germany, xviii (Altenburg 2), 11].

178. Moscow 49468. Pelike. *ARV²* 1463.31. A. Long-haired rider in anaxyrides and alopekis-style cap, mounted on a rearing stallion and thrusting a spear underarm at a gryphon to the front.

179. London F 85. Pelike. *ARV²* 1463.33. A. Amazon on stallion thrusting a spear underarm at a gryphon to her front.

180. Berlin, Freie Univ., from Capua. Pelike. *ARV*² 1464.42. A. Fight. Bareheaded cavalryman in chiton and chlamys, riding a stallion and thrusting a spear underarm at a hoplite who is falling under the impact of the spear and of the horse's hooves. To the rear of the falling hoplite are two other infantrymen. 370–360 [K. Peters, 'Zu attisch-rotfiguren Scherben in Berliner Privatbesitz', *AA* 109 (1958), 20].

181. St Petersburg (St 1863). Pelike. *ARV*² 1464.43. A. Rider in anaxyrides and oriental style cap, mounted on a stallion and thrusting a spear underarm at a hoplite who is on his knees beneath the hooves of the horse. To the rear of the hoplite are a second hoplite and a figure in oriental dress.

182. St Petersburg (St 1866). Pelike. *ARV*² 1464.44. Amazon, mounted on a rearing white stallion, thrusting a spear at an infantryman.

183. Moscow 11277. Pelike. *ARV*² 1464.45. A. Amazon on a rearing horse, thrusting overarm at an infantryman to her front. The weapon is not visible in the photograph in M. M. Kobylina, 'Pozdnie bosporskie peliki', *Mat. SSSR* 19 (1951), pl. 13.2, but the position of the arm suggests a spear.

184. Moscow 1517. Pelike. *ARV*² 1464.46. A. Rider in anaxyrides on a rearing horse is slashing overarm with a sword at an infantryman to the rear. This has caused the rider to slide towards the rear of the horse; in front of the horse two foot-soldiers engage in single combat.

185. Salonica, from Pella. Pelike. *ARV*² 1464.52. A. Amazonomachy, including an Amazon on a white horse slashing overarm with a sword at a hoplite to her rear; another hoplite lies prostrate beneath the hooves of her horse. c.350–330 ['Chroniques des fouilles et découvertes archéologiques en Grèce en 1954', *BCH* 79 (1955), 279].

186. Salonica 99 (R 146). Pelike. *ARV*² 1464.53. A. Bearded horseman in anaxyrides, pilos-style helmet, and boots, thrusting a spear underarm at an Amazon on rocky ground to his front. End of 5th cent. [D. M. Robinson, *Excavations at Olynthus*, v (Baltimore, 1933), 127–8, no. 146].

187. Athens, NM 1445 (CC 1860). Pelike. *ARV*² 1464.56. A. Amazon on a rearing white stallion, thrusting a spear overarm at two hoplites to her front; to her rear an Amazon on foot.

188. London F 14. Pelike. *ARV*² 1464.62. A. Amazon, mounted on a rearing white stallion, thrusting a spear underarm at a retreating hoplite on hilly ground.

189. Kavala 877Π. Pelike. *ARV*² 1465.68; *Para.* 494. A. Mounted Amazon(?) using an overarm motion to stab (with spear?) at opposing hoplite.

190. Athens, Pnyx 319, fr. Bell-krater. *ARV*² 1469.145. A. Long-haired rider, possibly carrying a spear (now missing) in the right hand. L. Talcott, B. Philippaki et al., 'Small Objects from the Pnyx', *Hesperia* Supplement x, 66 state that the rider is an Amazon but this is not obvious from their photograph (pl. 32). Late in the second quarter of 4th cent. [ibid. 66, no. 319].

191. Rhodes 14017. Bell-krater. *ARV*² 1469.157. A. Mounted youth in draped garment (chlamys?), beckoning with left arm and preceded by a woman beckoning with her right arm; two other youths on foot.

Near Group G (*II Delicate Style*)

192. London E 233. Hydria. *ARV*² 1471.3. Bearded man in anaxyrides and turban-style cap, mounted on a rearing white horse and thrusting a spear (with a butt-spike) overarm at a hoplite to his front; to the rear of the hoplite stands an archer. *ARV*² 1471.2, which Beazley describes as being the same as this vase, does not include a mounted combatant.

193. London E 247. Hydria. *ARV*² 1471.4. Amazon, mounted on a rearing white stallion with a leopard-skin saddle-cloth, thrusting a spear overarm at a hoplite to her front; to her rear an Amazon archer; above the horse is a diving bird, and a *pelte* lies beneath its hooves.

The Europa Painter[8]

194. Salonica, from Olynthos. Hydria. Robinson, *Excavations at Olynthus*, v. 126–7, pl. 92, no. 145 and 'The Residential Districts and the Cemeteries at Olynthus', *AJA* 36 (1932), 125, pl. 5.1; Schefold, *Untersuchungen*, 25 and 158, no. 195a. A. Amazonomachy: includes an Amazon on a rearing stallion, slashing overarm with an axe at a hoplite to her rear. c.370 [Schefold, *Untersuchungen*, 25].

The Group of Moscow 4302[9]

195. Moscow 4302. Pelike. *ARV*² 1474.1. Amazon, mounted on a rearing horse, riding at a hoplite with right arm raised above her head (her weapon no longer remains, or at least is not visible in the illustration in M. M. Kobylina, 'Pozdnie bosporskie peliki', *Mat. SSSR* 19 (1951), pl. 10.2).

The Amazon Painter

196. Odessa 3008. Pelike. *ARV*² 1478.11. A. Amazonomachy, includes a mounted Amazon slashing overarm with a sword to her rear.

---

[8] See Schefold, *Untersuchungen*, 158.
[9] Incorrectly given as 'Moscow 4332' in the heading in *ARV*².

197. St Petersburg (St 1810). Hydria. *ARV*² 1480.36. Amazonomachy, including Amazon on rearing stallion; she holds the reins and a spear in her left hand while the right is held upraised back towards the mêlée of foot.

The Chalki Group

198. Rhodes 13886. Onos. *ARV*² 1503.6; *Add.*² 383. C. Long-haired youth in chiton, petasos, and boots, mounted on a white horse with an animal skin secured by a chest-girth as a saddle-cloth. He is casting a broad-bladed javelin at a shield on a pole; the position of the fingers suggests the use of a javelin loop. Start of 4th cent. [G. Jacopi, 'La Necropoli di Pontamo', *Clara Rhodos*, 2 (1932), 134].

The Q Painter

199. Geneva MF 202. Stemless cup. *ARV*² 1519.18; *Para.* 500. I. Naked boy riding towards a semi-naked youth. See next entry.
200. Naples 2595. Stemless cup. *ARV*² 1519.19. I. Naked boy riding towards a beckoning male. For the subject of this and the last see A. D. Ure, 'Red-Figure Cups with Incised and Stamped decoration—II', *JHS* 64 (1944), 72.

Unattributed, Miscellaneous

201. St Petersburg (St 2178a). Hydria. Schefold, *Untersuchungen*, 21, no. 160, pl. 13; K. Schefold, *Kertscher Vasen* (Berlin, 1930), 22, pl. 2A. A. Youth in chiton riding a white horse, woman, winged Eros, horse's head, cheetah/leopard. B. The like, except the youth is in anaxyrides and there is a deer instead of the cheetah. c.370 [Schefold, *Kertscher Vasen*, 22].
202. Paris G 528. Bell-krater. Metzger, *Représentations*, 358, no. 31 and pl. 47.3; F. G. Welcker, *Griechische Vasengemälde*, iii (Göttingen, 1851), 523 ff., pl. 35; *CVA* France, viii (Louvre 5), Group iii Ie, p. 7, pl. 6.4, 7. Three youths (the first and third mounted on stallions, the sex of the middle horse is uncertain) casting javelins at a shield on a pole; all three have longish hair, wear chitones, and have garlands on their heads. The first has already thrown and his javelin lies broken beneath the target; the second (who is being crowned by winged victories) is about to cast, using an *amentum*; the third has his arm extended to the rear and the javelin clenched in his fist.
203. Athens, NM 1631 (CC 1478). Aryballos. Metzger, *Représentations*, 358, no. 30, pl. 47.2. Two youths throwing javelins at a shield on a pole. The first has longish hair and wears a chiton, boots, and cap (alopekis?); he is mounted on a stallion and has already cast a spear

(and missed). The second has longish hair and wears a chiton, boots, and petasos; he is riding up to throw his javelin. A broken javelin lies at the foot of the target and there are two shrubs in the background. According to Gardiner, *JHS* 27 (1907), 271, it is an Eretreian piece, but it is extremely close to the Athenian examples (159 and 202 above) and from the photograph I would follow Metzger in including it as an Athenian work. 4th cent. [Metzger].

APPENDIX 2
Attic Equestrian Reliefs

THIS appendix lists Attic reliefs with equestrian subjects and is intended both to provide a fairly representative selection of reliefs and a quick method of referring to a particular piece in the main part of the book. It does not pretend to be complete; compiling an exhaustive catalogue of reliefs was not my prime objective and considerations of space precluded a detailed treatment of such important monuments as the Parthenon frieze. The stones are listed in three general groups rather than chronologically—largely because many of them lack a firm date. The first of these groups comprises the reliefs recorded in Conze's *Die attischen Grabreliefs*, the second those in the National Museum at Athens, and the third those in other collections.

The entry for each relief includes, wherever possible, its location and accession number, a brief description, which concentrates on the equestrian part of the relief, its date (with the source given in square brackets), and details of illustrations. The information on illustrations always forms the last part of the entry and is separated from the rest of it by a colon. I have followed the same descriptive conventions as in Appendix 1.

The following abbreviations are specific to this appendix:

Clairmont   C. Clairmont, 'Gravestone with Warriors in Boston', *GRBS* 13 (1972), 49–58

Frel   J. Frel and B. Kingsley, 'Three Attic Sculpture Workshops of the Early Fourth Century BC ', *GRBS* 11 (1970), 197–218

P-D   D. Peppas-Delmousou, "«Ἐπιστήματα» τοῦ Τάφου τοῦ Μενύλλου Ἁλαιέως. Ἡ Βάση EM 13451", *AAA* 10 (1977), 225–41.

1. Conze 270. Stela; some surface damage. Farewell scene: a female (Paregoria) sits on a chair at the right. She faces left and is shaking hands with a male (Phrynion, 5.161), dressed in a chiton and chlamys, who faces her, Phrynion stands alongside (in front of) a horse whose reins he holds in his left hand. 4th cent. [*IG* II² 6449]: Conze, pl. LXII.

2. Conze 271 (Lost). Stela. Farewell scene: similar to no. 1 (the man is [..?..]e[n]ippos [..?..]eus, 5.59) [Conze]. 4th cent. [*IG* II² 7838]: Caylus, *Recueil d'Antiquités*, vi (Paris, 1764), pl. LVI.

3. Conze 441 (Paris, Louvre). Lekythos. Farewell scene: a female

seated on a chair at the right, a second (damaged) figure stands in attendance to the rear of the chair. The seated woman faces left and is shaking hands with a bearded man (Antias, 5.16) dressed in a chiton, standing alongside (in front of) a horse whose reins he holds in his left hand. To the rear of Antias and also facing right is another bearded man (Antiphon) dressed in a himation. 4th cent. [*PA* 973*a*, 1282*b*]: Conze, pl. CIII.

4. Conze 1001 (Moscow, Mus. Fin. Arts). Stela. Farewell scene: on the right a bearded man in a himation faces left towards another bearded man with chiton, chlamys, slung petasos, and bare feet. The latter faces right, carrying a spear with a butt-spike over his left shoulder, and stands alongside (in front of) a horse, only the forequarters of which are shown. *c*.375–360 [Frel, 212–13]: Frel, pl. 24.

5. Conze 1011 (Athens, NM 1074). Lekythos; damaged (head and shoulders of cavalryman, his mid-section, and most of horse are missing). Farewell scene: on right, facing left is a male (Autodikos? 5.33) in chiton and boots standing alongside (in front of) a horse. He is shaking hands with a bearded man in a chiton who faces right. *c*.400–350 [*PA* 2707].

6. Conze 1024. Lekythos. On the right a naked youth holding the reins of a horse which faces him from the left. Alongside (in front of) the horse and facing right is a male (Polymedes, 5.162) in a cuirass with pteryges and holding a spear(?) in his left hand. From Conze's drawing it looks to be late 4th/early 3rd cent.: Conze, pl. CCIII.

7. Conze 1073 (Athens, NM 835). Lekythos. Farewell scene: at right two hoplites shaking hands. At left, and facing left, is a woman seated in a chair with an attendant standing behind her. In the centre is a youth in a petasos (-style helmet?), cuirass, chiton, and boots, riding a stallion to the right. Post 440 [C. Bluemel, *Greek Sculptors at Work* (London, 1969), 77—but on p. vii incorrectly listing the relief as Conze, 1047]; *c*.320 [NM].

8. Conze 1098 (Paris, Louvre). Stela; damaged (figures' feet missing). Farewell scene: at right a standing female (Timagora) faces left and shakes the hand of a bearded male (Philochares, 5.149) dressed in chiton and chlamys, standing in front of his horse, only the forequarters of which are shown. According to Conze, Philochares held either the reins or a sword hilt in his left hand. 4th cent. [*PA* 14774]: Conze, pl. CCXXV.

9. Conze 1099 (Oxford, Ashmolean, Michaelis 140). Stela; bottom section damaged. Farewell scene: at right a standing female (Lysimache) facing left and shaking the hand of a (bearded?) male (Philodemos Sophilou Cholleides(*sic*), 5.150) in chiton. He faces right and stands alongside (in front of) his horse which also faces right. Mid-4th cent. [*IG* II² 7807]; early 4th cent. [Museum]: Conze, pl. CCXV.

10. Conze 1153 (Villa Albani). Stela; lower portion damaged. Battle scene: at right is a youth in chiton and chlamys(?) facing left and standing alongside (in front of) a rearing horse which faces right. He holds the (now missing) reins in his left hand and his right arm is raised above his head for an overarm blow with a (now missing) sword at a fallen youth in chlamys(?) and slung petasos. *c*.415–413 [Clairmont, 56]: Clairmont, pl. 3.2.

11. Conze 1154 (Athens, NM 1674). Lekythos; only the decorative figures at the top remain. At right is a youth (Chryseus) in a crested Ionian helmet, chlamys, and carrying an *aspis* aiming an overhead blow with his sword to the left. In the centre is a youth in chiton and chlamys depicted frontally, alongside (in front of) a horse, only the head and neck of which are shown. At left is a youth moving to the right but with his head turned to the left. He wears a chlamys and a slung petasos with a sword on a baldric and carries a spear over his left shoulder: Conze, 252.

12. Conze 1158 (Athens, Kerameikos P 1130). Stela; some surface damage to lower half. Dexileos monument; battle scene: mounted youth (Dexileos, 5.51) in centre riding down a hoplite to the right. Dexileos is bareheaded, wears a chiton, chlamys, and sword, and rides a stallion. His right arm is poised for a downward blow at his opponent with a (now missing) spear. 394/3: Pl. 11.

13. Conze 1159 (Athens, NM). Stela; worn quite badly in places. Battle scene: dismounted horseman in chiton, chlamys, and helmet, alongside (in front of) a rearing horse whose reins he seems to hold in his left hand. He faces right and his right arm is raised over his head for a downward blow with a (now missing) sword. Beneath the hooves of his horse is a shield but no enemy figure: Conze, 255.

14. Conze 1160 (Berlin, Staatliche Museen zu Berlin K. 30). Stela; damaged. Battle scene depicting a cavalryman [..?..]ulos Phlyeus, 5.188): what remains are the forequarters of a rearing horse moving to the right and traces of the rider's (bare?) head. Beneath the hooves a recumbent foe strikes up at the horse with a sword. End of 5th cent. [*IG* II² 7716]; *c*.415 [Clairmont, 56]: Conze, pl. ccxlix; Clairmont, pl. 4.2.

15. Conze 1161 (London, BM GR. 1816.6–10.384 = GR SC 638). Stela. Bearded rider (Aristokles, 5.29) in a cloak rides a horse to the right. Behind him follows a young attendant who carries a staff or a spear. Start of 4th cent. [*IG* II² 7151]: Conze, pl. ccl.

16. Conze 1161A. Stela. A youth (Menes), bareheaded, in chiton and chlamys, spear in right hand, reins in left, rides a stallion to the right. Although Menes is described as an Argive the relief is apparently Attic. 4th cent.(?) [Conze, 256]: loc. cit.

17. Conze 1162 (Brocklesby Park). Stela. Warrior: a bearded man

([X]en[o]kles Polyar[..?..] Alopek[ethen], 5.190) in helmet and chiton rides to the left. 4th cent. [*PA* 11213]: Conze, 257.

18. Athens, NM Θ 168. Lekythos. Farewell scene: bearded man (Menyllos, 5.117) dressed in chlamys and cloak standing alongside (in front of) a stallion facing left. He faces left and shakes hands with his father (Astyphilos), a bearded man in himation facing right. Part of the same monument as numbers 19, 34, and 35; P-D 225–41. *c*.340–330 [P-D 240]: P-D pl. 2β.

19. Athens, NM Θ 170. Lekythos. Farewell scene (Menyllos): as for the last except better executed: P-D pl. 2α.

20. Athens, NM 884. Lekythos-shaped stela. Farewell: at right a youth (Panaitios, 5.138) in petasos, girdled chiton, and barefoot, with a slung sword and holding a *kamax* and two javelins in his left hand. He stands alongside (in front of) a stallion, facing left and is shaking hands with an older male in a himation, behind whom stands a young attendant. *c*.395–390 [Sekunda, *AG* 60]: Pl. 9.

21. Athens, NM 1773. Base, reliefs on three sides, inscription on fourth. Bryaxis monument; depicting Demainetos, Demeas, and Demosthenes (5.43–4, 50). Left face: bearded horseman riding a stallion from left to right towards a tripod. He is bareheaded, barefooted, and dressed in a chiton with girdle. He appears to be holding the reins in his left hand and the horse's mane in his right. Rear face: as for the last except his right hand is flat on the horse's neck. Right face: as for the rear face, probably including position of hands but damage renders this uncertain. Mid-4th cent. [B. Petrakos, *National Museum Sculpture-Bronzes-Vases* (Athens, 1981), 112].

22. Athens, NM 1824. Lekythos. Farewell scene: in centre, a man (Pheidestratos) and a woman (Xenarete) facing each other and shaking hands. They are flanked on the right by a bearded man (Autodikos, 5.33) and on the left by a young horseman (Thereus, 5.183); both face inwards. Thereus, dressed in a petasos, chiton, and cloak, and apparently unarmed, is dismounted. He stands to the front of his stallion's head with his right hand on Pheidestratos' right shoulder. *c*.400–350 [*PA* 2707].

23. Athens, NM 2405. Stela; fragmentary. Battle scene: what remains is a horse's foreleg moving from left to right, superimposed on a hoplite aiming an overarm swordstroke at the horse.

24. Athens, NM 2586. Stela; considerable surface damage. Farewell scene: at right a seated man facing left and shaking hands with another bearded man in petasos, breastplate with shoulder and waist pteryges, chiton(?), long cloak, and boots. To his rear stands a boy holding a horse by its (now missing) reins.

25. Athens, NM 2744. Stela; some surface damage. Battle scene (monument to those killed at Corinth and Boiotia in 394/3): at right a

beardless cavalryman in petasos-helmet and chiton with slung bird-handled sword and bare feet. He is riding down a fallen hoplite to the left and holds a (now missing) spear in his right hand poised for a downward blow. To the rear of the fallen soldier is a second hoplite in support. 394/3: Pl. 13.

26. Athens, NM 3620A. Lekythos. Battle scene: a beardless cavalryman (Kephisodotos, 5.85) in petasos-helmet, chiton, long cloak, and mounted on a stallion rides down a falling infantryman; a light-armed infantryman stands to the rear of the horse, facing left. No weapons are visible but the right arm is raised for a downward blow with a spear (or possibly a sword). First half of 4th cent. [*IG* II² 5391].

27. Athens, NM 3708. Base, reliefs on three sides, blank on the fourth. Battle scenes: left panel: beardless cavalryman in petasos, muscle cuirass, chiton, and boots. He is riding down a semi-recumbent infantryman and has his arm raised for an overarm thrust, probably with a (now missing) spear. Front: beardless cavalryman in petasos, chiton, cloak, boots, and slung sword, riding down an infantryman as for the last. Right: beardless cavalryman in petasos, chiton, cloak and boots, riding down an infantryman as for the last. Late 390s [Frel, 204]: Pl. 2 (left panel).

28. Athens, NM 4464. Stela. A negro groom to right facing a stallion with a leopard or cheetah skin saddlecloth; above the horse's hind-quarters is painted a Boiotian helmet. *c.*300 or shortly afterwards [S. Karouzou, *National Archaeological Museum Collection of Sculpture* (Athens, 1968), 127]; Alexander's time or soon after [Sekunda, *AG* 15]: Pl. 16.

29. Athens, NM. Loutrophoros. Battle scene: a bearded horseman (Philon Aristokleous Meliteus, 5.156) dressed in petasos-helmet, girdled chiton, and slung sword, mounted on a rearing stallion facing right. His spear (no longer visible) is poised for a downward thrust at a beardless enemy kneeling at right and drawing sword. To the rear of Philon is a second, dying, horseman falling from his mount; beneath the second horse is a prone body. According to Y. Nikopou-lou, "'Επιτύμβια Μνημεῖα παρὰ τὰς Πύλας τοῦ Διοχάρους", *AAA* 2 (1969), 332, there is a third prone figure overlapping, but to the right of, the kneeling warrior. *c.*325–300 [Nikopoulou, *AAA* 2 (1969), 334]: Nikopoulou, *AAA* 2 (1969), fig. 3.

30. Eleusis 5101. Stela. Votive relief of [Pythodoro]s (5.168); surface damage, right half missing. Battle scene: at top of relief a bearded cavalryman in petasos, cuirass with pteryges, and boots, arm poised for downward thrust with spear(?) rides down an infantryman, behind him the forequarters of another horse. At the bottom is a similar scene although all that remains of the cavalryman is a booted

leg and the forelegs of his mount. *c*.420 [K. G. Kanta, *Eleusis* (Athens, 1979), 33]; *c*.413–410 [Clairmont, 55]: Pl. 12.

31. San Lorenzo. Stela; damaged. What remains is a rider's torso and booted legs; he is dressed in chiton and chlamys, and mounted on a stallion (whose head and forelegs are missing), riding to the right. Post-394, but not too long after [Frel, 202]: ibid. pl. 15.2.

32. Paris, Louvre 744. Stela; right side missing. Battle scene: a cavalryman and *hamippos* advancing to right. The cavalryman (face missing) has a slung petasos, a chiton, and chlamys(?), while the light-armed *hamippos* runs behind the horse holding on to its tail. Before *c*.362 [Sekunda, *AG* 54, 57]: Pl. 10.

33. Budapest, Mus. Fin. Arts 4744. Stela; lower portion missing. Battle scene: mounted youth in petasos, girdled chiton, and chlamys, with slung sword, rides to the right on a horse with an animal skin saddlecloth, spear poised for a downward thrust at what was probably a fallen enemy beneath the hooves of his horse. To the front of the horse and facing left is a light-armed soldier wielding a club(?) either at the horse or the fallen warrior. Before *c*.362 [Sekunda, *AG* 54, 58]: ibid. 58.

34. Copenhagen, Ny Carlsberg 2786. Lekythos. Farewell scene (Menyllos): similar to 18 and 19 except Menyllos is rather larger than Astyphilos: P-D pl. 2γ.

35. (?) Once Athens Market. Lekythos. Farewell scene (Menyllos): as for nos. 18, 19, and 34.

36. Athens, Stoa of Attalos I 7167. Stela. Tribe of Leontis in the *anthippasia*: rank of five horsemen riding to the right, each cavalryman overlapping the man to his left. The right-hand figure is a bearded man (phylarch?) dressed in an alopekis (or helmet?), chiton, and high boots; the two to his left are bareheaded youths in chitones. The two figures on the left-hand end of the rank are fragmentary (both heads are missing) but the one on the extreme left is also in a chiton. Early 4th cent. [Shear, *Hesperia*, 41 (1971), 272]: ibid. pl. 56*c* (a smaller version is in Bugh, *Horsemen*, fig. 7).

37. Cambridge, Fitzwilliam Museum GR 20.1865. Lekythos; foot restored. Farewell scene: a bearded male (Hegemon of Epikephisios) in himation facing right, shaking hands with a short-haired youth in chlamys and slung petasos, standing alongside (in front of) a stallion, whose reins he holds. To the rear of Hegemon stands a boy with a dog on a leash. *c*.400 [Museum].

APPENDIX 3
The Parthenon Frieze

THE identity of the riders on the Parthenon frieze is an important and interesting question, not only for the history of the Athenian cavalry, but also in terms of the interpretation of the frieze itself. For years it was simply assumed that they were cavalrymen participating in the Panathenaic procession, and Martin, for example, claimed that the frieze recorded the first time the new cavalry corps took part in the event.[1] However, the traditional interpretation has been challenged since Boardman's suggestion that the mounted figures represent the heroized dead from Marathon and Simon's claim that they portray mounted *epheboi*.[2]

Boardman's theory is that the horsemen, the *apobatai* (equestrian competitors who leaped in and out of chariots), and any males in the procession not carrying objects, leading animals, or playing musical instruments, are the dead from Marathon in the guise of heroes. They are celebrating the Panathenaia, and the other, non-heroic, participants 'are there simply to demonstrate the immediate role of the great cavalcade, as worshippers of the city goddess.'[3] He advances three main arguments to support this theory: that the Parthenon was closely associated with Marathon, that too many aspects of the procession are unrepresented for it to portray a real Panathenaic procession, and that the number of heroized figures is 192, exactly the same number as the dead from Marathon.[4] The first of these is certainly correct but the other two are open to serious objection.

The question of the omitted features of the procession, such as the *kanephoroi* (the girls who carried the *kanoun* or offering basket) and the ship with the *peplos* (the dress for the statue of Athena), have been discussed in considerable detail, most recently by Brommer and Simon, and most can be explained satisfactorily.[5] For example, as Boardman himself admits, it is not even certain that the practice of using a ship to carry the *peplos* existed in the fifth century.[6] Similarly, Simon (building

[1] Martin, *Cavaliers*, 134.
[2] Boardman, 'The Parthenon Frieze', 39–49; Simon, *Festivals*, 59–60.
[3] Boardman, 'The Parthenon Frieze', 44–8.
[4] Ibid. 42–3 (omissions), 43–4 (Marathon links), 48–9 (Marathon dead).
[5] F. Brommer, *Der Parthenonfries* (Mainz am Rhein, 1977), 147–9; Simon, *Festivals*, 60–1.
[6] Boardman, 'The Parthenon Frieze', 42 n. 17; see also Brommer, *Parthenonfries*, 147.

on an argument originally suggested by Schelp) demonstrates that the *kanoun* is represented, although now damaged, on the East frieze.[7]

The existence of exactly 192 heroized dead is also problematical. First, not all of the frieze is extant and estimates of the number and type of the missing figures vary. Boardman bases his calculations on Schuchhardt's reconstruction and points out that Peris's reconstruction is very similar.[8] However, given the precision required by Boardman's argument, accuracy is vital here and these reconstructions are not exactly the same. Peris, for example, restores three more figures on the North frieze and eight more on the South than Schuchhardt does.[9] Second, it seems rather dubious that Boardman has to omit other participants in the procession to arrive at his figure of 192.[10] He includes the *apobatai*, but not their drivers, omits dismounted functionaries like musicians, *hydriaphoroi*, and herdsmen, but includes marshals and even a small boy. I find it hard to believe that both marshals and horsemen were intended to symbolize Marathon heroes.[11] In fact, it seems altogether too allusive on the part of the sculptors to portray the dead from Marathon as cavalrymen or officials when other friezes simply portrayed them as what they were—hoplites.[12]

Another important objection to Boardman's thesis is the age of the riders. All except two are portrayed as beardless youths and, as Simon points out, 'heroization does not mean total rejuvenation.'[13] The depiction of cavalrymen as young men and their officers as older, bearded, men was very common in Athenian art and literature and Robertson's identification of the two bearded men as the hipparchs[14] seems highly likely—despite Simon's objections. She identifies one bearded rider as the polemarch, ignores the identity of the other, and rejects Robertson's

---

[7] Between figures 49 and 50 on Slab VII of the East frieze; Simon, *Festivals*, 60–1, pl. 22.1. Cf. Brommer, *Parthenonfries*, 148.

[8] Boardman, 'The Parthenon Frieze', 48 and n. 38, referring to W. H. Schuchhardt, 'Die "Entstehung des Parthenonfrieses"', *JDAI* 45 (1930), 218–80 and F. J. Peris, *Die Disposition des Parthenonfrieses* (Bonn, 1974).

[9] Schuchhardt, *JDAI* 45 (1930), 277 n. 1, has 138 on each while Peris, *Disposition*, has 141 for the North and 146 for the South (counted from his diagram).

[10] Brommer, *Parthenonfries*, 149 n. 15 also finds this a weakness in Boardman's case.

[11] Boardman, 'The Parthenon Frieze', 42 argues against a Greek artist using 'the same device in the same scene to mean two different things', yet he assumes here that an artist uses two different devices in the same scene to mean the same thing.

[12] See Bugh, *Horsemen*, 77–8 n. 134.

[13] Simon, *Festivals*, 59. She is also surprised at the omission of Herakles and Theseus if the frieze really indicates a link with Marathon.

[14] M. Robertson, *The Parthenon Frieze* (London, 1975), 48 (unnumbered; it is the page describing Slabs V–VI and VIII–IX of the West frieze). See also 199–201 above.

theory because 'the *hipparchoi* were not involved in specific cult functions, whereas the polemarch was.'[15] However, it is quite clear that the hipparchs were involved in conducting state processions[16]—the very activity depicted in the frieze. There is a clear contrast between their age and that of their companions, as is the case in an analogous relief (no. 36) of the Leontis cavalry squadron winning an equestrian review. This sculpture depicts one bearded male in an alopekis (or possibly a helmet) leading a rank of youths; he is almost certainly the victorious phylarch. Given the similar contrast on the Parthenon frieze, and the fact that there are two bearded men, dressed identically (in alopekis, chiton, chlamys, and boots), Robertson's identification of the two bearded riders as hipparchs is clearly preferable.[17]

It is for these reasons that I find Boardman's argument unproven, although he does cast some doubts on the traditional view that the frieze represents a normal Panathenaic procession. Simon's alternative explanation is also unconvincing. In her opinion, these riders are a section of mounted *epheboi* not cavalrymen,[18] but several factors militate against this. The first is that the *ephebeia* may well not have existed as a formal military training institution when the Parthenon was being constructed in the mid-fifth century.[19] The second is that, even if it had done so, it would not have included equestrian training. There is simply no evidence for, and in fact much against, the existence of ephebic equestrian training in the classical period.

Owning a horse was very costly and mounted training could have been provided only to those who already possessed mounts. As these must have constituted a small minority of ephebes, it seems highly unlikely that cavalry instruction was included in their general training programme and this is confirmed by the extant evidence. Around 365, Xenophon suggested providing an instructor to teach the younger cavalry recruits how to mount from the spring.[20] This was an important skill, and one which would surely have been taught to these recruits already, if they had just completed two years as mounted ephebes. Even more telling is

---

[15] Simon, *Festivals*, 59 and n. 12.

[16] Dem. 4. 26.

[17] The two figures are 8 and 15 on Slabs IV and VIII of the West frieze. The best photographs are in Brommer, *Parthenonfries*, pls. 13–14, 23–6.

[18] Simon, *Festivals*, 59–60.

[19] For the debate on the date the *ephebeia* was instituted see O. W. Reinmuth, 'The Genesis of the Athenian Ephebia', *TAPhA* 83 (1952), 34–50, esp. 34 n. 2; Pélékidis, *Histoire de l'éphébie attique*, 7–79; P. Vidal-Naquet, 'The Black Hunter and the Origin of the Athenian Ephebeia', *PCPhS* NS 14 (1968), 49–64. Although the *ephebeia* apparently existed in some form in the fifth century, as Beck points out, *OCD*² 386, 'there is no clear evidence of any organized training institution before *c*.335 BC.'

[20] Xen. *Hipparch.* 1. 17.

the *Athenaion Politeia* ascribed to Aristotle and written about forty years later. This contains a passage describing the course of the ephebes' training from acceptance by a deme to graduation as full citizens. It states that they were trained 'to fight as hoplites, shoot the bow, throw the javelin, and fire the catapult'—nearly every military skill in fact except riding. The list of ephebic officials in the same work does not include a riding instructor, and at the end of the first stage of their training the ephebes were presented with a shield and a spear.[21] These were part of the infantry panoply not cavalry weapons. The conclusion must surely be that there were no mounted ephebes at this time.

There is in fact no evidence for any sort of equestrian training for the *epheboi* until the mid-first century. A rather fragmentary inscription of this date records '[practice(?)] in horsemanship' amongst a list of ephebic activities, while two others mention 'exercise' or 'training in horsemanship'.[22] However, such training can be attested only for a very short period within the first century and may well have originated during the ten-year democracy between Caesar and Antony. Earlier ephebic texts, dating from 123/2 to post 94/3, do not apparently mention equestrian training.[23] Particularly telling is the omission of equestrian training from *IG* II[2] 1039, which Reinmuth argues precedes the series of inscriptions which incorporates 1040–1025, 1041, and 1042[24] (the first and last of which do record equestrian training). *IG* II[2] 1039 is virtually complete and has no space for the restoration of riding activities in the lines which cover training (45–50). If Reinmuth is correct in assigning *IG* II[2] 1039 to the aristocratic government established by Sulla at Athens,[25] then the equestrian training seems to have emerged under the democratic government restored by Caesar.

Simon's main evidence for mounted *epheboi* (she does not mention the inscriptional material) seems to be that they are known to have escorted processions and that the mounted figure on the Little Metropolis calendar frieze cannot be a cavalryman exercising (Deubner's suggestion) as 'there are no other profane representations in the frieze'.[26] However, the figure could easily represent a cavalry contingent with the cavalcade. *Hippeis*

[21] *Ath. Pol.* 42. 2–4.
[22] *IG* II[2] 1040–1025, ll. 27–9 (τῆς ἐν τοῖς ἱππικοῖς [ἐμπειρίας]); 1043, l. 21; 1042, l. 21. The former is a composite inscription, joined by O. W. Reinmuth, 'An Ephebic Text of ca. 43/2 BC: *IG* II[2], 1040 and 1025', *Hesperia*, 34 (1965), 255–72; *IG* II[2] 1040 restores γυμνασίας (exercise) instead of ἐμπειρίας (practice).
[23] *IG* II[2] 1006; 1008; 1009; 1011; 1028; 1029; 1030 (the last 2 more fragmentary than the others); and J. H. Oliver 'Selected Greek Inscriptions', *Hesperia*, 2 (1933), 503–4, no. 16.
[24] Reinmuth, *Hesperia*, 34 (1965), 264–5.
[25] Ibid. 264.
[26] Simon, *Festivals*, 25.

too, participated in state processions and would therefore be part of the religious event and not a profane addition. Finally, as noted, the two bearded riders on the frieze are best explained as the two hipparchs, and as Boardman remarks, the horsemen are portrayed in 'ten ranks or clusters,' with sufficient slight variations in dress to further distinguish the groups from each other. This seems to be an attempt to portray the ten tribal *phylai* or squadrons.[27]

For these reasons, and because of the evidence for cavalry participation in the Panathenaic procession discussed in Chapter 4, the traditional interpretation of the riders on the Parthenon frieze should stand. They are cavalrymen, not heroized dead from Marathon or mounted ephebes.

[27] Boardman, 'The Parthenon Frieze', 40.

APPENDIX 4

The Cost of Cavalry Service at Athens

FOR much of the classical period the Athenians regarded the *hippeis* as a necessary component of their armed forces, and were prepared, on a state basis, to contribute to its financial upkeep. This was done through the provision of an establishment loan, or *katastasis*, to assist with the initial capital outlay required, and a daily ration allowance, or *sitos*, to help with continuing feed costs. *Sitos* was paid from at least 410/9, the *katastasis* from at least the mid-420s.[1] However, on close examination, it is clear that the state paid only part of the cost of its cavalry and relied heavily upon the willingness of the wealthy to shoulder much of the burden of its upkeep.

This appendix examines the financial cost of cavalry service to the individual *hippeus*,[2] concentrating in particular on the two major items of expenditure involved: the cost of purchasing and of feeding a horse. While the evidence is not entirely problem-free, it is possible to reconstruct these costs with a reasonable degree of precision for the 330s. Although the exact costs identified for this period should not perhaps be applied too rigidly to other years, they do provide a good indication of the expense of cavalry service relative to the cost of living, and this probably holds true for most of the period from about 450 to 320.[3] The picture which emerges confirms the general impression conveyed by the contemporary Athenian literature—membership of the equestrian milieu was an expensive pastime which few citizens could afford.[4]

---

[1] *Sitos*: *IG* I³ 375 (accounts of the Treasurers of Athena, 410/9). *Katastasis*: Lysias, 16. 6–7 (referring to 404/3); Eupolis fr. 268 (dated to *c*.429–425, J. M. Edmonds, *Fragments of Attic Comedy*, i (Leiden, 1957), 407 note e). Bugh, *Horsemen*, 56–7 argues that it dates to the institution of the corps of 300 (in 457 by his reckoning, ibid. 47) but the suggestion (Kroll, 99) that the grant was contemporary with the establishment of the 1,000 strong corps (*c*.445–438) is more likely. The creation of the corps of 300, presumably drawn from the very wealthiest members of·society (cf. Bugh, *Horsemen*, 66), pre-dated the period when state-payment became a widely accepted practice in Athens, and monetary support to the richest Athenians would probably not have been countenanced at this date.

[2] See 'attitudes to the cavalry *c*.404–363', Ch. 4 for the often high social costs involved in cavalry service.

[3] However, the *sitos* payment was larger prior to 403/2 (Lysias fr. 6 = Grenfell and Hunt, *Hibeh Papyri*, 51–2, no. 14, ll. 70 ff.), which meant that feeding a horse was slightly cheaper then.

[4] See 'wealth', Ch. 4.

TABLE 6. Athenian barley prices in the fourth century

Date	Grain Type	Price (per *medimnos*)	Source
c.330	Barley	18 drachmas	[Dem.] 42. 20
	Grain (including barley)	6 drachmas	[Dem.] 42. 31
c.330	Barley[a]	5 drachmas	*IG* II² 408, ll. 13–14
329/8	Barley	3 drachmas	*IG* II² 1672, ll. 282–3
	Barley	3 drachmas 5 obols	*IG* II² 1672, l. 298

[a] The word *krithas* (barley) is reconstructed in this case.

The costs involved in being a cavalryman derived from the purchase of arms and armour and from owning a horse. On campaign, a fully accoutred *hippeus* might have some or all of the following: helmet, cuirass, a spear, two (or more) javelins, and a sword.[5] Although it is impossible to ascertain the cost of such a panoply (evidence for the cost of arms and armour is notoriously scanty and occasionally contradictory), it cannot have been cheap.[6] For example, one of the items recorded on the *hermokopidai* stelae is a *doration* (throwing spear) valued at 2 drachmas 5 obols.[7] This weapon alone cost about the same as 0.5–1 *medimnos* of barley—enough to provide a reasonably generous grain ration to an active adult male for between twenty-four and forty-eight days.[8] Many cavalrymen, though, carried two javelins into battle[9] and almost certainly had spares with their baggage. Given that javelins were thrown, and therefore particularly prone to loss or damage, purchasing such items was presumably a fairly constant financial outlay during a career in the cavalry.

Horse-owning involved the mount's purchase price, its feed, maintenance of a stable (or rent of one), the cost of riding tackle, and the cost of a

[5] See 'weaponry', Ch. 2 for the variety of equipment.

[6] Cf. W. K. Pritchett, 'The Attic Stelai: Part II', *Hesperia*, 25 (1956), 306–7.

[7] W. K. Pritchett, 'The Attic Stelai: Part I', *Hesperia*, 22 (1953), 253, stela II, l. 226. His statement, *Hesperia*, 25 (1956), 307, that it is valued at 2 drachmas seems to be an error as the photographs at pl. 70 of Pritchett, *Hesperia*, 22 (1953), and in B. D. Meritt, 'Greek Inscriptions', *Hesperia*, 5 (1936), 383, show that the price was 2 drachmas and 5 obols.

[8] Calculated on the 'standard' ration of 1 *choinix* per day (see L. Foxhall and H. A. Forbes, 'Σιτομετρεία: The Role of Grain as a Staple Food in Classical Antiquity', *Chiron*, 12 (1982), 62–3; Markle, *Crux*, 294–5), at prices in 330 (see Table 6).

[9] Cf. the sample of Attic vase-paintings in App. 1.

groom.[10] Additional expenses could also be incurred if specialist veterinary treatment was sought in the case of illness or injury.[11] The cost of some of these are impossible to recover—for example the cost of buying a groom, consulting a vet, maintaining a stable, and the price of a complete set of horse harness.[12] Fortunately, there is solid evidence for the initial cost of buying a horse (and its subsequent depreciation), and the recurring expense of feeding it can also be reconstructed, although with less certainty. Together these form the bulk of the expenditure involved in cavalry service.

The best evidence for the value of horses is provided by the lead cavalry tablets excavated in the Kerameikos and Agora wells in 1965 and 1971 respectively.[13] The Kerameikos tablets consist of 574 lead tablets from just after the middle of the third century; the Agora tablets consist of 111 lead tablets, 26 from the mid-fourth century and 85 from the third.[14] In both finds the tablets were rolled up or folded with the name of a man on the outside. On the inside were usually listed a colour, a symbol, and a number. Braun convincingly interpreted the information as follows: the man's name on the outside, in the genitive case, is that of a cavalryman and the information on the inside refers to his mount. This information consists of its colour, brand (or the word *asemos* if unbranded), and its value.[15] As Kroll points out, the identification of the men as cavalrymen is confirmed by two of the tablets (no. 565 of the Kerameikos series and no. 62 of the Agora series) which include the title *prodromos*. These men were scouts and possibly numbered five per *phyle* or squadron.[16]

---

[10] However, the experienced horseman could train one of his existing slaves (cf. Xen. *PH* 5. 1)—presumably a cheaper practice than purchasing a ready trained *hippokomos*. Because of the variables involved no attempt has been made to reconstruct the cost of land and infrastructure needed to provide fodder for mounts in peacetime; these were presumably not solely committed to the upkeep of horses anyway.

[11] This may have been a rather later development in Greece—Gossen, *RE* viii. 1714 states that the first specialist veterinary treatise was apparently by Herakleides of Tarentum, (writing *c*.75 BC, *OCD*² 500). However, there are equine veterinary texts from Ugarit (*c*.1380) and Assyria (*c*.700)—see M. B. Gordon, 'The Hippiatric Texts from Ugarit', *Annals of Medical History*, 4 (1942), 406–8 (I am indebted to Ann Nyland for this reference). Presumably most minor treatment was carried out by the owner or groom. On ancient veterinarian science as applied to horses, see Vigneron, *Cheval*, 40–50.

[12] On stables see Vigneron, *Cheval*, 20–3; *IG* I³ 395, l. 1 shows that stables were rented out, but unfortunately the price is lost. Pasture too could be leased (*IG* I³ 418, l. 3). Pritchett, *Hesperia*, 25 (1956), 313–14 proposes the restoration [λαβί]ς παραστόμια at line 198 of stela II and argues that it was part of a bridle; it cost 2 obols.

[13] Published in Braun, *MDAI(A)* 85 (1970), 129–269 and Kroll, 83–140.

[14] On the dating see Kroll, 100–6.

[15] Braun, *MDAI(A)* 85 (1970), 199.

[16] Kroll, 85; *GSAW* i. 131; Sekunda, *AG* 54.

Kroll suggested in his publication of the Agora finds that the purpose of the tablets was to record the results of the official valuation of the horses (*timesis ton hippon*),[17] and the third-century figures are often preceded by the word *timema* (value) or by an abbreviation of it. This *timesis* is attested in decrees which honour the cavalry officers of 282/1 and 188/7,[18] but from the dating of the earlier Agora tablets to shortly after the middle of the fourth century it must now be regarded as a fourth-century institution. Kroll's argument that the lead tablets were used to record the value of each horse, so that its owner might be reimbursed if it was killed or maimed on active service,[19] is very convincing, and to my knowledge no alternative interpretation has been proposed. These records then provide excellent evidence for the value of cavalry horses in the second half of the fourth century and in the third century. This affords a much more comprehensive picture of horse prices than was previously provided by the occasional literary references.

However, there appears to be a 1,200-drachma ceiling on the recorded values. This is the highest amount inscribed (the 1,300 identified by Braun on the Kerameikos tablet 170 is apparently a misreading) and Kroll's suggestion that 1,200 drachmas represented the limit of the state's liability is surely correct.[20] The literary evidence suggests that this sum was fairly standard for a high-quality horse, but others cost more. For example, Alexander's famous horse, Boukephalos, was variously valued at 13 and 16 talents.[21] However, these were exceptionally high prices and the accuracy of the lead tablets is confirmed by Isaios' court-room gibe that the defendant had never owned a horse worth more than 3 minae (= 300 drachmas). This would therefore seem to have been the minimum price for a decent horse around 390/89.[22]

The sum of 1,200 drachmas was definitely on the expensive side and the prices recorded in Table 7 illustrate considerable variations in cost. In the fourth century sample the values range from 100 to 700 drachmas, with the median (the middle price in the total range) and the mode (the most frequently paid price) both at 500 drachmas, (the mean or average is 408 drachmas). The third century range is larger, from 100 to 1200 drachmas, with the median at 600 and the mode at 500 drachmas (the mean is 676 drachmas).

[17] Kroll, 97–100.
[18] Threpsiades and Vanderpool, *AD* 18 (1963), 99–114; C. Habicht, 'Neue Inschriften aus dem Kerameikos', *MDAI(A)* 76 (1961), 127–43.
[19] Kroll, 98–9.
[20] Ibid. 88–9, 99.
[21] Prices: Ar. *Clouds*, 21–3, 1224–5; [Lysias], 8. 10. Xen. *Anab.* 7. 8. 6 records a horse worth 50 Darics (1,250 drachmas). Boukephalos: Chares, cited in Aulus Gellius, 5. 2. 1–2; Pliny, *Nat. Hist.* 8. 154.
[22] Isaios, 5. 43; although 372 is also a possible date, cf. R. C. Jebb, *The Attic Orators from Antiphon to Isaeos* ii (New York, 1962), 350.

TABLE 7. Horse prices on the Kerameikos and Agora tablets
(*a*) Summary of the data

Value (dr.)	Fourth Century			Third Century		
	No. of horses per value	% of total no. of horses[a]	Total per value (dr.)	No. of horses per value	% of total no. of horses[a]	Total per value (dr.)
1,200				62	12.5	74,400
1,100				5	1	5,500
1,000				49	10	49,000
900				19	4	17,100
800				39	8	31,200
750				1	0.2	750
700	1	5	700	49	10	34,300
650				1	0.2	650
600	3	16	1,800	72	14.5	43,200
550				3	0.6	1,650
500	6	31.5	3,000	92	18.5	46,000
450				2	0.4	900
400	2	10.5	800	40	8	16,000
300	2	10.5	600	45	9	13,500
250	1	5	250	3	0.6	750
200	1	5	200	12	2	2,400
150	2	10.5	300			
120				1	0.2	120
100	1	5	100	5	1	500
TOTAL	19		7,750	500		337,920

[a] rounded to nearest whole number where possible.

(*b*) Measures of central tendency (in drachmas)

	4th cent.	3rd cent.
Median	500	600
Mode	500	500
Mean	408	676

Note: This Table includes only those prices which are complete or which allow of only one restoration. There are 26 fourth-century tablets, all from the Agora, with two (21, 22) listing two names, one (3) with an incomplete price, and eight (5, 6, 18, 21b, 23, 24, 25, 26) with no visible price, giving a total sample of nineteen animals with complete prices.

There are 659 third-century tablets (85 from the Agora and 574 from the

These figures show that, although the most common price paid for a horse recorded on the tablets remained static at 500 drachmas, the group which paid this price was (proportional to the rest of the sample) much smaller in the third century than in the fourth.[23] The third century figures exhibit a clear tendency towards the purchase of more expensive horses, with the upper price range increasing from 700 to 1200 drachmas, causing the median horse-price to rise by 100 drachmas. Several explanations are possible, including a rise in the price of horses, a rise in the level of wealth amongst the *hippeis*, or that the third-century corps was more socially exclusive.[24] None of these is entirely satisfactory because horses continued to be available, and purchased, at the lower end of the price range. If prices did increase, it was apparently only at the upper end of the scale, and if a higher proportion of third century cavalrymen was prepared to buy horses in this price bracket, some were still buying horses in the same lower range as their fourth-century predecessors.

The third-century cavalry then was clearly not composed entirely of those drawn from the upper echelons of the cavalry class, although it is quite possible that the proportion of such men in the cavalry had increased. Inscriptional evidence shows that the third century corps was a much smaller body, ranging from 100 to 300 men in size[25] and, given

---

Kerameikos; hereafter abbreviated as A. and K.). Including the 44 prices on those tablets with two or more entries (A. 59, 62, 63, 64, 65, 66, 81; K. 13, 24, 27, 44, 88, 104, 122, 149 [3 entries], 151, 156 [3 entries], 181, 200, 260, 268, 288, 297, 329, 338, 339, 341, 352, 410, 427, 445, 449, 451, 465, 467, 496, 501, 503, 539, 541, 552, 563) gives a total of 703 prices. However, 51 tablets have incomplete prices (A. 58, 60, 100, 101; K. 33, 39, 74, 83, 84, 85, 89, 106, 117, 118, 122(2), 129, 142, 149(2), 181(1), 199, 203, 204, 223, 236, 238, 239, 268(1), 279, 293, 353, 356, 373, 386, 398, 407, 411, 416, 420, 421, 439, 512, 516, 531, 534, 539(2), 542, 544, 550, 555, 559, 570) and 149 entries have no visible price (A. 31, 34, 40, 41, 54, 63a, 64a, 65(a & b), 66(a & b), 67, 74, 75, 77, 81a, 83, 84, 92, 99, 102, 107; K. 2, 4, 5, 6, 8, 12, 17, 19, 21, 29, 34, 38, 41, 42, 48, 51, 52, 55, 64, 68, 69, 71, 77, 80, 91, 93, 95, 96, 99, 100, 107, 108, 112, 116, 123, 130, 134, 141, 144, 146, 153, 159, 166, 168, 169, 173, 177, 180, 182, 184, 188, 189, 190, 191, 192, 200(1), 205, 206, 214, 216, 218, 219, 224, 226, 235, 237, 248, 256, 267, 275, 282, 285, 286, 288(2), 295, 297(1 & 2), 300, 303, 311, 313, 316, 323, 328, 329(1), 332, 333, 341(2), 344, 346, 354, 357, 359, 363, 372, 382, 384, 387, 390, 400, 409, 410(1), 423, 427(1), 440, 445(1), 449(1), 450, 454, 464, 467(1), 485, 490, 496(1), 500, 501(1), 503(2), 511, 517, 520, 522, 533, 537, 546, 549, 552b, 569). Excluding the rather problematical K. 110, 145 and 388 leaves a total sample of 500 prices. (In these three cases the number appears to be reversed, although it is possible that the Δ in the ΔHH on K. 110 and 145 may be a mistake for X, or even an abbreviation for drachmas (cf. K.494 and 574 which have ΔPA X and ΔP XHH).

[23] Reducing from 31.5% in the 4th cent. to 18.5% in the 3rd.
[24] Kroll, 89 argues for the last of these.
[25] In 282/1 the hipparchs and phylarchs were honoured for raising the cavalry from 200 men to 300 men (see Threpsiades and Vanderpool, *AD* 18 (1963), 104, ll. 6 ff.).

278 *Appendix 4*

TABLE 8. Values used in calculations

General
1 *medimnos* = 48 *choinikes*[a]
1 Attic *choinix* = 1.087 litres[b]
1 lb. = 453.6 grammes
1 lb. of barley = 0.665 litres[c]
1 hand = 10.16 cm.

Calorific requirements/quantities[d]
A family of 6 requires 15,495 calories per day
1 *choinix* of wheat or barley supplies 2,803 calories

---

[a] Foxhall and Forbes, *Chiron*, 12 (1982), 84, table 1.
[b] Loc. cit.
[c] Calculated on the basis of 1 lb. of barley = 0.7 US quarts, Schryver and Hintz, *Feeding Horses*, 18. At the standard conversion rate of 1 US quart to 0.95 litres, 1 lb. of barley = 0.665 litres.
[d] Foxhall and Forbes, *Chiron*, 12 (1982), 86–7 and 49 n. 26.

Athens' considerably reduced role at this time, it had a much less important military function than in the fourth century. The third century was arguably a safer time (both physically and politically) for men to display their wealth while serving in the cavalry than the fourth, and this may well help to explain the variation between the Kerameikos and Agora prices. However, a rise in the wealth of the upper section of the cavalry class and an associated rise in the cost of the best horseflesh cannot entirely be discounted as factors.

The sum of 500 drachmas, the median price and price most commonly paid for the fourth-century horses, equates to 83.33 *medimnoi* (= 4,000 *choinikes*) of wheat at 6 drachmas per *medimnos*, the most common price during the period in question.[26] Using Foxhall and Forbes's calculations of the calorific values of grain, this represents approximately 24 months' supply of food for an 'average' family of six.[27] If the family ate barley, a cheaper but much less popular grain,[28] 500 drachmas would have

[26] Markle, *Crux*, 293–4.
[27] Foxhall and Forbes, *Chiron*, 12 (1982), 86–7 and 49 n. 26, record the family's daily requirement as 15,495 calories (a generous estimate) and that 1 Attic *choinix* of wheat supplied 2,803 calories. The calorific content of hard wheat and barley is identical, ibid. 85, table 2. For the values used see my Table 8; the family of six excludes slaves and 1 month is taken as 30 days. My calculations assume that the grain supplied their entire calorific requirements, which in reality it would not (Foxhall and Forbes, 74, estimate that it may have constituted 70–75% of the diet under normal circumstances). However, even with these assumptions, the calculations give a good approximation of the value of a horse in real terms.
[28] See Ar. *Wasps*, 715–18; *Lysis*: 1203–15; cf. Bede, *A History of the English Church and People*, 4. 28.

purchased between 41.66 and 83.33 *medimnoi* (= between 2,000 and 4,000 *choinikes*) at the highest and lowest of the normal prices recorded in fourth-century Athens (see Table 6).[29] This would have supplied them with sufficient food for between about 12 and 24 months. Similarly, the price of the median horse on the fourth-century tablets is 90 drachmas more than the median price for houses recorded in both the *hermokopidai* stelae of 414 and the fourth-century *poletai* sales.[30] Isaios' 300 drachmas minimum for a decent horse would have fed our average family for about 14.5 months on wheat and between about 14.5 and 29 months on barley. At 100 drachmas, even the cheapest horse on the fourth-century tablets would have done so for about 5 months on wheat and between nearly 5 and just over 9.5 months on barley.

This clearly involved the *hippeus* in a considerable outlay, well beyond the reach of many citizens, and one which state assistance only temporarily relieved. Although the exact details of how the *katastasis* was administered are uncertain, it was patently a loan and not a gift.[31] Bugh argues that it was a loan of 1,200 drachmas, designed to cover the cost of a horse's active service life of some 15 years, and also implies that the average cavalryman would retire from service at about the time when his horse was at or approaching zero value.[32] Some may have done this, but the lead tablets provide many examples of *hippeis* buying new or newer horses during their period of service.[33] In addition, I am not convinced that in the days before proper veterinary care warhorses would have had such a long life—nor that each *hippeus* received 1,200 drachmas. At this rate, raising 1,000 cavalrymen would entail an outlay of 200 talents—a large sum even for imperial Athens. It seems much more likely that each cavalryman was loaned either a fixed amount (lower than 1,200 drachmas) or, alternatively, all or part of what his horse actually cost—perhaps up to a maximum of 1,200 drachmas.

Whatever the size of the loan, if a cavalryman kept his horse until it had depreciated to the point where it was worth nothing, he would end up having to pay the full cost of his mount himself when reimbursing the state for his *katastasis*. This is quite within the bounds of possibility as some served in the cavalry for many years and the depreciation rate was

[29] Excluding the 18 drachmas described as three times the normal price in [Dem.] 42. 20, 31.

[30] See Pritchett, *Hesperia*, 25 (1956), 270, table A (*Hermokopidai*), 272, table D (*Poletai* sales), and 275. Only items 3–4 in Table A and 1–4, and 6 in table D have been used to calculate the median house-price—the others are either incomplete or include the cost of an estate.

[31] Harpokration on Lysias, 16. 6–7, s.v. *katastasis*. The most recent treatment is by Bugh, *Horsemen*, esp. 53–8 and 66–70 (but see also his index). See too Martin, *Cavaliers*, 335–45.

[32] Bugh, *Horsemen*, 66–70.

[33] Cf. the Erechtheid *hippeis* in Kroll, 90, table 1.

quite high.[34] Those who retired from the cavalry while their original horse was still valuable enough to significantly offset their debt to the state were therefore probably in the minority. In most cases then, whether he kept his horse until it had no value or replaced it beforehand, the cavalryman was still going to be considerably out of pocket when repaying the establishment loan.

The purpose of the loan was not apparently to save the cavalryman from paying for his horse but rather to allow a man of good prospects, but without sufficient ready capital, to purchase a suitable mount. This was done presumably on the expectation that he would have acquired this sum by the time he came to leave the corps. The scheme would be particularly effective in encouraging the enlistment of those young men from wealthy families who had not yet come into their patrimony. Such youths were, by virtue of fitness, temperament, and prospective means, prime recruits for the corps.[35] In most cases, the *katastasis* grant would not free the *hippeus* from buying his horse, but only postpone the date of payment; at best it provided only partial assistance to the *hippeus* during his period of service.

Purchasing a horse was therefore expensive and so too was its continued feeding, although determining this cost is more complex and the result less certain. The two main problems involved in making this calculation are that first, no ancient author specifies the content or quantity of a horse's daily diet, and second, we only know the price of grain at a few specific points during the period under consideration. However, assuming that the ancient horse was fed on a mixture of grain and fodder and that the grain involved was barley (with the fodder coming from the owner's own property)[36] it is possible to arrive at a rough estimate of the daily cost of feeding a horse. It is only a rough estimate, though, as the evidence is rather scattered and in some cases not entirely free from ambiguity. However, the resultant figure is at its most accurate for around 330, the same approximate date as the fourth-century tablets from the Agora.

[34] Lysias, 14. 10; in the 3rd cent. depreciation averaged 100 drachmas per year and could be as high as 200, Kroll, 94.

[35] Cf. Xen. *Hipparch*. 1. 9–12. The general youth of the cavalrymen is borne out by the artistic evidence.

[36] Barley: Aisch. *Agamemnon*, 1639–41; cf. Babrius, 74, 76, 83. Mules too were fed on barley: Babrius, 62; Aelian, *On Animals*, 6. 49. Grazing a horse on one's own land must have been fairly common, cf. Xen. *Oik*. 5. 5, and lucerne (*Medike poia*) is a likely candidate for the feed. On this see Ar. *Kn*. 606; *AGH* 94; and J. A. S. Evans, 'Cavalry About the Time of the Persian Wars: A Speculative Essay', *CJ* 82 (1987), 102–3 (but using the US term 'alfalfa'). Apart from the Polybios passage discussed below, other evidence suggests barley was the standard horse feed of the Roman army, at least *c*.AD 205—see papyrus 64A in A. Perkins (ed.), *The Excavations at Dura-Europos* (Final Report v, part 1; New Haven, Conn., 1959), 230–1.

The first step in determining the cost of feeding an Athenian cavalry mount is to calculate the horse's dietary requirements. More recent cavalry practice, according to Engels, suggests 10 lb. (4.5 kg.) or 6.1 Attic *choinikes* of grain as the average daily requirement (in addition to fodder) for a horse on active service.[37] This is the same as the prescribed amount in the British Army in AD 1914,[38] but there were of course fluctuations caused by the exigencies of campaigning. For example, horses in only two of the units involved in the pursuit (a particularly vigorous phase of war) after the Third Battle of Gaza in 1917 actually received 10 lb. of grain a day (see Table 1). However, Engels's figures do not really tally with our only ancient evidence, Polybios, 6. 39. 13–14. This records a monthly allocation of 7 and 5 Attic *medimnoi* of barley to Roman and allied cavalry respectively.[39] This means that the daily Roman ration was 11.2 *choinikes* while that of the allies was 8.[40] Presumably Roman horses did not eat more than the allied horses and, in view of the fact that ancient soldiers' rations were not the minimum but the maximum required (allowing some excess for emergencies),[41] it seems likely that the allied rations were closer to real requirements than the higher Roman figure.

However, there is a problem in that the daily wheat rations for the men in the Polybios passage cited are 1.06 *choinikes* for an infantryman, 2.13 *choinikes* for an allied horseman, and 3.2 *choinikes* per Roman cavalryman. Only the first of these figures represents the 'standard' ration requirement for a man, but if the infantry ration is taken as the starting point they are almost exactly in the ratio of 1:2:3.[42] This suggests that the allied trooper's ration included enough for an attendant while that of his Roman counterpart included enough for two extra people. Both Anderson and Kroll have assumed that the Roman cavalryman had a mounted groom and that half of the barley allocation was for his horse, thereby giving a daily ration of 5.6

---

[37] Engels, *Logistics*, 18, 126, converted into *choinikes* according to the ratios in Table 8.

[38] General Staff, War Office, *Field Service Pocket Book 1914* (London, 1917), 171.

[39] The full figures are 2 *medimnoi* of wheat and 7 of barley for a Roman and 1.3 *medimnoi* of wheat and 5 of barley for an allied trooper. The wheat is undoubtedly intended for the men as the infantry receive only it (32 *choinikes* per month) and no barley. Even today wheat is regarded as too expensive for horse feed and can only be fed to horses when processed, H. F. Schryver and H. F. Hintz, *Feeding Horses* (New York State College of Agriculture and Life Sciences, Animal Sciences: Equine Research Program 1, Information Bulletin 94; New York, 1975?), 9.

[40] Assuming a 30-day month.

[41] Foxhall and Forbes, *Chiron*, 12 (1982), 56–7 and 74; the same practice is followed today by the Australian Army.

[42] Foxhall and Forbes, *Chiron*, 12 (1982), 62–3. The 1.06 *choinix* ration of the infantryman is very close to the 1 *choinix* 'standard' Greek daily ration, ibid. 62.

choinikes.[43] This in itself appears reasonable as two mounted attendants seems excessive.[44] The Roman cavalryman therefore had either one mounted attendant with a good margin of grain left over, nearly one man's daily ration in fact, or had two attendants, probably only one of which was mounted. However, for the reason already given, it is better to treat the allied rations as closer to the real daily requirements of a horse. This gives a figure of 4 *choinikes* each for the horses belonging to the cavalryman and his attendant—considerably lower than Engels's figure of 6.1 *choinikes* per diem. The reason for this apparent contradiction is that classical Greek horses were not as large as modern cavalry horses and, almost certainly, were not worked so hard or loaded so heavily on campaign; in short, Engels's estimates are too high.

Despite Engels's confident assertion that 'the size of the average horse has not changed from Alexander's day to our own,'[45] the Greek evidence suggests otherwise. This evidence is, however, very limited: few osteological studies have been undertaken (Leipe's study, cited by Engels, is a north European not a Greek study) and artistic representations of horses can only provide a rough indication of size.[46] However, what little osteological evidence there is indicates a range from 1.1 to 1.45 m. at the withers, (that is 10 hands 3½ in. to 14 hands 1 in., with most being around 1.34 m. or 13 hands 1 in.; see Table 9).[47] A horse of around 13

[43] *AGH* 94, 137; Kroll, 97–8 n. 36; cf. F. W. Walbank, *A Historical Commentary on Polybius*, i (Oxford, 1957), 722, following Veith; Evans, *CJ* 82 (1987), 102 n. 51.

[44] But not impossible on the ration scales given (particularly if the attendant's mounts were fed less than the cavalryman's); these allow 3.7 *choinikes* per animal.

[45] Engels, *Logistics*, 127.

[46] Like Engels, loc. cit. (following Markham), I do not believe most artistic representations can be used to reconstruct ancient horse sizes. The debate whether the horses on the Parthenon frieze are Skyros ponies (see J. Coulentianou, 'The Misfits of Skyros', *The Athenian*, May 1981, 18–22) illustrates the problems in trying to do so. The argument for accuracy founders when the artistic problems of portraying a mounted rider on the same frieze as a dismounted figure are considered. As Ashmole, *Architect and Sculptor*, 128–9, points out: if the horse is portrayed as actual size it dwarfs the walkers and means the rider cannot fit in the top of the frieze. The solution adopted on the Parthenon frieze was to reduce the size of the horses. J. Stanley apparently reiterated this point in a letter on this debate to the *TLS* of 4 July 1975, cited in Coulentianou, 18–19. As their surface area is not so restricted, mosaics and wall-paintings could perhaps give a better indication, but few of these survive from the classical period.

[47] J. H. Crouwel, *Chariots and Other Means of Land Transport in Bronze Age Greece* (Amsterdam, 1981), 33 states that the Lerna bones (at 1.45 m. or 14 hands 1 in.) accord well with contemporary Anatolian and Egyptian osteological evidence. This is certainly true for the Buhen horse, see J. Clutton-Brock, 'The Buhen Horse', *Journal of Archaeological Sciences*, 1 (1974), 89–100. This horse, killed in a battle at Buhen in Egypt *c.*1675, was 1.45–1.51 m. high (= 14 hands 1 in.–14 hands 3½ in.), ibid. 89, 96. Two other Egyptian horses, dating *c.*1430–1400 and 1580–1350 respectively, were approximately 1.43 m. (= 14 hands ½ in.) and 1.36 m. (= 13 hands 1½ in.) at the withers, ibid. 95.

hands 1 in. is some 2 hands 1 in. smaller than the average cavalry charger in the early part of this century.[48] This osteological evidence also accords well with Arrian, *Anab.* 5. 13, which records that during a river crossing the water came up to the chests of the men while the horses were only just able to keep their heads above water.

Because of this, and the lower campaign workload of the Greek cavalry horse in comparison to its more modern counterpart, it is misleading to assume their rations were the same. A much better comparison in terms of horse size, workload, climate, and to some extent topography, would be with the small horse or the mounted infantry pony on field service in India. The prescribed ration for these horses in 1914 was 8 lb. (3.63 kg.) and 6 lb. (2.72 kg.) of dry feed (gram or barley, and bran) per day respectively.[49] Converted into volumetric measures (using the values in Table 8) this equals a daily dry feed ration of 4.89 *choinikes* for the small horse and 3.67 *choinikes* for the mounted infantry pony. These fit quite neatly with the figures for Roman and allied cavalry discussed above.

It is therefore possible to accept 4 *choinikes* of barley as the approximate

TABLE 9. Greek horse sizes[a]

Place	Date	Estimated Height[b]	
		metres	hands
Lerna[c]	*c.*1400–1100[d]	1.45	14 hands 1 in.
Lefkandi[e]	*c.*1000–900	1.1–1.4	10 hands 3½ in.–13 hands 3 in.
Knossos (North Cemetery)[g]	*c.*670[f]	1.33	13 hands ½ in.
		1.34	13 hands 1 in.
		1.33	13 hands ½ in.
		1.35	13 hands 1 in.

[a] I would like to thank Mrs Sheilagh Crowther for supplying me with the figures for horses to be included in her sections on animal bones in the two forthcoming BSA Supplementary Volumes for Lefkandi and Knossos.
[b] At withers.
[c] Gejvall, cited in Crouwel, *Chariots*, 33.
[d] Based on the table in S. Hood, *The Arts in Prehistoric Greece* (Harmondsworth, 1978), 15.
[e] BSA Supplement, *Lefkandi II*, part 2 (forthcoming).
[f] Conversation with the excavator, Dr Carington Smith.
[g] BSA Supplement, *Knossos: The North Cemetery*, (forthcoming).

[48] 15 hands 2 in. and 1,000 lbs. (= 1.57 m. and 453.6 kg.), Chenevix-Trench, 72.
[49] General Staff, War Office, *Field Service Pocket Book 1914*, 171.

daily ration of grain required for a horse on active service.[50] Although
the peacetime ration could have been lower if a *hippeus* was prepared to
accept a drop in his mount's condition,[51] and variations undoubtedly
occurred under campaign conditions, 4 *choinikes* will serve as a general
rule of thumb. It now remains to calculate the cost of providing 4
choinikes of barley per day. The evidence for the cost of barley at Athens
in the classical period basically consists of two inscriptions and two
passages of a speech ascribed to Demosthenes. Although the sample is
small, it can nevertheless give a good indication of the price range in the
second half of the fourth century. The information derived from these
sources is summarized in Table 6.

As can be seen, the price could fluctuate considerably. In the case of
IG II² 1672 (dated to 329/8), the first figure represents the price of the
main *aparchai* (votive gifts or first-fruits), the second figure the price of
those from Imbros which had arrived late.[52] Prices on Delos in 250 also
show a monthly variation, and we know that changes in price within the
same day were not unheard of.[53] However, the 18 drachmas cited in
[Demosthenes] 42. 20 was presumably unusually high—in section 31 of
the same speech it is stated that Phainippos sold grain at three times the
normal price. As Jardé points out, this gives 6 drachmas as the 'normal'
price, one which he finds in accord with the figures recorded in *IG* II²
408,[54] although on the evidence presented above it is at the upper end of
the scale.

Using 4 *choinikes* of barley as the average daily ration, and a price
range of 3–6 drachmas per *medimnos*, the cost of a horse's daily ration
(excluding grazing) would have been between 1.5 and 3 obols. This
represents about four times the cost of providing a reasonably generous
daily ration of the same grain for a man. However, the Athenian cavalryman almost certainly had to maintain two mounts—his own and that of
his groom or *hippokomos*. Thucydides records that the groom normally

[50] Supplemented by grazing and/or fodder which on campaign would normally
have been acquired by foraging.

[51] See Xen. *Hipparch.* 1. 13. When grain prices were high there was presumably
a temptation to compromise—cf. Babrius, 76 on the piteous plight of the horse of
a later period used as a pack animal by his master. However, conscientious
cavalrymen undoubtedly looked after their chargers very carefully, cf. Xen. *PH* 4.
1–3, and when necessary may have fed them more than the 4 *choinix* campaign
figure to maintain them in top condition.

[52] A. F. V. Jardé, *Les Céréales dans l'antiquité grecque* (Paris, 1925), 181 n. 6.

[53] Lysias, 22. 12; G. R. Stanton, 'Retail Pricing of Grain in Athens', *Hermes*,
113 (1985), 121–3 shows that the prices do not represent the sixfold profit
normally assumed. Delos: *IG* XI ii 287, ll. 59–71 (cited in Markle, *Crux*, 294) has
hulled barley ranging from 2 drachmas to 3 drachmas 1 obol; for similar monthly
variations to *alphita* (barley meal) and wheat prices on Delos see Foxhall and
Forbes, *Chiron*, 12, (1982), 90, table 4.

[54] Jardé, *Céréales*, 181 n. 5.

carried his master's rations[55] and this presumably was also the case for the horse's feed-ration, which would have been even bulkier and more of a handicap for the *hippeus* in combat. It seems likely, therefore, that the groom too was mounted and this is supported by Xenophon's remark that a cavalry force could be made to appear larger by equipping the *hippokomoi* with spears or imitation spears and placing them between the horsemen—whether 'at the halt or manœuvring.'[56]

If the grooms were on foot, not only would they have difficulty keeping up while manœuvring but, given Xenophon's later suggestion that infantrymen can be hidden by placing them among the cavalry,[57] they would not achieve the effect of making the cavalry force look larger (except at considerable distances), but would merely be swallowed up by it. At closer distances, their spears would be seen to be held on an obviously lower level than those of their mounted companions. Finally, in mobile operations, especially the frequent cavalry tasks of raids and reconnaissance missions, the *hippokomoi* must have been mounted in order not to have been left behind.

Therefore the cavalryman was required to spend between 3 and 6 obols per day in around 330 to feed his two horses and in times of severe shortage perhaps as much as 18 obols (3 drachmas). Even at the lower price this is very close to the daily peacetime *sitos* or ration grant rate of 4 obols and it seems very likely that, for at least part of each year, it was normal for the cavalryman to pay upwards of 2 obols per day in addition to the state benefit to feed his animals. This sum, according to Markle, would have bought more than a day's supply of food for a man at about the same date.[58]

So, even taking *sitos* and *katastasis* payments into account, a member of the cavalry class had to be well off. In the fourth-century he was committed to at least an expenditure of 100 drachmas for his horse (although the horse at this value on the tablets was probably nearing the end of its service life)[59] with the most common outlay at 500 drachmas. He also had the cost of buying his groom's mount, although the vast majority of *hippokomoi* were undoubtedly mounted on cheap horses or perhaps, as Anderson suggests, even on pack animals.[60] Depreciation on the mounts was also fairly heavy: in the third-century at least, it averaged 100 drachmas a year[61]—in itself ten months' wages for a skilled crafts-

---

[55] Thucy. 7. 75. 5.
[56] Xen. *Hipparch.* 5. 6; cf. *AGH* 137.
[57] Xen. *Hippach.* 5. 13.
[58] Markle, *Crux*, 295.
[59] On the basis of 3rd cent. depreciation rates, Kroll, 94, this horse would have been valueless at the next *timesis*.
[60] *AGH* 137.
[61] Kroll, 94.

man, or equivalent to over two years' fairly generous wheat ration for an adult male. In addition, although the *sitos* payment would cover the cost of his horse feed for part of the year, for the rest of it (particularly in wartime or other time of shortage), he was likely to pay a minimum of 2 obols a day to feed his mount. He was also liable for the cost of stabling, grazing, riding tackle, keeping a groom, and possibly even of specialist veterinary treatment when required—in addition to his military equipment.

Being a cavalryman was therefore a costly exercise, even with state aid, and horse-ownership or cavalry service clearly qualifies an individual for inclusion in J. K. Davies's propertied class. It also means that Athens expected a not inconsiderable financial sacrifice from its serving cavalrymen.

APPENDIX 5

A Prosopography of the Athenian
*Hippeis c.*500–300

THIS appendix lists those men who are attested either as serving Athenian cavalrymen or as members of the equestrian milieu.[1] In some respects it can be seen as a supplement to Davies's *Athenian Propertied Families*, since it incorporates those men omitted because Davies did not then consider the level of wealth required to be a *hippeus* sufficient for membership of his 'propertied' class.[2] A complete listing of the cavalry class in its widest sense[3] would therefore comprise the men in *APF* and those in this appendix. However, it is beyond the scope and purpose of this appendix to provide a comprehensive listing of the wider hippic class by amalgamating Davies's corpus and my own. My intention was rather more specialized than Davies's and the catalogue which follows lists men who were not only of hippic class but who were also firmly part of the equestrian milieu. Davies's list consists of those who could afford to be in the cavalry, mine represents those who either were in it, or who were closely linked with horses and equestrian pursuits. This appendix also provides the prosopographical information which helped form my conclusions concerning the social composition and character of the *hippeis*.

Before listing the known *hippeis*, it is appropriate to examine briefly the evidence from which the catalogue was derived and the main conclusions arising from it. The first important point is that, although it is a relatively limited sample of the total number of Athenian cavalrymen during the 5th and 4th centuries, it does constitute a reasonably representative group. Davies believed that his numbers did not represent even 'an adequate random sample'[4] but this is not the case for my list. It is not so much concerned with the men as examples of Athenians who possessed a certain level of wealth (although they did), but rather as serving cavalrymen or as active participants in an equestrian lifestyle. All those listed below have a direct link to the cavalry or to the equestrian

---

[1] To qualify under the latter category required evidence of horse ownership, including (for example) participation in equestrian activity or being portrayed with a horse on a monument.

[2] On his changed opinion regarding this, see Davies, *Wealth*, p. vi.

[3] That is, all those wealthy enough to own a horse.

[4] *APF* p. xxvii.

milieu and, while we admittedly know most about the more famous members of this group, the less well-known and less wealthy are also represented.

This is partially a result of the types of evidence which have survived: literary and epigraphical. Although these do supplement each other, they tend to give rather a different impression of the cavalry class. The literary evidence generally records the activities or identities of the rich and famous among the cavalry, or those who particularly distinguished themselves in warfare or some other area. For example, the presence of Gryllos and Diodoros, Xenophon's sons, in the cavalry at Mantineia in 362 would presumably have gone unrecorded if their father had been a less well-known Athenian.[5] Other individuals are attested as cavalrymen and cavalry officers only because of their participation in court cases sufficiently important, or lucrative enough, to warrant the attention of the more famous Attic orators.[6] The epigraphical evidence is ostensibly a useful complement to the literary record because it often records the existence and, to a lesser extent, the activities of ordinary cavalrymen and their less well-known officers. Unfortunately, this can also be a disadvantage since the names of many of the personnel mentioned in cavalry inscriptions are otherwise unknown. The inscriptions are therefore sometimes of less obvious value, except of course as a strong reminder that not all *hippeis* were as prominent as an Alkibiades or a Meidias, and in their contribution to building a picture of the cavalry class as a whole.

Another general factor is that the evidence is not equally distributed over the period in question. For example, the majority of known phylarchs and hipparchs within the 4th and 5th centuries are dated to the hundred years or so between *c*.425 and 325. On the other hand, approximately half of the known cavalrymen are dated to the period between *c*.350 and 300. This uneven distribution is particularly true of the epigraphical material which, because it often existed in only one copy, was even more subject to an irregular survival pattern than some of the literature. Because of this, the temporal distribution of cavalrymen known to us from inscriptional or epigraphic sources is rather limited. For example, twenty-one of those serving cavalrymen fully or partially identified between *c*.450 and 300 are known from one stela, *IG* II² 1955, which recorded the cavalry on Salamis *c*.320. A further eight are inscribed on *IG* II² 5222, the monument to the *hippeis* killed in 394, while twenty-six appear on the lead cavalry tablets excavated in the Agora.

However, in spite of these considerations, it is possible to draw valid conclusions from a prosopographical study of the Athenian cavalry—provided that certain general qualifications are kept in mind. The first of

---

[5] Alkibiades' service at Delion is a similar case, Pl. *Symp.* 221a.
[6] For example, Meidias (112), Alkibiades IV (9), and Euandros (65).

these is that many of the conclusions can at best indicate trends, and the second, that they are more likely to provide us with information about the more socially important and well-to-do sections of the cavalry.

One theory which is supported by the consolidated prosopographical evidence is the relative social homogeneity and associated sense of identity of the hippic class in general and the cavalry in particular. I argued in Chapter 4 that it is possible to regard the cavalry in general as a relatively uniform group, and this is corroborated by the tradition of cavalry service in some families and by the apparently extensive links between families of cavalry class.

There are, for example, at least ten families which had more than one serving cavalryman (see Table 10). This is quite a large number, considering that the evidence is often insufficient to show whether members of the equestrian class related to known cavalrymen were also serving members of the cavalry corps. However, on the odd occasion the evidence can be excellent: the well-known Bryaxis monument (relief 21), for instance, records a family which held a cavalry officer's post over two generations. The front of the slab publicizes a father and his two sons, each of whom was victorious in the *anthippasia* as the phylarch of Erechtheis in the early to mid-4th century.[7]

Such a family commitment could be high, particularly in wartime. This is illustrated by the three known sons of one Polystratos of Deiradiotai—all of whom probably served in the cavalry during the latter stages of the Peloponnesian War. The eldest son, also called Polystratos, was in the cavalry dispatched to Sicily in 414/13, and another son, probably called Lykios, was in the cavalry in 410/9. A third son, Philopolis, is recorded as being a soldier in the Hellespont in the same year. Given his brothers' cavalry service, it seems likely that he was part of the Athenian mounted contingent which served there in 410/9.[8]

In addition to those families with a tradition of sustained cavalry service, there are several whose members were involved in equestrian activities over successive generations. These include Lysis (I) of Aixone (no. 106) and his son Demokrates (no. 49) who are recorded in Plato, *Lysis*, 205c, as winning equestrian victories at several games, and Themistokles (no. 178) and his son Kleophantos (no. 93). Plato, *Parmenides*, 126c, records that both Antiphon (no. 23) and his grandson Antiphon (II) Pyrilampous (no. 24) had a passionate interest in horses and, finally, Perikles' sons (nos. 140 and 189), both trained as good horsemen according to Plato, *Meno*, 94b, were the great grandsons of Kallias (I) Phainippou who was an Olympian and Pythian victor in the mid-sixth century (see *PA* 7833). Autodikos of Erchia (no. 33) and his (probable) son

---

[7] Demainetos and his sons Demeas and Demosthenes (nos. 43, 44, and 50).

[8] [Lysias], 20. 4, 24, 28–9; Xen. *Hell*. 1. 2. 5, 7.

Thereus (no. 183) both appear on equestrian grave-reliefs in the first half of the 4th century and are therefore almost certainly horse-owners.

Marriage links between 'cavalry families' are also evident, although again a general lack of detailed information about individuals, and particularly the women, can frustrate attempts to confirm a suspected link. For example, even in the case of a family as well known as Xenophon's (see Table 10, no. 5), we do not know the names of his son's wives, let alone their social status and family connections.

TABLE 10. Athenian families with a tradition of cavalry service[a]

Name	Relation	No.	Post	Date
1. Menexenos		116	Phylarch	429
Dikaiogenes	grand-nephew	53	Trooper(?)	*c.*390
2. Alkibiades(III)		10	Trooper	424
Alkibiades (IV)	son	9	Trooper	390s
3. Polystratos		163	Trooper	414/3
Lykios	brother(?)	102	Trooper	*c.*410/9
Philopolis	brother	157	Trooper(?)	410/9
4. Xenophon		191	Hipparch	mid-5th cent.
APF lost name 1	son-in-law	195	Trooper	pre-*c.*390
Philomelos	grandson-in-law	155	Trooper(?)	pre-349/8
Xenophon	grandson(?)	193	Trooper	mid-4th cent.
5. Xenophon		192	Trooper(?)	*c.*404/3
Gryllos	son	72	Trooper	362
Diodoros	son	55	Trooper(?)	362
6. Demainetos		43	Phylarch	early 4th cent.
Demeas	son	44	Phylarch	mid-4th cent.
Demosthenes	son	50	Phylarch	mid-4th cent.
7. Theophon		182	Phylarch	370s(?)
Hagnias	?	24 (§3)	Phylarch	*c.*286–261
8. Sokles		172	Trooper	*c.*320
Charamantides	cousin	37	Trooper	*c.*320
9. Euktaios		68	Trooper	*c.*320
Nikias	2nd cousin(?)	127	Trooper	*c.*320
10. Demetrios(I)		46	Hipparch	pre-325/4(?)
Demetrios (III)	grandson(?)	3 (§2)	Hipparch	mid-3rd cent.

[a]The family groups are listed in chronological order (of the first member) and the entry in the relationship column is the relationship of the individual to the first name in his family list. Unless otherwise specified, the reference number supplied for each man is from Part 1 of the catalogue of cavalrymen in App. 5.

However, some evidence does remain; *IG* II² 1955, a record of cavalrymen serving on Salamis *c*.320, includes two sets of cousins serving together. Sokles (no. 172) and Charamantides (no. 37) are first cousins, while Euktaios (no. 68) and Nikias (no. 127) are very probably second cousins. Similarly, Xenophon son of Euripides (no. 191), a hipparch in the second half of the fifth century was the father-in-law of an unnamed cavalryman (no. 195), and his granddaughter (by that marriage) married Philomelos (no. 155), another cavalryman. The frequency of such links becomes even more apparent if one broadens the area to include those who were of hippic status and part of the equestrian milieu, but who cannot be proved conclusively to have been in the cavalry; these are listed in Table 11. While I am not suggesting that these inter-family relationships were caused by the fact that the families concerned contained cavalrymen or cavalry officers (this is anyway impossible for nos. 1–3), these links do lend support to the argument for the relative social homogeneity of the hippic class as a whole.

There are also some slight indications that family traditions of cavalry service survived the decline in popularity which followed cavalry involvement in the oligarchic movements at the end of the 5th century. There are at least four families with members who served in the 5th century and other members who served in the 4th, after the coup. Given the evidence for the cavalry's sense of identity and their apparent closing of ranks against the criticism of the early 4th century, it is quite possible that there were more families like this. However, the difficulties involved in tracing the activities of individuals, let alone families, have undoubtedly reduced the number of examples. The first of the four known cases is that of Xenophon (no. 192), who was almost certainly a member of the cavalry under the Thirty. This did not, though, prevent his sons (nos. 55 and 72) from joining the cavalry on their return to Athens in 362.[9] Although the hostility to the cavalry was probably fading by then, Gryllos and Diodoros were probably in a fairly vulnerable position at this stage of their return to Athenian society, and yet chose to serve with the cavalry rather than with the politically safer hoplites.

Another example involving a well-known family is that of Alkibiades (IV), son of the famous Alkibiades (a cavalryman at Delion in 424), who served with the cavalry in the early 4th century (nos. 9 and 10). However, this is possibly less solid evidence of the survival of a family tradition as Lysias asserts that the service was performed reluctantly, and from a desire to serve in the safest part of the army.[10] Whether this claim is true or not, and it could of course be rhetorical exaggeration, Alkibiades the Younger apparently believed cavalry service desirable enough to risk the

[9] Xen. *Hell*. 7. 5. 15–17; Pausanias 1. 3. 4; Diog. Laert. 2. 52, 54.
[10] Lysias, 14. 7, 10.

TABLE 11. Links between Hippic families from the sixth to the fourth centuries[a]

1. The daughter of Megakles (II) (*PA* 9692; *APF* 9688 III) son of Alkmeon (I) Megakleous (I) (*PA* 651; *APF* 9688 II) who had Athens' first Olympic equestrian victory in 592[b] married (*c*.557) the grandson of the tyrant Peisistratos (who must have been of at least hippic class).[c]

2. Kimon (I) Stesagorou (*PA* 8426; *APF* 8429 VII), three times Olympic victor *tethrippo*[d] (in 536, 532, 528?) was the half brother (by the same mother) of Miltiades (I) Kypselou (*PA* 10209; *APF* 8429 V), Olympic equestrian victor in 560.[e]

3. Elpinike Miltiadou (II) (*PA* 4678), granddaughter of Kimon (I) Stesagorou (see 2 above); married, in the early 480s, Kallias (II) Hipponikou (I) (*PA* 7825; *APF* 7826 V) grandson of Kallias (I) Phainippou (*PA* 7833; *APF* 7826 II), an Olympic and Pythian equestrian victor.[f]

4. Hipparete (I) Hipponikou (II) (*PA* 7590), great-granddaughter of Kallias (I) Phainippou (I) (see 3 above) married, in the late 420s, Alkibiades (III) Kleiniou (II) (*PA* and *APF* 600; App. 5.10), cavalryman in 424 and Olympic victor in the chariot race in 416.[g]

5. Kallias (III) Hipponikou (II) (*PA* and *APF* 7826) brother of Hipparete (see 4 above) was the second husband (married in *c*.413–405) of one Chrysilla (= the Chrysias of *PA* 15577), who was previously married to Ischomachos (*PA* 7725/6/7; *APF* 7826 XI–XIV; App. 5.75), a probable cavalryman.[h]

6. Chabrias Ktesippou (I) (*PA* and *APF* 15086; App. 5.34), victor *tethrippo* at the Pythian games in 374,[i] was distantly related by marriage (in the late 370s) to Menexenos (I) Dikaiogenes (I) (*PA* 9976; *APF* 3773; App. 5.116), the phylarch killed at Olynthos in 429 (Chabrias' wife was Menexenos' great-granddaughter.)

[a] For a family to be included in this list one of its members must be attested as a member of the cavalry, as a horse racer or breeder, or as a horse-owner.
[b] Hdtos 6. 125; Pindar, *Pythian*, 7. 13 ff.; Isok. 16. 25.
[c] His sons were involved with horses, Idomeneus, *FGH* 338 F3; *PA* i. 948 and Peisistratos may well have owned a chariot (Plut. *Solon*, 30. 1). His lack of equestrian victories is not surprising (if he were in fact a *hippotrophos*) in view of the state of evidence for the period and the ascendancy of the team of Kimon Koalemos at that time, cf. Hdtos 6. 103.
[d] Hdtos 6. 103.
[e] Hdtos 6. 36, 103.
[f] Ibid. 6. 122. 1; L. Moretti, *Olympionikai: I vincitori negli antichi agoni Olympici* (Rome, 1957), 70, no. 103; Schol. to Ar. *Birds*, 283.
[g] Thucy. 6. 16. 2; Isok. 16. 32–4; Pl. *Symp.* 221a–b.
[h] Xen. *Oik.* 11. 14–20.
[i] [Dem.] 59. 33.

opprobrium this entailed at that time. The last two cases, families 1 and 4 in Table 10, involve less well-known individuals but this is interesting as it suggests that it was not only the prominent who felt able to expose themselves to possible criticism by serving in the mounted arm.

A final aspect of the hippic class indicated by the prosopographical record is the continued lure of horse-breeding and racing as a means of establishing an aristocratic image—even in the 4th century I have found two examples of apparent nouveaux riches (the orator Demades and the general Chabrias, nos. 42 and 34) entering the ranks of the *hippotrophoi*,[11] which is interesting given the scope for possible criticism entailed in becoming a horse-breeder. This was an occupation one might have thought should be avoided by those whose chosen profession required the support of the ordinary citizens.[12]

The catalogue which follows is divided into three parts. The first lists all known cavalrymen and men attested as horse-owners, or as participants in equestrian activities, from about 500 to 300. The upper date is approximately fifty years or so before the cavalry reform which instituted the corps of 1,000 men, while the lower date is about the time when the cavalry became a rather more socially exclusive group with a limited military role. These dates are used instead of the core period of 450–320 in order to give a better idea of the family links among the *hippeis* during the 5th and 4th centuries as a whole. The second and third parts are more specialized, listing the hipparchs from *c*.450 to 100 and the phylarchs from *c*.450 to 160 respectively. The lower dates of these sections are extended downward in the interests of providing a comprehensive reference. This would also have been possible with part 1, but to do so would have created an unmanageable list: there are over 300 mid-third century cavalrymen known from the Kerameikos tablets alone. Many of these are otherwise unattested so the inclusion of the 3rd-century material in part 1 would have added considerable extra bulk, but little useful information, to my work. As an additional space-saving device, where an individual listed in parts 2 and 3 also appears in part 1 (which is true of most), his biographical entry is not reproduced on his second and/or third appearance.

PART 1: *HIPPEIS c.*500–300

The format of entries in this part of the appendix is as follows: wherever possible each man is listed by name, patronymic, and demotic (the last two in the genitive), as they appear in the original source of

---

[11] Demades: *APF* p. 101 (*Suda*, Demades, 415); Chabrias: [Dem.] 59. 33.
[12] See 'attitudes to the cavalry *c*.404–363', Ch. 4.

evidence for his membership of the cavalry class. Where these are incomplete or fragmentary I have used the following conventions:

Square brackets: denote that something once recorded in the original source is now lost. Letters appearing inside such brackets are restorations; where letters cannot confidently be restored, a number indicates how many are missing while a question mark indicates an unknown number of missing letters.

Curved brackets: denote something which did not appear in the original source. Material appearing inside such brackets is normally either an expansion of abbreviated words or consists of a name, demotic, or patronymic, supplied from elsewhere to make identification more complete. Roman numerals inside curved brackets indicate an individual's position in his family; these do not appear in the original source but are supplied where necessary to avoid confusion between men of the same name.

Dot beneath a letter: denotes that the letter is not entirely clear in the original source.

The number, or numbers, in brackets following a name denote the man's reference number (*not* page number, unless otherwise indicated) in *PA, APF, AO,* or Kroll. This is followed by a brief biography which includes the major points of the individual's equestrian and military career, any pertinent references, and any other salient information.

Entries (including incomplete names) are in strict alphabetical order beginning with the first surviving letter, whether this is part of the name, patronymic, or demotic. Names lacking a patronymic or demotic are listed before examples of the same name which do possess a patronymic and/or demotic.

1. Adeistos (Kroll, 16). Cavalryman, mid-4th cent.
2. [A]gasias (Kroll, 15). Cavalryman, mid-4th cent.
3. Agathinos (Kroll, 14). Cavalryman, mid-4th cent.
4. Agathokles (Kroll, 22*a*). Cavalryman, mid-4th cent.
5. Ais[. . ? . .] (Kroll, 5). Cavalryman, mid-4th cent.; unidentifiable (there are 18 possible names in *PA* beginning with these letters).
6. Alechs[. . ? . .]. *Hippotoxotes*(?), listed on a funeral monument before the end of the 5th cent. (*SEG* 12 (1955), no. 73); after 431/0 (B. D. Meritt, 'Greek Inscriptions', *Hesperia*, 21 (1952), 341–2, no. 2).
7. Alexiades (?Anaphlystios) (Kroll, 12). Cavalryman, mid-4th cent.; this name is attested only for the deme Anaphlystos, see Kroll, 109; *Agora*, xv. 335.
8. Aleximen(es) (Kroll, 6). Cavalryman, mid-4th cent.
9. Alkibiades (IV) Alkibiadou (III) (*PA* 598; *APF* 600 viii–x). Cavalry-

man, 390s (Lysias, 14. 7–8, 10, and 15. 5). Son of the following entry.

10. Alkibiades (III) Kleiniou Skambonides (*PA* 600; *APF* 600 vii–ix). Cavalryman, 424 (Pl. *Symp.* 221a); Panathenaic victor 418(?); Olympic victor in chariot race 416; equestrian victor at Nemea and Delphi (on these see Kyle, *AAA* A4); *strategos* at least ten times from 420/19 onwards. *PA* lists him as Alkibiades (II) not (III). Father of the preceding entry.

11. Alkimos (Kroll, 1). Cavalryman, mid-4th cent. The only Alkimos listed in *PA* is far too late to be this man.

12. Amphis[th]enes (Kroll, 17). Cavalryman, mid-4th cent.

13. Anacharsis Me[. . ? . .] (?Kydathenaieus) (*PA* 822, 823(?); *AO* 129, p. 349). Victorious phylarch, mid-4th cent. (*IG* II² 3135; 3136). *PA* dates him to the mid-2nd cent. but this seems unlikely and may be a misprint. The only other men of this name attested in *PA* are the father of Prokleides, a *grammateus* c.354/3, and who would therefore seem rather too early, and *PA* 823 who is attested towards the end of the 4th cent. If he is the latter his deme is Kydathenaion; on this see also *IG* II² 1576, ll. 23–4 and W. S. Ferguson, 'An Introduction of the Secretary Cycle', *Klio*, 14 (1914/15), 394 n. 3.

14. Andokides (IV) Leogorou (II) Kydathenaieus (*PA* 828; *APF* 828). The orator, born c.440, owned a horse when young (Andok. 1. 61). *PA* lists him as Andokides (III) not (IV).

15. Anthemion Diphilou (*PA* 938). Horse-owner(?), after 480/79, who dedicated a statue of a horse on the Akropolis to commemorate rising from thetic rank to the *hippeis* (*Ath. Pol.* 7. 4; Pollux, 8. 31). However, in this case the horse seems more likely to have been symbolic of his change in status than an indication of actual horse-ownership. If his son was Anytos (*PA* 1324; *APF* 1324) then his deme is Euonymon (see *APF* 40).

16. Antias (*PA* 973a, 1282b). Horse-owner(?), depicted on a 4th-cent. relief (Paris, Louvre; Conze, no. 441, pl. ciii = *IG* II² 10700; App. 2.3).

17. Antid[o]ros Thriasios (*AO* 175, p. 414). Hipparch, 4th cent. (J. H. Kroll and F. W. Mitchel, 'Clay Tokens Stamped with the Names of Athenian Military Commanders', *Hesperia*, 49 (1980), 92–3; *SEG* 30 (1980), no. 114). No further identification is possible: he could be linked with *PA* 1023–5, all of whom are 4th cent. and lack a demotic. However, as the name Antidoros is attested in ten demes (*APF* 35, no. 1024), such links would be far from certain.

18. Antikrates Sokratous Hermeios (*AO* 200, p. 414). Hipparch, 4th cent. (H. A. Thompson, 'Excavations in the Athenian Agora: 1952', *Hesperia*, 22 (1953), 49–51); possibly an ancestor of the Antikrates

Hermeios who was a cavalryman *c*.260–240 (Braun, *MDAI(A)* 85 (1970), 243, no. 25).

19. Antimachos (*PA* 1106). Horse-owner, 425; the *choregos* who refused Aristophanes (Ar. *Acharn.* 1150 ff.).
20. Antimachos [. . 4 . .]os Pelekethen (*AO* 210, p. 246). Phylarch or taxiarch, 373/2 (E. Schweigert, 'Greek Inscriptions', *Hesperia*, 8 (1939), 3–5, no. 2: patronymic given there as [. . 4 . .]o, but from the photograph it looks as though *AO* p. 246 is correct to list it as [. . 4 . .]os).
21. Antiphanes (*PA* 1215). Probably a horse-owner, was certainly involved in a case concerning a horse, for which Deinarchos wrote a speech (F. Blass, *Die attische Beredsamkeit*, 2nd edn., iii. 2 (Leipzig, 1898), 304, no. 22).
22. Antiphanes (?Akamantidos) (*PA* 1221; *AO* 226, p. 209). Phylarch, killed at Corinth 394 (*IG* II² 5222). If, as *PA* assumes, all the men on this inscription were from the same tribe then he is from Akamantis. However, as *APF* 422 points out, there is no overriding necessity to believe it is a purely tribal inscription.
23. Antiphon (I) Pyrilampous (*PA* 1275; *APF* 8792 VIII). Skilled and passionate horseman (Pl. *Parmen.* 126c), early 5th cent.; for grandson see next entry.
24. Antiphon (II) Pyrilampous (*PA* 1284; *APF* 8792 VIII). Skilled and passionate horseman like his grandfather in the preceding entry (Pl. *Parmen.* 126c); born *c*.425 (*APF* 330).
25. Antisthenes (I) (?Antiphatous Kytherrhios) (*PA* 1184/94/96/97; *APF* 1194). Cavalryman; later general, pre-355(?) (Xen. *Mem.* 3. 4. 1), *c*.370 (*AO* p. 291). I accept Davies's identification here contra *PA*.
26. Archetion (*PA* 2435). Fellow cavalryman of Meidias in 348 (Dem. 21. 134).
27. [Aris]to.e[. . 12 . .] Anagyr(asios) (*PA* ii. 512). Cavalryman on Salamis *c*.320 (*IG* II² 1955).
28. Aristokles (Kroll, 3). Cavalryman, mid-4th cent.
29. Aristokles Menonos Peiraieus (*PA* 1880). Horse-owner(?), depicted as a rider on a relief of the early 4th cent. (BM; Conze, no. 1161, pl. CCL = *IG* II² 7151; App. 2.15).
30. Aristolochos (?Charidemou (I) Erchieus) (Kroll, 18). Cavalryman, mid-4th cent. The most likely identification with a known Aristolochos would be with the son of Charidemos of Erchia, the banker and trierarch listed as *APF* 1946 (*PA* 1946/47/49/51); the dates and level of wealth would certainly fit. The other two possibilities are PA 1948, a victor in the Olympic *stadion* in 344, and *PA* 1950.
31. Aristophon (Kroll, 7). Cavalryman, mid-4th cent.
32. [. . 4 . .]as [. . 5 . .]imo [Myrrhi]nosios (*AO* 3706, p. 246). Phylarch

or taxiarch, 373/2 (E. Schweigert, 'Greek Inscriptions', *Hesperia*, 8 (1939), 3–5, no. 2). Could be Charias (*PA* 1532) who fits both the date and deme.

33. Autodikos Erchieus (*PA* 2707). Horse-owner(?), represented on reliefs *c*.400–350 (Athens, NM 1074 and 1824, the first of which = Conze, no. 1011; App. 2.5, 22); probably father of Thereus (no. 183).

34. Chabrias Ktesippou (I) Aixoneus (*PA* 15086; *APF* 15086). Victor in the Pythian four-horse chariot race, 374 ([Dem.] 59. 33; see also Kyle, *AAA* A71); *strategos* at least five times from 390/89. He married the great-granddaughter of Menexenos (no. 116), a phylarch in 429.

35. Chairedemos Euangelou ek Koiles (*PA* 15125). Horse-owner(?), dedicated a *dourios hippos* (wooden horse) on the Akropolis at the end of the 5th cent. (Scholia to Ar. *Birds*, 1128; *IG* I² 535).

36. Chairephon (Kroll, 21*b*). Cavalryman, mid-4th cent.

37. Charamantides Sokleou (I) Euonyme(us) (*PA* 15284). Cavalryman on Salamis, *c*.320 (*IG* II² 1955); his cousin Sokles, no. 172, is also recorded on the same stone.

38. Chares (Kroll, 26). Cavalryman, mid-4th cent.

39. Char[ide]m[os] [E]uni[k. . ? . .] (*AO* 636, p. 246). Phylarch or taxiarch, 373/2 (E. Schweigert, 'Greek Inscriptions', *Hesperia*, 8 (1939), 3–5, no. 2; *AO* p. 246 records the name as Char[idem]o[s]. The photograph in Schweigert is not clear enough to judge which is correct.

40. Cheimon (Kroll, 22*b*). Cavalryman, mid-4th cent.

41. Deinokles (Kroll, 19). Cavalryman, mid-4th cent. As Kroll, 111 points out, the only other example of the name Deinokles is on *IG* II² 1960, l. 47, dated to 128/7.

42. Demades (I) Demeou (I) Paianieus (*PA* 3263; *APF* 3263). Horse-breeder; Olympic victor in a horse race, *c*.328 (on the date see Moretti, *Olympionikai*, no. 467; Kyle, *AAA* A13); apparently no relation to the next entry (*APF* p. 99).

43. Demainetos (I) Demeou (III) Paianieus (*PA* 3276; *APF* 3276; *AO* 720, p. 291). Phylarch, victorious in the *anthippasia* at the start of the 4th cent. (*IG* II² 3130; App. 2.21); father of Demeas (no. 44) and Demosthenes (no. 50) who were also phylarchs.

44. Demeas (IV) Demainetou (I) Paianieus (*PA* 3323; *APF* 3276; *AO* 725, p. 291). Phylarch, victorious in the *anthippasia*, mid-4th cent. (*IG* II² 3130; App. 2.21); son of the preceding entry and brother of Demosthenes (no. 50), both also phylarchs.

45. Demetrios [?Anti]phanou Alopekethen (*AO* 727, p. 414). Phylarch honoured in a decree proposed by Moschos of Anaphlystos (no. 121) *c*.330 (*SEG* 3 (1927), no. 115; *AO* p. 414 dates him 'possibly'

to the period 336/5–322/1 and restores the patronymic as [Anti]pha-
nou).

46. Demetrios (I) Phanostratou Phalereus (*PA* 3455; *APF* 3455; *AO*
740, pp. 402, 414). Hipparch (*IG* II² 2971), either 'not long before
325/4' (S. Dow and H. Travis, 'Demetrios of Phaleron and his
Lawgiving', *Hesperia*, 12 (1943), 147) or 315/4 (*IG* II² 2971). On
the date see also *APF* 108 and *AO* p. 402. Victor in various chariot
events at the Panathenaic, Delian, and Hermaian games (*IG* II²
2971; see also Kyle, *AAA* A14). Commemorated in many equestrian
statues (Diog. Laert. 5. 75); *strategos* three times (*IG* II² 2971),
325/4, 324/3, 323/2(?), *AO* p. 453. Demetrios (III) Demetriou (II)
Phalereus (part 2, no. 3), a phylarch and hipparch in the 3rd cent.,
is almost certainly his grandson.

47. [Democh]ares (I) (?Demonos (III)) Paia(nieus) (*PA* 3718; *APF*
3737B; *AO* 744, p. 241). Hipparch(?), who swore a treaty with
Amyntas between 375 and 370. (*IG* II² 102, l. 19, restoration by
Koumanoudis). Probably to be identified as the Demochares (I)
Demonos (III) Paianieus who was trierarch in 356/5 ([Dem.] 47.
22 ff.) and the brother of Phrynion Demonos (III) Paianieus (no.
160), an equestrian victor at the Pythian games.

48. Demokles (?Akamantidos) (*PA* 3492). Cavalryman, killed at Corinth in 394 (*IG* II² 5222). If, as *PA* assumes, all the men on this
inscription were from the same tribe then he is from Akamantis.
However, as *APF* 422 points out, there is no overriding necessity to
believe it is a purely tribal inscription.

49. Demokrates (I) Lysidos (I) Aixoneus (*PA* 3519; *APF* 3519/9574).
Victor with four horse chariot team and/or race horse at some (or
all) of the Pythian, Isthmian, and Nemean games, second half of
the 5th cent. (Pl. *Lysis*, 205c; see also Kyle, *AAA* A15). Pl. *Lysis*,
205c also describes him, his father Lysis (no. 106), and other
unnamed family members, as wealthy horse-breeders and equestrian victors.

50. Demosthenes (III) Demainetou (I) Paianieus (*PA* 3596; *APF* 3276;
AO 794, p. 291). Phylarch, victorious in the *anthippasia*, mid-4th
cent. (*IG* II² 3130; App. 2.21), son of Demainetos (no. 43) and
brother of Demeas (no. 44), both also phylarchs.

51. Dexileos Lysaniou (I) Thorikios (*PA* 3229). Cavalryman, killed at
Corinth in 394 aged 20; depicted in a combat scene on funerary
monument (Athens, Kerameikos P 1130 = *IG* II² 5222 and 6217;
App. 2.12; Pl. 11). His brother, Lysistratos, apparently lent money
to another cavalryman, Mantitheos of Thorikos (no. 109), for his
father's funeral *c*.357 ([Dem.] 40. 52).

52. Dieitrephes (?(II) Nikostratou Skambonides) (*PA* 3755; *AO* 830,
pp. 187–8). Phylarch, then hipparch, pre-414; afficionado of chariot

racing (Ar. *Birds*, 798–800, 1440–3). *PA* identifies him with the
man of the same name who was *strategos* in 414/13 (Thucy. 7. 29. 1)
and under the oligarchy in 411 (Thucy. 8. 64. 2). *AO* p. 187,
follows this but adds the patronymic Nikostratou, presumably on
the basis of Nikostratos son of Dieitrephes who was general several
times in the first half of the Peloponnesian War (Thucy. 3. 75. 1; 4.
53. 1, 119. 2; 5. 74. 3) and apparently accepts the suggestion that
his demotic was Skambonides (D. M. Macdowell, 'Nikostratos',
CQ 59 (1965), 41–51; see also Fornara, 'Athenian Board of Generals', 57).

53. Dikaiogenes (III) Dikaiogenous (II) Kydathenaieus (*PA* 3774, *APF*
3773). Horse-owner (and possible cavalryman?), *c.*390 (Isaios, 5.
43); his great-uncle is Menexenos (no. 116), phylarch in 429.

54. [Diocha]res (Kyle, *AAA* A19). Equestrian victor *c.*366–338. Possibly
connected with the wealthy mining family from Pithos discussed at
APF 4048, although the name is also attested for Oion (*PA* 4448).

55. Diodoros Xenophontos (I) Erchieus (*PA* 3941). Cavalryman, 362
(Diog. Laert. 2. 54 implies he was a cavalryman at Mantineia; cf. 2. 52
where he and his brother are called the *Dioskouroi*). Both his father,
Xenophon (no. 192), and brother, Gryllos (no. 72), were cavalrymen.

56. Diotimos (III) Diopeithous (I) Euonymeus (*PA* 4384; *APF* 4386;
AO 926). Hipparch in charge of cavalry on Salamis, *c.*338/7 or
shortly after (Dem. 18. 116; his hipparchy is not recorded in *AO*
which presumably therefore dates him post 322/1). *Strategos* at
least three times (*IG* II² 408, 1623, 1628). Note that *APF* p. 163
lists him as Diotimos (II) on one occasion (bottom of page).

57. Diphilos (II) Philotadou [L]amptreus (*PA* 4483). Cavalryman on
Salamis, *c.*320 (*IG* II² 1955).

58. Endelos (?Akamantidos) (PA 4697). Cavalryman, killed at Corinth
in 394 (*IG* II² 5222). If, as *PA* assumes, all the men on this
inscription were from the same tribe then he is from Akamantis.
However, as *APF* 422 points out, there is no overriding necessity to
believe it is a purely tribal inscription.

59. [. . ? . .]e[n]ippos [. . ? . .]eus. Horse-owner(?), depicted on a 4th cent.
relief—now lost (*IG* II² 7838; Conze, no. 271; App. 2.2).

60. [. . ? . .]enou Pro[spaltios/balisios]. Hipparch, late 4th or early 3rd
cent. (E. Vanderpool,'Victories in the Anthippasia', *Hesperia*, 43
(1974), 313; *AO* does not list him and so presumably dates him
post 322/1).

61. Epikrates Diophantou Peiraieu(s) (*PA* 4910). Cavalryman on
Salamis, *c.*320 (*IG* II² 1955).

62. Epilykos Nikostra[tou Gargettios] (*PA* 4926; *AO* 1050, p. 414).
Hipparch, *c.*350–325 (M. Crosby, 'Greek Inscriptions', *Hesperia*, 6
(1937), 462, no. 10).

63. [. . ? . .] Erechthidos. Probably phylarch in *anthippasia* c.321/20 or 318/17 (*IG* II² 379, ll. 1–4. Davies, *Wealth*, 154 dates him to 322/1 while *AO* does not list him and so presumably dates him post 322/1).

64. Eualkides Alkimachou ek Keram(eon) (*PA* 5260). Cavalryman on Salamis, c.320 (*IG* II² 1955). He may be the same man as *PA* 5259 and possibly father of *PA* 12799.

65. Euandros (I) (?Erithalionos Euonymeus) (*PA* 5267/71; *APF* 5267). Cavalryman under, and supporter of, the Thirty (Lysias, 26. 10). If this Euandros is, as seems likely, the same as *PA* 5271 then he was *tamias* of Athena in 411 under the Four Hundred and was archon in 382/1 (Diod. Sic. 15. 20. 1; Dem. 24. 138).

66. Eukles Lysiou Meliteus (*PA* 5727). Cavalryman on Salamis, c.320 (*IG* II² 1955).

67. [Eue]tion Pythangelou Kephisieus (*PA* 5461/2; *APF* 5463; *AO* 1132, p. 414). Hipparch, c.350–325 (M. Crosby, 'Greek Inscriptions', *Hesperia*, 6 (1937), 462, no. 10). *APF* p. 190 plausibly argues that he was the *strategos* of 323/2 listed as *PA* 5461, but see *AO* p. 408, suggesting he was *nauarchos*.

68. Euktaios (III) Nikiou (I) Xypetaion (*PA* 5774; *APF* 10814). Cavalryman on Salamis, c.320 (*IG* II² 1955). Nikias (no. 127), also a cavalryman on Salamis in 320, is very probably his second cousin (see *APF* pp. 407–8). I accept *APF*'s Euktaios (III) contra PA's Euktaios (II).

69. Eustrophos Eugenidou Peiraieu(s) (*PA* 5996). Cavalryman on Salamis, c.320 (*IG* II² 1955).

70. Euthykrates Perg[asethen] (*AO* 1252, p. 414). Phylarch, c.380 (B. D. Meritt, 'Greek Inscriptions', *Hesperia*, 9 (1940), 57–8, no. 6) or c.336/5–322/1 (*AO* p. 414); neither Meritt nor Develin supply reasons for their datings.

71. Glaukippos (Kroll, 8). Cavalryman, mid-4th cent.

72. Gryllos (II) Xenophontos (I) Erchieus (*PA* 3096). Cavalryman, killed at Mantineia 362 (Paus. 1. 3. 4; 8. 9. 5, 10, 11. 6; 9. 15. 5; Diog. Laert. 2. 53–5). His father, Xenophon (no. 192) and brother, Diodoros (no. 55), were both cavalrymen.

73. [Ha]gnodemos Pa[ianieus] (*AO* 1327, p. 414). Phylarch c.380 (B. D. Meritt, 'Greek Inscriptions', *Hesperia*, 9 (1940), 57–8, no. 6) or 336/5–322/1 (*AO* p. 414); neither Meritt nor Develin supply reasons for their dating. Davies, *Wealth*, 154 mistakenly lists him as [Ha]gnodoros.

74. [. . < 8 . .]ikles (*AO* 3241, p. 254). Hipparch(?), swearing oath to treaty between Athens and Leukas 368 (*IG* II² 104, ll. 1–2). The missing eight letters preceding the name also include the ending of the previous name, Nike[. . ? . .] (no. 126), the other hipparch(?) in 368.

75. Ischomachos (*PA* 7725/6/7; *APF* 7826 xi–xiv). Cavalryman, early 4th cent. (Xen. *Oik.* 11. 14–15, 20). Although quite possibly a fictional character, he does seem identifiable with a real person of liturgical class (Table 11, no. 5; see also *APF* pp. 266–7).

76. Isokrates Theodorou (I) Erchieus (*PA* 7716; *APF* 7716). The orator; he was a horseman in his youth in the 420s (Plut. *Mor.* 839c). Possibly also an equestrian victor according to Kyle, *AAA* P98.

77. Kallias (II) Hipponikou (I) Alopekethen (*PA* 7825; *APF* 7826 v). Olympic chariot victor in 500, 496, and 492 (Kyle, *AAA* A31), or in 496, 492, 484 (*APF* p. 258, following Robert). However, schol. Ar. *Clouds*, 64 which mentions these victories is rather confused.

78. Kallias Kallikratou Koloneth(en) (*PA* 7870). Cavalryman on Salamis, *c.*320 (*IG* II² 1955).

79. K[a]l[lias S]oinautou Kolonethe(n) (*PA* 7871). Cavalryman on Salamis, *c.*320 (*IG* II² 1955).

80. Kallisthenes Ch[. . ? . .]. Hipparch or phylarch(?), after mid-4th cent.: recorded on the edge of Agora i. 5816, which has [*ho*]*i hippeis* inside a wreath on the front face (B. D. Meritt, 'Greek Inscriptions', *Hesperia*, 30 (1961), 247, no. 44; *SEG* 21 (1965), no. 701). Could possibly be the Kallisthenes Charopidou Trinemeias who proposed a decree of the Boule in 328/7 (= *PA* 8106; *AO* 1558, p. 398).

81. Kallistratos (Kroll, 10). Cavalryman, mid-4th cent. The Kallistratos in the next entry could be a homonymic ancestor but the name is a very common one; no. 83, for example, could also be a 5th-cent. ancestor.

82. Kallistratos Empedou (I) Oethen (*PA* 8142; *AO* 1566, p. 156). Hipparch, killed in Sicily 413 (Pausanias 7. 16. 4–5; Plut. *Mor.* 844b). Plutarch mistakenly gives his demotic as Aphidnaios; on this see Davies, *Wealth*, 154.

83. Kallistratos Leontidos (*PA* 8150). Cavalryman executed by those in the Peiraieus, 403 (Xen. *Hell.* 2. 4. 27).

84. Kephisodoros Marathonios (*PA* 8376; *AO* 1594, p. 264). Hipparch for 363/2, killed at Mantineia (Paus. 8. 9. 10; Ephoros, *FGH* 70 F85).

85. Kephisodotos Kononos Aith(alides). Cavalryman, depicted in a combat scene on a relief (Athens, NM 3620A, App. 2.26) in the first half of 4th cent. (*IG* II² 5391).

86. Kimon (II) Miltiadou (IV) Lakiades (*PA* 8429; *APF* 8429). Horse-owner and probable cavalryman, dedicating horse's bridle on the Akropolis in 480 (Plut. *Kim.* 5). For the possibility that he was *strategos* in that year see *AO* p. 64. Many of his 6th-century ancestors were major *hippotrophoi* (see Table 11, nos. 2–3) and his son Lakedaimonios (no. 99) was hipparch *c.*450.

87. [Kineas Nikom]achou Lamptreu[s]. Hipparch, *c*.350–275 (E. Vanderpool, 'Victories in the Anthippasia', *Hesperia*, 43 (1974), 312); *strategos* during the same period (EM 13367; not included in *AO* which presumably therefore dates him post 322/1). For the family see *APF* 12883 and *PA* 8436.

88. [Klea]ndros (Kyle, *AAA* A35). Equestrian victor, *c*.366–338.

89. [K]learchos (*PA* 8475). Equestrian victor, *c*.366–338 (Kyle, *AAA* A36); post 338 (*PA*). Possibly a member of the trierarchic family of Oe discussed in *APF* 10552, but the name is attested in at least five other demes.

90. Kleon Kleainetos Kydathenaion (*PA* 8674; *APF* 8674). Cavalryman(?), 430s/420s (Scholia to Ar. *Kn*. 225; see also Tzetzes on *Clouds*, 549a): on this see W. R. Connor, *The New Politicians of Fifth Century Athens* (Princeton, NJ, 1971), 152 n. 32 and Bugh, *Horsemen*, 107.

91. Kleonymos Kleoxeno(u) Marathonios (*AO* 1669, p. 246). Phylarch or taxiarch, 373/2 (E. Schweigert, 'Greek Inscriptions', *Hesperia*, 8 (1939), 3–5, no. 2; *AO* p. 246). None of the entries in *PA* could be this man, but 8607 could be his father.

92. Kleophantos Kleophontos Eleus[i](nios) (*PA* 8633). Cavalryman on Salamis, *c*.320 (*IG* II² 1955).

93. Kleophantos Themistokleous (I) Phrearrhios (*PA* 8635; *APF* 6669 VI). Good horseman (Pl. *Meno*, 93d), died *c*.459; possibly an equestrian victor according to Kyle, *AAA* P99. His father, Themistokles (no. 178), was part of the equestrian milieu.

94. [. . ? . .]kles Erchi(eus) (*AO* 3500, p. 241). Hipparch, swearing oath to treaty between Athens and king Amyntas of Macedonia, *c*.375–370 (*IG* II² 102, l. 18).

95. Komaios (?Komonos Semachides) (Kroll, 13; *PA* 8693(?); *APF* 8693(?)). Cavalryman, mid-4th cent. Komaios is an unusual name, attested only once in *PA*, a trierarch *c*.356–346 and *prytanis* in 334/3 (*IG* II² 1622, l. 707; *Agora*, xv 44, l. 70; J. S. Traill, 'The Bouleutic List of 304/3 BC', *Hesperia*, 35 (1966), 224 ff., l. 317); the dates and wealth of this man would suit an identification with the cavalryman on the lead tablet.

96. Krates Heortiou Peiraieus (Kyle, *AAA* A37). Equestrian victor (*apobates*) in the Panathenaia, early 4th cent.

97. Kratinos (?Erchieus) (*PA* 8753; *AO* 1700, p. 314). Hipparch, 349/8 (Dem. 21. 132 and scholia). The demotic Erchieus was suggested by D. Lewis (*AO* p. 314).

98. Kritoboulos Kritonos Alopekethen (*PA* 8801(?), 8802; *APF* 8823). Horse-owner, pre-399 (Xen. *Oik*. 2. 6; 3. 9).

99. Lakedaimonios Kimonos (II) Lakiades (*PA* 8965; *APF* 8429 XI–XII; *AO* 1766, p. 104). Hipparch, *c*.450 (*IG* I² 400; *AO* p. 104 opts

for a date in the early 440s); *strategos* 433/2 (*IG* I³ 364, l. 8 = R. Meiggs and D. Lewis, *A Selection of Greek Historical Inscriptions* (Oxford, 1969), 61). His father, Kimon (no. 86), was a horse-owner and probably a cavalryman in 480. Many of his sixth cent. ancestors were major *hippotrophoi* (see Table 11, nos. 2–3).

100. Lakrates. Cavalryman, died (fighting on Pausanias' side) in 403 (F. Willemsen, 'Zu den Lakedämoniergräbern im Kerameikos', *MDAI(A)* 92 (1977), 135–40; cf. *GSAW* iv. 133–4, esp. n. 123).

101. [. . 5 . .]los Promachou Eleus[inios] (*PA* 12245; *APF* 12245). Panathenaic (and Eleusinian?) victor in the two-horse chariot race, first half of 4th cent. (*IG* II² 3126; see also Kyle, *AAA* A73).

102. Lykios (?Polystratou (I) Deiradiotes) (*PA* 9211; *APF* 12076). Commanded the cavalry of the Ten Thousand, 401/400 (Xen. *Anab.* 3. 3. 20); he is also highly likely to be Polystratos of Deiradiotai's (unnamed) son who served in the Athenian cavalry in Boiotia and Attica *c.*410/9 ([Lysias], 20. 4, 28). If so, his brother Polystratos (no. 163) was also in the cavalry, while the other, Philopolis (no. 157), was very probably a serving cavalryman too.

103. Lykophron (*PA* 9255; *AO* 1828, p. 414). Phylarch, by about 340; hipparch *eis Lemnon* for two to three years in the 330s (Hyper. 1. 17; prior to 333 according to *AO* p. 414).

104. Lykos (*PA* 9240). Horse-owner or cavalryman(?). Depicted at an altar to Hermes on a red-figure vase by Onesimos (*ARV*² 324.63) *c.*500–475. The other scenes are equestrian and suggest practice near the Stoa of the Herms, see *PP* 80. All of the other men of the same name in *PA* are too late, with the possible exception of 9239.

105. Lysimachos (*PA* 9486; *AO* 1871, p. 185). Hipparch, 404/3; member of the Thirty (Xen. *Hell.* 2. 4. 8, 26).

106. Lysis (I) Aixoneus (*PA* 9567/73; *APF* 9574). Victor with four-horse chariot team and/or race horse at some (or all) of the Pythian, Isthmian, and Nemean games, *c.*470s/460s (Pl. *Lysis*, 205c; see also Kyle, *AAA* A42). Pl. *Lysis*, 205c also describes him, his son Demokrates (no. 49), and other unnamed family members as wealthy horse-breeders and equestrian victors.

107. Lysitheos (?Akamantidos) (*PA* 9403). Cavalryman, killed at Corinth in 394 (*IG* II² 5222). If, as *PA* assumes, all the men on this inscription were from the same tribe then he is from Akamantis. However, as *APF* 422 points out, there is no overriding necessity to believe it is a purely tribal inscription.

108. Makartatos (*PA* 9658). Cavalryman killed at Tanagra(?), 457 (Pausanias 1. 29. 6).

109. Mantitheos (?Thorikios) (*PA* 9674; *APF* 9667). Cavalryman, 394 (Lysias, 16. 13); lent money by the brother of Dexileos (no. 51), *c.*357. Probably not the same Mantitheos whose son Mantias

married the daughter of Pamphilos the hipparch (no. 136); on this see *APF* 9667.

110. Megakles (IV) Hippokratous (I) Alopekethen (*PA* 9695; *APF* 9688 x). Pythian victor in the four-horse chariot race, 486 (Schol. to Pindar, *Pythian*, 7; see also Kyle, *AAA* A43). *PA* lists him as Megakles (V). See the next entry for his son.

111. Megakles (V) Megakleous (IV) Alopekethen (*PA* 9697; *APF* 9688 x). Olympic victor in the *tethrippo*, 486 (Schol. to Pindar, *Pythian*, 7; see also Kyle, *AAA* A44). *PA* lists him as Megakles (VII). See the previous entry for his father.

112. Meidias (I) Kephisodorou (I) Anagyrasios (*PA* 9719; *APF* 9719; *AO* 1921, p. 314). Hipparch, 349/8 (Dem. 21. 171 ff.), at age of 50 (ibid. 154, 162).

113. Meixis[. . ? . .] (Kroll, 23). Cavalryman, mid-4th cent.

114. Melanopos (*PA* 9781). Cavalryman, killed at Tanagra(?), 457 (Pausanias, 1. 29. 6).

115. Melesias (?Akamantidos) (*PA* 9808). Cavalryman, killed at Corinth in 394 (*IG* II² 5222). If, as *PA* assumes, all the men on this inscription were from the same tribe then he is from Akamantis. However, as *APF* 422 points out, there is no overriding necessity to believe it is a purely tribal inscription.

116. Menexenos (I) Dikaiogenous (I) Kydathenaieus (*PA* 9976; *APF* 3773Af; *AO* 1982, p. 119). Phylarch, killed at Spartolos in 429 (Isaios, 5. 42). His grand-nephew, Dikaiogenes (no. 53) was adopted by Menexenos' son Dikaiogenes (II). This Dikaiogenes (II) was also wealthy enough to be of hippic status (*APF* 3773), but is not directly attested as a cavalryman or horse-owner. His great-granddaughter married Chabrias (no. 34), an equestrian victor.

117. Menyllos Astyphilou Halaieus. Horse-owner(?), depicted on reliefs, Athens, NM Θ 168, Θ 170, Copenhagen, Ny Carlsberg 2786, and Athens market, c.340–330 (*IG* II² 5497; 5498; 5499, published together by Peppas-Delmousou, *AAA* 10 (1977), 226–41; App. 2.18–19, 34–5).

118. Mn[e]s[ipp]o[s] (Kyle, *AAA* A49). Equestrian victor, c.366–338.

119. Moiragenes Ika[rieus] (*AO* 2046, p. 414). Phylarch, c.380 (B. D. Meritt, 'Greek Inscriptions', *Hesperia*, 9 (1940), 57–8, no. 6) or 336/5–322/1 (*AO* p. 414); neither Meritt nor Develin supply reasons for their dating.

120. Moschion. Phylarch, (quite probably fictional) in Menander, *Samia*, 15.

121. Moschos Antiphanous Anaphlystios (*APF* 1227). Cavalryman, c.330 (*SEG* 3 (1927), no. 115, ll. 3–4).

122. [. . c.9 . .]n Oethen (*AO* 3726, p. 414). Phylarch, c.325 (B. D. Meritt, 'Greek Inscriptions', *Hesperia*, 15 (1946), 176–7).

123. Nausikles Nausigenou Anagy(rasios) (*PA* 10550). Cavalryman on Salamis, *c*.320 (*IG* II² 1955).

124. Neokleides (?Akamantidos) (*PA* 10633). Cavalryman, killed at Koroneia in 394 (*IG* II² 5222). If, as *PA* assumes, all the men on this inscription were from the same tribe then he is from Akamantis. However, as *APF* 422 points out, there is no overriding necessity to believe it is a purely tribal inscription.

125. Nikandros (Kroll, 11). Cavalryman, mid-4th cent.

126. Nike[.. < 8 ..] (*AO* 2067, p. 254). Hipparch(?), swearing oath to treaty between Athens and Leukas in 368 (*IG* II² 104, ll. 1–2). The missing eight letters at the end of his name also include the start of the following name, [.. ? ..]ikles (no. 74), the other hipparch(?) for 368.

127. Nikias (II) Euktaiou (II) Xypetaion (*PA* 10815; *APF* 10814). Cavalryman on Salamis, *c*.320 (*IG* II² 1955); his (probable) second cousin, Euktaios (III) son of Nikias (I), also served on Salamis that year (no. 68).

128. Nikomachos (?Akamantidos) (*PA* 10942). Cavalryman, killed at Corinth in 394 (*IG* II² 5222). If, as *PA* assumes, all the men on this inscription were from the same tribe then he is from Akamantis. However, as *APF* 422 points out, there is no overriding necessity to believe it is a purely tribal inscription.

129. Nikostratos (*PA* 11005). Cavalryman, nicknamed 'the fair', killed at Phyle 404/3 (Xen. *Hell.* 2. 4. 6).

130. Nikostratos (II) Nikostratou (I) Cholar(geus) (*PA* 11058). Cavalryman on Salamis, *c*.320 (*IG* II² 1955).

131. [.. 4 ..]okle[s] [.. 5 ..]tio [ek K]edon (*AO* 3575, p. 246). Phylarch or taxiarch, 373/2 (E. Schweigert, 'Greek Inscriptions', *Hesperia*, 8 (1939), 3–5, no. 2; *AO* p. 246, which I follow for the number of lost letters; cf. Bugh, *Horsemen*, 228).

132. Onetorides (?Akamantidos) (*PA* 11462; *APF* 11473G). Cavalryman killed at Corinth, in 394 (*IG* II² 5222). If, as *PA* assumes, all the men on this inscription were from the same tribe then he is from Akamantis. However, as *APF* 422 points out, there is no overriding necessity to believe it is a purely tribal inscription and he may well be the son of Onetor (II) of Melite (*APF* 421–2 and table III).

133. Orthoboulos ek Krameon (*PA* 11489; *APF* 9667, p. 364; *AO* 2220, p. 207). Phylarch, or possibly hipparch, 395/4 (Lysias, 16. 13; cf. *APF* p. 364).

134. [.. 16 ..]ou Eleu[sin](ios). Cavalryman on Salamis, *c*.320 (*IG* II² 1955).

135. [.. ? ..]ous A[.. ? ..]. Hipparch, late 4th/early 3rd cent. (E. Vanderpool, 'Victories in the Anthippasia', *Hesperia*, 43 (1973), 313).

136. Pamphilos Keiriades (*PA* 11545; *APF* 9667, p. 365; *AO* 2239,

p. 207). Hipparch, 395/4 (Lysias, 15. 5); *strategos* 389/8 (Xen. *Hell.* 5. 1. 2).

137. Panaitios (*PA* 11566/7; *AO* 2245, p. 130). Hipparch(?), *c.*425/4 (Ar. *Kn.* 243). Sommerstein (*Aristophanes: Knights*, 155–6 nn. 242–3) identifies him with the Panaitios involved in profaning the mysteries (= *PA* 11567) but he could be entirely fictional (cf. Simon, no. 170, and *AO* p. 130).

138. Panaitios. Cavalryman, depicted armed for war on a relief (Athens, NM 884; App. 2.20; Pl. 9) *c.*395–390 (Sekunda, *AG* 60).

139. Pandios (?Akamantidos) (*PA* 11574). Cavalryman, killed at Corinth in 394 (*IG* II² 5222). If, as *PA* assumes, all the men on this inscription were from the same tribe then he is from Akamantis. However, as *APF* 422 points out, there is no overriding necessity to believe it is a purely tribal inscription.

140. Paralos Perikleous (I) Cholargeus (*PA* 11612; *APF* 11811 vii). A good horseman, 3rd quarter of 5th cent. (Pl. *Meno*, 94b); his father Perikles (no. 142) was possibly a horse-owner and his brother Xanthippos (no. 189) was also a good horseman.

141. Patroklees Hierokleous Philiades (*AO* 2274, p. 414). Hipparch, 4th cent. (H. A. Thompson, 'Excavations in the Athenian Agora: 1952', *Hesperia*, 22 (1953), 49–51).

142. Perikles (I) Xanthippou (I) Cholargeus. (*PA* 11811; *APF* 11811). Horse-owner(?), mid-5th cent.; had both his sons (Paralos, no. 140, and Xanthippos, no. 189) trained as good horsemen while they were youths (Pl. *Meno*, 94b).

143. Phainippos Kallipou (*PA* 13978; *APF* 14734B, p. 552). Cavalryman, prior to early 320s; horse-breeder ([Dem.] 42. 24).

144. Phanes (?Akamantidos) (*PA* 14002). Cavalryman, killed at Corinth in 394 (*IG* II² 5222). If, as *PA* assumes, all the men on this inscription were from the same tribe then he is from Akamantis. However, as *APF* 422 points out, there is no overriding necessity to believe it is a purely tribal inscription.

145. Pheidon Thriasios (*PA* 14178; *AO* 2346, p. 349). Hipparch *eis Lemnon*, mid-4th cent. (J. H. Kroll and F. W. Mitchel, 'Clay Tokens Stamped with the Names of Athenian Military Commanders', *Hesperia*, 49 (1980), 89–91). He is also very probably the phylarch in Mnesimachos fr. 4.

146. Phi[. . 3 . .]on Philist[. . ? . .]. Hipparch(?), late 4th/early 3rd cent. (E. Vanderpool, 'Victories in the Anthippasia', *Hesperia*, 43 (1974), 312; he is omitted from *AO* and therefore presumably dated to post-322/1). His status as hipparch seems fairly certain from the heading HIPP[. . ? . .] at l. 5 on the stone as the similar (but not identical) Agora i. 3495 has the heading HIPPARCHOI along with two names. If there are exactly 3 letters missing from his name then

the only possible name attested in *PA* is Philemon; the father's name could be Philistides, Philistion, Philistiōn, Philistis, Philistiō or Philistos.

147. Phileas Diokleous Elaiousios (*PA* 14237; *APF* 4021). Cavalryman on Salamis, *c*.320 (*IG* II² 1955).

148. Philinos [. . ? . .]nos [Anaphlys]tio[s] (*AO* 2371, p. 246). Phylarch or taxiarch, 373/2 (E. Schweigert, 'Greek Inscriptions', *Hesperia*, 8 (1939), 3–5, no. 2). *AO* p. 246 gives the patronymic as [. . ? . .]nes but the photograph accompanying Schweigert's article supports the latter's reading of [. . ? . .]nos.

149. Philochares Philonidou Kephisieus (*PA* 14774). Horse-owner(?), depicted on a 4th-cent. relief (Paris, Louvre; Conze, no. 1098, pl. ccxxv; App. 2.8).

150. Philodemos Sophilou Cholleides(*sic*). Horse-owner(?) depicted on a mid-4th-cent. relief (*IG* II² 7807; Conze, no. 1099, pl. ccxv; App. 2.9).

151. Philok[. . ? . .] (Kroll, 25). Cavalryman, mid-4th cent.; there are nine possible names in *PA* which start with this combination of letters so he must remain unidentifiable. However, his dates fit with those of the next two entries.

152. Philokles (Kroll, 20). Cavalryman, mid-4th cent. Could be the same man as in the preceding and following entry.

153. Philokles (?Phormionos Eroiades) (*PA* 14521/41; *APF* 14541; *AO* 2422, p. 414). Hipparch, three or four times and *strategos* ten times by 324/3 (Dein. 3. 12). Could be the same man as in the two preceding entries.

154. Philoktemon (I) Euktemonos Kephisieus (*PA* 14641; *APF* 15164, pp. 562–3). Cavalryman, trierarch on many occasions including at the time of his death in action, probably in the 370s (Isaios, 6. 9, 27).

155. Philomelos (II) Philippidou (I) Paianieus (*PA* 14670; *APF* 14670). Horse-owner (and cavalryman prior to this?), lending Meidias a horse for a parade in 349/8 (Dem. 21. 174); trierarch. His wife's maternal grandfather, Xenophon (no. 191), was a hipparch and *strategos*, and his father-in-law (*APF* lost name 1, no. 195) was also a cavalryman and equestrian competitor.

156. Philon Aristokleous Meliteus. Cavalryman, depicted in a combat scene on a funerary loutrophoros *c*.325–300 (Athens, NM, Y. Niko-poulou, "'Επιτύμβια Μνημεῖα παρὰ τὰς Πύλας τοῦ Διοχάρους", *AAA* 2 (1969), 329–34; C. Clairmont, 'Gravestone with Warriors in Boston', *GRBS* 13 (1972), 53 n. 4, i; App. 2.29).

157. Philopolis Polystratou (I) Deiradiotes (*APF* 12076, pp. 467–8). Served in Boiotia and in the Hellespont in 410/9 ([Lysias], 20. 4, 29) and most probably in the cavalry (see the introduction to this

App.). His brother Polystratos (no. 163) was a cavalryman, as was another brother, Lykios(?), (no. 102).

158. Philostratos Teisandrou Peira(ieus) (*PA* 14743). Cavalryman on Salamis, *c*.320 (*IG* II² 1955).

159. Phokos (II) Phokionos (*PA* 15081; *APF* 15081). Equestrian victor (*apobates*) at the Panathenaia (Plut. *Phok.* 20), *c*.320s (Kyle, *AAA* A70).

160. Phrynion Demonos (III) Paianieus (*PA* 15021; *APF* 3737, pp. 143–4). Victor in the four-horse chariot race at the Pythian games, *c*.371–339 ([Dem.] 59. 33). His brother(?), Demochares (no. 47), was probably a hipparch *c*.375–370.

161. Phrynion Kallipp[idou K]ephisieus (*PA* 15016). Horse-owner(?), depicted on a 4th-cent. relief (*IG* II² 6449; Conze, no. 270, pl. LXII; App. 2.1).

162. Polymedes. Cavalryman, depicted on a (late 4th cent.?) relief (Conze, no. 1024, pl. CCIII; App. 2.6).

163. Polystratos (II) Polystratou (I) Deiradiotes (*PA* 12076; *APF* 12076, pp. 467–8). Cavalryman in Sicily, 414/13 ([Lysias], 20. 4, 24). His brother Lykios(?) (no. 102), was a cavalryman and his brother Philopolis (no. 157) was probably one too.

164. Prokleid[e]s (*PA* 12190). Equestrian victor (*sunoridi*), *c*.366–338 (Kyle, *AAA* A56); post-338 (*PA*).

165. Prokles Erxigenou Kollyteus (*PA* 12230). Cavalryman on Salamis, *c*.320 (*IG* II² 1955).

166. Prokles Gniphonos (Thoraieus) (*PA* 12213). Hipparch(?), recorded on a mid-4th-cent. dedication (*IG* II² 12523). The anaglyph portrays horsemen riding to the right and is likely to be a dedication by a hipparch (cf. P. Wolters, 'Litteratur und Funde', *MDAI(A)* 12 (1887), 268), although he could be a phylarch or (less likely) an ordinary cavalryman (see also B. D. Meritt ,'Greek Inscriptions', *Hesperia*, 15 (1946), 217 n. 30).

167. Pronap[es] (?Pronapidou Prasieus) (*PA* 12250/51/53; *APF* 12250; *AO* 2627, p. 104). Hipparch, shortly after the mid-5th cent. (*IG* I² 400). He is very probably the Pronapes Prasieus who is recorded as a victor in the four-horse chariot event at the Nemean, Isthmian, and Panathenaic games *c*.450–440 (*IG* II² 3123), *c*.450–400 (Kyle, *AAA* A57).

168. [Pythodoro]s (I) Epizelo(u) (I) (Halaieus Araph.) (*PA* 12402/10; *APF* 12402; *AO* 2671, p. 187). Hipparch, *c*.420–410, depicted in combat on a votive relief (Eleusis 5101 = *IG* I² 816; App. 2.30; Pl. 12); *strategos* 414 (Thucy. 6. 105. 2).

169. Pythodoros Hippothontidos (*PA* 12405; *AO* 2667, p. 158). Phylarch, *c*.412 (*IG* I² 950, l. 180; for the date see Davies, *Wealth*, 153).

170. Simon (*PA* 12687; *AO* 2712, p. 130). Hipparch(?), *c.*425 (Ar. *Kn.* 242 and schol.), although he could be an entirely fictional character (cf. Panaitios, no. 137, and *AO* p. 130).

171. Smikythos Sosippou Aixoneus (*PA* 12784). Cavalryman on Salamis, *c.*320 (*IG* II² 1955).

172. Sokles (II) Aleximachou (I) Euonymeus (PA 13070). Cavalryman on Salamis, *c.*320 (*IG* II² 1955), his cousin Charamantides, no. 37, also served there in the same year.

173. S[o]k[r]ates (I) Eudramonos Aphidnai(os) (*PA* 13105). Cavalryman on Salamis, *c.*320. (*IG* II² 1955).

174. Sostratos Petalou. Chariot victor(?) in the Panathenaic games, early 5th cent. (Raubitschek, *Dedications*, 196). For doubts concerning this victory see Kyle, *AAA* P108.

175. Strat[. . ? . .] (Kroll, 21*a*). Cavalryman, mid-4th cent.; unidentifiable (there are eleven possible names in *PA* which begin with this combination of letters).

176. Teisias (II) Teisimachou Kephalethen (*PA* 13479; *APF* 13479). Horse-owner, purchased a chariot team through Alkibiades in 416 (Isok. 16. 1–3; see also Kyle, *AAA* A63); *strategos* 417/6 (Thucy. 5. 84. 3). He was also brother-in-law of Charikles, a member of the Thirty, and was himself connected with the oligarchy, as a councillor in 404/3 (Isok. 16. 43).

177. Theangelos (?Akamantidos) (*PA* 6600). Cavalryman, killed at Corinth in 394 (*IG* II² 5222). If, as *PA* assumes, all the men on this inscription were from the same tribe then he is from Akamantis. However, as *APF* 422 points out, there is no overriding necessity to believe it is a purely tribal inscription.

178. Themistokles (I) Neokleous (I) Phrearrhios (*PA* 6669; *APF* 6669). Several references place Themistokles in the equestrian milieu in the first half of the 5th cent. (Plut. *Them.* 2. 7; 5. 2; 17. 3; Idomeneus, *FGH* 338 F4); one of his sons, Neokles, died of a horse bite and another, Kleophantos (no. 93), was attested as a good horseman (Plut. *Them.* 32. 1; Pl. *Meno*, 93d). Kyle, *AAA* P91 suggests he may have been an equestrian victor.

179. Theogenes (Kroll, 4). Cavalryman, mid-4th cent. He could be the same as the hipparch Theogenes Theomedous Eleusinios in the next entry as the dates are consistent (although Theogenes is a common name).

180. Theogenes Theomedous Eleusinios (*PA* 6705). Hipparch on Salamis, *c.*320 (*IG* II² 1955). May be the same as the cavalryman in the previous entry.

181. Theophilos Eua[ngelou] Herṃ[eios] (*AO* 2955, p. 246). Phylarch or taxiarch, 373/2 (E. Schweigert, 'Greek Inscriptions', *Hesperia*, 8 (1939), 3–5, no. 2).

182. Theophon (*PA* 7180; *APF* 2921 xi; *AO* 2962, p. 291). Phylarch, 370s(?) (Isaios, 11. 41). A descendant by marriage was Hagnias (IV) of Oion (Part 3 no. 24), phylarch between 286 and 261.

183. Thereus (?Autodikou Erchieus) (*PA* 2707). Horse-owner(?), depicted on a relief (Athens, NM 1824; App. 2.22) *c*.400–350; son(?) of no. 33.

184. Thoudes (?Thoudiadou Alopekethen) (Kroll, 2). Cavalryman, mid-4th cent. Kroll, 107 identifies him with the *prytanis* of *c*.331 in *Agora*, xv no. 55, l. 41, but this may be the same man as *PA* 7249—although the demotic here is restored as [Ankyl]ethen.

185. Thrasippos (Kroll, 9). Cavalryman, mid-4th cent. The date could allow identification with *PA* 7291/92/93/97/97*a*.

186. Thrasymedes Kal[l]istrato Acharneus (*AO* 3050, p. 246). Phylarch or taxiarch, 373/2 (E. Schweigert, 'Greek Inscriptions', *Hesperia*, 8 (1939), 3–5, no. 2).

187. Timokrates (II) Antiphontos Krioeus (*PA* 13772, *APF* 13772). Olympic victor in two-horse chariot race (*IG* II² 3127), in 352 (Kyle, *AAA* 65); syntrierarch in the 370s (*IG* II² 1604, l. 83).

188. [. . ? . .]ulos Phlyeus. Cavalryman(?) depicted in a combat scene on relief at the end of the 5th cent. (Berlin, Staatliche Museen zu Berlin K. 30; Conze, no. 1160, pl. ccxlix = *IG* II² 7716; App. 2.14).

189. Xanthippos (II) Perikleous (I) Cholargeus (*PA* 11170; *APF* 11811 vii) A good horseman, 3rd quarter of 5th cent. (Pl. *Meno*, 94b); his father, Perikles (no. 142), was possibly a horse-owner and his brother Paralos (140) was also a good rider.

190. [X]en[o]kles Polyar[. . ? . .] Alopek[ethen] (*PA* 11213). Cavalryman(?): depicted wearing a helmet on a 4th-cent. equestrian relief (Brocklesby Park; Conze, no. 1162 = *IG* II² 5574; App. 2.17).

191. Xenophon (?Euripidou Meliteus) (*PA* 11313; *APF* 5951; *AO* 3144, p. 104). Hipparch, mid-5th cent. (*IG* I² 400); *strategos* 441/40 and 439/8 (Androtion, *FGH* 324 F38; *ATL* ii D18, l. 45) and possibly in 440/39 (see *APF*'s entry). Killed at Spartolos in 429 while general for 430/29 (Thucy. 2. 79). His son-in-law, (*APF* lost name 1, no. 195), was also a cavalryman while his granddaughter married Philomelos (no. 155), a horse-owner. Xenophon Meli[t]eus (no. 193), also a cavalryman, is possibly a homonymic grandson.

192. Xenophon (I) Gryllou (I) Erchieus (*PA* 11307). Almost certainly a cavalryman under the Thirty (the detailed descriptions of the cavalry actions in *Hell*. 2 make this extremely likely, especially in the light of his horse ownership and family service). Horse-owner (*Anab*. 3. 3. 19); both his sons, Diodoros (no. 55) and Gryllos (no. 72), were in the cavalry.

193. Xenophon Meli[t]eus (Kroll, 24). Cavalryman, mid-4th cent.; possibly grandson of the hipparch Xenophon (?Euripidou Meliteus) (no. 191) as they share the same name and deme.

194. Xenotimos (II) Karkinou (I) Thorikios (*PA* 11269; *APF* 8254A). Horse-owner, dedicated parts of horse's harness to Artemis Brauronia, pre-398/7 (*IG* II² 1388, l. 74; 1400, l. 62; 1455, ll. 25–7; 1458, ll. 1–2).

195. (?) (Father of the speaker of Lysias, 19; *APF* lost name 1, pp. 200, 592). Cavalryman; equestrian victor at the Isthmian and Nemean games, pre-*c.*390 (Lysias, 19. 63). His father-in-law, Xenophon (no. 191), was a hipparch, his son-in-law, Philomelos (no. 155), was a horse-owner. On the chance that his deme was Myrrhinous, see Kyle, *AAA* A78.

196. [. . ? . .] (*APF* lost name 8, p. 594). Hipparch, honoured by the cavalry on Salamis and Imbros; gymnasiarch; *strategos*, pre-318 (*IG* II² 3206).

197. [. . ? . .] (*APF* lost name 11, p. 594). Hipparch; trierarch, *c.*320 (*IG* II² 3209; Davies, *Wealth*, 155).

198. [. . ? . .] (*APF* lost name 21, p. 595). Victor in the two-horse chariot event at the Ilieia and in the horse race at the Klarian and Ephesian games, end of 4th cent. (*IG* II² 3138; Davies, *Wealth*, 168).

PART 2: HIPPARCHS c.450–100

Entries in this part of the appendix have a similar format to those in part 1: each man is listed alphabetically by name, patronymic, and deme (where possible), and using the same conventions. If the man's hipparchy post-dates 300 then a full entry appears here. However, if his hipparchy pre-dates 300 no further information is given, apart from the date of the hipparchy and any family links with other members of the cavalry class. In this case, the number in brackets following the name represents his number in part 1 of this appendix and the reader should check there for the rest of his details.

1. Antid[o]ros Thriasios (17). 4th cent.
2. Antikrates Sokratous Hermeios (18). 4th cent.
3. Demetrios (?(III) Demetriou (II) Phalereus) (*PA* 3453; *APF* 3455(F), pp. 109–10). Born not later than 286, probable grandson of the next entry. Hipparch, phylarch, and *strategos* several times, mid-3rd cent. (*IG* II² 1285; Athenaios, 4. 64).
4. Demetrios (I) Phanostratou Phalereus (46). Shortly before 325/4, or in 315/4; *strategos* three times. Probable grandfather of the previous entry.
5. [Democh]ares (I) (?Demonos (III)) Paia(nieus) (47). Hipparch(?), between 375 and 370.
6. Dieitrephes (?(II) Nikostratou Skambonides) (52). Pre-414; see also part 3 no. 18.

7. Diotimos (III) Diopeithous (I) Euonymeus (56). *c.*338/7 or shortly afterwards.

8. [. . ? . .]enou Pro[spaltios/balisios] (60). Late 4th/early 3rd cent.

9. Epilykos Nikostra[tou Gargettios] (62). *c.*350–325.

10. [Eue]tion Pythangelou Kephisieus (67). *c.*350–325.

11. [. . < 8 . .]ikles (74). Hipparch(?), 368.

12. Kallisthenes Kleoboulou Prospaltios (*PA* 8104*a*). Crowned by the *Boule* and people for service as phylarch, hipparch, and twice as *strategos*, mid-3rd cent. (*IG* II² 2854); see also part 3 no. 28.

12a Kallisthenes Ch[. . ? . .] (80). Hipparch or phylarch(?), after mid-4th cent.

13. Kallistratos Empedou (I) Oethen (82). Killed in Sicily, 413.

14. Kephisodoros Marathonios (84). Killed at Mantineia, 362.

15. [Kineas Nikom]achou Lamptreu[s] (87). *c.*350–275.

16. [. . ? . .]kles Erchi(eus) (94). Between *c.*375 and 370.

17. Komeas Chai[r].ou Lamptreus (*PA* 8956). Hipparch *eis Lemnon*, start of the 3rd cent. (*IG* II² 672, ll. 5 ff.). On the basis of names attested in *PA* the patronymic is either Chai[re]ou or (the less common) Chai[ri]ou.

18. Kratinos (?Erchieus) (97). 349/8.

19. Lakedaimonios Kimonos (II) Lakiades (99). *c.*450 (*IG* I² 400); early 440s (*AO* p. 104).

20. Lykophron (103). Hipparch *eis Lemnon*, during the 330s (twice), pre-333 according to *AO* p. 414; see also part 3 no. 30.

21. Lysimachos (105). 404/3.

22. [. . ? . .]maniou Peiraieus (*PA* 9665). End of 2nd cent.

23. Meidias (I) Kephisodorou (I) Anagyrasios (112). 349/8.

24. Nike[. . < 8 . .] (126). Hipparch(?), 368.

25. Nikogenes Arkesantos Euonymeus (*PA* 10848). 282/1 (Threpsiades and Vanderpool, *AD* 18 (1963), 104, no. 1, ll. 25–6).

26. Nikogenes (I) Nikonos (I) Philiades (*PA* 10850). *c.*160; also held magistracies prior to this (*c.*180 and later); *agnothetes* in 161/60.

27. Ophelas Habronos (III) Batethen (*PA* 11501). *c.*160; *Exegetes Pythochrestos* (Interpreter of the Pythian Oracles) in 128/7.

28. [. . ? . .]ous A[. . ? . .] (135). Late 4th/early 3rd cent.

29. Pamphilos Keiriades (136). 395/4.

30. Panaitios (137). Hipparch(?), *c.*425/4.

31. Patroklees Hierokleous Philiades (141). 4th cent.

32. Pheidon Thriasios (145). Hipparch *eis Lemnon*, mid-4th cent.; see also part 3 no. 40.

33. Phi[. . 3 . .]on Philist[. . ? . .] (146). Hipparch(?), late 4th/early 3rd cent.

34. Philokles (?Phormionos Eroiades) (153). Pre-324/3 (3–4 times).

35. Prokles Gniphonos (Thoraieus) (166). Hipparch(?), mid-4th cent.

36. Pronap[es] (?Pronapidou Prasieus) (167). Shortly after the mid-5th cent.
37. [Pythodoro]s (I) Epizelo(u) (I) (Halaieus Araph.) (168). c.420–410.
38. Simon (170). Hipparch(?), c.425.
39. [T]elesidemos Ami[n]iou Hekalethen (*PA* 13523). Hipparch *eis Lemnon*, c.166 (*IG* II² 1224, ll. 10–11).
40. Theogenes Theomedous Eleusinios (180). Hipparch on Salamis, c.320.
41. Theophrastos (?Lamptreus) (*PA* 7166; (?)Braun, *MDAI(A)* 85 (1970), no. 212, (?)151.1). Hipparch in 222/1(?) and 220/19; *strategos* late 3rd cent. He may be the Theophrastos who was a cavalryman c.260–240 (Braun, 212), however, it is a fairly common name; if this identification is correct then his deme is Lamptrai.
42. Thou[kritos] (?Alkimachou Myrrhinousios) (*PA* 7261). Hipparch, 268/7 (*IG* II² 1279, ll. 1–2); *strategos* four times, mid-3rd cent. (*IG* II² 2856).
43. Xenophon (?Euripidou Meliteus) (191). Mid-5th cent.
44. [. . ? . .] (*APF* lost name 8, p. 594) (196). Pre-318.
45. [. . ? . .] (*APF* lost name 11, p. 594) (197). c.320(?).

PART 3: PHYLARCHS c.450–160

Entries in this part of the appendix have the same format as those in part 2.

1. Alexandros Alexandrou Erchieus (*PA* 504). Shortly after c.161/60.
2. Anacharsis Me[. . ? . .] (?Kydathenaieus) (13). Mid-4th cent.
3. Antimachos [. .4 . .]os Pelekethen (20). Phylarch or taxiarch, 373/2.
4. Antimachos (II) Acharneus (*APF* 1122). 282/1.
5. Antiphanes (?Akamantidos) (22). 394/3.
6. Aration Simou Aigeidos (*PA* 1576). 161/60.
7. Aristophanes (II) Leukonoieus (*APF* 2092). Phylarch; gymnasiarch; twice *strategos* (237/6 and 236/5).
8. [. .4 . .]as [. . 5 . .]imo [Myrrhi]nosios (32). Phylarch or taxiarch, 373/2.
9. Boularchos Damoklea Akamantidos (*PA* 2910). c.168/7–164/3.
10. Char[ide]m[os] [E]uni[k. . ? . .] (39). Phylarch or taxiarch, 373/2.
11. Charikles Aiantidos (*PA* 15406). c.160.
12. Deimachos Deim[achou L]eukonoieus (*PA* 3253). c.161/60.
13. Demainetos (I) Demeou (III) Paianieus (43). Early 4th cent.
14. Demeas (IV) Demainetou (I) Paianieus (44). Mid-4th cent.
15. Demetrios [?Anti]phanou Alopekethen (45). c.330.
16. Demetrios (? (III) Demetriou (II) Phalereus) (Part 2 no. 3). Mid-3rd cent.
17. Demosthenes (III) Demainetou (I) Paianieus (50). Mid-4th cent.

18. Dieitrephes (?(II) Nikostratou Skambonides) (52; part 2 no. 6). Pre-414.
19. [. . ? . .] Erechthidos (63). Probably phylarch in *anthippasia*, *c*.321/20 or 318/17.
20. [. . 3 . .]es Amph[iou Eleu]sinios. Served on a board of twelve (probably phylarchs or taxiarchs) in the early 3rd cent. (*IG* II² 3852, l. 4).
21. Eubios Telesidemou Ptolemaiidos (*PA* 5289). *c*.160.
22. Euthykrates Perg[asethen] (70). *c*.380 or *c*.336/5–322/1.
23. [Gl]auko[n Eteokleous Haithalides] (*PA* 3019). Phylarch; *strategos*; *agnothetes*; victor in *anthippasia* at Olympia and the Great Panathenaia, pre-*c*.280/79 (*IG* II² 3079).
24. Hagnias (IV) ex Oiou (*APF* 2921 xii). Between 286 and 261, cf. Theophon, Part 1 no. 182.
25. [Ha]gnodemos Pa[ianieus] (73). *c*.380 or *c*.336/5–322/1.
26. Harmoxenos Harmoxenou Kekropidos (*PA* 2238). *c*.160.
27. Kallisthenes Ch[. . ? . .] (80). Hipparch or phylarch(?), after mid-4th cent.
28. Kallisthenes Kleoboulou Prospaltios (Part 2 no. 12). Mid-3rd cent.
29. Kleonymos Kleoxeno(u) Marathonios (91). Phylarch or taxiarch, 373/2.
30. Lykophron (103; Part 2 no. 20). By about 340(?).
31. Lysippos (III) Lysip[pou] (I) Kettios (*APF* 9560). 282/1.
32. [. . 4 . . m]achos [. . 12 . . Ai]xoneus. Served on a board of twelve (probably phylarchs or taxiarchs) in the early 3rd cent. (*IG* II² 3852, l. 3).
33. Menexenos (I) Dikaiogenous (I) Kydathenaieus (116). 430/29.
34. Moiragenes Ika[rieus] (119). *c*.380 or *c*.336/5–322/1.
35. Moschion (120). Phylarch, (quite probably fictional) in Menander, *Samia*, 15.
36. [. . *c*.9 . .]n Oethen (122). *c*.325.
37. [. . 4 . .]okle[s] [. . 5 . .]tio [ek K]edon (131). Phylarch or taxiarch, 373/2.
38. Orthoboulos ek Kerameon (133). Phylarch (or possibly hipparch), 395/4.
39. [. . 3 . .]otheos Do[rotheou Ana]phlystos. Served on a board of twelve (probably phylarchs or taxiarchs) in the early 3rd cent. (*IG* II² 3852, l. 6).
40. Pheidon (?Thriasios) (?145; ?part 2 no. 32). Pre-329 (Mnesimachos fr. 4).
41. Philinos [. . ? . .]nos [Anaphlys]tio[s] (148). Phylarch or taxiarch, 373/2.
42. Platon Alexionos Hippoth[ontidos] (*PA* 11848). *c*.160.
43. Prokles Gniphonos (Thoraieus) (166). Mid-4th cent. (but perhaps more likely a hipparch or, less likely, a cavalryman).

44. Pythodoros Hippothontidos (169). *c*.412.

45. [S]atyros Hi[er]okl[e]ous Ke[k]ropido[s] (*PA* 12583). 168/7–164/3.

46. [Tel]emachos (III) D[. . 8 . .] Aphignaios(*sic*) (*APF* 13560). Served on a board of twelve (probably phylarchs or taxiarchs) in the early 3rd cent. (*IG* II² 3852, l. 5).

47. Theodor[. . ? . .] Charikleous Aiantidos (*PA* 6809). *c*.160.

48. Theophilos Eua[ngelou] Herm[eios] (181). Phylarch or taxiarch, 373/2.

49. Theophon (182). 370s(?).

50. Thrasykles (II) Thrasyllou (II) Dekeleieus (*PA* 7321; *APF* 7341). 282/1; *agnothetes*, 271/70.

51. Thrasymedes Kal[l]istrato Acharneus (186). Phylarch or taxiarch, 373/2.

APPENDIX 6

The Hipparch *eis Lemnon*

AN interesting feature of the Athenian cavalry command structure is the hipparch sent to Lemnos (*eis Lemnon*). This officer commanded a cavalry contingent on the island, probably from about the mid-fourth century, and was a third, and slightly junior, hipparch elected especially for this function.

The *Ath. Pol.* describes the election of the *hipparchos eis Lemnon* as follows: 'they also elect a hipparch for Lemnos to take charge of the cavalry on Lemnos.' Taken with the rest of the passage, the natural sense of the section quoted is that this hipparch was elected in addition to the two already mentioned. The fact that it follows a description of how two hipparchs are elected from all the citizens (*ex hapanton*) and ten phylarchs, one per tribe (*hena tes phyles*), clearly indicates that this was a separate, third, hipparchy and not a subsequent vote distributing duties to the two hipparchs already mentioned. Although there was such an election to allocate the ten *strategoi* to various posts after their initial election, the *Ath. Pol.* deals with this in a very different way from the section on the hipparch *eis Lemnon*. First, it is treated in the same section as the original election for the *strategeia*, whereas the mention of the Lemnian hipparchy occurs after the election of the phylarchs and not with the discussion on the election to the hipparchy. Second, when referring to the distribution of duties to the generals the *Ath. Pol.* uses the verb διατάττω ('to appoint to separate duties/offices') rather than the phrase χειροτονοῦσι δὲ καί ('they also elect') which is used to introduce all other sections concerning elections to an office, including the election of the *Hipparchos eis Lemnon*.[1]

Demosthenes 4. 26–7, though, gives a very different impression from the testimony of the *Ath. Pol.* Having noted at section 26 that two hipparchs were elected, Demosthenes tells the Athenians at section 27 that 'it is necessary for one of your hipparchs to sail to Lemnos'. Although at first sight this seems to suggest that one of the two hipparchs mentioned in section 26 was serving in Lemnos, this was certainly not the case.

The *Ath. Pol.* passage describes general practice while Demosthenes is making a point about a particular occasion. It is therefore possible, even

---

[1] *Ath. Pol.* 61. 4–6, esp. 6: Χειροτονοῦσι δὲ καὶ εἰς Λῆμνον ἵππαρχον, ὃς ἐπιμελεῖται τῶν ἱππέων τῶν ἐν Λήμνῳ.

if one of only two hipparchs was in Lemnos, that this was an unusual situation—perhaps because of the death or illness of one of the elected officers in that year. However, it is equally possible, and perhaps more likely, that we are reading too much into Demosthenes' remarks. The impression left with anyone who assumes that there were only two hipparchs is that one of these was sent, but Demosthenes does not actually state that one of the two cavalry officers was sent to Lemnos—he mentions two hipparchs and slightly later states one hipparch was dispatched to Lemnos. The passage therefore cannot be taken as proof that the officer sent to Lemnos was one of only two hipparchs elected.

On balance then, the *Ath. Pol.* passage has greater validity for this question and the existence of a third hipparch, elected for service on Lemnos, is in fact confirmed by other fourth century evidence. While Demosthenes, 4. 27, Hypereides, 1. 17–18, and the clay tokens of Pheidon of Thria all show that the *hipparchos eis Lemnon* actually served his term of office on the island itself, other sources confirm that two hipparchs served at Athens.[2] Xenophon for example describes the hipparchs each leading half of the cavalry in equestrian displays. Such a division of the *hippeis*, whether for public displays or for tactical purposes,[3] would have been inconceivable if one of the two hipparchs was stationed in Lemnos. Further circumstantial support is given to this interpretation by the implicit assumption throughout Xenophon's *Hipparchikos* that the hipparch will serve at Athens. No mention is made of the duties required at Lemnos, which suggests that the hipparchy there was a separate office.

The date the hipparchy *eis Lemnon* was created is uncertain, but the earliest literary reference to it, Demosthenes, 4, was delivered in 351, about the same date as the first inscriptional evidence.[4] Wilhelm's suggestion, that the third hipparch inscribed on *IG* I² 400 (mid-5th century) was the *hipparchos eis Lemnon*,[5] seems highly unlikely. First, if one of the three was stationed on Lemnos then it would be improbable

---

[2] Clay tokens: J. H. Kroll and F. W. Mitchel, 'Clay Tokens Stamped with the Names of Athenian Military Commanders', *Hesperia*, 49 (1980), 86–96. The tablets are dated to shortly after the middle of the fourth century and probably served to identify official messengers sent to the hipparch on Lemnos, ibid. 89, 94–6.

[3] Xen. *Hipparch.* 3. 6, 11; cf. inscription I 3495 (dated to the late fourth/early third century), published in E. Vanderpool, 'Victories in the Anthippasia', *Hesperia*, 43 (1974), 313; *Ath. Pol.* 61. 4. See also 'leadership' and 'training', Ch. 2.

[4] The first known hipparch is the Pheidon of Thria (App. 5.145) in the mid-4th cent., whose clay symbolae are referred to above. The other known holders of the office are Lykophron (5.103) in the 330s, Komeas (5 part 2.17) at the start of the 3rd cent., and Telesidemos (5 part 2.39) *c.*166.

[5] Cited in Bugh, *Horsemen*, 50; the original publication was unfortunately unavailable to me.

for all of them to be campaigning together. Second, the dates of both *IG*
I² 400 and the founding of the Lemnian cleruchy are not certain enough
to allow us to assert that the inscription post-dates the establishment of
the cleruchy—if it did it could only be by a few years at the most.[6] Given
that the mid-fourth century is the period when the office is first mentioned in our sources, this seems the most likely date for its creation.[7]

[6] The register in *ATL* 1 shows that the total tribute of the Lemnian *poleis* was
nearly halved between 450/49 and 444/3, suggesting that the cleruchy was established at this time; cf. Bugh, *Horsemen*, app. B.

[7] Bugh, *Horsemen*, 218 reaches the same conclusion.

SELECT BIBLIOGRAPHY

THIS bibliography is intended as a guide to the most important reading on the subject and to provide a ready reference for those works cited more than once in the book. Items which are listed in the 'abbreviations', and (unless of particular interest) those which occur only once in the notes, do not appear again here.

ADKINS, A. W. H., *Merit and Responsibility* (Oxford, 1960).

ALFIERI, N., *Spina: museo archeologico nazionale di Ferrara* (Bologna, 1979).

ALFÖLDI, A., *Die Herrschaft der Reiterei in Griechenland und Rom nach dem Sturz der Könige*, (*Antike Kunst*, Beiheft 4; Bern, 1967).

ANDERSON, J. K., 'Notes on Some Points of Xenophon's 'Περὶ Ἱππικῆς', *JHS* 80 (1960), 1–9.

—— *Xenophon* (London, 1974).

ASHMOLE, B., *Architect and Sculptor in Classical Greece* (London, 1972).

BEST, J. G. P., *Thracian Peltasts and their Influence on Greek Warfare* (Groningen, 1969).

BIVAR, A. D. H., 'The Stirrup and its Origins', *Oriental Art*, NS 1 (1955), 61–5.

BOARDMAN, J., 'The Parthenon Frieze—Another View' in Höckmann, U., and Krug, A. (eds.), *Festschrift für Frank Brommer* (Mainz am Rhein, 1977), 39–49.

BRAUN, K., 'Der Dipylon-Brunnen B1, die Funde', *MDAI(A)* 85 (1970), 129–269.

BROMMER, F., *Der Parthenonfries* (Mainz am Rhein, 1977).

BUGH, G. R., 'Andocides, Aeschines, and the Three Hundred Athenian Cavalrymen', *Phoenix*, 36 (1982), 306–12.

—— *The Horsemen of Athens* (Princeton, NJ, 1988).

CAHN, H. A., 'Dokimasia', *RA* (1973), 3–22.

CARTLEDGE, P., 'Hoplites and Heroes: Sparta's Contribution to the Technique of Ancient Warfare', *JHS* 97 (1977), 11–27.

CAWKWELL, G., *Philip of Macedon* (London, 1978).

CROUWEL, J. H., *Chariots and Other Means of Land Transport in Bronze Age Greece* (Amsterdam, 1981).

DAVIES, J. K., *Wealth and the Power of Wealth in Classical Athens* (Salem, Mass., 1981).

DE STE. CROIX, G. E. M., 'Demosthenes' Τίμημα and the Athenian Eisphora in the Fourth Century BC', *C&M* 14 (1953), 30–70.

DEMAND, N. H., *Thebes in the Fifth Century* (London, 1982).

DENISON, G. T., *A History of Cavalry*, 2nd edn. (London, 1913).

ENGELS, D. W., *Alexander the Great and the Logistics of the Macedonian Army* (Berkeley, Calif., 1978).

FALLS, C., *Military Operations Egypt and Palestine from June 1917 to the end of the War*, 2 vols. (London, 1930).

FERRILL, A., *The Origins of War* (London, 1985).

FORNARA, C. W., 'The Athenian Board of Generals from 501 to 404', *Historia Einzelschriften*, 16 (Wiesbaden, 1971).

FOXHALL, L., and FORBES, H. A., '*Σιτομετρεία*: The Role of Grain as a Staple Food in Classical Antiquity', *Chiron*, 12 (1982), 41–90.

FREL J., and KINGSLEY, B. M., 'Three Attic Sculpture Workshops of the Early Fourth Century BC', *GRBS* 11 (1970), 197–218.

FULLER, J. F. C., *Armoured Warfare* (London, 1943).

—— *The Decisive Battles of the Western World*, ed. J. Terraine, vol. 1 (London, 1970).

GARDINER, E. N., 'Throwing the Javelin', *JHS* 27 (1907), 249–73.

GARLAN, Y., *War in the Ancient World*, trans. J. Lloyd (London, 1975).

General Staff, War Office, *Field Service Pocket Book 1914* (London, 1917).

GOMME, A. W., *A Historical Commentary on Thucydides*, vols. 1–3 (Oxford 1945–56).

—— Andrewes, A., and Dover, K. J., *A Historical Commentary on Thucydides*, vols. 4–5 (Oxford, 1970–81).

GRENFELL, B. P., and Hunt, A. S., *The Hibeh Papyri*, part 1 (London, 1906).

GULLETT, H. B. S., *Not as a Duty Only: An Infantryman's War* (Melbourne, 1976).

GULLETT, H. S., *The AIF in Sinai and Palestine* (The Official History of Australia in the War of 1914–1918, vol. 7; St Lucia, 1984).

HANSON, V. D., *The Western Way of War* (New York, 1989).

HARRIS, H. A., 'Greek Javelin Throwing', *G&R* 10 (1963), 26–36.

HENDERSON, G. F. R., *The Science of War*, ed. N. Malcolm (London, 1912).

HIGNETT, C., *A History of the Athenian Constitution* (Oxford, 1958).

HOLLADAY, A. J., 'Hoplites and Heresies', *JHS* 102 (1982), 94–103.

HOLMES, R., *Firing Line* (Harmondsworth, 1987).

HOOD, R. G., *Greek Vases in the University of Tasmania*, 3rd edn. (Hobart, 1982).

IDRIESS, I. L., *The Desert Column* (Sydney, 1985, first pub. 1932).

JARDÉ, A. F. V., *Les Céréales dans l'antiquité grecque* (Paris, 1925).

KAYLL, A. J., *A Technique for Studying the Fire Tolerance of Living Tree Trunks* (Department of Forestry, Canada, Publication 1012; Ottawa, 1963).

KEEGAN, J., *The Face of Battle* (Harmondsworth, 1978).

KRENTZ, P., 'Casualties in Hoplite Battles', *GRBS* 26 (1985), 13–20.

KROLL, J. H., and MITCHEL, F. W., 'Clay Tokens Stamped with the Names of Athenian Military Commanders', *Hesperia*, 49 (1980), 86–96.

KROMAYER, J., and VEITH, G., *Heerwesen und Kriegführung der Griechen und Römer* (Munich, 1928).

LAWRENCE, A. W., *Greek Aims in Fortification* (Oxford, 1979).

LAWRENCE, M., *Flyers and Stayers: The Book of the World's Greatest Rides* (London, 1980).

LAZENBY, J. F., *The Spartan Army* (Warminister, 1985).

LIDDELL HART, B. and A. (eds.), *The Sword and the Pen: Selections from the World's Greatest Military Writings* (New York, 1976).

LORIMER, H. L., 'The Hoplite Phalanx with Special Reference to the Poems of Archilochus and Tyrtaeus', *ABSA* 42 (1947), 76–138.

LUTTWAK, E., *A Dictionary of Modern War* (London, 1972).

MARKLE, M. M., 'Jury Pay and Assembly Pay at Athens', in Cartledge, P. A., and Harvey, F. D. (eds.), *Crux: Essays presented to G. E. M. de Ste. Croix on his 75th Birthday* (History of Political Thought, vol. 6, Issue 1/2; Exeter, 1985), 265–97.

MARSDEN, E. W., *The Campaign of Gaugamela* (Liverpool, 1964).

MARTIN, A., *Les Cavaliers athéniens* (Bibliothèque des Écoles Françaises d'Athènes et de Rome, fasc. 47; Paris, 1886).

METZGER, H., *Les Représentations dans la céramique attique du IVe siècle*, 2 vols. (Bibliothèque des Écoles Françaises d'Athènes et de Rome, fasc. 172; Paris, 1951).

MILNS, R. D., 'Alexander's Macedonian Cavalry and Diodorus xvii. 17. 4', *JHS* 86 (1966), 167–8.

MINGAZZINI, P., *Catalogo dei vasi della collezione Augusto Castellani* (Rome, 1930).

MORETTI, L., *Olympionikai: I vincitori negli antichi agoni Olympici* (Rome, 1957).

NIKOPOULOU, Y., "'Ἐπιτύμβια Μνημεῖα παρὰ τὰς Πύλας τοῦ Διοχάρους'', *AAA* 2 (1969), 329–34.

OBER, J., *Fortress Attica* (Leiden, 1985).

OMAN, C. W. C., *The Art of War in the Middle Ages*, rev. by J. H. Beeler (New York, 1968).

PÉLÉKIDIS, C., *Histoire de l'éphébie attique* (Paris, 1962).

PEPPAS-DELMOUSOU, D., "'«Ἐπιστήματα» τοῦ Τάφου τοῦ Μενύλλου Ἀλαιέως. Ἡ Βάση EM 13451'' *AAA* 10 (1977), 226–41.

PERIS, F. J., *Die Disposition des Parthenonfrieses* (Bonn, 1974).

PRITCHETT, W. K., 'The Attic Stelai: Part I', *Hesperia*, 22 (1953), 225–99.

—— 'The Attic Stelai: Part II', *Hesperia*, 25 (1956), 178–328.

RAHE, P. A., 'The Annihilation of the Sacred Band at Chaeronea', *AJA* 85 (1981), 84–7.

RAUBITSCHEK, A. E., *Dedications from the Athenian Akropolis* (Cambridge, Mass., 1949).

REINMUTH, O. W., 'An Ephebic Text of ca 43/2 BC: *IG* II² 1040 and 1025', *Hesperia*, 34 (1965), 255–72.

RHODES, P. J., 'Problems in Athenian *Eisphora* and Liturgies', *AJAH* 7 (1982), 1–19.

RICHTER, G. M. A., *Attic Red-figured Vases: A Survey*, rev. edn. (New Haven, Conn., 1958).

ROSE, V., *Aristotelis Fragmenta*, 3rd edn. (Leipzig, 1886).

SARGENT, R. L., 'The Use of Slaves by the Athenians in Warfare', *CPh* 22 (1927), Part I, 201–12, Part II, 264–79.

SARIKAKIS, T., *The Hoplite General in Ancient Athens/The Generals of the Hellenistic Age* (Chicago, 1976).

SCHEFOLD, K., *Untersuchungen zu den Kertscher Vasen* (Berlin and Leipzig, 1934).

SCHRYVER, H. F., and HINTZ, H. F., *Feeding Horses* (New York State College of Agriculture and Life Sciences, Animal Sciences: Equine Research Program 1, Information Bulletin 94; New York, 1975?).

SEKUNDA N. V., 'Some Notes on the Life of Datames', *Iran*, 26 (1988), 35–53.

SELTMAN, C. T., *Greek Coins*, 2nd edn. (London, 1960).

SHACKLEY, M., 'Arms and the Men: 14th-Century Japanese Swordsmanship Illustrated by Skeletons from Zaimokuza, near Kamakura, Japan', *World Archaeology*, 18 (1986), 247–54.

SHEAR, T. L., 'The Athenian Agora: Excavations 1970', *Hesperia*, 40 (1971), 241–79.

SIEWERT, P., *Die Trittyen Attikas und die Heeresreform des Kleisthenes* (Vestigia, Beiträge zur alten Geschichte, 33; Munich, 1982).

SIMON, E., *Festivals of Attica* (Madison, Wis., 1983).

SPENCE, I. G., 'Athenian Cavalry Numbers in the Peloponnesian War: *IG* I³ 375 Revisited', *ZPE* 67 (1987), 167–75.

—— 'Perikles and the Defence of Attika during the Peloponnesian War', *JHS* 110 (1990), 91–109.

STANTON, G. R., 'Retail Pricing of Grain in Athens', *Hermes*, 113 (1985), 121–3.

THOMPSON, W. E., 'The Neokoroi of Poseidon Hippios', *Hesperia*, 40 (1971), 232–4.

—— 'More on the Prytaneion Decree', *GRBS* 20 (1979), 325–9.

THREPSIADES, J., and VANDERPOOL, E., "Πρὸς τοῖς Ἑρμαῖς" *AD* 18 (1963), 99–114.

TURNBULL, S. R., *The Book of the Samurai* (London, 1982).

VANDERPOOL, E., 'Victories in the Anthippasia', *Hesperia*, 43 (1974), 311–13.

Vasić, R., 'Grylus and Epaminondas in Euphranor's "Cavalry Battle"', *ŽA*, 29 (1979), 261–8.

——'Some Observations on Euphranor's Cavalry Battle', *AJA* 83 (1979), 345–9.

Vigneron, P., *Le Cheval dans l'antiquité gréco-romaine* (Annales de l'Est, l'Université de Nancy, Mém. 35; Nancy, 1968).

von Bothmer, D. *Amazons in Greek Art* (Oxford, 1957).

Vos, M. F., *Scythian Archers in Archaic Attic Vase Painting* (Groningen, 1963).

Watson, D. J., 'Inflammability of Cereal Crops in Relation to Water-content', *EJEA* 18, no. 71 (1950), 150–62.

Westlake, H. D., *Thessaly in the Fourth Century BC* (London, 1935).

——*Essays on the Greek Historians and Greek History* (Manchester, 1969).

Whitehead, D., 'Κλοπὴ Πολέμου: "Theft" in Ancient Greek Warfare', *C&M* 39 (1988), 43–53.

Wilson, N. G. (ed.), *Scholia in Aristophanem* i. 1. B; *In Acharnenses* (Groningen, 1975).

Wintringham, T., and Blashford-Snell, J. N., *Weapons and Tactics* (Harmondsworth, 1973).

Woodward, A. M., 'Financial Documents from the Athenian Agora', *Hesperia*, 32 (1963), 144–86.

GLOSSARY

agathos
good/noble/well-born; in a political context at Athens it was often used by political theorists and the upper classes to denote the man best fitted by birth and education to be a full citizen or political leader.

alopekis
(plural alopekides) fox-skin cap, originally from the Thracian region (worn by the right-hand rider on Plate 8).

amentum
a loop attached to a javelin to allow the thrower to impart spin to the weapon and increase the distance thrown.

andreia
manliness, bravery.

anthippasia
mock-battle performed at Athens by cavalry squadrons as a public contest (for which a prize was awarded).

antidosis
(at Athens) exchange of property/possessions. If assigned to a public liturgy a man could nominate another (whom he believed to be financially better off) to either perform the liturgy in his place or exchange property with him. If the second man refused, the matter would be decided in court.

aparche
(plural *aparchai*) votive gift to a god or goddess; at Athens 1/60th of the *phoros* from the empire was given as an *aparche* to Athena.

apobatai
(sing. *apobates*) equestrian competitors (at Athens) who leaped in and out of moving chariots.

arete
virtue/excellence or courage.

asemos
(of horses) unbranded.

aspis
large shield carried by hoplites (depicted on Plates 2, 8, and 11–13).

biga
two-horse chariot.

Boule
the Council of 500 at Athens which prepared the agenda for the assembly and handled the day to day administrative business between assembly meetings.

Bouleuterion
the building where the current standing committee of the *Boule* was housed during its chairmanship or prytany (each tribal group of 50 held this once during the council's year of office).

chiton
(plural chitones) tunic, often worn with a belt,

favoured by youths and cavalrymen (see Plates 9, 11, and 13).

chlamys · (plural chlamydes) cloak originating from Thessaly, usually worn over a chiton and favoured by cavalrymen (see the youths on Plate 3 and the hipparch on Plate 14).

choinix · (plural *choinikes*) measure of volume, used for grain; its size varied but at Athens it was 1/48th of a *medimnos* (= 1.087 litres).

chora · the territory of a *polis*; its agricultural hinterland.

dekadarch · (*dekadarchos*, plural *dekadarchoi*) literally 'leader of ten'; a rank in the Spartan infantry. Xenophon recommended in the *Hipparchikos* that dekadarchs should be used as subordinate commanders in the cavalry squadrons at Athens.

diadochoi · (literally 'successors') the men who took over and ruled the various parts of Alexander the Great's empire after his death.

dokimasia · the examination of a cavalryman and his horse before listing on the cavalry rolls (or of an archon before entry to office).

doru · (plural *dorata*) spear.

doxa · opinion, reputation.

drachma/s · (*drachme*, plural *drachmai*) unit of weight or money (1 = 6 obols).

eisphora · property tax, originally levied only in wartime on the wealthiest citizens; from the mid-fourth century it became a regular tax, levied annually.

ekdromos · (plural *ekdromoi*) a soldier who charged out of the ranks (as part of a group) to drive off an enemy.

embades · high boots, much favoured by Athenian cavalrymen (see the right-hand youth, Plate 3).

ephebeia · the state youth-training system at Athens, probably founded as a formal training institution in the middle or second half of the 4th cent. It involved two years' training/garrison duty for youths between the ages of 18 and 20.

epheboi · (sing. *ephebos*) ephebes, or boys between the ages of 15 and 20; at Athens, also youths undergoing the *ephebeia*.

epilektoi · picked or chosen troops who formed a permanent or semi-permanent force in many Greek states in the fourth century; the Theban 'Sacred Band' was one of the first.

grammateus a secretary (in some cases elected) to a magistrate or board.

hamippoi (sing. *hamippos*) an infantryman (usually light) who operated with cavalry (see Plate 10).

hermai stone or bronze pillars, usually square, with a bust on top; originally representing the god Hermes but later also other gods. Male *hermai* had genitals and the mutilation of these in Athens in 415 resulted in public trials and the banishment of Alkibiades.

hermokopidai those involved in the mutilation of the *hermai* at Athens in 415.

himation (plural himatia) outer garment, often worn over the chiton (see the older men, Plates 1 and 3–4).

Hipparcheion the cavalry headquarters at Athens, probably sited near the Stoa of the Herms in the north-west of the Agora.

hipparchos (plural *hipparchoi*) hipparch, or cavalry commander, at Athens and elsewhere. At Athens there were two, elected by the citizens, and holding joint command for one year (there was no limit on the number of times an individual could hold the office).

hipparmostes a cavalry commander at Sparta, apparently equivalent to the hipparch at Athens (although the method of election and duration of office are unknown).

hippeus (plural *hippeis*) cavalryman; it can also be used to mean a rider and in the plural denotes either the cavalry or (at Athens) members of the second highest of the census classes established by Solon (originally all those with an annual agricultural production between 300 and 500 *medimnoi*).

hippotoxotes (plural *hippotoxotai*) horse-archer.

hippotrophos (plural *hippotrophoi*) horse-breeder (a mark of considerable wealth).

hoplite (*hoplites*, plural *hoplitai*) heavy infantryman equipped with *aspis* and spear and perhaps (but not always) breast-plate, helmet, and greaves.

hyperetes (plural *hyperetai*) assistant or aide (either a free man or a slave, depending on the context).

kamax (literally 'pole') term used by N. V. Sekunda to denote a cavalryman's thrusting spear (depicted on Plate 9); perhaps similar to the *sarissa*, but in some cases may be identified with the *hoplite* spear or *doru*.

katana	long Japanese sword, worn in the belt.
katastasis	grant of money paid to help Athenian citizens set themselves up as cavalrymen; it had to be repaid on leaving the service.
kopis	sword, probably of Persian origin, of the same or similar type as the *machaira*.
kylix	flat drinking-cup, often painted on both interior and exterior (see Plates 1, 3–5).
lekythos	(plural lekythoi) oil-flask, often used as the shape for stone funeral monuments.
lochagoi	(sing. *lochagos*) subordinate commanders; at Athens, commanders of *lochoi*.
lochoi	(sing. *lochos*) infantry sub-unit; at Athens it may have been the *trittys* contingent of a tribal regiment.
machaira	(plural *machairai*) sword, probably with curved blade, not unlike a larger version of the Gurkha kukri.
medimnos	(plural *medimnoi*) measure of volume; at Athens, 48 *choinikes* (= 52.176 litres).
mina/e	(*mna*, plural *minai*) unit of weight and money (1 = 100 drachmas).
mora	(plural *morai*) a unit (infantry or cavalry) of the Spartan army (the cavalry *mora* was probably 120 strong).
mystai	initiates into a mystery cult, the most famous being the Eleusinian mysteries (of Persephone and Demeter) at Athens.
naukrariai	forty-eight, pre-Solonic, local administrative areas of Attica, each of which provided one ship and two cavalrymen for the armed forces. They probably ceased to exist as an administrative unit after Kleisthenes' reforms in 507 and their naval function was probably ended by Themistokles' reforms in 483.
neokoroi	temple-wardens.
obol	(*obolos*) unit of weight and money (= 1/6th of a drachma).
palton	(plural *palta*) javelin.
Panathenaia	a festival, celebrated every year at Athens. Every fourth year a larger version, the Great Panathenaia, was held incorporating a procession, public games (including athletic, equestrian, and musical events), and sacrifices.

pandemei   (of armies) to march out at full-strength; with the entire state's forces.

peltast   (*peltastes*) light infantryman originating in Thrace; equipped with a crescent shaped shield (*pelte*), sword, javelin, or thrusting spear.

pentakosiomedimnoi   members of the highest of the census classes established by Solon (originally all those with a minimum annual agricultural production of 500 *medimnoi*).

Perioikoi   inhabitants of the outlying villages of Lakedaimonia who did not have the same rights as full Spartiates.

petasos   (plural petasoi) broad-brimmed hat (see Plates 2–4, 8–10, 14–15) originating from north Greece; later used as the model for a helmet (Plate 13), favoured by the Athenian cavalry.

philotimia   love of honour, desire for fame/reputation.

phoros   tribute (paid by members of the Delian League/Athenian empire during the fifth century).

phyle   (plural *phylai*) tribe; also (at Athens) a 100-man tribal cavalry contingent or squadron.

pilos   close-fitting conical cap made of felt, sometimes used as a helmet-liner.

poletai   board of magistrates who sold and conducted the sale or lease of state property (including confiscated property), usually by auction.

polis   (plural *poleis*) city or city-state.

pompai   (sing. *pompe*) processions.

prodromoi   (sing. *prodromos*) cavalry scouts.

prostates   president or presiding officer; a variety of civil boards at Athens were headed by a *prostates*.

proxenoi   (sing. *proxenos*) a local citizen who represented the interests of another state in his *polis*.

psilos   (plural *psiloi*) light-armed soldier; could range from archers, slingers, or peltasts to men equipped with nothing more than a dagger or stones.

pteryges   (literally 'wings') strips of leather which hung down from the shoulders or the bottom edge of a breastplate to protect the upper arms/thighs.

sarissa   long Macedonian lance, carried by both infantry and (at least some) cavalry; perhaps similar to the *kamax*.

sarissophoroi   (sing. *sarissophoros*) soldiers carrying the *sarissa*; a cavalry unit of the Macedonian army.

sitos   (literally 'grain') an allowance for food for soldiers or, at Athens, for cavalry horses (*hippois sitos*).

sophos	skilled/wise (often regarded as an attribute of the good citizen, see also *agathos*).
stadion	stadium; a sprint race run the length of the stadium.
stela	(plural stelae) stone slab, usually with an inscription and/or relief on it (see Plates 9–13).
strategeia	the office of *strategos* (general/admiral) at Athens.
strategos	(plural *strategoi*) one of a board of ten generals/ admirals at Athens, elected annually (with no limit on the number of times the same man could hold office).
sunoridi	(in a) two-horse chariot event.
tachi	Japanese sword, worn slung from the waist.
talent	(*talanton*) unit of weight and money (= 60 minae or 6,000 drachmas).
taxiarchos	(plural *taxiarchoi*) taxiarch, commander of a *taxis* or infantry company at Athens.
taxis	(plural *taxeis*) an infantry sub-unit of approximately company size at Athens; the term may also have been used of a cavalry squadron or *phyle*.
tethrippo	(in a) four-horse chariot event.
thetes	(at Athens) members of the lowest of the census classes established by Solon (originally all those with an annual agricultural production below 200 *medimnoi*).
timema	price, value.
timesis	valuation; at Athens the *timesis ton hippon* was a valuation of cavalry horses to fix the price to be paid to a cavalryman if his mount was killed or maimed on campaign.
toxotes	(plural *toxotai*) archer.
trierarch	(*trierarchos*) a citizen who paid for, and normally captained, a ship in the Athenian navy for one year. It was a liturgy which an individual could be asked to hold only once in any 3-year period.
xiphos	straight sword.
zeira	(plural zeirai) a cloak, often patterned, originating in Thrace and from time to time popular with the Athenian cavalry (see Plate 7).
zeugitai	(at Athens) members of the third of the census classes established by Solon (originally all those with an annual agricultural production between 200 and 300 *medimnoi*).

INDEX

A number in brackets following an entry indicates that it appears in an appendix: the first number indicates which appendix, the second number (after the point) indicates the individual number within the appendix. Note that Greek words are normally transliterated rather than latinized (see p. xx above) so for Cunaxa, Cimon etc. see Kounaxa, Kimon.

Carthaginians 111 n.
  Sicilian cavalry deployed against 30,
    136
casualties:
  combat/plague effects on Athenian
    cavalry 99
  hoplite casualty rates 172
  maximized by cavalry in pursuit
    phase 157–9
  reduction of: by armour 60, 65; in
    withdrawal, by cavalry 151, 159–
    62
casualty lists (Athens) 57, 219
cavalry:
  attacks on infantry (method/
    effectiveness) 48–9, 102–17, 118,
    120, 126–9, 153, 155–7, 161–3,
    177–8
  battlefield positioning 90, 153–6,
    175–6, 214–15; *see also* cavalry:
    tactics and use
  combat potential 102–21, 162–3;
    definition of 34–5; factors affecting
    35–103; *see also* cavalry, Athenian:
    social influences on
  flexibility 35, 86–97, 102, 109, 117,
    118–19, 153
  formations: diamond/rhomboid 25,
    109, 178; tetragonal and
    wedge 22, 27, 59 n., 118, theory
    of 103–4, 107–9, 177–8; training
    in 77–8
  impressive/intimidating
    appearance 101, 112–14, 118, 186
  leadership xxiv–xxv, 35, 65–75, 102,
    117, 119, 144; contribution to
    flexibility 86–7; *see also* cavalry:
    motivation; cavalry, Athenian:
    leadership
  medieval 105–6
  mobility 35, 36–49, 102, 109, 143,
    144; compared to infantry 115–17,
    123, 126, 142, 153; contribution to
    flexibility 86–7, 119, 163;
    contribution to shock 107, 117;
    suitability for raids/
    reconnaissance 133, 135, 136, 145
  motivation (to fight) 35, 79–86, 102,

    117, 119; aided by protection 60,
    65
  numbers 97–8, 101–2; *see also*
    cavalry, Athenian: numbers
  post-medieval 105, 106–7, 112; *see
    also* Australian Light Horse
  protection 35, 60–5, 118
  psychological domination of
    infantry 113–14
  recruitment (Spartan, in Ionia) 4 n.
  tactics and use: in independent
    operations 126–37, internal
    security 136–7, mobile
    defence 127–33, raids 135–6,
    reconnaissance 133–5; in
    supporting operations
    (hoplite) 140–63, battle
    phase 151–62, march phase 141–
    51; *see also* cavalry: attacks on
    infantry
  training 35, 102, 117; contribution
    to flexibility 86–7; officer
    training 72; Spartan 4 n., 143; *see
    also* cavalry, Athenian: training
  weaponry 32–3, 35, 49–60, 102, 109,
    110, 117, 118; contribution to
    flexibility 86–7; use affected by
    lack of stirrups 44–5, 103–4, 109;
    see also weapons, cavalry
cavalry, Athenian:
  anti-Kleon 212–15
  attitudes to 164–5, 169, 172, 180–
    230; *c.*445–405 BC 211–16; *c.*404–
    363 BC 216–24; *c.*362–300 BC
    224–9; *see also* cavalry, Athenian:
    perception of
  class 287–93; catalogue 293–315;
    definition of 180–3; perception of,
    see cavalry, Athenian: perception
    of; prominence in society 184–90;
    self-perception 199, 201–2; third-
    century 277–8
  command structure: command
    relations with *strategoi* 70–1; pre-
    *c.*445–438 BC 9, 14–15; post-*c.*445–
    438 BC 9–10, 73–4, 87–94, 118–19,
    230; *see also* hipparch, phylarch
  decline, under Macedon 10, 277–8